BERLITZ®

MADRID

Berlitz Trademark Reg. U.S. Patent Office and other countries. Marca Registrada. Library of Congress Catalog Card No. 76-21363.

Printed in Austria.

Deluxe Guide
1989/1990

How to use this guide

- All the practical information, hints and tips that you will need before and during the trip start on page 99.
- For general background, see the sections Madrid and the Madrileños, p. 6, and A Brief History, p. 11.
- All the sights to see are listed between pages 17 and 49, with suggestions on day trips from Madrid from page 49 to 78. Our own choice of sights most highly recommended is pinpointed by the Berlitz traveller symbol.
- Entertainment, nightlife and all other leisure activities are described between pages 79 to 91, while information on restaurants and cuisine is to be found on pages 92 to 98.
- Finally, there is an index at the back of the book, pp. 126–128.

Although we make every effort to ensure the accuracy of all the information in this book, changes occur incessantly. We cannot therefore take responsibility for facts, prices, addresses and circumstances in general that are constantly subject to alteration. Our guides are updated on a regular basis as we reprint, and we are always grateful to readers who let us know of any errors, changes or serious omissions they come across.

Text: Ken Bernstein
Photography: Dany Gignoux
Layout: Doris Haldemann
We are particularly grateful to Mr. Juan Manuel Alvarez Gallo for his help in the preparation of this book. We also wish to thank the Spanish National Tourist Office for its valuable assistance.

Cartography: Falk-Verlag, Hamburg.

Contents

Maps

Photo, pp. 2–3: El Escorial

Madrid and the Madrileños

At an altitude of more than 2,100 feet, this boom town on the Castilian plateau is Europe's highest capital. The combination of high altitude and mountain breezes generates a unique atmosphere. The city is alive with light, the sunshine filtering down through a pale sky barely dense enough to float a cloud on.

Life starts right down on earth. Madrid is a hospitable hotbed of cafés and restaurants, theatres and nightclubs. This is the world capital of bullfighting. The shops are among the finest in Europe. But save strength for the cultural pursuits, starting with the Prado Museum and the Royal Palace. Then set forth on easy excursions to the other highlights of central Spain, towns, steeped in history, of infinite beauty and charm.

Like Brasilia, Washington or other "artificial" towns, the city of Madrid is a man-made capital conceived in political compromise. King Philip II promoted Madrid from a provincial town to his national command post in the middle of the 16th century at a time when his empire was still expanding. Since then, Madrid hasn't stopped growing. Latest reports show the population as being just under 4 million; the area, 205 square miles.

Madrid's business has always been government, but new industries have been drawn to the magnet of power. Today's *Madrileño* (inhabitant of Madrid) may work in

Beauties of Madrid: face in the flea-market crowd, fountain at sunset.

an engine or plastics factory, an insurance company's headquarters or a tourist hotel. With so much economic opportunity right in the geographical centre of the country, it's no wonder the capital is a melting pot of Spaniards from all over the nation. The young man you ask for directions may be a stranger here himself.

Don't be afraid of getting lost in Madrid. Outside every metro (underground) station there stands an oversize city map. Signs at bus stops explain where you're going and where the buses are coming from. The streets are well marked, often wittily, too, with illustrated wall tiles. A sign permanently displayed in a Puerta del Sol umbrella shop announces: *"Mañana lloverá"* (tomorrow it will rain). And if it doesn't, don't be disappointed. The streets are washed regularly with giant hoses.

Before the shrill traffic jams begin, early-morning Madrid sounds old-fashioned and neighbourly. A gypsy junk-collector chants his call. Caged canaries twitter. A grinding, tortured roar from a café means the espresso machine is boiling milk for coffee. Europe's most sleepless people, the *Madrileños,* are filing off to work only six hours after another late night out. The "night-people" image, no matter how deep-rooted, is not actually the real reason *Madrileños* are called *gatos* (cats). Academics claim the nickname originated in the 11th century when soldiers from Madrid spectacularly scaled the walls of an enemy fort, climbing like flies—or cats.

The city and its people run to extremes. It could well have something to do with the weather, which is usually either too cold or too hot (roughly one third of the population flees the city every August). The exaggerated contrasts extend to geography as well: the big city ends suddenly in open country, with no semi-detached suburbs to soften the edges. *Madrileños* seem to be bubbling one moment and sulking the next. They go to church but they go to the striptease, too. At a moment's notice, hand-kissing politeness gives way to the law of the jungle, for instance in the metro, where the train doors slam shut ten seconds after they open, and then, the devil take the hindmost. They may fume about the cost of living, but *Madrileños* never falter in their support of a thriving community of street beggars. They may bemoan the pace of modern life, but they find time to sit over coffee for an hour in an *tertulia,* or informal conversational club, discussing literature or football or the pace of modern life.

Observe the *Madrileños* cramming the promenades and outdoor cafés at the hour of the *paseo,* when the offices

A troubador troupe, called a tuna, *sets off to play in medieval garb.*

Winter scene, back-street Madrid: time changes only the wall slogans.

begin to empty. Elegant businessmen escort impeccably coiffed women of all ages. And all those children in tow! Spaniards may be having fewer children (official awards used to be given for fecundity) but they still take them everywhere. (Don't be concerned about the toddlers on the streets and in restaurants late at night, Madrid's junior "cats" make up for it at their afternoon siesta break.)

Enjoy Madrid in all its many aspects: human, historical, architectural and religious. There are enough museums alone to keep you busy for all your stay; but don't neglect the prodigious sights close enough for day trips. Be certain to see Toledo, Spain's former capital set on a crag, with its haunting memories of El Greco and with all Spain built into its houses and churches. Don't miss Segovia, a royal stronghold with its fairy-tale castle and classic Roman aqueduct. Tour the ancient walled city of saints, Avila. Closer to Madrid, you have to visit the Escorial, monastery, college and palace built for Philip II, and on the way, stop at El Valle de los Caídos (the Valley of the Fallen), Spain's memorial to her soldiers killed in the Civil War of 1936–39.

Situated as it is, in the epicentre of Spain, Madrid is the perfect base for explorations into the heart and soul of the country.

A Brief History

Until its sudden elevation to the status of capital city in 1561, the history of Madrid was long but undistinguished.

Remains from the Paleolithic, Neolithic and Bronze Ages have been unearthed in the Manzanares Valley around Madrid. The prehistoric population evidently appreciated the district's fresh air and water resources.

Nevertheless, even in the local scheme of things, Madrid's significance was negligible over many centuries crucial to the development of the Spanish people. The Romans built their most advanced province on the Iberian peninsula, but left no monuments in Madrid. Armies of North African nomads, spreading the Muslim religion in a relentless tide, invaded the peninsula in A.D. 711. Within ten years, they had overrun almost all of Spain. If Madrid played any role in this, no record of it remains.

The first solid references to this obscure settlement on the Castilian plateau, guarded by the brooding Guadarrama mountain range, don't appear until the 10th century. Even the name is vaguely recorded—perhaps Magerit or Magrit, but close enough to Madrid. The hamlet is mentioned in the chronicles because of its military significance, near the main line of resistance to the Christian reconquest. Since the struggle was to last for centuries, the defending Muslim army had time to build a full-scale fort, or *alcázar,* on the heights of Madrid commanding the Manzanares Valley.

Time passed and the crusading spirit driving south could not be held back forever. After several unsuccessful skirmishes, the Christian forces of Alfonso VI captured Madrid in 1083. The Alcázar became a fort of the Crown of Castile. During a counter-offensive a few years later, the town was overrun by the Muslims, but the Christianized Alcázar held, and shortly afterwards, the Moors were expelled once more, this time for good. But they were not to be driven from southern Spain for nearly another four centuries.

Meanwhile, Madrid enjoyed prominence for a short while in 1308 when King Ferdinand IV and his Cortes, an early version of parliament, held a formal meeting in the town. From then on, the kings of Spain began to visit

Madrid, where the air was invigorating and the hunting excellent.

Ferdinand and Isabella, known in Spain as the Catholic Monarchs who united all the provinces of Spain, first appeared in Madrid in 1477. They appreciated the town's loyalty to the Crown, but the idea never occurred to anyone, let alone the two monarchs, that Madrid might one day become the capital. Toledo served quite well enough.

Spain's Golden Age

Under Ferdinand and Isabella, Spain changed dramatically. In one year alone (1492), the royal pair presided over the discovery of the New World, the final conquest over the Moors, and the expulsion of the Jews. The country was entering its Golden Age, nearly a century of Spanish economic and political supremacy, accompanied by marvels of art and literature.

Ferdinand and Isabella per-

Ancient Romans built this graceful aqueduct, still in use, in Segovia.

sonify Spanishness *(Hispanidad)*. By contrast, their grandson, who assumed the throne in 1516, was as un-Spanish as it is possible to imagine. Born in Flanders in 1500, Charles I could barely express himself in Spanish. The first of the Hapsburgs, he packed his retinue with Burgundian and Flemish nobles. Soon after his arrival in Spain, the young man inherited the title of Holy Roman Emperor, as Charles V; this crown necessarily kept him busy away from the royal residences of Toledo, Segovia, Valladolid and Madrid. While the monarch was away on one of his many business trips, his increasingly dissatisfied subjects protested violently. The revolt of the *comuneros,* or townsmen, broke out in a number of Spanish cities, including Madrid. The rebels occupied the Alcázar, which had by then been converted to a royal palace. The insurrection was put down and the leaders executed, but the king got the message. He tried thereafter to pay more attention to his Spanish constituency.

Madrid's Rise to Capital

In 1556, Charles abdicated in favour of his son, Philip II, which was good news for Spain and even better for Madrid. Philip proclaimed Madrid his capital in 1561, converting an unimpressive town of less than 15,000 into the headquarters of the world's greatest empire of the time. For Madrid, the future soared onwards and upwards; for Spain, upwards, then downwards. Philip II takes credit for the rousing naval victory at Lepanto (Spaniards and Venetians versus the Turks), but only 17 years later he allowed Spain to be subjected to the humiliating defeat of its "invincible" Armada at the hands of Sir Francis Drake and the small English navy. He left behind him as a monument the Escorial, the visionary super-palace and monastery in the foothills of the Sierra de Guadarrama, north-west of Madrid.

Philip's son, Philip III, was unfaithful to Spain's new capital. For several years he held court in Valladolid, though eventually he returned to Madrid. It was he who organized the construction of the Plaza Mayor—the magnificent main square which still dignifies the centre of the city. Other tasteful, 17th-century buildings nearby, such as the Foreign Ministry and the Town Hall, show that the cap-

Reflection in a pool: Don Quixote statue in Madrid hails Cervantes.

ital was at last being taken seriously.

The Hapsburgs bowed out in 1700 with the death of Charles II. The subsequent War of the Spanish Succession resulted in the enthronement of the Bourbon candidate, Philip V. When the Alcázar of Madrid burned down in 1734 (with the loss, incidentally, of many art treasures), Philip decided to make the best of a bad thing. He ordered a new palace, ever more lavish. The result is Madrid's Royal Palace. You can tour it whenever Philip's descendant, King Juan Carlos I, is not using it for official ceremonies.

Madrid owes a lot to the civic-mindedness of Charles III, who ruled from 1759 to 1788. He paved and lit the streets, installed public fountains, built what became the Prado Museum, and laid out promenades and gardens.

Goya painted the next king, Charles IV, looking strangely like his transatlantic contemporary, George Washington. But Charles was much less successful in politics. His 20-year reign, weak at best, ended

Man of Action, Man of Letters

MIGUEL DE CERVANTES SAAVEDRA fought at the Battle of Lepanto (1571), was wounded, captured, imprisoned; he escaped, was enslaved and finally ransomed. Returning to Spain, he worked as an army quartermaster but spent several spells in jail on financial charges. Then, at the age of 58, he wrote the world's best-selling novel, *Don Quixote*.

In his modest house in Madrid's Calle del León, Cervantes died on April 23, 1616, perhaps the saddest day in literary history—for on the same date, the world also lost William Shakespeare.

in all-round disaster: abdication, arrest and war.

Napoleon invaded Spain and invested his older, taller and more agreeable brother, Joseph, as King José I. On May 2, 1808, Madrid rose up against the interloper. The Peninsular War (called by the Spaniards the War of Independence) went on murderously, but inconclusively for six years. Finally, with the help of the British under the Duke of Wellington, the Spanish expelled the occupying forces. In truth, Joseph Bonaparte meant well—he built so many plazas that the *Madrileños* nicknamed him *El Rey Plazuelas*—but the people loathed a government imposed from abroad. José I spent 17 years of exile in, of all unlikely places, New Jersey.

A modern-day horseman, in parade in Madrid, typifies Spanish pomp.

Monument to the national tragedy: Civil War memorial of Valle de los Caídos lies north-west of Madrid.

Decline and Decadence

The son of Charles IV, Ferdinand VII, was seated on his rightful throne in the Royal Palace of Madrid in 1814. But the war and the repercussions of the French Revolution had helped to create in Spain the nucleus of a liberal and national party. The power struggles at home and rebellious colonies abroad were symptomatic of the 19th century as a whole. By the time of the Spanish-American War of 1898, the empire of the Golden Age had been whittled to insignificance. King Alfonso XIII, who linked the 19th and 20th centuries, inaugurated the Madrid metro (its underground railway) and University City. But he was undone by the chronic unrest of his subjects. Neither constitutional government nor dictatorship proved workable and, in 1931, the king went into exile following anti-royalist results in municipal elections.

The Civil War

Under the new Republic, bitter, hard ideological conflicts divided parties and factions, with the church also involved. Finally, in 1936, a large section of the army under General Francisco Franco rose in revolt against the government. On Franco's side were monarchists, conservatives, the Church and the right-wing Falangists. Against him was a collection of republicans, liberals socialists, communists and anarchists.

The Civil War developed into one of the great causes of the 20th century with support for both sides coming from outside Spain. Often unaware of—or indifferent to—the particular Spanish origins of the struggle, many Europeans saw the Civil War as a crucial conflict between democracy and dictatorship, or from the other side, as a conflict between law and order and the forces of social revolution and chaos. The bloodshed lasted three years and cost several hundred thousand lives. Madrid was in Republican hands for most of the war, but the government was evacuated in the early stages of a Nationalist siege which, to the accompaniment of frequent bombing, lasted until March, 1939.

Even when the war ended, the hardship continued. But Spain's new *caudillo* (leader), Generalísimo Franco, managed to keep Spain out of the Second World War despite Hitler's efforts at persuasion. Spain was admitted to the United Nations in 1955, opening the gates to an overwhelming tourist invasion, with profound effects on both the economy and national mentality.

When Franco died in 1975, Prince Juan Carlos, the grandson of King Alfonso XIII, became monarch. The new king's commitment to democracy has brought Spain into line with the rest of Western Europe and assured the country of membership in the European Economic Community.

What to See

Madrid has so many facets that, for centuries, Spaniards have informally referred to it in the plural—*Los Madriles.*

Since there's so much to take in, you'll have to divide the *Madriles,* geographically or chronologically, horizontally or vertically. A good way to start is to sign on to one of the half-day guided tours to help get your bearings. Once you have a general idea of the layout of the town, you can set forth on your own according to your interests: art, history, shopping, nightlife, or all of them. Our suggestions follow.

But whatever else you do, begin by savouring the oldest of the *Madriles.* Start on foot in the heart of the original Madrid.

Old Madrid

Little is left of medieval Madrid except the mood. You feel it in the narrow streets which meander south from the Calle Mayor (Main Street). Dimly lit shops sell what they've always sold: religious habits, books, cheeses, military medals, statues, capes (Dracula-style or even for princesses). Artisans chip away at their woodwork. A gypsy beggar-woman, holding somebody else's baby, insistently asks for a coin. A waiter pins up the hand-written menu in the doorway of an inn. A greengrocer builds a pyramid of tomatoes. A blind lottery-ticket salesman, tapping his white cane to attract attention, recites a poem promising instant riches.

In its formalized version, Madrid's most famous lottery-ticket establishment faces the **Puerta del Sol** (Gate of the Sun). On big days, crowds of customers wait outside the shop called *La Hermana de Doña Manolita* (Mrs. Manolita's Sister). Some historic jackpot tickets have been issued here, and the clients are waiting for new miracles.

The gate from which the Puerta del Sol takes its name may have been decorated with

Spanish Dramatists

Spain's three top dramatists of the Golden Age make Shakespeare seem like something of a dawdler in contrast.

Lope de Vega (1562–1635) devised a new three-act format and turned out in the region of 1,500 plays.

Tirso de Molina (1571?–1648) wrote over 300 plays, including the first about the world's most famous lover, Don Juan.

Pedro Calderón de la Barca (1600–81) is credited with more than 100 comedies, tragedies and religious allegories.

Madrileños all three of them, these men had chequered careers. Lope de Vega joined the Armada. Tirso de Molina served as a monk on the island of Santo Domingo. Calderón enlisted as a cavalry man and was later ordained a priest.

Madrid's main square preserves the elegant 17th-century architecture.

a sculpted or painted sun design. But this is an academic point, for the gate—part of the ancient town wall—was torn down in 1570. For centuries, this plaza, hub of ten converging streets, has been Madrid's nerve-centre. All the radial highways of Spain are measured from Puerta del Sol, "Kilometre 0".

The no-nonsense, neo-Classical building on the south side of the square is headquarters of the security police. Nonetheless, thousands of *Madrileños* gather here for a ritual every New Year's Eve. They try to swallow a dozen grapes while the clock atop the building strikes 12. Then pandemonium breaks out.

In the central area of Puerta del Sol, overpowered by all the traffic, is a statue based on Madrid's coat of arms. It shows a bear standing against a *madroño* tree (an arbutus, or strawberry tree). This same

gourmet bear is seen all over Madrid, on the rear doors of every taxi, for instance.

The **Plaza Mayor** (Main Square), a few blocks away, is an architectural symphony in bold but balanced tones. Broad arcades surround a cobbled rectangle 200 yards long and 100 yards wide. It was built in the beginning of the 17th century, based on the graceful style of Juan de Herrera—symmetry, slate roofs, slender towers. (Juan de Herrera was Philip II's architect, responsible for the Escorial.) Plaza Mayor may be entered by any of nine archways, but mercifully not by motor vehi-

City on the move: Madrid is an expanding urban centre in a timeless setting, with the Castilian plateau stretching into the distance.

cles. Until relatively recent years, this was the scene of pageants, bullfights, even executions—residents disposing of more than 400 balconies overlooking the square used to sell tickets for such events. A statue of King Philip III, who ordered the Plaza to be built, occupies the place of honour but is no obstacle to events—ranging from pop concerts to theatre festivals—which are organized from time to time by the municipality. Take a seat at one of the outdoor cafés in the square and enjoy the proportions of Madrid's most elegant architectural ensemble.

Further along Calle Mayor, the old Plaza de la Villa (City Hall Square) juxtaposes stately 16th- and 17th-century buildings of varied style. The Casa y Torre de los Lujanes (the House and Tower of the Lujanes), 16th-century Gothic, has an imposing stone por-

Sunday in Madrid

Some cities have sedate Sundays. Not Madrid. Try to take in the excitement.

The Rastro. Sunday mornings, the streets of Old Madrid, beginning just south of the cathedral, are transformed into one of the world's biggest flea markets. Tens of thousands of bargain-minded *Madrileños* join the out-of-towners in pricing clothing, antiques, pots and pans, and junk of all sorts. Care to buy a used gas mask?

The Stamp Market. Hundreds of collectors assemble in the Plaza Mayor on Sunday mornings to buy and sell stamps, coins, banknotes, cigar bands and even used lottery tickets. Watch the enthusiasts with their tweezers and magnifying glasses.

The Book Fair. Just south of the Botanical Garden, the bibliophiles throng to open-air stalls along Calle de Claudio Moyano. New and used books bought and sold: trash, comics, foreign fiction and valuable old tomes.

So much for the morning. After drinks, snacks and, of course, lunch, you'll have to decide whether to watch Real Madrid play football, or go to a bullfight, or follow the race-horses at the Zarzuela Hippodrome.

tal. The **Casa de Cisneros,** built in the mid-16th century by a nephew of the intrepid inquisitor and warrior, Cardinal Cisneros, belongs to the ornate and delicate style of architecture known as Plateresque. Finally, the **Ayuntamiento** (City Hall) represents the Hapsburg era, with the towers and slate spires characteristic of the 17th-century official buildings all around Madrid.

There are more than 200 churches in Madrid, but very

Sightless lottery-ticket salesman hopes for big Christmas business. Below: lull in activity at Rastro.

few could be classified among the essential tourist attractions. Madrid is too young a city to have a great medieval cathedral. The present (provisional) cathedral of Madrid in Calle de Toledo, the **Catedral de San Isidro,** needed major rebuilding after severe damage in the Civil War. It has a massive dome, a single nave and, among many relics, the revered remains of the city's patron saint, San Isidro Labrador (St. Isidore the Husbandman).

Just down Calle de Toledo from the cathedral is the site of the **Rastro,** Madrid's phenomenal flea market, which buzzes with bargain-hunters every Sunday morning (see page 22). Also in the neighbourhood are some popular local tapas bars and the workshops of Madrid's artisans, from guitar makers to bookbinders.

A formidable Madrid church of the mid-18th century is the **Basílica de San Francisco el Grande** (Basilica of St. Francis of Assisi). The curved façade, an original version of a neo-Classic design, somewhat curtails the effect of the church's most superlative feature. Once inside, you'll realize that the dome is out of the ordinary. Indeed, its inner diameter of more than 100 feet exceeds the size of the cupolas of St. Paul's (London) and Les Invalides (Paris). Oversized statues of the apostles in white Carrara marble are stationed around the rotunda. Seven richly ornamented chapels fan out from the centre. In the Chapel of San Bernardino de Siena, notice the large painting above the altar, a lively scene of the saint preaching. The second figure from the right, dressed in yellow, is said to be a self-portrait of the artist, the immortal Francisco de Goya.

Another landmark of old Madrid is the Hospital de San Carlos (Calle de Santa Isabel 52). It has been renovated to house the **Centro de Arte Reina Sofia,** a venue for exhibitions of contemporary art.

Central Madrid

Except for the intensity of the traffic, the ample **Plaza de la Cibeles** is splendid. The fountain in the centre shows Cybele, a controversial Greek fertility goddess, serenely settled in a chariot pulled by two lions. The sculptural ensemble is probably the best-known fountain in all Spain.

Trees and fountains gracing Plaza de España ease Madrid pressures.

The most unavoidable building on the plaza is the cathedral-like Palacio de Comunicaciones, sarcastically nicknamed *Nuestra Señora de las Comunicaciones* (Our Lady of Communications). This ponderous post office, inaugurated in 1919, is dismal inside; its high ceilings, overhead walkways and general inhumanity give it the air of a prison.

While the Communications Palace shows off, the Army headquarters across the square camouflages itself behind 100-year-old iron railings. The army, improbably, occupies a huge mansion in

Ciudad Universitaria
Calle del Pintor Rosales
Museo de América
C. de Sta. Cruz de Marcenado
C. de Alberto Aguilera
Glorieta de Ruiz Jiménez
Calle de Quintana
C. de la Princesa
Palacio de Liria
Templo de Debod
C. de Ventura Rodríguez
Museo Cerralbo
Plaza de España
Bernardo
Calle de San
C. de los Reyes
San
Calle del Paz
Estación del Norte
Paseo San Vicente
Paseo San Vicente
Bailén
Gran Vía
de
C. de Torija
Convento de la Encarnación
Tudescos
Pl. del Callao
Campo del Moro
Palacio Real
Plaza de Oriente
Teatro Real
Las Descalzas Reales
Calle del Arenal
Pta. del Sol
Mayor
Nuestra Señora de la Almudena
de
Plaza de la Villa
Calle
Plaza Mayor
Calle de Segovia
Ronda de Segovia
Calle del Sacramento
Toledo
Calle de Atocha
Calle
San Isidro
Plaza Tirso de Molina
Puerta de Moros
Calle de S. Francisco
San Francisco el Grande
Ronda de Segovia
de
Pl. de Cascorro
C. de Mesón de Paredes
C. de Embajadores
Gran Vía de San Francisco
Calle
Ribera de Curtidores
Glorieta Puerta de Toledo

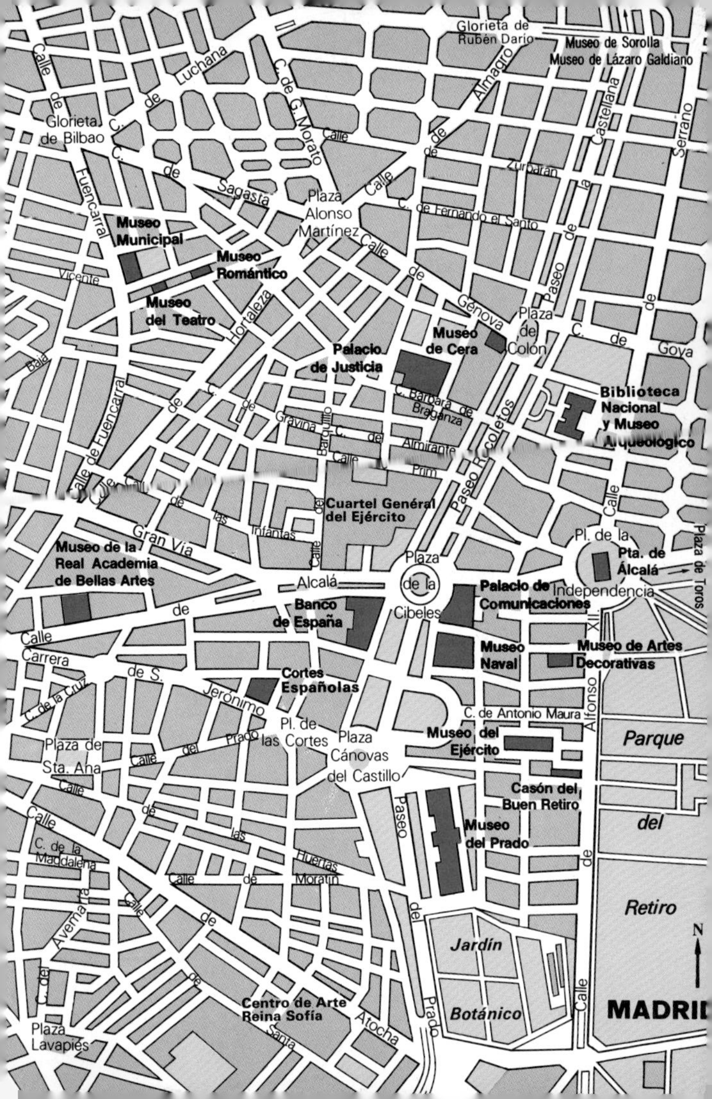

Glorieta de Rubén Darío
Museo de Sorolla
Museo de Lázaro Galdiano
Calle de Luchana
Glorieta de Bilbao
C. de G. Morato
Calle de Almagro
Paseo de la Castellana
Serrano
C. de Sagasta
Fuencarral
C. de Zurbarán
Plaza Alonso Martínez
C. de Fernando el Santo
Calle de Génova
Museo Municipal
Museo Romántico
Vicente
Museo del Teatro
Hortaleza
Plaza de Colón
C. de Goya
Museo de Cera
Palacio de Justicia
Baja
Calle de Fuencarral
C. Bárbara de Braganza
Biblioteca Nacional y Museo Arqueológico
Gravina
Barquillo
C. del Almirante
Calle Prim
Paseo Recoletos
Cuartel Genéral del Ejército
Infantas
Gran Vía
Museo de la Real Academia de Bellas Artes
Plaza de la Cibeles
Pl. de la Independencia
Pta. de Álcalá
Plaza de Toros
Calle de Alcalá
Palacio de Comunicaciones
Banco de España
Calle Carrera de S. Jerónimo
Museo Naval
Museo de Artes Decorativas
Cortes Españolas
C. de la Cruz
Alfonso XII
C. de Antonio Maura
Pl. de las Cortes
Plaza Cánovas del Castillo
Calle del Prado
Plaza de Sta. Ana
Museo del Ejército
Parque del Retiro
Casón del Buen Retiro
Museo del Prado
Calle de las Huertas
C. de la Magdalena
Calle de Moratín
Paseo del Prado
Calle de Atocha
Ave María
Jardín Botánico
Centro de Arte Reina Sofía
Santa
Plaza Lavapiés
N
MADRID

an enviable garden dotted with statues of scantily clad nymphs. This may explain why there are so many sentries guarding this coy private park.

Also facing Plaza de la Cibeles, the headquarters of the Bank of Spain combines neo-Classic, Baroque and Rococo styles. It looks about as solid as any bank can be. The financial district, Madrid's City, or Wall Street, begins here on **Calle de Alcalá.** Pompous buildings in this very high-rent district contain the head offices or branches of more than 100 banks plus insurance companies, the Finance Ministry and, a few streets away, the **Bolsa de Comercio** (Stock Exchange). Incidentally, the women selling lottery tickets are posted round the severely columned portal of the Stock Exchange, and suggest one more little gamble to arriving and departing tycoons.

But Calle de Alcalá is not entirely dedicated to Mammon. Next door to the Ministry of Finance is the clumsily named **Museo de la Real Academia de Bellas Artes de San Fernando**—call it the

Fountain and sculpture of Cybele glittering in the Madrid eventide.

Museum of the Royal Academy. The academy owns a celebrated batch of Goya's paintings, including the *Burial of the Sardine,* full of action and humour, and a superb self-portrait of the artist in his vigorous old age. Velázquez, Magnasco, Murillo and Rubens are also represented among hundreds of works on display.

And then there's the Royal Academy's magnificent collection of paintings by Zurbarán, which rivals that of the Prado. Representative of the artist's austere, devotional style are the *Vision of the Blessed Alonso Rodríguez* and a series of portraits of friars.

Now let's return to the **Gran Vía,** main east-west thoroughfare and lifeline of modern Madrid. The bustling Gran Vía (Main Avenue) is a mixture of hotels, shops, theatres, nightclubs and cafés—the street for strolling and window-gazing. Connoisseurs of traffic jams will appreciate the nightmarish rush-hour along this busy street. Pony-tailed policewomen frantically gesticulate and whistle in a doomed effort to stir the immovable traffic; drivers at their wit's end lean on their horns in sympathy and add to the cacophony. And a special bonus: in Madrid, thanks to the siesta break, the rush-hour happens not twice, but *four* times a day.

You can get your bearings on the Gran Vía by looking *up*. The highest tower in sight belongs to Madrid's first *rascacielos* (skyscraper), the headquarters of the telephone company. La Telefónica, as it is called, sprouts antennas and parabolic reflectors.

At **Plaza del Callao** (named after Peru's principal port), the pedestrian traffic reaches its peak. This is the centre for department stores, cinemas, cafés and bus stops: yet only a couple of streets south of Callao's turbulence, the **Convent of Descalzas Reales** clings onto a 16th-century tranquillity. The institution was founded by Princess Joanna of Austria, the daughter of Holy Roman Emperor Charles V, and subsidized by generous patrons. In 1961, it was opened to the public as a national museum. Cloistered nuns of the Santa Clara order, still on the premises, stay out of sight during visiting hours. As for tourists, their first view of the convent's splendours begins with the theatrical grand stairway. Upstairs are heavy timbered ceilings and walls covered with works of art, mostly of religious or royal significance. In one hall, there are a dozen 17th-century tapestries based on original Rubens drawings. The museum contains outstanding paintings by Titian, Brueghel the Elder, Zurbarán and Sánchez Coello. The shrine of the convent church is particularly well endowed in religious relics and jewels.

Girls wait with mixed emotions for start of film at a Madrid cinema.

From Plaza del Callao, the Gran Vía continues downhill towards the **Plaza de España** through more shopping, strolling and nightlife territory. Two controversial skyscrapers, of 26 and 34 storeys, have changed the atmosphere of the plaza, a sanctuary of grass, flowers, trees and fountains. A favourite sight, especially with visiting photographers, is the Cervantes Monument. A stone sculpture honouring the author looms behind bronze statues of his immortal creations, Don Quixote and Sancho Panza, astride their horse and donkey, respectively.

Calle de la Princesa, which begins at Plaza de España, is actually an extension of the Gran Vía aimed north-west. The house at Calle de la Princesa, 22, is literally palatial; it calls to mind a scaled-down Buckingham Palace. Tucked away in a comfortable park behind high railings, the **Palacio de Liria** is the residence of the Duchess of Alba. The family picture gallery includes works by Rembrandt, Titian, Rubens, Van Dyck, El Greco and Goya. The palace is closed to the public except by special arrangement.

Calle de la Princesa's smart trajectory ends where the University district begins. The landmarks here are the Air Force headquarters (a modern copy of the Escorial) and Madrid's youngest triumphal arch. It commemorates the Franco victory of 1939.

Madrid's Own Words

Sereno. Madrid's night-watchmen used to appear at the clap of the hands to unlock front doors of hotels and apartment houses. Tradition suffered a crushing blow in 1976, when the *serenos* were enlisted as auxiliary police. *Madrileños* now carry their own keys... and secrets.

Tasca. A bar specializing in *tapas,* tasty snacks consumed while standing in a litter of prawn shells and olive stones.

Tertulia. The unofficial club of conversationalists meeting in a café. The tradition is withering as life's pace accelerates.

Tuna. Band of troubadours in medieval costume, usually university students, who serenade clients in bars and restaurants for tips.

Zarzuela. A uniquely Spanish form of operetta, often on themes indigenous to Madrid.

The Prado

Madrid's pride, the Prado Museum, is indisputably the world's greatest collection of Spanish paintings. (Picasso's *Guernica* is in the Prado Annex—Casón del Buen Retiro—see p. 43.) In addition, there are hundreds of famous foreign works.

A serious student of art might well plan an entire Madrid itinerary around repeated visits to the Prado; but the tourist in a rush, trying to include so many highlights, may have to settle for a couple of hours. If the fast visit consists of aimless trudging through nearly 100 rooms, squinting for familiar pictures, the trip could be exhausting and only mildly edifying.

You should, for best results, do some planning. Here is one way out of the labyrinth: a suggested two-hour tour of the top 15 old masters, designed so a visitor can examine the most masterpieces per mile. Unfortunately the Prado is undergoing renovations and many of the pictures described below may have been moved temporarily from their accustomed places. Some of them may not be on view and certain rooms, or even entire wings, may be closed. The museum is open from 9 a.m. to 7 p.m. (2 p.m. on Sunday and some holidays). Closed Monday.

First climb the stairway to the side entrance at the north end of the building (facing Calle de Felipe IV and the Ritz Hotel).

In the main rotunda (Room 1), spare a glance for the sculpture of honour, a bronze by the Italian Leone Leoni showing the Emperor Charles V stamping out the Turkish foe. The emperor's armour is removable; underneath, he's as naked as a Greek god.

Spanish art forms the backbone of the art treasures in store, but since we're near the early Flemish masters, let's turn right and take a brief look into Room 41. Painted in the middle of the 15th century, the *Descent from the Cross* by **Van der Weyden,** with its griefstricken faces, shows unbelievable powers of draughtsmanship.

The Spanish call **Hieronymus Bosch** "El Bosco"—which is the way you will see his works labelled in Rooms 43 and 44. This Dutch genius, portraying the terrors and superstitions of the medieval peasant mind, calls to memory the hallucinations of Salvador Dalí, but Bosch was 400 years ahead of his time. The large triptych called *The Garden of Delights* is the all-time masterpiece of surrealism, full of sensuous fantasies and apocalyptical nightmares.

Sharing space here with his contemporary Bosch, the German painter **Albrecht Dürer** tackles more tangible subjects. His carefully posed self-portrait at the age of 26 shows every ruffle of his shirt and every curl in his flowing hair. He is also represented here by two charming nudes, *Adam* and *Eve*.

Return again across the rotunda to the north-east corner of the main floor, Room 2. **Raphael** (1483–1520) painted the explosive character study called *The Cardinal.* Centuries of investigation have failed to uncover the identity of the subject, with his fishy eyes, aquiline nose and cool, thin lips.

Room 3: In the late 15th century, in Venice, **Antonello da Messina** portrayed *Christ Sustained by an Angel.* With its realistic detail, the whole mood is one of intense sadness. In this room are three great tablets by the Florentine master **Botticelli.** *The Story of Nastagio degli Onesti* illustrates a tale from the *Decameron* of Boccaccio. The

Past Masters of Spanish Painting

In the Prado, the greatest of the great Spanish painters—Goya, El Greco, Murillo and Velázquez—are represented by literally dozens of works, many of them world-famous masterpieces:

Francisco de Goya (1746–1828). A philanderer in his youth, Goya had to flee Saragossa in 1763 for the anonymity of Madrid. He went on to become the king's principal painter. He worked mainly in the neo-Classical manner, and eventually developed a distinctive style that anticipated Impressionism.

El Greco (1541–1614). Born in Crete, resident in Italy, El Greco is a very Spanish painter nonetheless. He worked in Toledo, his adopted city, for 37 years, toiling away at the immense and intensely personal religious canvases that are his hallmark. Asymmetrical compositions, vivid colours and a mood of ecstacy typify his work.

Bartolomé Murillo (1617–1682). An uneven painter, Murillo is, alas, better known for his late pictures in the *estilo vaporoso* (melting style). Ignore the soft-focus and sentimental madonnas and beggar boys and concentrate instead on the naturalistic street urchins and heartfelt religious works.

Diego Velázquez (1599–1660). Apprenticed at age 14 to the Sevillan Pacheco, Velázquez showed his genius early on. A realist approach and virtuoso handling made his reputation. Of his varied output, the portraits stand out for their psychological penetration. Striking too, is the brilliant colour and brushwork that grows ever freer.

---

three panels are a Renaissance storyboard full of colour and action set in an enchanting landscape.

Room 4: *The Annunciation* by **Fra Angelico** is half-way in style between the Middle Ages and the Renaissance. The sunbeam is gold, the columns are graceful and, in the background, Adam and Eve wear robes.

Room 5: **Correggio's** masterpiece, *Noli me tangere,* shows Mary Magdalene awestruck at the sight of the resurrected Christ. The painting pulls the figures out from a lush, forested background.

Rooms 7, 8 and 9: For an artist who painted official portraits and religious works, **Titian** seemed to have no difficulty changing gear to the

downright lascivious. His *Baccanal* may be a reaction to his more serious assignments, but it is about as far as an orgy can go within the bounds of a museum. Two variations on a theme, *Venus Enjoying Herself with Music* and *Venus Enjoying Herself with Love and Music*, maintain the sensuous effect, though by current standards they might be considered as self-parody. Titian's *Portrait of the Emperor Charles V*, on horseback at the Battle of Mühlberg (1547), set the standard for court painters of the next century. While you're enjoying the Prado's splendid Titian collection, don't miss his self-portrait painted at the age of 89. Unlike many of his contemporaries who were doomed to an early death in poverty, this sprightly Venetian is reputed to have lived to 98.

Our route passes through Room 11, where you can get a glimpse of the experiments in light and shade of the devout Spanish painter, **Francisco de Zurbarán.**

Rooms 9B and 10B: El Greco enthusiasts will want to take a trip to Toledo for the fullest view of his works, but the Prado displays a good cross-section. Here is *Knight with Hand on Chest,* the distinguished *caballero* all in black, signed in Greek capital letters "Domenikos Theotokopoulos", the artist's real name. Another signed painting is a delicate portrait of St. Mary. The large painting, *Adoration of the Shepherds,* is a prime example of El Greco's unique

Left: still life outside the Prado. Detail from the fantasy Garden of Delights *by Dutch master Bosch.*

Salmer, Barcelona

lighting effects. In addition, there are pictures of the apostles, saints and other religious subjects, a two-room survey of the mystical and passionately coloured world of the 16th-century genius.

Continue now through the main hall (Rooms 26 and 27) and turn left in the very centre of the building: Room 12 is the place of honour of one of the finest Spanish artists, **Diego Velázquez.** Here are paintings of the high and the mighty along with studies of fun-loving ordinary mortals. As court painter to Philip IV, Velázquez was obliged to devote most of his time to official portraits. But he enlivened his subjects with almost impressionistic brushwork and colour, and his landscapes and skies are exquisite. One of the Prado's most-discussed works is his *Surrender of Breda,* commemorating a Spanish victory over Dutch forces in 1625. The chivalry of the winning general, the exhaustion of the loser, the less disguised emotions of their retinues, the extraordinary array of upraised lances of the Spaniards and the burning landscape show us Velázquez at his most profound. More Velázquez—princes and princesses, plus freaks and saints—are hung in Rooms 13 and 14, leading to the climax with Spain's all-time favourite painting. It has a room to itself, Room 15. *Las Meninas* (The Maids of Honour) is the triumph of Velázquez over light and space. You could spend an hour trying to determine how he managed to create the illusion of three dimensions. (A large mirror has been placed in the back of the room to help you study the depth factor.) But apart from the tricks, this giant canvas is a delight in itself and a crowning achievement of the artist, who painted himself with palette in hand at the left side of his own masterpiece.

The layout of the museum suggests a change now to Flemish and Dutch painters before returning to the art of Spain. Actually, there is a Spanish connection. **Peter Paul Rubens,** whose pictures are shown in Rooms 16 to 20, came to Spain twice and met Velázquez. His noble ancestry enabled him to follow a career as a diplomat as well as an artist. The Prado is well endowed with the works of Rubens on biblical and mythological themes, as well as royal portraits. Outstanding here is the huge *Adoration of the Magi,* as well as a painting of a radically different type, *The Three Graces*. Three fleshy nudes are shown in an equally lush landscape; the blonde on the left is said to be Rubens's second wife, Helena.

Room 23: **Rembrandt** is represented in the Prado by only two paintings. *Artemis* was signed by the newly wed artist in 1634. The self-portrait of an older Rembrandt is the familiar broad face glowing from a dark-brown background.

From Rembrandt, follow the corridor labelled Room 31 to the large hall (32) dedicated to **Francisco de Goya.** In the year 1786, he became an official painter to the Spanish court. *The Family of Charles IV,* his most celebrated royal portrait, is daringly frank. Only the royal children look anything like attractive; the adults presumably are true-to-life. The lady with head averted represented a not-yet-announced in-law. Taking a leaf from Velázquez, Goya stations himself on the left side of this painting.

To continue the Prado's survey of Goya, you'll have to

Spain's favourite painting, Las Meninas, *is a triumph of illusionism.*

go out into the main corridor (Rooms 29 and 28) and then down the stairs (called Room 45) to the ground floor. In its abstruse way, the route passes through Room 59 and the passageway numbered 58 to a gratifyingly large wing (Rooms 53 to 57A) devoted to Goya.

One of history's great protest pictures, *The Executions of the 3rd of May,* shows the shooting of Spanish patriots in 1808 by the French. Goya witnessed this tragedy of the War of Independence from the window of his cottage, then went to the scene by moonlight to sketch the victims.

Nothing in life escaped him—honour and joy, city

Goya's scandalous Naked Maja *still draws curious crowds in the Prado.*

and country, kings and peasants, disasters and cruelty, all recorded with compassion and colour, and on occasion boisterous good humour. Of all Goya's paintings—in fact of all the paintings in the Prado—none is more discussed and disputed than *The Naked Maja* (Room 57A). Nudes had been almost nonexistent in Spanish painting, and the principal gossip for over 160 years has concerned the identity of the model. The face is awkwardly superimposed on the body, suggesting that the lady was thus disguised. Rumours of a scandalous affair between Goya and the Duchess of Alba are always mentioned in this context and always denied. The other half of the famous pair is *The Clothed Maja,* the same lady provocatively robed.

So much for the scandalous. Now roam around the Goya rooms at will, to see how the people of Madrid lived at the end of the 18th century. Look at his sketches, engravings, cartoons for tapestries, and finally the "Black Paintings" of his last phase—the mad murals Goya produced in the bitterness of old age and deafness. His visions of death and monsters are a long way from the innocence of his lively sketches of children's games, but they all made up his prolific and impassioned reportage of life itself.

For your next visit to the Prado, make amends to some of those regretfully overlooked: Brueghel, Caravaggio, Coello, David, Van Dyck, Gainsborough, Herrera, Mengs, Murillo, Reynolds, Ribera, Teniers, Tiepolo and Watteau. Then return to your favourite pictures by the three greatest Spaniards, El Greco, Velázquez and Goya.

Missing Masters

Fate and turbulent times dealt unkindly with the last remains of Spain's three greatest painters.

El Greco died in Toledo in 1614. He was buried in a local church, but the coffin was transferred to another, which was destroyed. His bones were never found.

Velázquez (died in 1660) was entombed in a Madrid parish church which was demolished; the remains were lost.

Goya died in 1828 in Bordeaux, France, where he was interred. In 1899, the remains were sent back to Spain, but the skull was missing.

Other Museums and Sights

Royal Palace

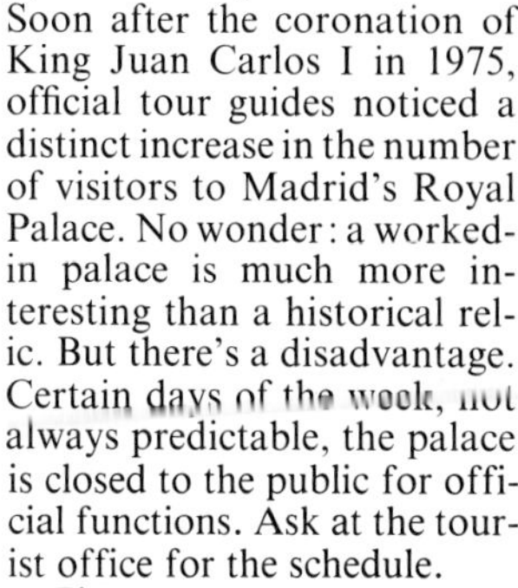

(Palacio Real)

Soon after the coronation of King Juan Carlos I in 1975, official tour guides noticed a distinct increase in the number of visitors to Madrid's Royal Palace. No wonder: a worked-in palace is much more interesting than a historical relic. But there's a disadvantage. Certain days of the week, not always predictable, the palace is closed to the public for official functions. Ask at the tourist office for the schedule.

The Royal Palace is often called El Palacio de Oriente (Palace of the East) in spite of its westerly location. It is set among formal gardens on a bluff overlooking the Manzanares Valley. The old Moorish fortress on the site burned down in 1734, whereupon King Philip V ordered the construction of an immense new palace in French style. His command produced this imperious residence, loaded with art and history.

For security reasons, visitors are forbidden to wander on their own, but are escorted in groups according to language. The basic one-hour tour takes in only a fraction of the 2,000 rooms. It begins with the climb up the main staircase—bright, airy and ceremonious beneath an arched ceiling. Each step is a single slab of marble. The marble lions on the bannisters don't match; one is French, the other Spanish.

The apartments of Charles III consist of one lavish room after another. The outstanding **Gasparini Room** is named after the artist (Matias Gasparini of Naples) who mobilized stone-cutters, sculptors, glass-blowers, clock-makers, silver-smiths, cabinet-makers and embroiderers to produce this example of Rococo at its most overwhelming. Floor, walls and ceiling swirl with special effects.

The **Ceremonial Dining Room,** seating 145 guests, was built for the wedding of Alfonso XII and his second wife, Maria Christina, in 1879. Do notice the 15 chandeliers, ten candelabra and 18th-century Chinese porcelain jars along walls hung with Brussels tapestries.

The so-called **Official Chamber,** all red velvet and gold, is still used when ambassadors come to present credentials. The **Throne Room** occupies the very centre of the south façade of the palace. Red velvet and mirrors in matching gilt frames cover the walls. The ceiling, painted by Tiepolo in 1764, aims to depict "the greatness of the Spanish monarchy with its provinces and states". Four gilded bronze lions defend the throne.

For a basic fee, you can see all the sights on the standard tour. An extra charge is made for additional sights within the palace:

The Crown Jewels. Dramatically displayed behind glass in a modern vault, an impressive collection of sceptres, crowns, jewels and relics.

Museum of Paintings. They go back to religious works which belonged to Queen Isabella I. In the room dedicated to Velázquez, note the large painting of a rearing, riderless horse; the artist died before he could paint in the royal horseman. Works by Zurbarán, El Greco and Goya round out the collection.

Scene of regal ceremonies and portentous events: Royal Palace as viewed under a typical Madrid sky.

Hall of the Halberdiers. Mostly ancient Flemish and Spanish tapestries in a remarkable state of preservation, the colours still rich.

Royal Library. Twenty-four rooms containing 300,000 works—rare editions, manuscripts and maps. Valuable musical instruments on show include two violins by Stradivarius, kept under glass but tuned and played periodically.

Royal Pharmacy. With a re-creation of a 17th-century alchemist's distillation room. Cupboards lining two rooms are filled with matching glass and porcelain apothecary jars specially ordered by Charles IV in 1794.

Royal Armoury. If the children—or anyone else for that matter—have begun to droop from all the mileage, the art and the history, this should perk them up. Swashbuckling swordsmen and jousting horsemen are commemorated here in a display of authentic battle flags, trophies, shields and weapons. The armoury is officially called the finest collection of its type in the world.

More for Art Lovers

Private collections, state-run galleries and religious institutions add to Madrid's renown as an art centre. Almost all

Miró and other moderns of Spain cheer Contemporary Art Museum.

museums are open from about 10 a.m. to 2 p.m.; for specific hours, see p. 114.

In nearly all of the Madrid museums, the legends are in Spanish only. Hint: *Siglo III a. C.* = 3rd century B.C. *Siglo III d. C.* = 3rd century A.D.

Museo Lázaro Galdiano, Calle de Serrano, 122. An astonishingly wide-ranging and priceless private collection bequeathed to the nation. Ancient jewellery including a Celtic diadem from the 2nd century B.C. Medieval and Renaissance masterpieces in ivory and enamel, gold and silver. Rare church vestments, medieval weapons. Paintings: a Rembrandt portrait of Saskia van Uylenburgh, dated the year they were married. *Vision of Tondal* is Hieronymus Bosch at his most diabolical. Goya: a rich repository of official portraits, colourful sketches of real life, and haunting scenes of witches and horrors. El Greco: a sensitive *St. Francis of Assisi* and an early (1562) picture from his Venetian period; English painters: Reynolds, Gainsborough and Constable, and an unexpected entry by the American Gilbert Stuart. But the museum's greatest pride, spotlighted in its own niche on the ground floor, is a portrait of angelic beauty, painted around 1480 by Leonardo da Vinci, entitled *The Saviour*.

Casón del Buen Retiro (Prado Annex), Calle de Felipe IV. Awkwardly subtitled "Section of 19th-Century Spanish Art of the Prado" and housed in a gravely colonnaded palace.

Picasso's *Guernica*, now back after 44 years in New York, is undoubtedly the star of the show. Apart from that, more Goya: paintings of death and daily life. Portraits, frequently unflattering, by Vicente López (Goya's prize pupil). A hall of historical paintings, strong on melodrama, blood and Spanish honour. And on to early Spanish impressionists.

Museo Sorolla, Paseo del General Martínez Campos, 37. The only Madrid museum devoted to a single painter, this mansion was the home and studio of Joaquín Sorolla (1863–1923). Close to 300 paintings on view, showing the Valencian impressionist's areas of immense talent—seaside scenes and landscapes.

Museo de Arte Contemporáneo (Museum of Contemporary Art), Avenida de Juan de Herrera, Ciudad Universitaria. This starkly modern museum is warm and attractive inside a somewhat forbidding skyscraper. Beautifully arranged and documented displays from early 20th-century realism to post-pop art. Picasso, Miró and Dalí, of course, plus many talented Spanish artists of lesser fame. First-class sculpture throughout and in the surrounding gardens.

Museo Cerralbo, Calle de Ventura Rodríguez, 17. Another nobleman's collection bequeathed to his country. It's more like visiting an art collector's house than a museum; few works are identified or marked. But there are paintings by El Greco, Murillo, Ribera, Zurbarán, Titian and Caravaggio. The mansion's split-level library would make any bibliophile jealous.

Convento de la Encarnación (Convent of the Incarnation), Plaza de la Encarnación. Founded in 1611 by Margaret of Austria, this convent-church-museum has accumulated an interesting art collection. Hundreds of religious relics. In the 18th-century Baroque church, you may hear the nuns praying, but you'll never see them; they are cloistered on the other side of the grillwork.

Panteón de Goya—Ermita de San Antonio de la Florida, Paseo de la Florida. In an unglamorous area between the railway yards and the river, Goya's greatest fresco covers the cupola of an 18th-century chapel. Four large mirrors, arrayed at crucial points to permit detailed scrutiny, allow you to study the painting without straining your neck. An identical chapel has been built alongside this one so that the local congregation is no longer bothered by tourists paying homage to Goya. His tomb was installed here in 1919.

Understanding the Past

Museo Arqueológico, Calle de Serrano, 13. Emphasizing the art of the ancient inhabitants of Spain. Charming statuettes and jewelry belonging to the 2nd-century B.C. Carthaginian settlers of the island of Ibiza. Miraculously preserved mosaics from 2nd-century A.D. Roman Spain. An unforgettable item, *La Dama de Elche* (The Lady of Elche), a stone sculpture found in Alicante Province in 1897. This thoroughly noble goddess, with beautiful cheekbones, lips and eyes, wearing a fanciful headdress, may be 2,500 years old. Items from the more recent past cover Visigothic religious works and the intricacies of Muslim Spanish workmanship.

A pre-Columbian figure from Costa Rica on view at Museum of America.

On the museum grounds—or, more correctly, *under* the ground—they have reproduced the painted scenes discovered in a cave in Altamira, in northern Spain: prehistoric paintings of animals, dating back perhaps 15,000 years and representing man's first illustrations of the world around him. A facsimile especially worth seeing now that the caves are closed to visitors.

Museo de América (closed for renovation), Avenida de los Reyes Católicos, 6 (Ciudad Universitaria). To Spaniards, "America" means Central and South America. Peru and Mexico provided outstanding pre-Columbian statues and artefacts. Two rare Mayan manuscripts (codices) are displayed in their entirety under glass—mysterious symbols and delightful illustrations which have long fascinated scholars.

Templo Egipcio de Debod. Threatened with submersion during the building of the Aswan High Dam, this 25-century-old Egyptian temple was dismantled and shipped to Madrid, stone by stone. It has been reconstructed amidst palm trees and other alien flora in the gardens of the Cuartel de la Montaña. The sight *from* the temple is also something special: a panoramic view over Madrid.

Arts and Crafts

Museo Nacional de Artes Decorativas, Calle de Montalbán, 12. Full of the things antique collectors dream of finding at the flea market *(Rastro)*—but here they are real. The best of old Spanish glassware, woodwork, tapestry, porcelain, jewelry.

Museo Romántico, Calle de San Mateo, 13. Spaniards seem incurably nostalgic for the age of love seats, Rococo mirrors and petticoated young princesses. Among the whimsical 19th-century relics are some genuinely interesting works of art.

Real Fábrica de Tapices (Royal Tapestry Factory), Calle de Fuenterrabía, 2. All that has changed since Philip V founded this workshop in 1721 is the method of dyeing the wool. Goya worked here, creating the designs on which tapestries were based. They are still being copied, along with contemporary designs, on commission.

Just for Curiosity

Museo de Carruajes (Carriage Museum), Campo del Moro. This installation, on the far side of the Royal Palace, houses royal transport of all kinds up to the eve of the age of automobiles. See a 16th-century litter thought to have borne the Emperor Charles V when he was suffering from gout. Much more recent history was made by the gala coach of Alfonso XIII, still showing signs of damage from a 1906 assassination plot. Here are coaches with the evocative Spanish names *berlina, lando, vis-a-vis, faeton* and *milord*. A stage-coach, ancient sedan chairs, sleds and saddles round off the well-organized curiosities.

Fábrica Nacional de Moneda y Timbre (also known as Casa de la Moneda, or Mint Museum), Paseo del Doctor Esquerdo, 36. A modern, attractive money museum on the top floor of the actual mint. While you explore the 22 halls with 25,000 numismatic exhibits, you can actually thrill to the vibration of the great presses downstairs manufacturing pesetas. Among the oddities on view: a 12th-century Chinese banknote, early American dollars and a proliferation of Russian banknotes issued in the confusion of the revolutionary period.

Museo Colón de Figuras de Cera (Wax Museum), Plaza de Colón. Privately run collection of realistic wax figures representing historical and contemporary celebrities, with special audiovisual effects.

Museo Naval, Calle de Montalbán, 2. Inside the Navy headquarters, this museum reflects the old glory of Spanish seamen—explorers and their ships. A treasure here, a map dating from 1500, discloses a startling amount of knowledge about the newly discovered western hemisphere.

Museo Municipal (Municipal Museum), Calle de

Fuencarral, 78. The best part is the exterior of the building, built by Pedro Ribera in the mid-18th century. The memorably ornamental portal is the last word in Rococo pomp.

Museo Taurino (Bullfighting Museum), part of Plaza de Toros Monumental de Las Ventas (bullring). Historic posters, capes, swords, paintings and photos for *aficionados* of the *corrida*.

Cervantes waits for inspiration at his desk in Wax Museum display.

Landmarks and Parks

Paseo de la Castellana, Madrid's principal north-south avenue, runs for several miles through the heart of the city. Heading northwards from Plaza de Colón, you come to a newer section of town. Patrician town-houses in the central area give way to luxurious modern apartment blocks with landscaped balconies.

Nuevos Ministerios (New Ministries). A bureaucrat's dream along Paseo de la Castellana, this mammoth 20th-century project dignifies the Ministries of Housing, Labour and Public Works, reminiscent of Washington, D.C.

Once a royal forest, Casa de Campo now has public lake, zoo, funfair.

Plaza de Colón. Separating La Castellana from the Paseo Recoletos is a wide-open space that has been the recent scene of far-reaching public-works projects. The city airline terminal operates below ground, far beneath an 1885 statue of Christopher Columbus and a monument to the discovery of the New World.

There is also the Centro Cultural de la Villa (City Cultural Center), with facilities for concerts, theatre, art exhibitions and films.

Puerta de Alcalá. This super-monumental triumphal arch, surmounted by warrior-angels, honours Charles III. Until the late 19th century, this was the very edge of town. Now the Plaza de la Independencia, in which the arch stands, is a bedlam of mid-town traffic.

One of a dozen entrances to **Parque del Retiro** faces Plaza de la Independencia. Until little over a century ago, the Retiro was a royal preserve. Now it's the easiest place for *Madrileños* to take a family outing (see page 91).

Another central breathing space, the **Real Jardín Botánico** (Royal Botanical Garden) adjacent to the Prado, was founded two centuries ago. It is packed with enlightening displays of flowers and plants from many regions.

Las Cortes Españolas, the Spanish Parliament, occupies a mid-19th-century building very near the Prado Museum. Before the Corinthian columns stand two ornamental lions, cast from the metal of guns captured from some of Spain's 19th-century enemies.

The **Puente de Segovia** (Segovia Bridge), Madrid's oldest bridge, dates from 1584. Juan de Herrera, the man who built the Escorial, designed this sturdy, granite span. It crosses Madrid's very own river, the Manzanares, a trickle of a river, no competition for the Mississippi, the Amazon or even the Thames. As Lope de Vega wrote, *"Tenéis un hermoso puente con esperanzas de río"*. ("You have a fine bridge, with hopes for a river.")

Ciudad Universitaria, the University City, was built on the ruins of the district that suffered the worst damage in the Civil War.

A drive around indicates the ambitious expanse of the campus and the mixture of architectural styles.

Parque Casa de Campo. Another former royal preserve, forested by Philip II in 1559. It is reachable by bus, suburban railway line or cable car *(teleférico)*. Thousands of acres of woodland interspersed with attractions and amenities. Hire a boat on the park lake. Swim in the pool. Practice bull-fighting. Ride the Ferris wheel and eat toffee-apples at the funfair. See the modern (1972) zoo, where 150 kinds of animals show off behind moats, not bars.

Excursions

Toledo

Pop. 45,000

(70 km. south-west of Madrid)

All of Spain—tradition, grandeur and art—is crammed into this small city set on a Castilian hilltop. This one-time imperial capital remains the religious centre of Spain and an incomparable treasure-house of the fine arts. You may get lost exploring the back streets, little changed over the centuries, but you'll never forget the aesthetic adventure.

If you see only one Spanish city outside Madrid, make it Toledo. And if you visit only one church in all Spain, make it the **Cathedral of Toledo.** You can locate the cathedral from any part of town, thanks to its Gothic tower, topped by a spire strangely ringed by spikes. But at ground level, the building is hemmed in by Toledo's clutter of back streets, so you cannot obtain a sufficiently dramatic view from any vantage point. No matter; the glory of this church can be seen inside it—the stained glass, wrought iron, sculpture and painting produced by platoons of geniuses.

Toledo's eminence as the centre of Christian Spain goes back to the first synods and ecclesiastical councils, held there as early as the year 400. But with the Muslim invasion of Spain in 711, Christianity went underground. After the reconquest of Toledo in 1085, with the legendary warrior El Cid leading the way, mosques were turned into churches. In 1222, funds were appropriated for a fitting cathedral. The construction lasted two and a half centuries; the ornamentation took longer.

In the centre of the five-aisled Gothic basilica, the **coro** (choir) is a marvel of woodcarving. Illustrations of the Christian triumph at Granada in 1492, on the lower choir stalls, were created by Rodrigo Alemán only three years after the great event itself. The higher stalls came later, carved by the Renaissance masters Alonso Berruguete (left) and Felipe Bigarny. The 13th- or 14th-century statue known as *The White Virgin* is believed to be French. Notice her smile.

Across the transept, the **main altar** outdoes the coro's considerable splendour. A magnificent polychrome retable tells New Testament stories in fervent detail, rising in five tiers. Immeasurable talent and toil went into this masterpiece of teamwork.

Just behind the back wall of the main chapel, the **Transparente** is the cathedral's most unforgettable innovation. Although the work is fantastically elaborate, it was done by one man. Narciso Tomé took all the credit as architect, sculptor and painter. What this 18th-century artist did was to open the ceiling and draw heavenly light into the sanctuary, at the same time leading our eyes up to an amazing launching pad for the soul. While the cathedral's 750 stained-glass windows illuminate with sublime restraint, Tomé's bronze, marble and jasper ensemble of colour, shape and symbolism startles as it inspires.

The **Sala Capitular** (Chapter-House) is a strangely oriental room with an intricate ceiling in the style called *mudéjar* (the work of Christianized Muslims after the Reconquest). Around the walls are portraits of the archbishops of Toledo, starting with St. Eugene (A.D. 96) and featuring Cardinal Cisneros, who ordered the construction of this hall.

In the **Tesoro** (Treasury Room), reliquaries, chalices and crowns take second place

León Valladolid
Adanero
SEGOVIA
Sierra de Guadarrama
Riofrío
La Granja
(S. Ildefonso)
El Paular
Villacastín
Puerto de
Navacerrada
Salamanca
San Rafael
Navacerrada
AVILA
Guadarrama
Valle de los
Caídos
El Escorial
Río Manzanares
Burgos
El Pardo
Barraco
Cebreros
Aeropuerto de Barajas
MADRID
Valencia
Cuenca
San Martín de
Valdeiglesias
Sotillo de
la Adrada
Getafe
Navalcarnero
Escalona
Río Guadarrama
Illescas
Chinchón
Maqueda
MADRID
AND VICINITY
Aranjuez
Albacete, Córdoba, Granada
Mocejón
TOLEDO
0
10 miles
N
Consuegra, Ciudad Real

to the lavish monstrance (also ordered by Cisneros). This towering vessel, made of 5,600 individual parts, was the work of the German silversmith Enrique de Arfe (Heinrich von Harff). It was subsequently gilded. Precious stones add to the glitter. The monstrance is said to weigh 17 *arrobas* (over 440 pounds).

The **sacristy** is a museum of art, air-conditioned for the sake of the paintings, not the people. The pictures are clearly labelled (a rarity in Spanish churches), so you won't have to keep asking, "Could this really be another genuine El Greco?" It certainly could. In all, there are 16 of them in this small collection. In addition to portraits of the Virgin, Christ with the Cross, and the apostles, there is a large and outstanding El Greco work over the main altar of the sacristy—*Expolio* (The Saviour Stripped of His Raiment). The museum also displays first-rate paintings by Goya, Titian and Velázquez.

Tourists are charged a fee

Among Toledo's glories: main altar of cathedral has splendid retable.

for admission to closed areas of the cathedral, such as the choir, treasury and museum.

The cathedral's only competitor for domination of the Toledo skyline is the **Alcázar,** a fortress destroyed and rebuilt many times. It began as a Roman redoubt, but its present style was devised in the 16th century. Since then it has been used as a royal palace, army post, school and prison. During the Spanish Civil War, it was a stronghold of the pro-Franco forces, who held out during a 72-day siege which all but destroyed the Alcázar. The Nationalist commandant, Colonel José Moscardó Ituarte, received a telephone call from the enemy announcing that his son, held hostage, would be executed unless the fortress surrendered. In a supremely Spanish reply, the colonel advised his son to "pray, shout *'Viva España'* and die like a hero". More than a month after the son was killed, the siege was lifted. You can visit the shrapnel-scarred office of the unyielding colonel and see other relics of the drama—an ancient Swedish radio transmitter, bound copies of the *Illustrated London News* riddled with bullet holes, two vintage Harley-Davidson motorcycles, the primitive underground hospital and the small, dark room in which two babies were born while the fighting raged.

The triangular-shaped main plaza of Toledo has also been rebuilt after Civil War destruction. The **Plaza de Zocodover** is where the Moorish market *(zoco)* was held in the Middle Ages. It was also the scene of the great fiestas, tournaments and executions of criminals and infidels. Suggestively, the horseshoe arch leading from the square towards the river is called El Arco de la Sangre (Arch of Blood).

Just down the hill beyond the arch in Calle de Cervantes, the 16th-century **Hospital de la Santa Cruz** (Hospital of the Holy Cross), now a museum, maintains a most elaborate façade. The main portal is of stone carved in the style called Plateresque, because it seems as delicate as a silversmith's work (*platero* means silversmith). Inside, great wooden ceilings add to a feeling of opulent spaciousness. The provincial archaeological museum is housed here, but greater interest accrues to the art collection. Here, too, El Greco fans are in for a happy surprise—a wide selection of his works, highlighted by the

TOLEDO
Puerta de Bisagra
Madrid
Avila
Paseo de la Rosa
Ciudad Real
Castillo de San Servando
Calle de Gerardo Lobo
Paseo de Recaredo
Santo Domingo
Santa Clara
Puente de Alcántara
Hospital de Santa Cruz
Arco de la Sangre
Paseo del Carmen
Calle Real
Santo Domingo el Antiguo
C. de Tendillas
Calle de la Plata
Calle del Comercio
Pl. de Zocodover
C. de Cervantes
Academia Militar
San Ildefonso
San Román
Alcázar
San Juan de los Reyes
Paseo de la Ronda Nueva
Calle del Angel
Palacio Arzobispal
Catedral
Santa María la Blanca
Parroquia de Santo Tomé
Taller del Moro
Ayuntamiento
Mérida
Museo y Casa de El Greco
Sinagoga del Tránsito
San Juan de la Penitencia
Río Tajo
Santa Isabel
Calle del Pozo
San Andrés
San Lucas
Seminario
N

Altarpiece of the Assumption, painted just a year before the artist's death.

At the bottom of Calle de Cervantes is the Paseo del Carmen, a promenade on a bluff overlooking the River Tagus, which flows all the way to Lisbon. From here, you get a fine view of the Bridge of Alcántara, with elements built in the 9th and 13th centuries. And across the river, the Castle of San Servando—originally a monastery, then a medieval fortress, designed to defend Toledo from any attack from the east. While the bridge, the fortress and other monuments are carefully preserved, the authorities have been unable to defend the Tagus from industrial pollution and detergent foam.

Every Tuesday, the Paseo del Carmen is the site of the big outdoor **market.** Here you can spy on the shouting, shoving and colour of unselfconscious provincial Spain. The street market caters to practical local needs—basic clothing and household goods. For tourist requirements, you'll have to try the shops elsewhere in Toledo. They sell swords, of course—bullfighter models or miniatures for letter openers, or historic reproductions. You can watch the artisans making a variety of damascene items. The ceramics are inventive. Or you might like to own an old-fashioned illustrated lady's folding fan.

The **Parish Church of Santo Tomé** is a landmark because of its stately *mudéjar* tower. Here they charge a fee for the sight of a single picture. But what a painting! El Greco's *Burial of the Count of Orgaz* manages to combine in a magic fusion the mundane and the spiritual. It depicts grave-faced local noblemen attending the count's funeral (which occurred nearly three centuries before the picture was painted). Tradition says two saints made an appearance at the funeral. El Greco shows St. Augustine and St. Stephen, in splendid ecclesiastical garb, lifting the count's body. Above, angels and saints crowd the clouds. The whole story is told in perfect pictorial balance and with El Greco's unpredictable colours.

Toledo was El Greco's adopted home town, where he spent the most productive years of his prolific career. Just down the hill from Santo Tomé, a house in which he may have lived has been reconstructed and linked to a museum dedicated to the painter. The authentic 16th-century furnishings and a tranquil garden assist the mood. Several of the master's paintings are on display, among them *A View and Map of Toledo,* showing how little the city has changed since his day. Dramatically displayed on an easel stands his *Portrait of St. Peter.*

The **El Greco House** was originally built by Samuel Levi, a remarkable 14th-century Jewish financier and friend of King Peter I of Castile. Since the 12th century, Toledo had been a centre of Jewish poets, historians and philosophers. Jews, Arabs and Benedictine monks worked together in translation teams. As Europe awakened from the Dark Ages, Toledo provided a key link in the transmission of vital knowledge of Arabic science and Greek philosophy to the Western world.

During those halcyon days, Samuel Levi, as devout as he was rich, built a synagogue next to his home. It now bears the curious name of **La Sinagoga del Tránsito** (Synagogue of the Dormition). Muslim artists created a ceiling of cedar imported from Lebanon; they adorned the walls with filigrees intricate beyond belief, as well as inscriptions in Hebrew from the Psalms. Upstairs, a large gallery was reserved for the women of the congregation. You may be surprised to find Christian tombstones in the floor. After the expulsion of the Jews from Spain, the synagogue was converted into a church. Nowadays, the **Sephardi Museum** is attached to Samuel Levi's synagogue, with exhibits of medieval tombs, scrolls and vestments.

Like the Tránsito, **La Sinagoga de Santa María la Blanca** (St. Mary the White) received its present name after its conversion to a church. No signs of the Jewish presence remain, yet this five-aisled building, with its 24 columns supporting horseshoe arches, was the main synagogue of 12th-century Toledo. Constructed by Muslim artisans, it looks more like a mosque than a synagogue or church. In the 15th century, bloodthirsty mobs raided the synagogue and massacred the Jewish population. After the pogrom, the old structure served a bizarre variety of purposes—as Catholic chapel, con-

Toledo skyline is almost unchanged since days of El Greco. So are the laundry methods in rural Castile.

vent for "fallen" women, army barracks and quartermaster's depot. This now empty building evokes the most dramatic memories.

A final church of Toledo, with regal connections: Ferdinand and Isabella built **San Juan de los Reyes** (St. John of the Kings) out of their private fortune in commemoration of the 1476 victory over the Portuguese in the Battle of Toro. The architectural style is a combination of Gothic, Renaissance and *mudéjar* elements. Look for a poignant souvenir on the outer wall—the chains which held Christian prisoners of the Moors. The cloister here is a superb double-decker of mostly late Gothic style, with elaborate stone carvings; a delightfully placid spot.

Two-storey cloister of San Juan de los Reyes is another gem of Toledo.

On the way out of town, between the 16th-century gateway called La Puerta Nueva de Bisagra and the bullring, there stands the **Hospital de Tavera,** part-palace, part-orphanage, part-church, built by a 16th-century Archbishop of Toledo, Juan Pardo de Tavera. The library contains fascinating old books as well as the bound volumes of the hospital's financial accounts, which record in meticulous script expenditures for fish and chocolate. In the dining room hangs a portrait by Titian of the Emperor Charles V and a painting of the Princess Clara Eugenia by Claudio Coello. Elsewhere in the palace, perhaps inevitably, El Greco is strongly represented. His portrait of the Virgin is stirringly beautiful; his *Baptism of Christ* is one of the artist's last works. A curiosity here is Ribera's portrait of a bearded woman. Notice, too, a small statue of

Near Toledo, a bicyclist tilts his imagination at Castilian windmills.

Christ resurrected, an experiment in sculpture by the great El Greco.

If you're driving back to Madrid from Toledo and would like a brief halt almost exactly mid-way, the village of **Illescas** (33 km. from Toledo) holds a surprise in store for you. Few visitors discover the village or its **Hospital de la Virgen de la Caridad** (Convent of the Virgin of Charity), in whose church hang five El Grecos. The locals seem only mildly interested in the artistic treasure in their midst. They tend to prefer another picture on display—a straightforward painting of the church itself.

Segovia

Pop. 40,000
(88 km. north-west of Madrid)

The delights of Segovia rise up unexpectedly on all sides. Before you have time to digest the glory of the natural setting, the magnificent skyline will have captivated you. Then, just when this mirage of medieval Spain comes into focus, your attention is drawn to some equally breathtaking monument or building. These are wonders to be savoured one at a time.

First, the site. Segovia juts out from the clean-air plateau in the heart of Old Castile. This is pure Castilian country—wide-open spaces made for cavaliers, interrupted only occasionally by a clump of trees, a lonely farmhouse, a monastery or a castle. The Sierra de Guadarrama, where you can ski in the winter, fills half the horizon.

Segovia's three greatest monuments are—in chronological order—the aqueduct, the Alcázar and the cathedral.

The **Roman aqueduct,** a work of art and a triumph of engineering, marches right through the centre of town. Looked at from our era of instant obsolescence, the builders of this public-works project merit special admiration. The aqueduct is composed of thousands of granite blocks arranged in graceful arches, sometimes two-tiered. It is nearly half a mile long and as much as 150 feet high. This is the last lap of a conduit bringing water from a mountain stream to the walled city. Almost as astonishing as the engineering achievement is the fact the aqueduct has been in constant use not just for 100 years, but 100 generations!

Only a couple of details have been changed. A modern pipeline has been installed in the channel atop the aqueduct; and in the 16th century, a statue of Hercules in a niche over the tallest arch was replaced by a Christian image. Nearly 2,000 years after the aqueduct was finished, it still brings water to Segovia.

The **Alcázar,** Segovia's incomparable royal castle, was built in the most natural strategic spot. It dominates a ridge overlooking the confluence of two rivers, with an unimpeded view of the plateau in all directions. The Romans are thought to have been among the first to build a watchtower here. The present storybook castle is a far cry from the simple stone fortress which took shape in the 12th century. As it grew bigger and more luxurious, it played a more significant historical role. By the 13th century, parliaments were convened here. In 1474, Princess Isabella stayed in the Alcázar at the time of her coronation as Queen of Castile. Here in 1570, King Philip II married his fourth bride, Anne of Austria. Less ceremoniously, the Tower of King John II became a dungeon for 16th-century political prisoners. The most fanciful,

SEGOVIA
Convento de Santa Cruz
Santa
Lucía
San Juan de los Caballeros
San Justo el Salvador
San Augustín
Acueducto
Madrid
Museo Provincial
San Nicolás
C. la Muerte
Monasterio de El Parral
Río Eresma
de
Pl. de los Huertos
La Trinidad
Casa de los Picos
San Clemente
Av. de Fernández Ladreda
San Martín
Bravo
Juan
San Esteban
Pl. de Franco
San Millán
Ronda
Convento del Corpus Christi
Villacastín
Catedral
San Andrés
Clamores
La Vera Cruz
Ronda
de
Paseo
Río
Plaza del Alcázar
Alcázar
Arévalo
N

photogenic parts of the castle's superstructure are the work of restoration after a disastrous fire in 1862.

You can sit quietly on a bench in the small park facing the turreted tower and allow the spectacle to sink in. Then cross the drawbridge over the moat and tour the royal rooms, carefully restored with period furnishings. See the Throne Room, the Pinecone Room (named after the designs carved in the ceiling),

Fairy-tale silhouette of Segovia's royal castle. Below: a view from 12th-century St. Martin's Church.

the royal bedrooms, the chapel. In the armoury, see early mortars and cannons, and even earlier lances and crossbows. The view from the open terrace is fit for a king.

From whatever part of town you look at it, the **cathedral** presents a reassuringly beautiful sight. Its pinnacles and cupolas seem to belong to a whole complex of churches, but, in fact, it's all a single elegant monument. Begun in 1525 (but not consecrated until 1768), this is the last of the great Spanish Gothic cathedrals. Its grace and style have won it the nickname of Queen of Cathedrals. Incidentally, the "Queen" was even taller until a lightning bolt lopped off the main tower in 1614. The reconstruction plan warily lowered the profile more than 10 per cent.

Inside, the cathedral's majestic columns and arches are lit by fine stained-glass windows. You will be struck by the sight of two 18th-century organs in all their massive flamboyance. Less obvious are the altarpieces in the chapels, the most important element of which (just to the right of the entrance) is a 16th-century polychrome pietà by the Valencian Juan de Juni.

Alongside the cathedral, delicate arches line the cloister. Admirable but invisible here is a background of persistent and meticulous handiwork. This cloister belonged to the former cathedral which was destroyed; it was moved here, stone by stone, in the 16th century and put back together.

The adjacent museum and chapter-house contain the religious art and relics that one would expect—but with a few surprises. The tapestries are 17th-century Gobelins. On show is the Baroque carriage propelled through the streets of Segovia every Corpus Christi, with its huge 17th-century silver monstrance. Here also is the pathetic reminder of a 14th-century tragedy: the tomb of the infant Prince Pedro, son of Enrique II. He slipped from the arms of his nurse as she admired the view from an open window of the Alcázar. The nanny scarcely hesitated before she leaped after him to death in the moat below.

Only a few streets away to the east, a much older church than the cathedral graces Segovia's most charming square. **St. Martin's Church** is a 12th-century Romanesque beauty with glorious portals and porches. Notice the ingeniously carved stone figures atop the pillars. Plaza de San Martín, which slopes down to Calle de Juan Bravo, is surrounded by noble mansions of the distinct Segovia style. As for Juan Bravo himself, whose flag-waving statue looms here, he defied the Emperor Charles V in the 16th century. Bravo of Segovia and Juan de Padilla of Toledo led an insurrection against absentee rulers and crushing taxes. The so-called *Comunero* movement eventually fizzled out, and both the leaders of the conspiracy were executed; but the brave Bravo is remembered here as the top local hero.

On the subject of statues, notice the primitive sculptures in the square. They may resemble James Thurber's hippopotami, but they are really a legacy of the Celtiberians, who preceded the Romans in ancient Old Castile.

Next to the church, the prison-like building with those fierce, barred windows was, in fact, a prison when it was built in the 17th century. Now it houses a library and archives. Here and throughout the city, the façades of the buildings are subject to elaborate three-dimensional decoration, mainly with geometric forms. The most extreme example, the nearby Casa de los Picos, simply bristles with pointed protuberances.

The main square of Segovia, the **Plaza Mayor,** combines history with real-life bustle. Buildings as pleasing as the 17th-century Town Hall face the large oblong plaza where shoppers, businessmen and tourists take time out for coffee in the fresh air. At festival times, the square is where all the excitement and colour begin.

Total tranquillity permeates the **Monastery of El Parral,** founded in the mid-15th century, lying beyond the city walls, but within easy reach of the centre of town. The architectural details, including a Gothic cloister, are being restored in fits and starts. Especially dramatic is the 16th-century high retable in the monastery's church.

Finally, you should see, just outside the wall and almost in the shadow of the Alcázar, the **Vera Cruz Church,** an unusual 12-sided building, dating from the early 13th century. The Knights of the Holy Sepulchre held court in its unique double-decker chapel surrounded by a circular nave. The Maltese Order, owner of the church for centuries, renovated it in the 1950s. It's still moody.

So much of Segovia is superlative that the 11th-century city wall itself is almost relegated to second-class status. But it's all relative. The mile and a half of wall tends to be irregular, but evocative; here and there you'll come across some warlike, fierce stretches, but mostly the wall is homely and lived-in.

Avila

Pop. 32,000

(112 km. north-west of Madrid)

The fairy-tale stone **walls** protecting Avila are just too perfect: they make the city look like a Castilian Disneyland. But they were built in all seriousness in the last decade of the 11th century.

Advertising signs on the road to Avila call it "The Best-Walled City in the World" *(la ciudad mejor amurallada del mundo)*. The publicity may be true, but there's more to Avila than the 1½ miles of fortifications, averaging 40 feet in height, with 88 towers and an

Avila dignitaries lead procession in commemoration of St. Theresa.

estimated 2,500 niches suitable for sentries or marksmen.

If you're visiting Madrid in summer, you'll appreciate the cooler mountain air of Avila—Spain's highest provincial capital, at more than 3,700 feet above sea level.

Before the "modern" Avila was built behind its crenellated wall, Celtiberians had settled in the area and are credited with having sculpted the crude stone statues of bulls and pigs around the city.

The **cathedral** of Avila, built between the 12th and 16th centuries, includes Romanesque, Gothic and Renaissance elements. It nudges the city wall; the apse, in fact, is a part of the wall itself. Fine stained-glass windows accentuate the grace of the interior. The choir stalls, carved to illustrate the lives of the saints, are attributed to the 16th-century Dutch master known as Cornelius de Holanda. The high retable was

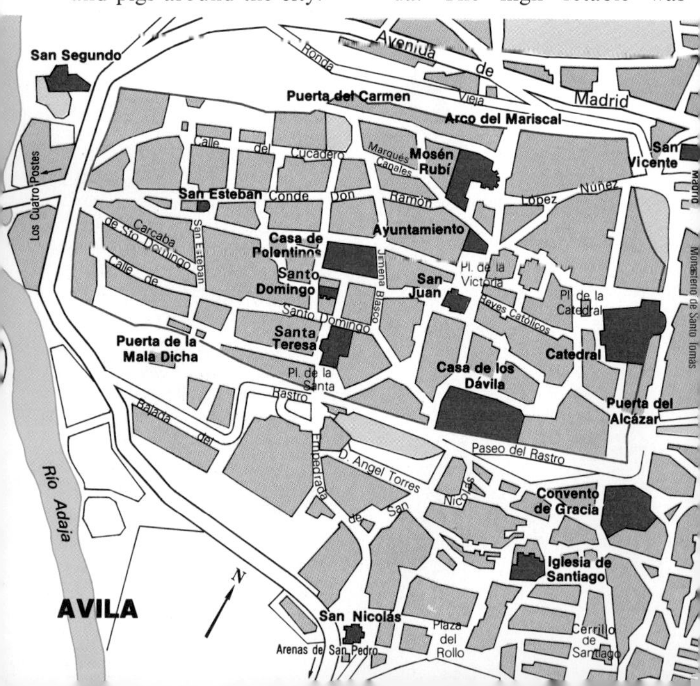

begun by Pedro Berruguete, Spain's first great Renaissance artist, but he died in 1504 before it could be finished. The brightly coloured scenes from the life of Jesus were completed by later painters, Juan de Borgoña and Santa Cruz. In the ambulatory behind the altar is a brilliantly sculpted alabaster monument, the tomb of Bishop Alonso de Madrigal, whose dark complexion won him the nickname *El Tostado* (The Toasted One). The 16th-century sepulchre portrays the bishop in full regalia, accurate right down to the embroidery on his robes.

Attached to the cathedral, a museum of relics and art works includes sculptures, paintings and valuable illuminated manuscripts. The place of honour, in an inviolable glass case, belongs to a silver monstrance as tall as a man. Juan de Arfe* was the artist; 1571, the year he finished it, and the tiny bells all ring.

The **Basílica de San Vicente** (St. Vincent's Basilica), just outside the city walls, is considerably smaller than the cathedral, but hardly less inspiring. The main (west) portico features lifelike statues of the apostles—barefoot, long-haired, bearded men, seemingly caught off guard by a candid sculptor. Inside, an extraordinary tomb commemorates the historically hazy case of St. Vincent of Saragossa and his two sisters, martyred in the 4th century. Knights of old placed their hands on this 12th-century sepulchre when they took their oaths. Reliefs all the way around the tomb illustrate in abundant detail the suffering of the martyrs. All of this is topped by a bizarre oriental-looking canopy added in the 15th century.

Melancholy history surrounds the **Royal Monastery of St. Thomas** (south-east, down the hill), the construction of which was sponsored by Ferdinand and Isabella. Their only son, Prince Don Juan, died here at the age of 19. His tomb in the monastery was carved from alabaster by Domenico di Sandro Fancelli of Florence. In a small chapel close to it, poignantly, the prince's two tutors are buried. Elsewhere in the church, Pedro Berruguete painted the reredos, showing episodes from the life of St. Thomas. It's worth climbing the old stone stairs to the choir loft to see the wood-carvings, particularly on the seats reserved for

* Grandson of Enrique de Arfe (Heinrich from Harff, near Cologne), who created the monstrance of Toledo.

the Catholic Monarchs themselves. Their coat-of-arms (the yoke and arrows later adopted as the motif of the Falange) appears here and elsewhere in the monastery.

Another historical note: This royal monastery was the headquarters of the monarchs' confessor and adviser, the noted Friar Tomás de Torquemada. As the first Grand Inquisitor of Spain, he was the enthusiastic leader of the 15th-century witch-hunt.

St. Thomas's is a three-cloister complex. The first is a small cloister, leading to the Silence Cloister with its garden. Beyond this is the third cloister built as a summer version of the royal court. Here, in the regal rooms, the Dominicans now run their **museum** devoted to Oriental art. This is not as inappropriate as it may seem at first. The Dominicans have long done missionary work in the Orient, and this is their collection of art works discovered in the field. A friar in a white cassock will escort you around, pointing out exceptional items—a huge Vietnamese incense-burner, Chinese ivory carvings of superhuman intricacy, a great Japanese jar portraying a fierce samurai, ancient pictures from Nepal, a Chinese bell from the 5th century B.C.

Many visitors associate Avila with Santa Teresa de Jesús (St. Theresa of Jesus). A much-adored mystic, reformer and personality, Teresa de Cepeda y Ahumada was born in Avila in 1515. The Convent of St. Theresa was built on the site of her birthplace. She spent some 30 years in the **Convent of the Incarnation,** outside the city walls, as a novice and later as prioress. Amongst the other landmarks, the Convent of San José was founded by St. Theresa in 1562, the first of 17 Carmelite convents she eventually established. She was canonized in 1622 and proclaimed a doctor of the Church in 1970. In Avila, you can see relics and manuscripts and even the habit St. Theresa wore in a remarkable life of prayer, penance and poverty.

After you've seen Avila up close—the cobbled streets, the mansions, the storks' nests in the belfries—drive or take a bus across the River Adaja to the monument called **Los Cuatro Postes** (The Four Posts). The simple, columned structure, of forgotten historic and religious significance, is secondary to the location. From this rocky hill you look back on the entire panorama of medieval Avila. Only from this vantage point, or an airplane, can you encompass the whole city in one admiring gaze. Under the pale blue sky of Old Castile, the invulnerable walled city looks too fabulous to be true.

Left: black-bereted Avila street vendor deploys toy clowns at fiesta. Since Middle Ages, storybook walls have enclosed living city of Avila.

El Escorial

(49 km. west of Madrid)

More than a palace, the Escorial is an entire royal city—living quarters, church, monastery, mausoleum and museum—all under one roof. In a distinctly Spanish version of Italian Renaissance style, it sums up the physical and spiritual superlatives of the empire's Golden Age (see opening photo, pages 2–3).

King Philip II ordered the Escorial built in celebration of Spain's victory over French forces in 1557 at the Battle of St. Quentin, in France. The king himself died here in 1598, to be buried in a family tomb tunnelled beneath the high altar of the basilica. The royal pantheon contains the remains of almost all Spain's kings, queens, princes and princesses over a period of four centuries.

As sombre and vast as the royal palace may be, the overbearing effect is eased by the adjoining, non-royal town of San Lorenzo de El Escorial. At an altitude of 3,460 feet, it's a popular getaway spot for *Madrileños* escaping the worst

Tapestries based on Goya's designs adorn room in the Escorial palace.

of summer. For a town of only 7,000 inhabitants, therefore, it enjoys more than its share of hotels, restaurants and bars.

Sheer statistics don't do full justice to the extravagant scale of the royal palace complex, built in only 21 years. The longest wall is over 970 feet from slim corner tower to tower. The dome of the palace church rises 302 feet. By official count, the building contains 86 stairways, more than 1,200 doors and 2,600 windows. Contemporary Spaniards called it the Eighth Wonder of the World.

The first plan for the Escorial is credited to the architect Juan Bautista de Toledo, but he died only four years after construction began. His successor, Juan de Herrera, is considered the greatest Spanish architect of the age. He also built the Royal Palace of Aranjuez and reconstructed the Alcázar of Toledo.

Inside the **basilica,** shaped like a Greek cross, the mood is one of devout magnificence. The immense main retable is composed of red marble, green jasper and gilded bronze. Fifteen statues, life-sized or larger, were the work of Leone and Pompeo Leoni, a father-and-son team of sculptors from Milan. The Leonis are also responsible for the bronze group on either side of the high altar. These portray the family of Charles V (on the left side) and the family of Philip II, kneeling majestically in prayer.

The 124 finely carved seats in the choir include a slightly roomier one for Philip II. In all, the basilica, with its brightly painted vaulted ceiling, fulfils its mission of embodying the king's religious fervour. Of the dozens of art works collected here, none attracts more admiration than the life-sized marble crucifix by Benvenuto Cellini of Florence. It is said that the great Renaissance artist originally planned the statue to adorn his own grave.

Exactly below the high altar, at the bottom of a flight of marble stairs, the **Pantheon of the Kings** is a subterranean churchyard of history. In the central hall, identical marble sarcophagi are stacked four high. Gilded angels hold lamps illuminating the terse Latin inscriptions. Of all the Habsburg and Bourbon kings who ruled Spain, only two are missing (Philip V is buried at La Granja de San Ildefonso, Ferdinand VI in Madrid). Adjoining chambers are assigned to lesser royal personages, with a gloomy area devoted entirely to the princes who died in childhood.

Above ground again, 40,000 rare books as well as manuscripts of immeasurable beauty and value are preserved in the **library** created by Philip II. The architect Herrera even took pains to design the bookcases, done in rare woods. The vaulted ceiling is a sight in itself—a painting symbolizing the arts and sciences, specifically Grammar, Rhetoric, Dialectic, Arithmetic, Music, Geometry and Astronomy. At opposite ends, Philosophy and Theology are extolled.

After seeing the church, mausoleum and library, visitors are shown through the **Palace of the Bourbons.** Here, one room is more lavish than the next. An outstanding element is the tapestries based on original designs by Goya and Rubens.

But the most striking wall-covering belongs to the **Hall of Battles.** Here, frescoes depict hundreds of soldiers, each detail carefully painted. The scene showing the Battle of Higueruela is based on the sketches by combat artists of 1431. Of course, the Spaniards won.

On the opposite side of the Courtyard of the Masks (named after the design of two fountains), the **apartments of Philip II** are modest in comforts, but rich in art works. The king died here among cherished paintings—a fantastic triptych by Hieronymus Bosch and works on religious themes by German, Flemish and Italian artists.

In addition to the fine paintings found elsewhere in the Escorial, the **New Museums** have been created to display the great works commissioned or collected by the Spanish monarchs. In the stately surroundings hang pictures by Bosch, Ribera, Tintoretto, Velázquez and Veronese. El Greco enthusiasts will find half a dozen of his canvases, including a unique portrait of Philip II at prayer in a sweeping celestial scene, as well as the classic *Martirio de San Mauricio* (Martyrdom of St. Maurice), full of sensitive detail. The New Museums amount to a worthy art gallery by any standards, a glorious afterthought to the historical and architectural significance of the Escorial.

Votive candles light faces of the devout in parish church near Avila.

Valle de los Caídos

(58 km. north-west of Madrid)

In a forested valley in the centre of Spain, Francisco Franco decreed that a memorial for the hundreds of thousands of victims, on both sides, of the Civil War be built on a site chosen personally by him. Thirty-five years later, in 1975, the Caudillo himself was buried beneath a simple stone slab in the monumental Church of the Valley of the Fallen. Officially, it is termed the "largest basilica ever built in the history of mankind", and this may be accurate. It was hewn out of the side of the mountain like a railway tunnel, yet claustrophobia is no great problem because the dimensions are so colossal and the decorations so unexpected.

The stone cross marking the basilica rises 492 feet from its base on top of a rocky outcrop. The cross is said to weigh 181,740 tons. Most other statistics are similarly impressive.

Farmer tills his land in idyllic countryside between Avila and Toledo.

From the parking area, where a souvenir shop sells Valley of the Fallen bottle openers and ashtrays, stairways lead to an esplanade with an area of 7½ acres. The arcaded façade of the church is big enough to fill one side of the esplanade. The style is reminiscent of Italian Fascist architecture. Inside the church, many statues and tapestries add to the subterranean pomp. There is plenty of room for decorations—the nave runs 860 feet into the mountain. Notable here are eight tapestries of the *Apocalypse of St. John* in brilliant colours. They were woven of gold, silver, silk and wool in Belgium in the mid-16th century and acquired by Spain's King Philip II.

A polychrome wood sculpture of *Christ Crucified* stands upon the high altar. The cross is said to come from a tree chosen and chopped down by Franco himself. Above this, the vast cupola is decorated by mosaics showing heaven-bound saints and martyrs of Spain.

Whatever your feelings are about the architectural, artistic, religious or political implications of the Valley of the Fallen, the superlatives add up to something unique and hard to forget.

Aranjuez

Pop. 30,000
(50 km. south of Madrid)

The deep-green water of the River Tagus, reflecting the noble buildings of Aranjuez, nourishes parks and formal gardens, as well as prize crops of asparagus and strawberries.

As you cross the bridge into Aranjuez on the road from Madrid, the roomy, geometric town plan becomes apparent. The balanced main square—actually a huge rectangle—is faced by arcaded buildings on two sides and the porticoed Church of St. Anthony at the south end.

But here the civic sights take second place to the royal parks and palaces. Ever since Ferdinand and Isabella, Spanish monarchs have been retreating to this oasis to escape Madrid's summer heat. Since the 18th century, they've enjoyed the luxury of a first-class country palace reminiscent of Versailles. In the mid-19th century, a railway line (later removed) ran right into the **Palacio Real** (Royal Palace). The iron horse was then considered so chic that it was a special delight for royal visitors to disembark directly at the bottom of the ceremonial staircase.

This is where the guided tours begin nowadays. They cover 22 rooms, enough to reveal a cross-section of royal taste in furniture, paintings, sculpture, tapestries, clocks, pianos, music-boxes and bric-a-brac. A few highlights:

Throne Room. All very ceremonious, except for the Louis XVI chairs beneath the royal canopy—surprisingly modest, really, for thrones.

Porcelain Room. Nobody could confuse this with any other room in any other palace. The decorations were created by the Buen Retiro porcelain factory of Madrid for King Charles III in 1760. The walls are covered with porcelain figures telling exotic stories: a Japanese samurai, Chinese mandarins, monkeys and birds. Seven mirrors, a weird porcelain chandelier, a circular couch and a fine marble floor complete the dazzling design.

Smoking Room. An Arabian Nights fantasy based on the Hall of the Two Sisters in the Alhambra at Granada. Red damask couches sprawl along the walls of this mid-19th-century reproduction.

Chinese Painting Salon. Hanging seven-deep along the walls, 200 ingenious rice-paper paintings were gifts from a Chinese emperor of the mid-19th century. The lantern-like chandelier, very original and oriental, comes from Japan.

A combined ticket covers all the sights in the palaces, gardens and museums. The **Museum of Court Dress,** downstairs in the Royal Palace, shows reproductions and, where possible, the actual costumes worn by Spain's kings and queens from the 16th to 20th centuries. One room is devoted to the costumes of the officials of the court—ambassadors, ministers, aides. A children's room decorated with the portraits of young princes contains their cradles, cribs and a rocking horse.

Less than 2 kilometres from the Royal Palace, the curiously named **Farmer's Cottage** *(La Casita del Labrador)* is set in the extensive Prince's Garden. Far from being a cottage, this is a condensed palace to which the kings retreated for parties and hunting weekends. Guided tours begin in the Billiard Room, filled by a behemoth billiard table illuminated by a formal chandelier.

Busts of ancient philosophers give the **Statue Gallery** its name, but the big attraction is what first seems to be a far-fetched fountain in the centre

Inspect Spanish regal fashions at museum in Aranjuez Royal Palace.

Salmer, Barcelona

of the room. It turns out instead to be a far-fetched clock, an 1850 folly, incorporating simulated water jets and a large music box.

This being an informal palace, the **ballroom** is scarcely large enough to accommodate 200 noble swingers. In their absence, a sturdy malachite desk and chair have been installed, a gift from the Russian Czar Alexander II to Queen Isabella II.

The **Platinum Room,** as sumptuous as it sounds, leads to the king's own toilet, wittily arranged as a plush throne.

Elsewhere in the Prince's Garden, in a modern building called the **Sailor's House** *(Casa de Marinos),* you can find out what became of the quaint "Tagus Squadron" of the royal fleet. The kings of Spain enjoyed being rowed down the river in gala launches. These flagships are preserved in the Sailor's House, along with related nautical mementoes. Here you can admire the last word in Rococo canoes, fancy feluccas and gilt gondolas.

Aside from the palaces and museums, Aranjuez is noted for its royal parks and gardens. The formal gardens are a wonder of flowers, clipped hedges, sculptures and fountains. The less disciplined forests of lindens, poplars or maples provide the kindest shade from the Spanish sun.

Chinchón

A nice side-trip (20 km.) from Aranjuez, through gently moulded hill country, leads to Chinchón. Here is charming proof that you don't have to travel hundreds of miles from Madrid to immerse yourself in the Spain of cargo-carrying donkeys on cobbled lanes. The town square could be a stage set. The two- and three-storey white stucco houses with wooden arcades surround an irregular, but vaguely oval plaza. Watch the laundry being washed in the town fountain. In season, bullfights are held right in the square, changing its Wild-West image to Old Spain.

Chinchón is celebrated as the home of various aniseed liqueurs. It also grows a much-vaunted species of garlic, sold locally in strung bouquets.

Scattered around the countryside here you'll notice over-sized earthen jars. These bee-hive-shaped vats, reminiscent of Roman amphoras, are made from a special type of clay quarried in this area. They're used for storing wine—or for decoration.

This Chinchón establishment sells ice-cream and more potent goods.

Three More Palaces

El Pardo, 15 kilometres north-west of Madrid, was the official residence of Generalísimo Franco for 35 years. It was built by Charles V in 1543 and reconstructed by Philip III after a fire in 1604. The main artistic attraction is a collection of tapestry amounting to hundreds of items; but to Spaniards, El Pardo may be more interesting for its memories of Franco's life—and death struggle.

La Granja de San Ildefonso, about 80 kilometres north of Madrid, is a huge palace set in classic formal gardens. Here, too, the tapestries—16th- to 18th-century masterpieces—are well worth seeing, collected by the Spanish royal family.

Riofrío, about 85 kilometres north of Madrid and 10 kilometres south of Segovia, has an 18th-century palace which is quite modest compared to the others. Part of it is now devoted to the **Museo de Caza** (Hunting Museum), with stuffed animals and ancient weapons. The palace is reached over the scenic road through the deer sanctuary. Drive carefully, and if you have any spare food along, the extrovert deer will eat out of the palm of your hand.

What to Do

Shopping

Madrid is Spain's superlative shopping centre, so leave some space in your luggage for gifts and souvenirs. What you buy will depend on your taste and budget, of course, but here's an alphabetical listing of items many visitors consider bargains or unique, or especially well made.

Alcohol. Bargains in brandy, sherry, wines and liqueurs bottled in Spain.

Antiques. Let the buyer beware, but Madrid's Rastro (flea market) attracts swarms of collectors. In nearby streets are more solid establishments dealing in old *objets d'art*.

Artificial pearls. From Majorca.

Bullfighter dolls, swords, hats—or posters, with your name imprinted as the star matador.

Capes. The old-fashioned Madrid *caballeros* sport a slightly sinister black version; women look glamorous in theirs.

Ceramics. Pots, bowls, tiles. Each Spanish region produces its own distinctive shapes, colours and designs, traditional or cheerfully modern.

Damascene. Inlaid gold designs in steel—knives, scissors, thimbles, jewelry. Watch them being made in Toledo.

Embroidery. Good handkerchiefs, napkins, tablecloths, sheets, all embellished with deft needlework.

Fans. The collapsible kind, as fluttered by *señoritas* over the centuries.

Fashion. Spanish *haute couture* has gained a significant niche in international competition.

Glassware. Blue, green or amber bowls, glasses, pots and pitchers from Majorca.

Handicrafts. No end to the originality and skill shown in items on sale in Madrid, the best works from artisans.

Hats. An offbeat souvenir—a bullfighter or Andalusian hat, just for fun.

Ironwork. Heavy on the baggage scales, but lamps, lanterns and candlesticks are appealing.

Jewelry. From cheap hippy-made bracelets to the most elegant necklaces.

Knives. Penknives, daggers and swords from Toledo, where the Crusaders bought theirs.

Leather. Check the varieties of coats, hats, gloves, wallets, handbags.

Men's wear. Suits tailored

to individual order, if you have the time and the money.

Needlework. The traditional lace mantillas for special occasions; or hand-sewn lingerie.

Paintings. Dozens of galleries around town sell the works of contemporary Spanish artists.

Quaint Quixote statues and knicknacks are found in every souvenir shop.

Reproductions. Cheap but handsome copies of great Spanish paintings, on canvas, sold at the Prado and in shops.

Rugs. Inventively designed floor coverings, from tiny throw-rug to full-scale carpet. Some are hand-woven.

Shoes. No longer such a bargain, but styles are admired. Be careful of sizes, which tend to be narrow.

Suede. Coats and bags may strike your eye.

Traditional trinkets. Millions of tourists keep coming back for the same old novelties—miniature swords, plastic-lined wine-skins, castanets and, irrationally, imitation Mexican sombreros.

Underwater gear. Snorkels, masks, flippers are bargains.

Among shopping joys of Madrid: olives for all tastes (left) and a Rastro specialist in bric-a-brac.

Valencian porcelain. Distinctive figurines of traditional or fashionable modern subjects.

Wicker baskets. Something original for carrying your other souvenirs.

Woodcarving. Statues of knights or saints.

Young fashions. Spanish children may be the world's best dressed. On sale are charming clothes, but very expensive.

Zany zoological figurines. Sophisticated ceramic animals made in Madrid.

Where and When to Shop

For a quick survey of what Spaniards are buying, amble

through the major department stores, with branches around Madrid.

For a look at the range of handicrafts, covering paperweights to full suits of armour, visit a shop of Artespaña, the official chain of showplaces for Spanish artisans.

For elegance, shop along Calle de Serrano and neighbouring streets. For variety, try the shops in the Gran Vía.

Madrid's biggest department store chains, El Corte Inglés and Galerías Preciados, now operate from 10 a.m. to 8 p.m. (9 p.m. on Fridays and Saturdays) without a break. But most shops follow the traditional Spanish hours, about 9.30 a.m. to 1.30 p.m. and 4 or 5 to 8 p.m.

Tax Rebates for Visitors

The Spanish government levies a value added tax (called "IVA") on most items. Tourists from abroad will be refunded the IVA they pay on purchases over a stipulated amount. To obtain the rebate, you have to fill out a form, provided by the shop. You keep one copy; the three others must be presented at the customs on departure, together with the goods. The rebate will then be forwarded by the shop to your home address.

The Bullfight

The *fiesta brava,* the bullfight, is an enduring symbol of Spain—flamboyance and fate, and violence with grace. And Madrid is indisputably the world's bullfighting capital. No matter how much of a sensation a bullfighter may have achieved in the provinces, he's a nobody until he wins the cheers of the *Madrileños.*

You may not like what you see, you may swear never to return to it, or you may become an outright *aficionado.* Whatever your reaction, you'll have to admit there's nothing like it in the world: man against bull, skill against instinct. For the bull, the outcome is certain; for the matador, less so.

At the outset of the fight, the matador meets the bull, takes his measure and begins to tire him using the big red and yellow *capote.*

After these preliminaries, the first *tercio* (third) begins when the *picador,* a mounted spearman in Sancho Panza costume, lances the bull's shoulder muscles. Then, in the second *tercio,* the deft *banderilleros* stab long darts into the animal's shoulders.

In the third *tercio,* the

matador returns to run the bull through a long series of passes, using the small, dark-red *muleta* cape, eventually dominating the beast. Finally, as the bull awaits its death, the *torero* lunges for the kill.

Waiting his turn in the bullring, matador fidgets over his costume. Below: running the bull in Avila.

Depending upon the quality and bravery of his performance, the matador may be awarded an ear, two ears or, as top prize, two ears plus the tail.

You may be upset, fascinated or simply confused by an afternoon at the bullfights. Admittedly, the spectacle is not for everyone—not even for every Spaniard. But it is something that remains very much a part of Spanish life.

The larger and more celebrated of Madrid's bullrings, the Plaza Monumental at Las Ventas, seats 32,000 spectators. The other *plaza de toros,* Vista Alegre, is in Carabanchel.

Buying a ticket could be a problem. Your hotel desk clerk can usually help—but at a significant mark-up for the ticket agent and a tip for the clerk. Travel agencies run tours for the afternoon, which include transport, tickets and a commentary. However you go, and whether you sit in the *sol* (sun) or *sombra* (shade), invest a few pesetas in comfort:

Dancers at Madrid flamenco show sum up the passionate soul of Spain.

hire a cushion so you don't spend the afternoon sitting on bare concrete.

Normally, Sunday afternoon is *corrida* time. But during the San Isidro fiestas in May, Madrid outdoes itself with a bullfight programme every day for more than a fortnight. Tickets are hard to come by.

Flamenco

Spain's best-known entertainment, after the bullfight, is flamenco—throbbing guitars, stamping heels and songs that gush from the soul. Many of the songs resemble the wailing of Arab music—which may be a clue to flamenco's origins, though not all "flamencologists" agree.

Madrid's flamenco nightclubs attract crowds of enthusiasts, including tourists who don't usually go to nightclubs or stay up after midnight. The anguished chants and compelling rhythms generate an electricity which crosses all frontiers of nationality or language.

There are two main groups of songs: one, bouncier and more cheerful, is known as the *cante chico* (a light tune). The second group of songs, called *cante jondo*, deals with love, death, all the human drama, done in the slow, piercing style of the great flamenco singers.

Purists say the talent in a *tablao flamenco* in Madrid is rarely up to top Andalusian standards. But it's a memorable night out, an overwhelming experience for the eyes, ears and heart.

Swinging Madrid

Europe's most indefatigable night people, the "cats" of Madrid, can choose from a profusion of bars and clubs. There are nightclubs with dancing girls, "intellectual" cafés, dark *boîtes* staffed with professional drinking partners, deafening discothèques, imitation pubs and beer halls, and jazz and folk-music clubs.

Travel agencies run Madrid-by-Night tours, taking in a couple of the top floorshows. Normally, the all-inclusive price covers dinner and a quota of drinks.

Casino
The Gran Madrid casino has turned the tables now, and American and French roulette, blackjack, chemin de fer and other games can be played in the swish halls of the casino, well purveyed with all the requisite bars, restaurants, etc. It's situated in the N-VI highway to La Coruña, half-an-hour's drive out of Madrid, and is open from 5 p.m. to 4 a.m. daily.

Cultural Activities

Concerts, Opera
Two resident symphony orchestras—the National Orchestra and the Spanish Radio and Television Symphony Orchestra—maintain a regular schedule of concerts for serious music fans in Madrid. Regular seasons of ballet and opera are also held.

Zarzuela
This uniquely Spanish form of operetta is much appreciated in Madrid, though its popularity has declined since the 1890's. The *zarzuela* comes in light-headed and in serious varieties. Even if you don't understand the language, it will entertain and enlighten.

Films
Almost all the films shown commercially in Spain have

Fiesta in windmill country of La Mancha brings out local folk dancers.

been dubbed into Spanish.

A certain number of cinemas in Madrid show foreign films in the original version, with Spanish subtitles. Normally, only avant-garde or controversial films are thus presented.

Theatre

Spain's dramatic tradition is long and glorious. In dozens of Madrid theatres, classical and contemporary foreign and Spanish works are performed, usually twice a night.

Fiestas

A fiesta in any Spanish city or village, however insignificant, will reveal a spirit and pageantry to be found nowhere else. If you happen to be around for the major spectacles, so much the better. But check local publications, ask at the tourist office or your hotel desk clerk to be sure you don't miss some unpretentious regional festival.

Here's a sample of noteworthy events in Madrid and surrounding provinces.

February

Zamarramala, Segovia Province. Santa Agueda festivals, medieval costumes and even older customs.

March

Illescas, Toledo Province. Fairs and bullfights for Festival of the Miracle of the Virgin of Charity.

March/April

Holy Week. Every town and city has striking processions of the penitent and other religious manifestations. In cities with famous cathedrals, such as Toledo and Segovia, the spectacle is unforgettable. The colourful town of Cuenca, 165 kilometres south-east of Madrid, is noted for its splendid processions and a religious music week.

May

Madrid. Fiestas of St. Isidore the Husbandman, the capital's patron saint. Half a month of neighbourhood parties, contests, plays, concerts and daily bullfights.

June

Toledo. Corpus Christi in Toledo. The Primate of Spain leads a solemn religious procession through the medieval streets.

Camuñas, Toledo Province. An ancient religious play is presented in mime, with spectacular costumes.

Segovia. Festivities of San Juan and San Pedro. Dances, bullfights.

July

Avila. Summer festival with poetry, art, theatre, sports, bullfights and funfair, all outdoors.

September

Candeleda, Avila Province. Pilgrimage of Our Lady of Chilla, medieval religious ceremonies plus dancing and bullfights.

October

Avila. Santa Teresa Week. Neighbourhood fairs, concerts, bullfights.

Consuegra, Toledo Province. Saffron Rose Festival in heart of windmill country of La Mancha.

Sports

Half a dozen **golf** clubs in the Madrid area operate all the year round. The greens are open to non-members on payment of a fee. Instruction is available. For advance planning, ask the Federación española de Golf, Capitán Haya 9, Madrid, for a detailed pamphlet, entitled "Golf in Spain".

Elsewhere in Madrid, a variety of sports facilities cater to many interests. You'll find **tennis** courts, **polo** grounds, **squash** courts, **swimming** pools, **bowling** alleys and **riding** stables.

Spectrum of outdoor sports: fun at Madrid pool and intensely serious putting on the green at plush club.

Hunting and Fishing

Big-game hunters make advance arrangements to stalk the rare *capra hispanica* (Spanish wild goat) in the Gredos National Preserve near Avila. Closer to Madrid, red partridge is a popular target. Water fowl are protected in a national preserve near Ciudad Real. Consult the Federación Española de Caza, Calle de la Princesa, 24.

In rivers near Madrid run trout, pike, black bass and royal carp. For further information, contact the Federación Española de Pesca, Calle Navas de Tolosa, 3.

Hunting and fishing permits are available from I.C.O.N.A., Calle de Jorge Juan, 39.

Skiing

From December to April, the Guadarrama Mountains north of Madrid become a major ski area. The scenery and facilities are first-rate, and all equipment may be hired. The most highly developed resort is Navacerrada, only 60 kilome-

Left: an excited crowd cheers football titans, Real Madrid, playing on their home field. Right: watching the rowing-boats drift by in Retiro Park.

tres from Madrid by car or bus. The only snag is that the slopes are simply packed with *Madrileños* every weekend and on holidays. Several other areas within easy range of the capital may be less congested. For further information, consult the Federación Española Deportes de Invierno, the Spanish Winter Sports Federation, Calle de Claudio Coello, 32.

Spectator Sports

Car racing. Championship trials at the Jarama circuit, on the Burgos road, 26 kilometres north of Madrid.

Dog racing. Daily at the Canódromo Madrileño, Vía Carpetana, 57, Carabanchel.

Football (soccer). The No. 1 sport in Spain. Real Madrid plays at Santiago Bernabéu Stadium, Paseo de la Castellana. Atlético de Madrid uses the Vicente Calderón Stadium, Paseo de los Melancólicos on the river in southwest Madrid.

Horse racing. Afternoons at the Hippodrome of La Zarzuela, on the La Coruña road, 7 kilometres from central Madrid.

Pelota. The incredibly fast Basque ball game, known in some circles as *jai alai*. Afternoons at Frontón Madrid, Calle del Doctor Cortezo, 10.

For Children

Casa de Campo. Swimming pool, sailing lake, funfair, ultra-modern zoo. For added excitement, take the cable car soaring above the city (*teleférico* station in Paseo del Pintor Rosales).

Retiro Park. Hire a rowing boat or a bicycle; sniff the flowers.

Wining and Dining

Plenty of hearty food made with fresh ingredients at reasonable prices: Such is the good news awaiting hungry tourists or international gourmets in Madrid.* Restaurants in this melting pot of Spain reproduce all the country's regional specialities. The capital has many delicacies of its own, as well. And if you're homesick for a pizza, a curry or whatever, the foreign restaurants cover more than a dozen nationalities.

Meal Times

Madrileños eat later than anybody. Though breakfast runs a fairly businesslike 8 to 10 a.m., lunch rarely begins before 2 p.m. and can go on to 4 or 4.30 p.m. Dinner might be attempted at 9 p.m., but 10 or 10.30 p.m. is the usual hour to start. The secret to survival: snack bars and cafés which keep everyone going between meals.

Where to Eat

All Spanish restaurants are officially graded by forks, not stars. One fork is the lowest grade, five forks, the top; however, ratings are awarded according to the facilities available, not the quality of the food. Many fork symbols on the door guarantee spotless tablecloths, uniformed waiters, lavish lavatories and high prices—but not necessarily better cooking.

Cafeterías in Spain are not self-service restaurants, but modern establishments serving fast meals, mostly at a counter.

Tascas are bars serving sumptuous snacks with wine or beer (see page 93).

Cafés serve coffee, drinks and snacks, and are almost always open.

Eccentricities

Spaniards customarily pack away filling, three-course meals. Don't feel obliged to keep up the same pace.

Regional cuisine varies greatly, but Spanish cooking is never overly spicy; a few Spanish dishes, on the contrary, may seem under-seasoned. Pepper is rarely served at the table. Garlic enters the picture frequently but subtly.

Menu prices are "all-inclusive". Your bill automatically includes all taxes and service

---

* For a comprehensive glossary of Spanish wining and dining, ask your bookshop for the Berlitz EUROPEAN MENU READER.

charges. But it's still customary to leave a tip. Ten per cent is considered generous.

All restaurants (as well as hotels) have an official complaint form *(hoja de reclamaciones)* available to dissatisfied clients. To be used only in outrageous cases.

Tascas and Tapas

A *tapa* is a bite-sized snack; a *tasca* is where you find it. *Tascas* are all over Madrid, and contribute to the excitement and temptation. One minute a *tasca* is empty, the next a crowd is fighting for space at the bar, the waiters are shouting to encourage business, and debris is piling up on the floor. It's all part of the essential atmosphere.

You don't have to know the Spanish names, for you can simply point to what you want. In fact, in a few cases, it might be better not to know what it is that looks and tastes so delicious. There are snails, deep-fried squid, mushrooms fried in garlic, baby eels, tripe, prawns and garlic, cold potato omelet, potato salad, meatballs.

In *tascas,* the food is more

Atmosphere and hospitality follow tradition in Old Madrid restaurant.

important than the drink, served in small glasses. Draught beer or house wine is appropriate. And don't be shy about tossing your olive stones, mussel shells and used napkins on the floor. If you don't, the counter-man will!

Castilian Specialities

Cocido Madrileño may be distinctive to Madrid, but nevertheless resembles the hotpot or stew found in other regions of Spain. The meal often starts with *sopa de cocido* (the broth resulting from boiling the ingredients for the next course), then the *cocido* itself: beef, ham, sausage, chickpeas, cabbage, turnip, onion, garlic, potatoes.

Sopa Castellana is a baked garlic soup, not as strong as it sounds. At the last moment, a raw egg is added; by the time it reaches the table, the egg is well poached.

Callos a la madrileña. By any other name, stewed tripe. But the spicy dark sauce makes all the difference. A great local favourite.

Besugo al horno. Sea-bream poached in a wine sauce.

Cochinillo asado. Tender Castilian sucking pig roasted to a golden crispness.

Cordero asado. Roast lamb, often a gargantuan helping.

From the Regions

Andalusia: *Gazpacho* (pronounced gath-PAT-cho) is the famous "liquid salad", so refreshing on a summer day. A chilled, highly flavoured soup to which chopped tomatoes, peppers, cucumbers, onions and croutons are added to taste.

Valencia: Renowned *paella* (pronounced pie-ALE-ya) is named after the black iron pan in which the saffron rice is cooked. In with the rice will be such ingredients as: squid, sausage, shrimp, rabbit, chicken, mussels, onion, peppers, peas, beans, tomatoes, garlic. Authentically, *paella* is served at lunchtime, cooked to order.

Asturias: *Fabada,* a variation on Madrid's *cocido,* but based largely upon white beans and sausage.

Navarra: *Trucha a la navarra,* grilled trout with a surprise slice of ham inside.

Galicia: *Caldo gallego,* a rich vegetable soup. Almost all Madrid restaurants, incidentally, serve a delicious soup of the day—vegetable, bean, lentil or chickpea.

Basque country: All manner of rich fish dishes come from this gourmet region of northern Spain. Try *bacalao al pil pil* (cod in hot garlic sauce), or *merluza a la vasca* (hake in a casserole with a thick sauce), or *angulas a la bilbaína* (eels in a hot olive-oil and garlic sauce, always eaten with a wooden fork).

Left: Sucking pig in show window of Segovia restaurant. Below: bar in Madrid offers tempting seafood.

Desserts

Like the seafood, which is rushed to Madrid from the Atlantic and Mediterranean every day, fresh fruit from all parts of the country turns up on restaurant tables: oranges, peaches, pears, strawberries, grapes and melons. Pastries overflowing with whipped cream are easy to find, hard to resist. A local speciality in Avila, an egg-yolk sweet called *yema de Avila,* is monumentally rich. Toledo is famous for a sweet, nutty relic of the Moors, spelled here *mazapán.*

Cheese is very expensive in Spain, no matter where it comes from. Look for *queso manchego,* from La Mancha, in its several varieties, from mild to sharp. Native goat cheeses, mostly anonymous, are cheaper.

P.S.: Breakfast

The most insignificant meal of the day in Spain, breakfast is just an eye-opener. Typically, it's *café con leche* (half coffee, half hot milk) and a pastry, grabbed on the run at the counter of a local bar. In deference to foreign tastes, most hotels also serve a full breakfast of juice, eggs, toast and coffee.

As for breakfast pastries, try *churros*. These fritters are

Churros, *left, are to be dipped. Musicians, below, are to be tipped.*

often made before your eyes by a contraption which shoots the batter into boiling oil. You absolutely must dunk *churros* in your coffee. (In late afternoon, or in the early hours after a very late night out, the Spaniards love a snack of *churros* with very thick, hot chocolate.)

Beverages

You needn't give a thought to "winemanship", or matching wits with the wine waiter to choose just the right vintage. When the average Spaniard sits down to a meal, he simply orders *vino,* and it means *red* wine to the average waiter. Often served chilled, this house wine can go with fish or meat, or anything. Relax and enjoy the unpretentiousness.

The nearest renowned vineyards to Madrid are Valdepeñas. If you're in a Galician restaurant, experiment with Ribeira wine—heavy red or white, from the area near Portugal. In Basque restaurants or bars, look for Txacoli, a slightly sparkling white.

The most famous of Spanish wines is sherry from Jerez de la Frontera, which is fortified with the addition of brandy. As an aperitif, try a *fino.* An *oloroso* goes well after dinner.

Sangría, a summertime refresher, is a winecup or a punch made with red wine, fruit juice, brandy and slices of fruit, diluted with soda and plenty of ice.

Spanish beer *(cerveza)* is good and cheap; usually served quite cold.

Spain is a bonanza for spirits and liqueur drinkers. Many foreign brands are bottled under licence in Spain and cost very little. By cruel contrast, imported Scotch and Bourbon are ultra-luxurious.

You may consider Spanish brandy too heavy or sweet compared with French cognac. But it's very cheap—often the same price as a soft drink.

Spanish *cava*—white sparkling wine—is mass-produced and cheap.

If you prefer non-alcoholic beverages with your meal or at a café, have no qualms about ordering a soft drink or mineral water, or fruit juice.

Finally, look for *horchata de chufa,* a chilled, sweet milky-white drink made from ground-nuts which taste similar to almonds. It's always drunk through a straw. Many bars stock it in small bottles, but the *aficionados* look for a real *horchatería* where it's home-made. A splendid Spanish thirst quencher.

To Help You Order…

Could we have a table?	**¿Nos puede dar una mesa?**
Do you have a set menu?	**¿Tiene un menú del día?**
I'd like a/an/some…	**Quisiera…**

beer	**una cerveza**	milk	**leche**
bread	**pan**	mineral water	**agua mineral**
coffee	**un café**	napkin	**una servilleta**
cutlery	**los cubiertos**	potatoes	**patatas**
dessert	**un postre**	rice	**arroz**
fish	**pescado**	salad	**una ensalada**
fruit	**fruta**	sandwich	**un bocadillo**
glass	**un vaso**	sugar	**azúcar**
ice-cream	**un helado**	tea	**un té**
meat	**carne**	(iced) water	**agua (fresca)**
menu	**la carta**	wine	**vino**

…and Read the Menu

aceitunas	olives	**jamón**	ham
albóndigas	meatballs	**judías**	beans
almejas	baby clams	**langosta**	spiny lobster
atún	tunny (tuna)	**langostino**	prawn
bacalao	codfish	**lomo**	loin
besugo	sea bream	**mariscos**	shellfish
boquerones	fresh anchovies	**mejillones**	mussels
calamares	squid	**melocotón**	peach
callos (a la madrileña)	tripe (with *chorizo* and tomatoes	**merluza**	hake
		ostras	oysters
		pastel	cake
cangrejo	crab	**pimiento**	green pepper
caracoles	snails	**pollo**	chicken
cerdo	pork	**pulpitos**	baby octopus
champiñones	mushrooms	**queso**	cheese
chorizo	a spicy pork sausage	**salchichón**	salami
		salmonete	red mullet
chuleta	chop	**salsa**	sauce
cocido madrileño	meat-and-vegetable stew	**ternera**	veal
		tortilla	omelette
cordero	lamb	**trucha**	trout
entremeses	hors-d'oeuvre	**uvas**	grapes
gambas	shrimp	**verduras**	vegetables

BLUEPRINT for a Perfect Trip

How to Get There

If the choice of ways to go is bewildering, the complexity of fares and regulations can be downright stupefying. A reliable travel agent can suggest which plan is best for your timetable and budget.

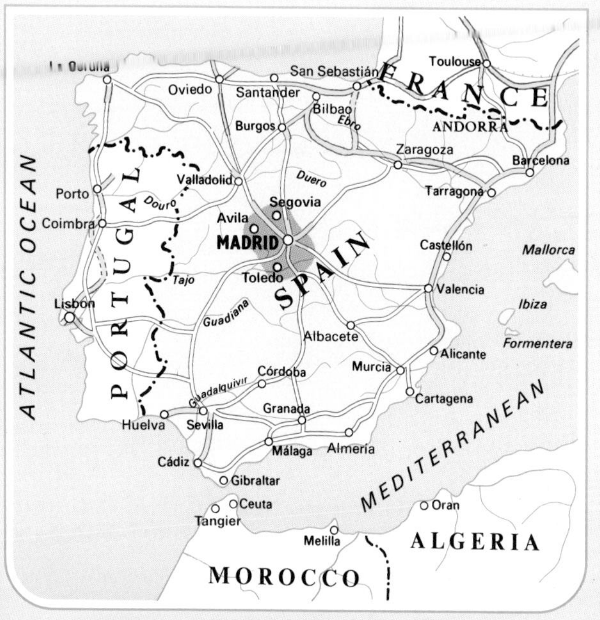

BY AIR

Scheduled flights

Madrid's Barajas Airport (see also p. 103) is on intercontinental air routes and is linked by frequent services to cities in Europe, North America, the Middle East and Africa.

Average journey times: Johannesburg–Madrid 12 hours, London–Madrid 2 hours, Los Angeles–Madrid 14 hours, Montreal–Madrid 6 hours, New York–Madrid 7 hours.

Charter flights and package tours

From the U.K. and Ireland: Many companies operate all-in package tours, which include flight, hotel and meals; check carefully to make sure that you are not liable to any surcharges. British travel agents offer guarantees in case of bankruptcy or cancellation by hotels or airlines. Most recommend insurance, too, for tourists who are forced to cancel because of illness or accident.

If you prefer to arrange your own accommodation and do not mind having to restrict your holiday to either one or two weeks, you can take advantage of the many charter flights that are available.

From North America: Package tours including hotel, car or other land arrangements can be very good value. In addition to APEX and Excursion fares, there's the Advance Booking Charter (ABC), which must be bought at least 30 days in advance.

BY ROAD

The main access road from France to Madrid is at the western side of the Pyrenees. A motorway (expressway) runs from Biarritz (France) via Bilbao to Burgos, from where you take the E25 straight down to Madrid, 240 kilometres (150 miles) away.

Express **coach services** operate between London and Madrid as well as between other European cities and Madrid. You can also travel by coach as part of a package holiday.

BY RAIL

The *Madrid-Talgo* links Paris with Madrid in about 11 hours. For most other connections you'll have to change trains at the border near San Sebastián.

Visitors from abroad can buy the *RENFE* (*Red Nacional de los Ferrocarriles Española,* the Spanish National Railways) *Tourist Card* for a reasonable price, valid for unlimited rail travel within the country for periods of 8, 15 or 22 days (1st and 2nd classes available).

The *Rail Europ S* (senior) card, obtainable before departure only, entitles senior citizens to purchase train tickets for European destinations at reduced prices.

Any family of at least 3 people can buy a *Rail-Europ F* (family) card: the holder pays full price, the rest of the family obtain a 50% reduction in Spain and 14 other European countries; the whole family is also entitled to a 30% reduction on Sealink and Hoverspeed Channel crossings.

Anyone under 26 years of age can purchase an *Inter-Rail* card which allows one month's unlimited 2nd-class travel.

People living outside Europe and North Africa can purchase a *Eurailpass* for unlimited rail travel in 16 European countries including Spain. This pass must be obtained before leaving home.

When to Go

If you can avoid Madrid in July and August—as many *Madrileños* do—you're more likely to carry away happy memories, as the heat can be stifling. In winter months, chill and greyness are often alleviated by bright, mild spells.

It is in spring or autumn that you are likely to find spectacularly delightful weather in Madrid: perfect temperatures, low humidity and some of the clearest sunshine in Europe.

Temperatures		J	F	M	A	M	J	J	A	S	O	N	D
average daily	°F	47	52	59	65	70	80	87	85	77	65	55	48
max. (afternoon)	°C	9	11	15	18	21	27	31	30	25	19	13	9
average daily	°F	35	36	41	45	50	58	63	63	57	49	42	36
min. (sunrise)	°C	2	2	5	7	10	15	17	17	14	10	5	2
Average hours of sunshine per day		5	6	6	8	9	11	12	11	9	7	5	4

Planning Your Budget

To give you an idea of what to expect, here's a list of average prices in Spanish pesetas (ptas.). They can only be *approximate,* however, as inflation creeps relentlessly up. Prices quoted may be subject to a VAT/sales tax (IVA) of either 6 or 12%.

Airport. Transfer to city terminal by bus 175 ptas., by taxi approx. 1,000 ptas.

Baby-sitters. From 500 ptas. per hour.

Car hire. *Seat Ibiza* 2,100 ptas. per day, 21 ptas. per km., 25,000 ptas. per week with unlimited mileage. *Ford Escort 1.1* 2,600 ptas. per day, 25 ptas. per km., 40,000 ptas. per week with unlimited mileage. *Ford Sierra 2.0* 4,700 ptas. per day, 47 ptas. per km., 54,000 ptas. per week with unlimited mileage. Add 12% tax.

Cigarettes. Spanish brands 100–150 ptas. per packet of 20, imported brands 175 ptas. and up.

Entertainment. Cinema 400 ptas. and up, theatre 700 ptas. and up, discotheque 1,000 ptas. and up, bullfight 2,000 ptas. and up, flamenco nightclub show (entry and first drink) 2,000 ptas. and up.

Hairdressers. *Woman's* haircut, shampoo and set or blow-dry 2,000–4,000 ptas., permanent wave 3,000 ptas. and up. *Man's* haircut 800–2,000 ptas.

Hotels (double room with bath per night). ***** from 10,000 ptas., **** from 9,000 ptas., *** from 6,000 ptas., ** from 3,500 ptas., * from 2,000 ptas.

Museums. Up to 500 ptas.

Restaurants. Continental breakfast 400–500 ptas., *plato del día* from 500 ptas., lunch/dinner in good establishment 2,500 ptas. and up, bottle of wine 200 ptas. and up, beer 25–200 ptas., coffee 85–125 ptas., Spanish brandy 125–200 ptas., soft drinks 110 ptas. and up.

Shopping bag. Loaf of bread 60–120 ptas., 250 grams of butter 325 ptas., dozen eggs 180–220 ptas., 1 kilo of beefsteak 1,400 ptas. and up, 100 grams of instant coffee 350 ptas. and up, 1 litre of fruit juice 200 ptas. and up, bottle of wine 250 ptas. and up.

Youth hostels. Approx. 1,000 ptas. per night.

An A–Z Summary of Practical Information and Facts

A star (*) following an entry indicates that relevant prices are to be found on page 102.
Listed after most entries is the appropriate Spanish translation, usually in the singular, plus a number of phrases that may come in handy during your stay in Madrid.

AIRPORT* *(aeropuerto).* Barajas Airport, 14 kilometres east of Madrid, handles domestic and international flights. Arriving passengers will find porters to carry their luggage to taxi ranks or bus stops. Taxis are readily available. Air-conditioned airport buses leave every 15 minutes for the city terminal beneath Plaza de Colón. The trip takes 30 to 45 minutes. A

The airport buildings are provided with the usual amenities—souvenir shops, snack bars, car-hire counters, currency-exchange offices and hotel-reservation desks. There is also a duty-free shop.

Porter!	**¡Mozo!**
Taxi!	**¡Taxi!**
Where's the bus for ...?	**¿Dónde está el autobús para ...?**

BABY-SITTERS*. This service can usually be arranged with your hotel. Rates may vary, depending upon the hotel. B

Can you get me a baby-sitter for tonight?	**¿Puede conseguirme una niñera** (or, **"canguro") para esta noche?**

CAR HIRE* *(coches de alquiler).* See also DRIVING. International and local car-hire firms have offices all over Madrid; your hotel receptionist can make arrangements. The law requires that you have an International Driving Permit, but in practice your national licence will probably be sufficient. Most agencies set a minimum age for car hire at 21. C

A deposit, as well as advance payment of the estimated hire charge, is generally required, although holders of major credit cards are normally exempt from this. VAT or sales tax (IVA) is added to the total. Third-party insurance is automatically included, but you have to request full collision coverage. The customer pays for the fuel. Ask about any available seasonal deals.

I'd like to rent a car.	**Quisiera alquilar un coche.**
for tomorrow	**para mañana**
for one day/a week	**por un día/una semana**
Please include full insurance coverage.	**Haga el favor de incluir el seguro a todo riesgo.**

CIGARETTES, CIGARS, TOBACCO* *(cigarrillos, puros, tabaco).* Spanish cigarettes can be made of strong, black tobacco *(negro)* or light tobacco *(rubio).* Canary Islands cigars are excellent and Cuban cigars are readily available. Pipe smokers find the local tobacco somewhat rough.

The rights of non-smokers today prevail over the right to smoke; legislation makes it illegal to smoke in many public places in Spain. Always observe the no-smoking sign, whether on public transport, in department stores or cinemas.

A packet of .../A box of matches, please.	**Un paquete de .../Una caja de cerillas, por favor.**
filter-tipped	**con filtro**
without filter	**sin filtro**

CLOTHING. First, the climate problem. In winter, Madrid can be uncomfortably cold, not only because of the temperature but also on account of the mountain winds which carry the chill to your bones. Pack warm clothes. The summer is so dependably scorching that you won't need a sweater until the evenings in late August or September.

Madrid's traditional formality of dress has relaxed under the influence of the younger generation. Still, resort wear would be inappropriate in this big, sophisticated city. Some restaurants require ties for men, and jackets are suggested for the opera. On visits to churches, be sure to wear modest clothing—no shorts, for instance—though women no longer have to wear headscarves.

Will I need a jacket and tie?	**¿Necesito chaqueta y corbata?**
Is it all right if I wear this?	**¿Voy bien así?**

COMMUNICATIONS. Post offices *(correos)* handle mail and telegrams, but not normally telephone calls.

Post office hours: most post offices are open from 9 a.m. to 2 p.m.

Madrid's cathedral-like main post office on Plaza de la Cibeles stays open from 9 a.m. to 1.30 p.m. and from 5 to 7 p.m., Monday to Friday; Saturday from 9 a.m. to 2 p.m.

The special **lista de correos** *(poste restante or general delivery)* window at the main post office is open from 9 a.m. to 8 p.m., Monday to Saturday, and from 10 p.m. to noon on Sundays and holidays.

For telegrams the main post office stays open round the clock and for stamp sales until midnight.

Mail: If you don't know in advance where you'll be staying, you can have your mail sent to you *lista de correos* at the main post office. Mail should be addressed as follows:

Mr. John Smith
Lista de correos
Plaza de la Cibeles
Madrid
Spain

Don't forget to take your passport as identification when you go to pick up your mail and be prepared to pay a small fee for each letter received.

Postage stamps *(sello)* are also on sale at any tobacconist's *(tabacos)*. Mail boxes are yellow and red.

Telephone *(teléfono)*. You can make local and international calls from public telephone booths in the street, from most hotels (often with heavy surcharges) and from some post offices. Area codes for different countries are given in the telephone directory. You'll need a supply of small change. For international direct dialling, pick up the receiver, wait for the dial tone, then dial 07, wait for a second sound and dial the country code (U.K. 44, Canada/U.S.A. 1), city code and subscriber's number. Madrid's main telephone office is located at:

Calle de Fuencarral and Gran Vía.
Open from 9 a.m. to 10 p.m. Monday to Saturday; from 10 a.m. to 2 p.m. and 5 to 9 p.m. on Sundays.

To reverse the charges, ask for *cobro revertido*. For a personal (person-to-person) call, specify *persona a persona*.

C

Telegrams *(telegrama).* Telegram and post office counter services work independent hours and usually overlap. You can also send telegrams by phone—dial 222 2000. If you are staying at a hotel, the receptionist can take telegrams. Telex service is also available in principal post offices.

Can you get me this number in ...?	**¿Puede comunicarme con este número en ...?**
Have you received any mail for ...?	**¿Ha recibido correo para ...?**
A stamp for this letter/postcard, please.	**Por favor, un sello para esta carta/tarjeta.**
express (special delivery)	**urgente**
airmail	**vía aérea**
registered	**certificado**
I want to send a telegram to ...	**Quisiera mandar un telegrama a ...**

COMPLAINTS. Tourism is Spain's leading industry and the government takes complaints from tourists very seriously.

Hotels and restaurants: The great majority of disputes are attributable to misunderstandings and linguistic difficulties and should not be exaggerated. As your host wants to keep both his reputation and his licence, you'll usually find him amenable to reason. In the event of a really serious and intractable problem, you may demand a complaint form *(hoja de reclamaciones),* which all hotels and restaurants are required by law to have available. The original of this triplicate document should be sent to the regional office of the Ministry of Tourism; one copy stays with the establishment against which the complaint is registered, while the final copy remains in your hands as a record. Merely asking for a complaint form resolves most matters.

In the rare event of major obstruction, when it is not possible to call in the police, write directly to the Secretaría de Estado de Turismo, Sección de Inspección y Reclamaciones:

Duque de Medinaceli, 2, Madrid.

Bad merchandise and car repairs: Consumer protection is in its infancy in Spain. If you think you've been taken advantage of, all you can do is appeal to the proprietor.

In the event of gross abuse, take your complaint to the local tourist office. They're often able to sort out this kind of problem.

CONVERTER CHARTS. For fluid and distance measures, see page 110. Spain uses the metric system. **C**

Temperature

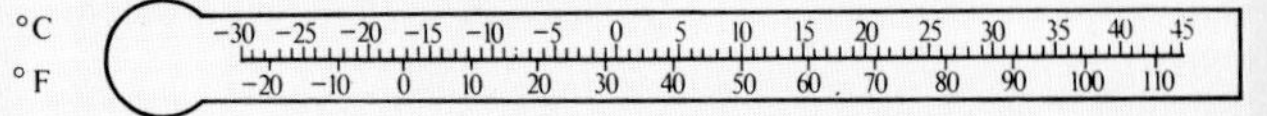

Length

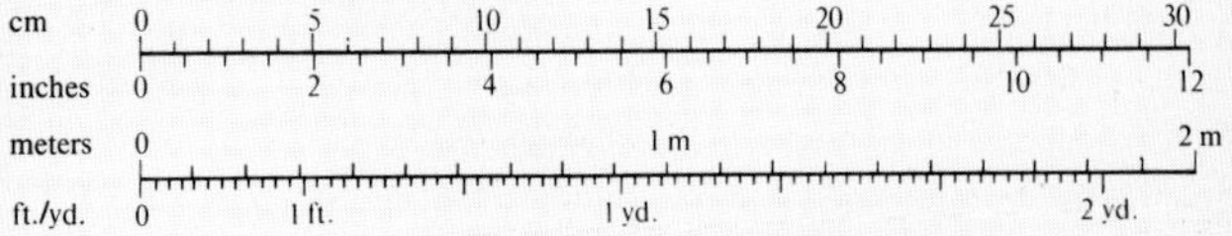

Weight

grams 0 100 200 300 400 500 600 700 800 900 1 kg

ounces 0 4 8 12 1 lb 20 24 28 2 lb.

CRIME and THEFT. Spain's crime rate has caught up with the rest of the world. Wherever crowds collect in Madrid—at the Rastro or the bullfight, in buses and metro—be vigilant for handbag-snatchers and pickpockets. And remember never to leave luggage visible in a parked car.

I want to report a theft.	**Quiero denunciar un robo.**
My ticket/wallet/passport has been stolen.	**Me han robado mi billete/ cartera/pasaporte.**

CUSTOMS *(aduana)* **and ENTRY REGULATIONS.** Most visitors need only a valid passport to visit Spain, and even this requirement is waived for the British, who may enter on the simplified Visitor's Passport. Though residents of Europe and North America aren't subject to any health requirements, visitors from further afield should check with a travel agent before departure in case inoculation certificates are called for.

Currency restrictions. Tourists may bring an unlimited amount of Spanish or foreign currency into the country. Departing, though, you must declare any amount beyond the equivalent of 500,000 pesetas. Thus if you plan to carry large sums in and out again it's wise to declare your currency on arrival as well as on departure.

C Here's what you can carry into Spain duty-free and, upon your return home, into your own country:

Into:	Cigarettes		Cigars		Tobacco	Spirits		Wine
Spain 1)	300	or	75	or	350 g.	1.5 l.	and	5 l.
2)	200	or	50	or	250 g.	1 l.	or	2 l.
Australia	200	or	250 g.	or	250 g.	1 l.	or	1 l.
Canada	200	and	50	and	900 g.	1.1 l.	or	1.1 l.
Eire	200	or	50	or	250 g.	1 l.	and	2 l.
N.Zealand	200	or	50	or	250 g.	1.1 l.	and	4.5 l.
S.Africa	400	and	50	and	250 g.	1 l.	and	2 l.
U.K.	200	or	50	or	250 g.	1 l.	and	2 l.
U.S.A.	200	and	100	and	3)	1 l.	or	1 l.

1) Visitors arriving from EEC countries.
2) Visitors arriving from other countries.
3) A reasonable quantity.

I've nothing to declare. **No tengo nada que declarar.**
It's for my personal use. **Es para mi uso personal.**

D **DRIVING IN SPAIN.** To take your car into Spain, you should have:

- an International Driving Permit (not obligatory for citizens of most Western European countries—ask your automobile association—but recommended in case of difficulties with the police as it carries a Spanish translation) or a legalized and certified translation of your home licence
- car registration papers
- Green Card (an extension to your regular insurance policy, making it valid for foreign countries)

Also recommended: With your certificate of insurance, you should carry a bail bond. If you injure somebody in an accident in Spain, you can be imprisoned while the accident is being investigated. This bond will bail you out. Apply to your home automobile association or insurance company.

A nationality sticker must be prominently displayed on the back of your car. Seat belts are compulsory. Not using them outside towns makes you liable to a fine. You must have a red reflecting warning triangle when driving on motorways (expressways). Motorcycle riders and their passengers are required to wear crash helmets.

Driving conditions: Drive on the right. Pass on the left. Yield right of way to all traffic coming from the right. Spanish drivers tend to use their horn when passing other vehicles.

Main roads are adequate to very good and improving all the time. Secondary roads can be bumpy. The main danger of driving in Spain comes from impatience, especially on busy roads. A large percentage of accidents in Spain occur when passing, so take it easy. Wait until you have a long, unobstructed view.

Spanish truck and lorry drivers will often wave you on (by hand signal or by flashing their right directional signal) if it's clear ahead.

In villages, remember that the car only became a part of the Spanish way of life some 30 years ago; the villages aren't designed for them, and the older people are still not quite used to them. Drive with care.

Speed limits: 120 k.p.h. (75 m.p.h.) on motorways (expressways), 100 k.p.h. (62 m.p.h.) or 90 k.p.h. (56 m.p.h.) on other roads, 60 k.p.h. (36 m.p.h.) in towns and built-up areas.

Driving in Madrid: Nerve-wracking traffic jams are part of the way of life in the capital. To avoid the worst, try to drive in or through the city during the hours of the extended siesta afternoon break (usually between 2 and 5 p.m.). Madrid drivers are not noted for their courtesy. They are as impatient as drivers in Rome, but less skilled in avoiding accidents.

Parking: If driving in Madrid sometimes resembles a bad dream, parking is a positive nightmare as more and more central areas become "residents' parking zones" and non-residents have to buy parking tickets from the local tobacconists. The price—modest—depends on length of stay intended and different colours indicate different lengths of stay (maximum 1½ hours; any excess heavily fined). To make things worse, it's very often impossible to know that one is in such a zone (the signposts are not easy to understand) so the only way to be sure is to ask. And it's worth doing so: even tourists' cars don't always escape the *grua* that hauls away cars badly parked, and more than one tourist has returned to where his car was only to find no car, but in its place a parking fine with just a stone to keep it there. Underground parking facilities, ever more abundant, charge a fee.

D

Traffic police: The armed Civil Guard *(Guardia Civil)* patrol the highways on powerful black motorcycles. Always in pairs, these toughlooking men are courteous and will stop to help anyone in trouble. They're severe on lawbreakers.

If fined, you will be required to pay on the spot. The most common offences include passing without flashing the directional-indicator lights, travelling too close to the car ahead and driving with a burnt-out head- or tail-light. (Spanish law requires you to carry a set of spare bulbs at all times.)

Accidents: In case of accident, dial the police emergency number, 092.

Fuel and oil: Fuel is theoretically available in super (97 octane), lead-free (95 octane), normal (92 octane) and diesel, but not every petrol station carries the full range. It's customary to give the attendant a coin or two as a tip.

Fluid measures

imp. gals. 0 5 10

liters 0 5 10 20 30 40 50

U.S. gals. 0 5 10

Distance

To convert kilometres to miles:

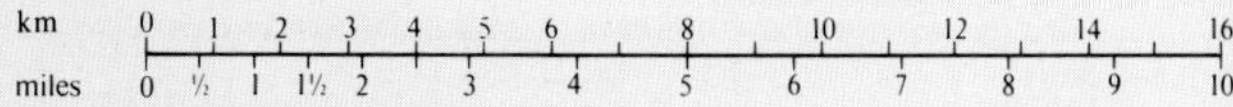

Breakdowns: Spare parts are most readily available for Spanish-built cars. For some other brands, spares may be difficult to find. Make sure your car is in top shape before you leave home.

If you have a breakdown on the highway, use one of the strategically positioned emergency telephones to call for help. Otherwise telephone the Guardia Civil.

Road signs: Most road signs are the standard pictographs used throughout Europe. However, you may encounter these written signs:

¡Alto!	Stop!
Aparcamiento	Parking
Autopista (de peaje)	(Toll) motorway (expressway)

Calzada deteriorada	Bad road
Calzada estrecha	Narrow road
Ceda el paso	Give way (Yield)
Cruce peligroso	Dangerous crossroads
Cuidado	Caution
Curva peligrosa	Dangerous bend
Despacio	Slow
Desviación	Diversion (Detour)
Escuela	School
Peligro	Danger
Prohibido adelantar	No overtaking (passing)
Prohibido aparcar	No parking
Puesto de socorro	First-aid post
Salida de camiones	Lorry (Truck) exit

(International) Driving Licence	**carné de conducir (internacional)**
car registration papers	**permiso de circulación**
Green Card	**carta verde**

Are we on the right road for …?	**¿Es ésta la carretera hacia …?**
Fill her up please, top grade.	**Llénelo, por favor, con super.**
Check the oil/tires/battery.	**Por favor, controle el aceite/ los neumáticos/la batería.**
I've had a breakdown.	**Mi coche se ha estropeado.**
There's been an accident.	**Ha habido un accidente.**

DRUGS. Until the 1980s, Spain had one of the strictest drug laws in Europe. Then possession of small quantities for personal use was legalized. Now the pendulum has swung back in the other direction: possession and sale of drugs is once again a criminal offense in Spain.

ELECTRIC CURRENT. Both 120- and 220-volt 50-cycle current may be encountered in Madrid, depending on the location and age of the building. Be sure to ask at your hotel desk before you plug in a razor or hair-dryer.

If you have trouble with an appliance, ask your hotel receptionist to recommend an *electricista.*

What's the voltage—120 or 220?	**¿Cuál es el voltaje—ciento veinte (120) o doscientos veinte (220)?**
an adaptor/a battery	**un adaptador/una pila**

E

EMBASSIES

Australia:	Paseo de la Castellana, 143; tel. 279 85 04
Canada:	Núñez de Balboa, 35; tel. 431 43 00
Eire:	Claudio Coello, 73; tel. 276 35 00/8/9
South Africa:	Claudio Coello, 91; tel. 225 38 30
U.K.*:	Fernando el Santo, 16; tel. 419 02 08
U.S.A.:	Serrano, 75; tel. 273 36 00

Where's the ... embassy?	**¿Dónde está la embajada ...?**
American/Australian/British/ Canadian/Irish/South African	**americana/australiana/británica/ canadiense/irlandesa/sudafricana**

EMERGENCIES. If your hotel receptionist isn't handy to help, and you have a real crisis, dial the police emergency number, 091.

Here are a few other numbers for urgent matters:

Fire	080
Ambulance	274 14 29
Accidents (municipal police)	092

Depending on the nature of the emergency, refer to the separate entries in this section such as CONSULATES, MEDICAL CARE, POLICE, etc.

Though we hope you'll never need them, here are a few key words you might like to learn in advance:

Careful!	**¡Cuidado!**	Police!	**¡Policía!**
Fire!	**¡Fuego!**	Stop!	**¡Deténgase!**
Help!	**¡Socorro!**	Stop thief!	**¡Al ladrón!**

G

GUIDES and INTERPRETERS *(guía; intérprete).* Qualified guides and interpreters for individual tours or business negotiations may be hired through certain travel agencies or from Asociación Profesional de Informadores Turísticos:

Ferraz, 82; tel. 241 12 14.

We'd like an English-speaking guide.	**Queremos una guía que hable inglés.**
I need an English interpreter.	**Necesito un intérprete de inglés.**

* Also for citizens of Commonwealth countries not separately represented.

H

HAIRDRESSERS* *(peluquería)*/**BARBERS** *(barbería).* Some hotels have their own salons, and the standard is generally good. Prices vary widely according to the class of establishment, but rates are often displayed in the window.

Not too much off (here).	**No corte mucho (aquí).**
A little more off (here).	**Un poco más (aquí).**
haircut	**corte**
shampoo and set	**lavado y marcado**
blow-dry	**modelado**
permanent wave	**permanente**
a colour rinse/hair-dye	**champú colorante/tinte**
a colour chart	**un muestrario**

HOTELS and ACCOMMODATION* *(hotel; alojamiento).* Spanish hotel prices are no longer government-controlled. Accommodation in Madrid ranges from a simple but always clean room in a *pensión* (boarding house) to the luxurious surroundings of a five-star hotel. Hotel-reservation desks are found at Barajas Airport, at Chamartín and Atocha railway stations and in the Torre de Madrid on Plaza de España. Before the guest takes a room he fills out a form with hotel category, room number and price and signs it.

When you check into your hotel you might have to leave your passport at the desk. Don't worry, you'll get it back in the morning.

Other accommodation:

Hostal and **Hotel-Residencia:** Modest hotels without a restaurant, often family concerns.

Pensión: Boarding house, few amenities.

Fonda: Village inn, clean and unpretentious.

Parador: Government-run inn, usually in isolated or touristically underdeveloped areas.

Youth hostels *(albergue de juventud).* A youth hostel operates year-round in Casa de Campo Park. Normally, a stay is limited to three nights, and you must present a youth-hostel membership card. For addresses and other information, contact the Oficina Central de Albergues Juveniles:

Calle Ortega y Gasset, 71, Madrid.

H In central Madrid, cheap accommodation may be found at simple *pensiones* (boarding houses) and *casas de huéspedes* (guest houses).

a double/single room	**una habitación doble/sencilla**
with/without bath/shower	**con/sin baño/ducha**
What's the price per night?	**¿Cuál es el precio por noche?**

HOURS. See also under COMMUNICATIONS and MONEY MATTERS. One of the really great Spanish discoveries, aimed at keeping people out of the afternoon sun, is the siesta—just the ticket for overtaxed tourists as well as for locals. Try a nap after lunch.

But if you insist on fighting the system, you can still accomplish things between 2 and 5 p.m. The siesta hours are the best time to drive in or through Madrid (see DRIVING). Restaurants start serving lunch about 1 p.m. and dinner between 8 and 10 p.m.

Office hours: Generally from 9 a.m. to 2 p.m. and 4.30 to 7 p.m., Monday to Friday in winter; from 8.30 a.m. to 3 p.m. in summer.

Shopping hours: 9.30 a.m. to 1.30 p.m. and 4 or 5 to 8 p.m. Monday to Friday, 9.30 a.m. to 2 p.m. on Saturdays; department stores generally open from 10 a.m. to 8 p.m. without a break, Monday to Saturday.

Tourist Information Offices: 10 a.m. to 1 p.m. and 4 to 7 p.m., Monday to Friday, and 10 a.m. to 1 p.m. on Saturdays.

Museums: Most are closed on Mondays and public holidays.

L **LANGUAGE.** After Chinese and English, the most widely spoken language in the world is Spanish—at home from Madrid to Manila, from Avila to Argentina. The Castilian spoken in Madrid (seat of the all-powerful Royal Spanish Academy of the Language) is understood wherever you may travel in Spain.

French, English and German are widely understood in hotels and tourist-oriented establishments.

Good morning/Good day	**Buenos días**
Good afternoon/good evening	**Buenas tardes**
Good night	**Buenas noches**
Thank you	**Gracias**
You're welcome	**De nada**
Please	**Por favor**
Good-bye	**Adiós**

The Berlitz phrase book, SPANISH FOR TRAVELLERS, covers all situations you are likely to encounter in your travels in Spain. The Berlitz Spanish-English/English-Spanish pocket dictionary contains a 12,500-word glossary of each language, plus a menu-reader supplement. **L**

Do you speak English? **¿Habla usted inglés?**
I don't speak Spanish. **No hablo español.**

LAUNDRY *(lavandería)* **and DRY-CLEANING** *(tintorería).* Most hotels will handle laundry and dry-cleaning, but they'll usually charge more than a laundry or a dry-cleaners. In many areas of Madrid, you can find launderettes *(launderama)* which will wash, dry and fold a 5-kilo (11-pound) load of clothing.

Where's the nearest laundry/dry-cleaners?	**¿Dónde está la lavandería/ tintorería más cercana?**
I want these clothes cleaned/washed.	**Quiero que limpien/laven esta ropa.**
When will it be ready?	**¿Cuándo estará lista?**
I must have this for tomorrow morning.	**La necesito para mañana por la mañana.**

LOST PROPERTY. Check first at your hotel reception desk. Then report the loss to the police. In Madrid, all lost property should go to Plaza Legazpi, 7.

Lost children face few perils in Spain, where the people are particularly fond of youngsters. A lost child would normally be delivered to the nearest police station, which is where you should go if you lose a child—or find one.

I've lost my wallet/handbag/ passport. **He perdido mi cartera/bolso/ pasaporte.**

M

MAPS. Road maps are on sale at most filling-stations and bookshops. The maps in this guide were prepared by Falk-Verlag, Hamburg, which also publishes a map of Madrid. The most detailed cartographic information is contained in the official atlas of Spain issued by the Ministry of Public Works.

A number of Madrid city maps are sold at news-stands. The municipal bus service issues a chart of all its routes. A city map with metro lines superimposed is posted outside every underground (subway)

M station, and a pocket-size map of the metro is available free on request at the ticket office in any metro station.

a street plan of ...	**un plano de la ciudad de ...**
a road map of this region	**un mapa de carreteras da esta comarca**

MEDICAL CARE. See also EMERGENCIES. To be completely relaxed, make certain your health-insurance policy covers any illness or accident while on holiday. If not, ask your insurance representative about travel insurance or have your travel agent arrange Spanish tourist insurance *(ASTES)* for you. *ASTES* covers doctor's fees and hospital treatment in the event of accident or illness.

For first-aid matters, paramedical personnel, called *practicantes*, can help. Hospitals, clinics and first-aid centres *(casa de socorro)* are concentrated in Madrid.

Pharmacies *(farmacia)*. After hours, one shop in each area is always on duty for emergencies. Its address is posted daily in all other chemists' windows and published in all newspapers.

Where's the nearest (all-night) pharmacy?	**¿Dónde está la farmacia (de guardia) más cercana?**
I need a doctor/dentist.	**Necesito un médico/dentista.**
an ambulance/hospital	**una ambulancia/hospital**
I've a pain here.	**Me duele aquí.**

MEETING PEOPLE. Politeness and simple courtesies still matter in Spain. A handshake on greeting and leaving is normal. Always begin any conversation, whether with a friend, shop girl, taxi-driver, policeman or telephone operator with a *buenos días* (good morning) or *buenas tardes* (good afternoon). Always say *adiós* (goodbye) or, at night, *buenas noches* when leaving. *Por favor* (please) should begin all requests.

Finally, don't try to rush Spaniards. They have no appreciation for haste, and consider it bad form when anyone pushes them. Take your time. In Spain, there's plenty of it.

How do you do?	**Encantado de conocerle (Encantada** when a woman is speaking).
How are you?	**¿Cómo está usted?**
Very well, thank you.	**Muy bien, gracias.**

MONEY MATTERS

Currency. The monetary unit of Spain is the *peseta* (abbreviated *pta.*).
Coins: 1, 5, 10, 25, 50 and 100 pesetas.
Banknotes: 200, 500, 1,000, 2,000, 5,000 and 10,000 pesetas.
A 5-peseta coin is traditionally called a *duro*, so if someone should quote a price as 10 duros, he means 50 pesetas. For currency restrictions, see CUSTOMS AND ENTRY REGULATIONS.

Banking hours are from 9 a.m. to 2 p.m. Monday to Friday, till 1 p.m. on Saturdays.

Most Madrid banks have departments for changing foreign currency into pesetas. Curiously, the exchange rate for traveller's cheques is more favourable than for banknotes. Always take your passport with you; it's the only acceptable form of identification. Outside banking hours, you may use exchange offices *(cambio)* at Chamartín railway station, the airport or your own hotel. The exchange rate is a bit less favourable than in the banks.

Credit cards: All the internationally recognized cards are accepted by hotels, restaurants and businesses in Spain.

Eurocheques: You'll have no problem settling bills or paying for purchases with Eurocheques.

Traveller's cheques: Many hotels, travel agencies, shops and banks accept them—though in Madrid some branch banks refer clients to the head office. Remember to take your passport along for identification if you expect to cash a traveller's cheque.

Only cash small amounts at a time, and keep the balance of your cheques in the hotel safe if possible. At the very least, be sure to keep your receipt and a list of the serial numbers of the cheques in a separate place to facilitate a refund in case of loss or theft.

Prices: Although Spain has by no means escaped the scourge of inflation, Madrid remains quite competitive with the other tourist capitals of Europe.

Certain rates are listed on page 102 to give you an idea of what things cost.

Where's the nearest bank/ currency exchange office?	**¿Dónde está el banco/la oficina de cambio más cercana?**
I want to change some pounds/dollars.	**Quiero cambiar libras/dólares.**

Do you accept traveller's cheques?	**¿Acepta usted cheques de viajero?**
Can I pay with this credit card?	**¿Puedo pagar con esta tarjeta de crédito?**
How much is that?	**¿Cuánto es?**

NEWSPAPERS and MAGAZINES *(periódico; revista).* All major British and Continental dailies are sold in Madrid on their publication day. U.S. magazines and the Paris-based *International Herald Tribune* are also available.

The weekly *Guía del Ocio* lists information for Madrid visitors.

Have you any English-language newspapers?	**¿Tienen periódicos en inglés?**

PHOTOGRAPHY. Most popular film brands and sizes are available, but they generally cost more than at home, so bring as much as you can with you.

The Spanish films Negra and Valca, in black-and-white, and Negracolor, are of good quality and cheaper than the internationally known brands.

In some churches and museums, photography is forbidden. If you go to a bullfight, be sure to sit on the shady side when taking pictures. You might need a filter to eliminate the red haze of the late afternoon sun.

Photo shops sell lead-coated plastic bags which protect films from X-rays at airport security checkpoints.

I'd like a film for this camera.	**Quisiera un carrete para esta máquina.**
a black-and-white film	**un carrete en blanco y negro**
a film for colour pictures	**un carrete en color**
a colour-slide film	**un carrete de diapositivas**
35-mm film	**un carrete de treinta y cinco**
super-8	**super ocho**
How long will it take to develop (and print) this film?	**¿Cuánto tardará en revelar (y sacar copias de) este carrete?**

POLICE *(policía).* There are three police forces in Spain: the *Policía Municipal,* who are attached to the local town hall and usually wear a blue uniform; the *Policía Nacional,* a national anti-crime unit recognized by their brown uniforms and berets; and the *Guardia Civil,* the national police force wearing patent-leather hats, patrolling highways as well as towns.

If you need police assistance, you can call on any one of the three. Spanish police are efficient, strict and particularly courteous to foreign visitors. **P**

Where's the nearest police station?	**¿Dónde está la comisaría más cercana?**

PUBLIC HOLIDAYS *(fiesta)*

January 1	*Año Nuevo*	New Year's Day
January 6	*Epifanía*	Epiphany
March 19	*San José*	St. Joseph's Day
May 1	*Día del Trabajo*	Labour Day
July 25	*Santiago Apóstol*	St. James's Day
August 15	*Asunción*	Assumption
October 12	*Día de la Hispanidad*	Discovery of America Day (Columbus Day)
November 1	*Todas los Santos*	All Saints' Day
December 6	*Día de la Constitución Española*	Constitution Day
December 25	*Navidad*	Christmas Day
Movable dates:	*Viernes Santo*	Good Friday
	Corpus Christi	Corpus Christi
	Inmaculada Concepción	Immaculate Conception (normally December 8)

In addition to these nation-wide holidays, Madrid celebrates May 2, as well as its patron saint's day—San Isidro Labrador (St. Isidore the Husbandman) on May 15—and *La Almudena* on November 9 as legal holidays.

RADIO and TV *(radio; televisión)*. Most hotels have television lounges. All programmes are in Spanish, except for very occasional showings of foreign films with subtitles. **R**

Travellers with medium-wave receivers will be able to pick up the BBC World Service after dark, from about 9.15 p.m. onwards. During the daytime, both the BBC and the Voice of America can be heard on short-wave radios.

R **RELIGIOUS SERVICES** *(servicio religioso).* The national religion of Spain is Roman Catholic, but other denominations and faiths are represented. Services in English are held in the following churches:

Catholic: North American Catholic Church, Av. Alfonso XIII, 165

Protestant: British Embassy Church (Anglican), Núñez de Balboa, 43

The Community Church (Protestant Inter-denominational), Padre Damián, 34

Emmanuel Baptist Church, Hernández de Tejeda, 4

Jewish: The synagogue is at Balmes, 3

T **TIME DIFFERENCES.** Spanish time coincides with most of Western Europe—Greenwich Mean Time plus one hour. In spring, another hour is added for Daylight Saving Time (Summer Time).

Summer Time chart:

New York	London	**Madrid**	Jo'burg	Sydney	Auckland
6 a.m.	11 a.m.	**noon**	noon	8 p.m.	10 p.m.

What time is it? **¿Qué hora es?**

TIPPING. Since a service charge is normally included in hotel and restaurant bills, tipping is not obligatory. However, it's appropriate to tip bellboys, filling-station attendants, bullfight ushers, etc., for their services. The chart below gives some suggestions as to what to leave.

Hotel porter, per bag	minimum 50 ptas.
Maid, for extra services	100–200 ptas.
Lavatory attendant	25–50 ptas.
Waiter	10% (optional)
Taxi driver	10%
Hairdresser/Barber	10%
Tourist guide	10%

 Keep the change. **Déjelo para usted.**

TOILETS. There are many expressions for toilets in Spanish: *aseos, servicios, W.C., water* and *retretes.* The first two terms are the most common.

In public conveniences, attendants expect a small tip. If you drop into a bar specifically to use the facilities, it is considered polite to buy a cup of coffee or a glass of wine as well.

Where are the toilets? **¿Dónde están los servicios?**

TOURIST INFORMATION OFFICES *(oficinas de turismo).* Spanish National Tourist Offices are maintained in many countries throughout the world. These offices will supply you with a wide range of colourful and informative brochures and maps in English on the various towns and regions in Spain. They will also let you consult a copy of the master directory of hotels in Spain, listing all facilities and prices.

Canada: 60 Bloor St. West, Suite 201, Toronto, Ont. M4W 3B0, tel. (416) 961-3131.

United Kingdom: 57, St. James's St. London S.W.1; tel. (01) 499-0901.

U.S.A.: 845 N. Michigan Ave., Chicago, IL 60611; tel. (312) 944-0215.

4800 The Galleria, 5085 Westheimer Rd., Houston, TX 77056; tel. (713) 840-7411.

665 5th Ave., New York, N.Y. 10022; tel. (212) 759-8822.

Tourist information offices in Madrid:

Torre de Madrid (Plaza de España); tel. 241 23 25
Calle Duque de Medinaceli, 2; tel. 429 49 51
Chamartín railway station
Barajas Airport; tel. 205 83 56

On-the-spot advice is available from multilingual experts who patrol the streets of tourist zones. Look for the blue-and-yellow uniform with the **i** symbol on the lapel.

TRANSPORT

Buses *(autobús).* The municipal transportation system, EMT, operates bus routes criss-crossing Madrid. On blue buses, you generally enter through the rear door and buy a ticket from a conductor seated behind a little desk. On red ones, you enter by the front door and pay the driver. Municipal buses operate from about 5.30 a.m. to 1.30 a.m.

A bargain ticket *(Bono Bus),* valid for ten rides on the red buses, is available at EMT booths—or, at a fractionally higher price, on buses with conductors.

Microbuses *(microbús).* These small, yellow buses are air-conditioned and more manœuvrable than conventional buses, hence faster and slightly more expensive.

Metro: Madrid's underground (subway) system combines speed with economy. The catch is that the metro can be oven-hot in summer. For the metro, too, there is a cheaper ten-ride ticket *(Billete de diez viajes).* Ask for a metro map at any station.

Taxi *(taxi).* Madrid's 12,000 taxis are easily recognized by the letters *SP* (for *servicio público*) on front and rear bumpers, the symbol of Madrid's bear on the rear doors and the livery—the taxicabs are painted either black or white with a red stripe. If a taxi is free, a green light on the right front corner of the roof is turned on and a *libre* ("free") sign is displayed.

The meter shows an initial charge at the drop of the flag, with fares varying according to distance and time elapsed. The figure displayed at the end of your trip may not be the full price. Legitimate added charges are compounded for night and holiday travel, pickups, etc.

Non-metered tourist cars, which often solicit business at major hotels and nightclubs, charge premium rates.

Trains *(tren).* Madrid's three principal railway stations are Chamartín (just off the Paseo de la Castellana). Norte (facing the Campo del Moro) and Atocha (south of the Prado). In general, rail service to nearby towns of interest is less convenient than parallel bus services. But the luxurious international *Talgo* and the long-distance *Ter* trains are highly regarded. Seat reservations are required for most Spanish trains.

EuroCity (EC)	International express, first and second classes
Talgo, Intercity, Electrotren, Ter, Tren Estrella	Luxury diesel, first and second classes; supplementary charge over regular fare

Expreso, Rápido	Long-distance expresses, stopping at main stations only; supplementary charge, usually second class only
Omnibus, Tranvía, Automotor	Local trains, with frequent stops, usually second class only
Auto Expreso	Car train
Coche cama	Sleeping-car with 1-, 2- or 3-bedded compartments, washing facilities
Coche comedor	Dining-car
Litera	Sleeping-berth car *(couchette)* with blankets, sheets and pillows
Furgón de equipajes	Luggage van (baggage car); only registered luggage permitted

When's the next bus to ...?	**¿Cuándo sale el próximo autobús para ...?**
Will you tell me when to get off?	**¿Podría indicarme cuándo tengo que bajar?**
Where can I get a taxi?	**¿Dónde puedo coger un taxi?**
What's the fare to ...?	**¿Cuánto es la tarifa a ...?**
Which is the best train to ...?	**Cuál es el mejor tren para ...?**
I want a ticket to ...	**Quiero un billete para ...**
single (one-way)	**ida**
return (round-trip)	**ida y vuelta**
first/second class	**primera/segunda clase**
I'd like to make seat reservations.	**Quiero reservar asientos.**

WATER *(agua).* Madrid's mountain spring water is less delicious nowadays because of chlorination. You can drink it from the tap with confidence. Spaniards often prefer bottled mineral water, which is tasty and healthful.

DAYS OF THE WEEK

Sunday	**domingo**	Wednesday	**miércoles**
Monday	**lunes**	Thursday	**jueves**
Tuesday	**martes**	Friday	**viernes**
		Saturday	**sábado**

MONTHS

January	**enero**	July	**julio**
February	**febrero**	August	**agosto**
March	**marzo**	September	**septiembre**
April	**abril**	October	**octubre**
May	**mayo**	November	**noviembre**
June	**junio**	December	**diciembre**

NUMBERS

0	**cero**	18	**dieciocho**
1	**uno**	19	**diecinueve**
2	**dos**	20	**veinte**
3	**tres**	21	**veintiuno**
4	**cuatro**	22	**veintidós**
5	**cinco**	30	**treinta**
6	**seis**	31	**treinta y uno**
7	**siete**	32	**treinta y dos**
8	**ocho**	40	**cuarenta**
9	**nueve**	50	**cincuenta**
10	**diez**	60	**sesenta**
11	**once**	70	**setenta**
12	**doce**	80	**ochenta**
13	**trece**	90	**noventa**
14	**catorce**	100	**cien**
15	**quince**	101	**ciento uno**
16	**dieciséis**	500	**quinientos**
17	**diecisiete**	1,000	**mil**

SOME USEFUL EXPRESSIONS

yes/no	**sí/no**
please/thank you	**por favor/gracias**
excuse me/you're welcome	**perdone/de nada**
where/when/how	**dónde/cuándo/cómo**
how long/how far	**cuánto tiempo/a qué distancia**
yesterday/today/tomorrow	**ayer/hoy/mañana**
day/week/month/year	**día/semana/mes/año**
left/right	**izquierda/derecha**
up/down	**arriba/abajo**
good/bad	**bueno/malo**
big/small	**grande/pequeño**
cheap/expensive	**barato/caro**
hot/cold	**caliente/frío**
old/new	**viejo/nuevo**
open/closed	**abierto/cerrado**
here/there	**aquí/allí**
free (vacant)/occupied	**libre/ocupado**
early/late	**temprano/tarde**
easy/difficult	**fácil/difícil**
Does anyone here speak English?	**¿Hay alguien aquí que hable inglés?**
What does this mean?	**¿Qué quiere decir esto?**
I don't understand.	**No comprendo.**
Please write it down.	**Escríbamelo, por favor.**
Is there an admission charge?	**¿Se debe pagar la entrada?**
Waiter!/Waitress!	**¡Camarero!/¡Camarera!**
I'd like …	**Quisiera …**
How much is that?	**¿Cuánto es?**
Have you something less expensive?	**¿Tiene algo más barato?**
Just a minute.	**Un momento.**
Help me please.	**Ayúdeme, por favor.**
Get a doctor quickly.	**¡Llamen a un médico, rápidamente!**

Index

An asterisk (*) next to a page number indicates a map reference.

098/810 LUD 69

Selection of Madrid Hotels and Restaurants

BERLITZ®

Where do you start? Choosing a hotel or restaurant in a place you're not familiar with can be daunting. To help you find your way amid the bewildering variety, we have made a selection from the *Red Guide to Portugal and Spain 1988* published by Michelin, the recognized authority on gastronomy and accommodation throughout Europe.

Our own Berlitz criteria have been (a) price and (b) location. In the hotel section, for a double room with bath but without breakfast, Higher-priced means above ptas. 10,000, Medium-priced ptas. 6,000–10,000, Lower-priced below ptas. 6,000. As to restaurants, for a meal consisting of a starter, a main course and a dessert, Higher-priced means above ptas. 4,000, Medium-priced ptas. 3,000–4,000, Lower-priced below ptas. 3,000. Special features (where applicable), and regular closing days are also given. For hotels and restaurants, checking first to make certain that they are open and advance reservations are both advisable. In Spain, hotel and restaurant prices include a service charge, but a value-added tax (IVA) of 6–12% will also automatically be added to the bill.

For a wider choice of hotels and restaurants, we strongly recommend you obtain the authoritative Michelin *Red Guide to Portugal and Spain,* which gives a comprehensive and reliable picture of the situation throughout the country.

HOTELS

HIGHER-PRICED

(above ptas. 10,000)

Alcalá
Alcalá 66
28009 Madrid
Tel. 435 10 60; tlx. 48094
153 rooms
Basque restaurant.

Emperador
Gran Vía 53
28013 Madrid
Tel. 247 28 00; tlx. 46261
232 rooms
Outdoor swimming pool. No restaurant.

Eurobuilding
Padre Damián 23
28036 Madrid
Tel. 457 78 00; tlx. 22548
540 rooms
Garden and terrace with outdoor swimming pool.

G. H. Velázquez
Velázquez 62
28001 Madrid
Tel. 275 28 00; tlx. 22779
145 rooms

Holiday Inn
av. General Perón
28020 Madrid
Tel. 456 70 14; tlx. 44709
310 rooms
Dinner accompanied by piano music. Outdoor swimming pool.

Meliá Castilla
Capitán Haya 43
28020 Madrid
Tel. 571 22 11; tlx. 23142
1,000 rooms
Outdoor swimming pool.

Meliá Madrid
Princesa 27
28008 Madrid
Tel. 241 82 00; tlx. 22537
265 rooms
Outdoor dining.

Miguel Angel
Miguel Angel 31
28010 Madrid
Tel. 442 00 22; tlx. 44235
300 rooms
Indoor swimming pool.

Mindanao
paseo San Francisco de Sales 15
28003 Madrid
Tel. 449 55 00 ; tlx. 22631
289 rooms
Outdoor and indoor swimming pools.

Novotel Madrid
Albacete 1
28027 Madrid
Tel. 405 46 00; tlx. 41862
240 rooms
Outdoor dining. Outdoor swimming pool.

Palace
pl. de las Cortes 7
28014 Madrid
Tel. 429 75 51; tlx. 22272
508 rooms

Pintor
Goya 79
28001 Madrid
Tel. 435 75 45; tlx. 23281
176 rooms

Plaza
pl. de España
28013 Madrid
Tel. 247 12 00; tlx. 27383
306 rooms
View. Outdoor swimming pool (summer only). No restaurant, but snacks available.

Princesa Plaza
Serrano Jover 3
28015 Madrid
Tel. 242 21 00; tlx. 44377
406 rooms

Ritz
pl. de la Lealtad 5
28014 Madrid
Tel. 521 28 57; tlx. 43986
156 rooms
Pleasant hotel. Outdoor dining.

Sanvy
Goya 3
28001 Madrid
Tel. 276 08 00; tlx. 44994
141 rooms
Outdoor swimming pool. Belagua restaurant.

Suecia
Marqués de Casa Riera 4
28014 Madrid
Tel. 231 69 00; tlx. 22313
67 rooms
Bellman restaurant.

Villa Magna
paseo de la Castellana 22
28046 Madrid
Tel. 261 49 00; tlx. 22914
198 rooms
Pleasant hotel.

Wellington
Velázquez 8
28001 Madrid
Tel. 275 44 00; tlx. 22700
258 rooms
Outdoor swimming pool. El Fogón restaurant.

OUTSKIRTS OF MADRID

Monte Real
Arroyofresno 17
28035 Madrid
Tel. 216 21 40; tlx. 22089
79 rooms
Quiet hotel. Elegant decor. Outdoor dining. Pretty garden. Outdoor swimming pool.

MEDIUM-PRICED
(ptas. 6,000–10,000)

Abeba
Alcántara 63
28006 Madrid
Tel. 401 16 50
100 rooms
No restaurant.

Agumar
paseo Reina Cristina 9
28014 Madrid
Tel. 552 69 00; tlx. 22814
252 rooms
No restaurant, but snacks available

Apartotel El Jardín
carret. N1
28034 Madrid
Tel. 202 83 36
41 rooms
Outdoor swimming pool. Garden. Hotel tennis courts. No restaurant.

Aramo
paseo Santa María de la Cabeza 73
28045 Madrid
Tel. 473 91 11; tlx. 45885
105 rooms
No restaurant, but snacks available.

Aristos
av. Pio XII-34
28016 Madrid
Tel. 457 04 50
24 rooms
Outdoor dining. El Chaflán restaurant.

Arosa
Salud 21
28013 Madrid
Tel. 232 16 00; tlx. 43618
126 rooms
No restaurant, but snacks available.

Bretón
Bretón de los Herreros 29
28003 Madrid
Tel. 442 83 00
56 rooms
No restaurant.

Capitol
Gran Vía 41
28013 Madrid
Tel. 521 83 91; tlx. 41499
142 rooms
No restaurant.

Carlos V
Maestro Vitoria 5
28013 Madrid
Tel. 231 41 00; tlx. 48547
67 rooms
No restaurant.

Carlton
paseo de las Delicias 26
28045 Madrid
Tel. 239 71 00; tlx. 44571
133 rooms

Chamartín
estación de Chamartín
28036 Madrid
Tel. 733 90 11; tlx. 49201
378 rooms
No restaurant.

Conde Duque
pl. Conde Valle de Suchil 5
28015 Madrid
Tel. 447 70 00; tlx. 22058
138 rooms
No restaurant, but snacks available.

Convención
O'Donnell 53
28009 Madrid
Tel. 274 68 00; tlx. 23944
790 rooms
No restaurant, but snacks available.

El Coloso
Leganitos 13
28013 Madrid
Tel. 248 76 00; tlx. 47017
84 rooms

El Gran Atlanta
Comandanta Zorita 34
28020 Madrid
Tel. 253 59 00; tlx. 45210
180 rooms
No restaurant.

El Prado
Prado 11
28014 Madrid
Tel. 429 35 68
45 rooms
No restaurant.

Emperatriz
López de Hoyos 4
28006 Madrid
Tel. 413 65 11; tlx. 43640
170 rooms
No restaurant, but snacks available.

G. H. Colón
Pez Volador 11
28007 Madrid
Tel. 273 59 00; tlx. 22984
390 rooms
Outdoor swimming pool. Garden.

Las Alondras
José Abascal 8
28003 Madrid
Tel. 447 40 00; tlx. 49454
72 rooms
No restaurant, but snacks available.

Liabeny
Salud 3
28013 Madrid
Tel. 232 53 06; tlx. 49024
158 rooms

Mayorazgo
Flor Baja 3
28013 Madrid
Tel. 247 26 00; tlx. 45647
200 rooms

Príncipe Pío
cuesta de San Vicente 16
28008 Madrid
Tel. 247 08 00; tlx. 42183
157 rooms

Puerta de Toledo
glorieta Puerta de Toledo 4
28005 Madrid
Tel. 474 71 00; tlx. 22291
152 rooms
Puerta de Toledo restaurant.

Washington
Gran Vía 72
28013 Madrid
Tel. 266 71 00; tlx. 48773
120 rooms
No restaurant.

Zurbano
Zurbano 79
28003 Madrid
Tel. 441 55 00; tlx. 27578
261 rooms

LOWER-PRICED
(below ptas. 6,000)

Alexandra
San Bernardo 29
28015 Madrid
Tel. 242 04 00
69 rooms
No restaurant.

Amberes
Gran Vía 68 – 7° piso
28013 Madrid
Tel. 247 61 00
44 rooms
No restaurant.

Anaco
Tres Cruces 3
28013 Madrid
Tel. 522 46 04
37 rooms
No restaurant.

Atlántico
Gran Vía 38 – 3° piso
28013 Madrid
Tel. 522 64 80; tlx. 43142
62 rooms
No restaurant.

California
Gran Vía 38 – 1° piso
28013 Madrid
Tel. 522 47 03
26 rooms
No restaurant.

Casón del Tormes
Río 7
28013 Madrid
Tel. 241 97 46
61 rooms
No restaurant.

Claridge
pl. del Conde de Casal 6
28007 Madrid
Tel. 551 94 00; tlx. 45585
150 rooms
No restaurant, but snacks available.

Cortezo
Dr Cortezo 3
28012 Madrid
Tel. 239 38 00; tlx. 48704
90 rooms
No restaurant, but snacks available.

Don Diego
Velázquez 45 – 5° piso
28001 Madrid
Tel. 435 07 60
58 rooms
No restaurant.

Francisco I
Arenal 15
28013 Madrid
Tel. 248 02 04; tlx. 43448
57 rooms

Galicia
Valverde 1 – 4° piso
28004 Madrid
Tel. 522 10 13
40 rooms
No restaurant.

Hostal Auto
paseo de la Chopera 69
28045 Madrid
Tel. 239 66 00
106 rooms
Mesón Auto restaurant.

Inglés
Echegaray 10
28014 Madrid
Tel. 429 65 51
58 rooms
No restaurant.

Italia
Gonzálo Jiménez de Quesada 2 –
2° piso
28004 Madrid
Tel. 522 47 90
59 rooms

Lisboa
Ventura de la Vega 17
28014 Madrid
Tel. 429 46 76
23 rooms
No restaurant. Breakfast not provided.

Lope de Vega
Gran Vía 59 – 9° piso
28013 Madrid
Tel. 247 70 00
47 rooms
View. No restaurant.

Madrid
Carretas 10
28012 Madrid
Tel. 521 65 20; tlx. 43142
72 rooms
No restaurant.

Mercator
Atocha 123
28012 Madrid
Tel. 429 05 00; tlx. 46129
90 rooms
No restaurant, but snacks available.

Moderno
Arenal 2
28013 Madrid
Tel. 231 09 00
98 rooms
No restaurant.

Paris
Alcalá 2
28014 Madrid
Tel. 521 64 96; tlx. 43448
114 rooms

Persal
pl. del Angel 12
28012 Madrid
Tel. 230 31 08
100 rooms
No restaurant.

Praga
Antonio López 65
28019 Madrid
Tel. 469 06 00; tlx. 45248
428 rooms
No restaurant, but snacks available.

Santander
Echegaray 1
28014 Madrid
Tel. 429 95 51
38 rooms
No restaurant.

Tirol
Marqués de Urquijo 4
28008 Madrid
Tel. 248 19 00
93 rooms
No restaurant, but snacks available.

RESTAURANTS

HIGHER-PRICED
(above ptas. 4,000)

Bajamar
Gran Vía 78
28013 Madrid
Tel. 248 59 03; tlx. 22818
Fish and shellfish.

Bidasoa
Claudio Coello 24
28001 Madrid
Tel. 431 20 81; tlx. 42948
Closed Sunday.

Cabo Mayor
Juan Hurtado de Mendoza 11
28036 Madrid
Tel. 250 87 76; tlx. 49784
Notably good cuisine. Original decor.

Café de Chinitas
Torija 7
28013 Madrid
Tel. 248 51 35
Dinner only. Flamenco. Supplement payable for floorshow. Closed Sunday and Christmas Eve.

Café de Oriente
pl. de Oriente 2
28013 Madrid
Tel. 241 39 74
Notably good, Basque-French cuisine. Elegant decor. Closed Saturday lunchtime, Sunday and August.

Club 31
Alcalá 58
28014 Madrid
Tel. 231 00 92
Closed August.

Don Victor
Emilio Vargas 18
28043 Madrid
Tel. 415 47 47
Outdoor dining. Closed Saturday lunchtime, Sunday and August.

El Amparo
Puigcerdá 8
28001 Madrid
Tel. 431 64 56
Excellent Basque-French cuisine. Closed Saturday lunchtime, Sunday, Holy Week and August.

El Bodegón
Pinar 15
28006 Madrid
Tel. 262 88 44
Closed Saturday lunchtime, Sunday, public holidays and August.

El Cenador del Prado
Prado 4
28014 Madrid
Tel. 429 15 49
Notably good cuisine. Pleasant restaurant. Closed Sunday and most of August.

Fortuny
Fortuny 34
28010 Madrid
Tel. 410 77 07
Small, elegantly decorated former palace. Pleasant terrace. Outdoor dining. Closed Saturday lunchtime, Sunday and public holidays.

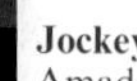

Jockey
Amador de los Ríos 6
28010 Madrid
Tel. 419 24 35
Notably good cuisine. Elegant decor. Closed Sunday, public holidays and August.

La Fragata
Capitán Haya 45
28020 Madrid
Tel. 270 98 36
Dinner with music.

L'Albufera
Capitán Haya 45
28043 Madrid
Tel. 279 63 74; tlx. 23142
Meals accompanied by piano music. Closed August.

Las Cuatro Estaciones
General Ibañez Ibero 5
28003 Madrid
Tel. 253 63 05; tlx. 43709
Notably good cuisine. Modern decor. Closed Saturday, Sunday and August.

Lúculo
Génova 19
28005 Madrid
Tel. 419 40 29
Notably good cuisine. Closed Saturday lunchtime, Sunday, public holidays and mid-August to mid-September.

Lur Maitea
Fernando el Santo 4
28010 Madrid
Tel. 419 09 38
Basque cuisine. Closed Saturday lunchtime, public holidays and August.

Príncipe de Viana
Manuel de Falla 5
28036 Madrid
Tel. 259 14 48
Notably good Basque cuisine. Closed Saturday lunchtime, Sunday, Holy Week and August.

Senorío de Bertiz
Comandante Zorita 6
28020 Madrid
Tel. 233 27 57
Notably good cuisine. Closed Saturday lunchtime, Sunday, public holidays and August.

Zalacaín
Álvarez de Baena 4
28006 Madrid
Tel. 261 48 40
Superb cuisine. Elegant decor. Outdoor dining. Closed Saturday lunchtime, Sunday, Holy Week and August.

MEDIUM-PRICED
(ptas. 3,000–4,000)

A' Casinã
Puente de los Franceses
28040 Madrid
Tel. 449 05 76
Galician cuisine. Outdoor dining.

Ainhoa
Bárbara de Braganza 12
28004 Madrid
Tel. 410 54 55
Basque cuisine. Closed Sunday and August.

Amalur
Padre Damián 37
28036 Madrid
Tel. 457 62 97
Closed Sunday, public holidays and August.

Bar del Teatro
Prim 5
28004 Madrid
Tel. 231 17 97
Situated in a wine cellar. Closed Saturday lunchtime and Sunday.

Bogavente
Capitán Haya 20
28020 Madrid
Tel. 456 21 14
Fish and shellfish.

Combarro
Reina Mercedes 12
28020 Madrid
Tel. 254 77 84
Galician cuisine. Closed Sunday evening and August.

Cota 13
estación de Chamartín
28036 Madrid
Tel. 315 52 18
Outdoor dining. Closed Saturday, Sunday, public holidays and August.

Currito
casa de Campo – Pabellón de Vizcaya
28011 Madrid
Tel. 464 57 04
Basque cuisine. Outdoor dining.

El Espejo
paseo de Recoletos 31
28004 Madrid
Tel. 410 25 25
Replica of old Paris café.

El Fogón
Villanueva 34
28001 Madrid
Tel. 275 44 00; tlx. 22700
Rustic Spanish style.

El Landó
pl. Gabriel Miró 8
28005 Madrid
Tel. 266 76 81
Elegant decor. Closed Sunday and August.

El Pescador
José Ortega y Gasset 75
28006 Madrid
Tel. 402 12 90
Notably good cuisine. Fish and shellfish. Closed Sunday and mid-August to mid-September.

Guipúzcoa
casa de Campo – Pabellón de Guipúzcoa
28011 Madrid
Tel. 470 04 21
Basque cuisine. Outdoor dining.

Gure-Etxea
pl. de la Paja 12
28005 Madrid
Tel. 265 61 49
Notably good, Basque cuisine. Closed Sunday and August.

Horcher
Alfonso XII – 6
28014 Madrid
Tel. 522 07 31
Notably good cuisine. Elegant decor.

Irizar
Jovellanos 3 – 1° piso
28014 Madrid
Tel. 231 45 69
Notably good, Basque-French cuisine. Closed Saturday lunchtime, Sunday and evenings of public holidays.

Jai-Alai
Balbina Valverde 2
28002 Madrid
Tel. 261 27 42
Basque cuisine. Outdoor dining. Closed Monday and mid-August to early September.

José Luis
Rafael Salgado 11
28036 Madrid
Tel. 250 02 42; tlx. 41779
Outdoor dining. Closed Sunday and August.

Korynto
Preciados 36
28013 Madrid
Tel. 521 59 65
Fish and shellfish.

Kulixka
Fuencarral 124
28010 Madrid
Tel. 447 25 38
Fish and shellfish.

La Boucade
Capitán Haya 30
28020 Madrid
Tel. 456 02 45
Closed Saturday lunchtime, Sunday, public holidays and August.

La Nueva Máquina
av. del Brasil 7
28020 Madrid
Tel. 455 10 02
Outdoor dining. Pleasant terrace. Closed Saturday lunchtime and Sunday.

Las Cuevas de Luis Candelas
Cuchilleros 1
28005 Madrid
Tel. 266 54 28
Old-Madrid decor. Waiters dressed as old-style bandits.

La Trainera
Lagasca 60
28001 Madrid
Tel. 276 80 35
Notably good cuisine. Fish and shellfish. Closed Sunday and August.

Los Borrachos de Velázquez
Principe de Vergara 205
28002 Madrid
Tel. 458 10 76
Andalusian restaurant. Closed Sunday.

Los Porches
paseo Pintor Rosales 1
28008 Madrid
Tel. 247 70 53
Outdoor dining.

Mayte Commodore
Serrano 145
28002 Madrid
Tel. 261 86 06
Elegant decor. Outdoor dining. Closed Sunday.

Mesón El Caserío
Capitán Haya 49
28020 Madrid
Tel. 270 96 29
Rustic decor. Outdoor dining.

Moanã
Hileras 4
28013 Madrid
Tel. 248 29 14
Galician cuisine. Closed Sunday, evenings of public holidays and July.

Nuevo Valentín
av. Concha Espina 8
28036 Madrid
Tel. 259 74 16
Outdoor dining.

O'Pazo
Reina Mercedes 20
28020 Madrid
Tel. 234 37 48
Fish and shellfish. Closed Sunday and August.

Ponteareas
Claudio Coello 96
28006 Madrid
Tel. 275 57 73
Galician cuisine.
Closed July, Sunday and public holidays.

Posada de la Villa
Cava Baja 9
28005 Madrid
Tel. 266 18 80
Old inn in Castilian style. Closed Sunday evening and August.

Rafa
Narváez 68
28009 Madrid
Tel. 273 10 87
Outdoor dining.

Sacha
Juan Hurtado de Mendoza 11
28036 Madrid
Tel. 457 51 52
Outdoor dining. Closed Sunday and August.

St.-James
Juan Bravo 26
28020 Madrid
Tel. 275 60 10
Outdoor dining. Closed Sunday.

Schwarzwald (Selva Negra)
O'Donnell 46
28009 Madrid
Tel. 409 56 13
Original decor.

Taberna del Alabardero
Felipe V - 6
28013 Madrid
Tel. 247 25 77
Typical tavern.

Villa y Corte de Madrid
Serrano 110
28025 Madrid
Tel. 261 29 77
Elegant decor. Closed Sunday in summer, and August.

Viridiana
Fundadores 23
28028 Madrid
Tel. 256 77 73
Notably good cuisine. Closed Sunday and August.

LOWER-PRICED
(below ptas. 3,000)

Alejandro
Mesonero Romanos 7
28013 Madrid
Tel. 231 51 04
Outdoor dining. Closed Sunday.

Alkalde
Jorge Juan 10
28001 Madrid
Tel. 276 33 59
Situated in a wine cellar. Closed Saturday evening and Sunday in July, and August.

Antonio
Santa Engracia 54
28010 Madrid
Tel. 447 40 68
Closed Sunday night, Monday and August.

Asador Guetaria
Comandanta Zorita 8
28020 Madrid
Tel. 254 66 32
Rustic Basque-style decor. Basque cuisine. Closed Sunday and August.

Aymar
Fuencarral 138
28010 Madrid
Tel. 445 57 67
Fish and shellfish.

Bodegón Navarro
paseo de la Castellana 121
28046 Madrid
Tel. 455 30 11
Rustic decor. Closed Sunday.

Botín
Cuchilleros 17
28005 Madrid
Tel. 266 42 17
Typical wine cellar in old-Madrid style.

Café de Oriente (Horno de Leña)
pl. Oriente 2
28013 Madrid
Tel. 247 15 64
Situated in a wine cellar.

Casa Domingo
Alcalá 99
28009 Madrid
Tel. 431 18 95
Outdoor dining.

Casa Lucio
Cava Baja 35
28005 Madrid
Tel. 265 32 52
Castilian decor. Closed Saturday lunchtime and August.

Café Viena
Luisa Fernanda 23
28008 Madrid
Tel. 248 15 91
Meals accompanied by piano music. Replica of an old-style café. Closed Saturday lunchtime, Sunday and August.

Casa Félix
Bréton de los Herreros 39
28003 Madrid
Tel. 441 24 79

Casa gallega
pl. de San Miguel 8
28005 Madrid
Tel. 247 30 55
Galician cuisine.

El Asador de Aranda
pl. de Castilla 3
28046 Madrid
Tel. 733 87 02
Roast lamb a speciality. Castilian decor. Closed Sunday evening and August.

El Hostal
Principe de Vergara 285
28016 Madrid
Tel. 259 11 94
Closed Sunday.

Hogar Gallego
pl. Comandante Las Morenas 3
28013 Madrid
Tel. 248 64 04
Outdoor dining. Galician cuisine. Closed Sunday evening.

La Fonda
Lagasca 11
28001 Madrid
Tel. 403 83 07
Catalan cuisine.

La Plaza de Chamberí
pl. de Chamberí 10
28010 Madrid
Tel. 446 06 97
Outdoor dining. Closed Sunday and Holy Week.

Las Cumbres
Alberto Alcocer 32
28036 Madrid
Tel. 458 76 92
Andalusian tavern.

Las Cumbres
av. de América 33
28002 Madrid
Tel. 413 07 51
Andalusian tavern. Closed Sunday evening.

Las Reses
Orfila 3
28010 Madrid
Tel. 419 10 13
Meat specialities. Closed Sunday, public holidays and August.

Los Galayos
Botoneras 5
28012 Madrid
Tel. 266 30 28
Outdoor dining.

Lucca
José Ortega y Gasset 29
28006 Madrid
Tel. 276 01 44
Modern decor. Meals accompanied by piano music.

Mesón Auto
paseo de la Chopera 71
28045 Madrid
Tel. 239 66 00
Rustic decor.

México Lindo
pl. República del Ecuador 4
28016 Madrid
Tel. 259 48 33
Mexican cuisine.

O'Xeito
paseo de la Castellana 47
28046 Madrid
Tel. 419 83 87
Galician-style decor. Fish and shellfish. Closed Saturday lunchtime, Sunday and August.

Pizzería Paolo
General Rodrigo 3
28003 Madrid
Tel. 254 44 28
Italian cuisine. Closed Sunday and August.

Salvador
Barbieri 12
28004 Madrid
Tel. 521 45 24
With paintings and photos of the bullfighting world. Closed Sunday and mid-July to early September.

Sixto
José Ortega y Gasset 83
28006 Madrid
Tel. 402 15 83
Outdoor dining. Closed Sunday evening.

Sixto Gran Mesón
Cervantes 28
28014 Madrid
Tel. 429 22 55
Castilian decor. Closed Sunday evening.

Taberna Carmencita
Libertad 16
28004 Madrid
Tel. 231 66 12
Typical tavern. Closed Sunday.

Toralla
Amador de los Ríos 8
28010 Madrid
Tel. 410 28 88
Galician cuisine. Closed Saturday evening and Sunday.

8/810

BERLITZ®

SPANISH
for travellers

By the staff of Berlitz Guides

How best to use this phrase book

- We suggest that you start with the **Guide to pronunciation** (pp. 6–8), then go on to **Some basic expressions** (pp. 9–15). This gives you not only a minimum vocabulary, but also helps you get used to pronouncing the language. The phonetic transcription throughout the book enables you to pronounce every word correctly.
- Consult the **Contents** pages (3–5) for the section you need. In each chapter you'll find travel facts, hints and useful information. Simple phrases are followed by a list of words applicable to the situation.
- Separate, detailed contents lists are included at the beginning of the extensive **Eating out** and **Shopping guide** sections (Menus, p. 39, Shops and services, p. 97).
- If you want to find out how to say something in Spanish, your fastest look-up is via the **Dictionary** section (pp. 164–189). This not only gives you the word, but is also cross-referenced to its use in a phrase on a specific page.
- If you wish to learn more about constructing sentences, check the **Basic grammar** (pp. 159–163).
- Note the **colour margins** are indexed in Spanish and English to help both listener and speaker. And, in addition, there is also an **index in Spanish** for the use of your listener.
- Throughout the book, this symbol ☛ suggests phrases your listener can use to answer you. If you still can't understand, hand this phrase book to the Spanish-speaker to encourage pointing to an appropriate answer. The English translation for you is just alongside the Spanish.

Library of Congress Catalog Card No. 85-81371

Second revised edition—6th printing 1988
Printed in Austria

Contents

Travelling around 65

Sightseeing 80

Relaxing 86

Making friends 93

Shopping guide 97

Acknowledgments
We are particularly grateful to José Carasa for his help in the preparation of this book, and to Dr. T.J.A. Bennett who devised the phonetic transcription.

Guide to pronunciation

This and the following chapter are intended to make you familiar with the phonetic transcription we devised and to help you get used to the sounds of Spanish.

As a minimum vocabulary for your trip, we've selected a number of basic words and phrases under the title "Some Basic Expressions" (pages 9–15).

An outline of the spelling and sounds of Spanish

You'll find the pronunciation of the Spanish letters and sounds explained below, as well as the symbols we're using for them in the transcriptions. Note that Spanish has some diacritical letters—letters with special markings—which we don't know in English.

The imitated pronunciation should be read as if it were English except for any special rules set out below. It is based on Standard British pronunciation, though we have tried to take into account General American pronunciation as well. Of course, the sounds of any two languages are never exactly the same; but if you follow carefully the indications supplied here, you'll have no difficulty in reading our transcriptions in such a way as to make yourself understood.

Letters written in bold should be stressed (pronounced louder).

Consonants

Letter	Approximate pronunciation	Symbol	Example	
f, k, l, m, n, p, t, x, y	as in English			
b	1) generally as in English	b	**bueno**	**bway**noa
	2) between vowels, a sound between **b** and **v**	bh	**bebida**	bay**bhee**dhah

c	1) before **e** and **i** like **th** in **th**in	th	**centro**	**thayn**troa
	2) otherwise, like **k** in **k**it	k	**como**	**koa**moa
ch	as in English	ch	**mucho**	**moo**choa
d	1) generally as in **d**og, although less decisive	d	**donde**	**doan**day
	2) between vowels and at the end of a word, like **th** in **th**is	dh	**edad**	ay**dhahdh**
g	1) before **e** and **i**, like **ch** in Scottish lo**ch**	kh	**urgente**	oor**khayn**tay
	2) between vowels and sometimes inside a word, a weak, voiced version of the **ch** in lo**ch**	g	**agua**	**ah**gwah
	3) otherwise, like **g** in **g**o	g	**ninguno**	neen**goo**noa
h	always silent		**hombre**	**om**bray
j	like **ch** in Scottish lo**ch**	kh	**bajo**	**bah**khoa
ll	like **lli** in mi**lli**on	ly	**lleno**	**lyay**noa
ñ	like **ni** in o**ni**on	ñ	**señor**	say**ñor**
qu	like **k** in **k**it	k	**quince**	**keen**thay
r	more strongly trilled (like a Scottish **r**), especially at the beginning of a word	r	**río**	**ree**oa
rr	strongly trilled	rr	**arriba**	ahr**ree**bhah
s	always like the **s** in **s**it, often with a slight lisp	s/ss	**vista** **cuantos**	**bees**tah **kwahn**toass
v	1) tends to be like **b** in **b**ad, but less tense	b	**viejo**	**byay**khoa
	2) between vowels, more like English **v**	bh	**rival**	ree**bhahl**
z	like **th** in **th**in	th	**brazo**	**brah**thoa

Vowels

a	like **ar** in c**ar**t, but fairly short	ah	**gracias**	**grah**thyahss
e	1) sometimes like **a** in l**a**te	ay	**de**	day
	2) less often, like **e** in g**e**t	eh	**llover**	lyoa**bhehr**
i	like **ee** in f**ee**t	ee	**sí**	see

o	1) like **oa** in **boat**, but pronounced without moving tongue or lips	oa	**sopa**	**soa**pah
	2) sometimes like **o** in **got**	o	**dos**	doss
u	like **oo** in **loot**	oo	**una**	**oo**nah
y	only a vowel when alone or at the end of a word; like **ee** in **feet**	ee	**y**	ee

N.B. 1) In forming diphthongs, **a**, **e**, and **o** are strong vowels, and **i** and **u** (pronounced before a vowel like **y** in **y**es and **w** in **w**as) are weak vowels. This means that in diphthongs the strong vowels are pronounced more strongly than the weak ones. If two weak vowels form a diphthong, the second one is pronounced more strongly.

2) The acute accent (′) is used to indicate a syllable that is stressed, e.g., *río* = **ree**oa.

3) In words ending with a consonant, the last syllable is stressed, e.g., *señor* = say**ñor**.

4) In words ending with a vowel, the next to last syllable is stressed, e.g., *mañana* = mah**ñah**nah.

Pronunciation of the Spanish alphabet

A	ah	J	**khoa**tah	R	**ayr**ray
B	bay	K	kah	S	**ays**say
C	thay	L	**ayl**lay	T	tay
CH	chay	LL	**ayl**yay	U	oo
D	day	M	**aym**may	V	bhay
E	ay	N	**ayn**nay	W	bhay **doa**blay
F	**ayf**fay	Ñ	**ayn**yay	X	**ay**kheess
G	gay	O	oa	Y	ee **gryay**gah
H	**ah**chay	P	pay	Z	**thay**tah
I	ee	Q	koo		

Some basic expressions

Yes.	**Sí.**	see
No.	**No.**	noa
Please.	**Por favor.**	por fah**bhor**
Thank you.	**Gracias.**	**grah**thyahss
No, thank you.	**No, gracias.**	noa **grah**thyahss
Yes, please.	**Sí, por favor.**	see por fah**bhor**
Thank you very much.	**Muchas gracias.**	**moo**chahss **grah**thyahss
That's all right/ Don't mention it.	**No hay de qué.**	noa igh day kay
You're welcome.	**De nada.**	day **nah**dhah

Greetings *Saludos*

Good morning.	**Buenos días.**	**bway**noass **dee**ahss
Good afternoon.	**Buenas tardes.**	**bway**nahss **tahr**dayss
Good evening.	**Buenas tardes.**	**bway**nahss **tahr**dayss
Good night.	**Buenas noches.**	**bway**nahss **noa**chayss
Good-bye.	**Adiós.**	ah**dhyoss**
See you later.	**Hasta luego.**	**ah**stah **lway**goa
This is Mr. ...	**Este es el Señor ...**	**ay**stay ayss ayl say**ñor**
This is Mrs. ...	**Esta es la Señora ...**	**ay**stah ayss lah say**ñoa**rah
This is Miss ...	**Esta es la Señorita ...**	**ay**stah ayss lah sayñoa**ree**tah
How do you do? (Pleased to meet you.)	**Encantado(a)* de conocerle.**	aynkahn**tah**dhoa(ah) day koanoa**thayr**lay

* A woman would say *encantada*

How are you?	**¿Cómo está usted?**	koamoa aystah oostaydh
Very well. And you?	**Muy bien. ¿Y usted?**	mwee byayn. ee oostaydh
How's it going?	**¿Cómo le va?**	koamoa lay bah
Fine, thanks. And you?	**Muy bien, gracias. ¿Y usted?**	mwee byayn grahthyahss. ee oostaydh
I beg your pardon?	**¿Perdóneme?**	payrdoanaymay
Excuse me. (May I get past?)	**Perdóneme.**	payrdoanaymay
Sorry!	**Lo siento.**	loa syayntoa
You're welcome.	**Está bien.**	aystah byayn

Questions *Preguntas*

Where?	**¿Dónde?**	doanday
How?	**¿Cómo?**	koamoa
When?	**¿Cuándo?**	kwahndoa
What?	**¿Qué?**	kay
Why?	**¿Por qué?**	por kay
Who?	**¿Quién?**	kyayn
Which?	**¿Cuál/Cuáles?**	kwahl/kwahlayss
Where is ...?	**¿Dónde está ...?**	doanday aystah
Where are ...?	**¿Dónde están ...?**	doanday aystahn
Where can I find/get ...?	**¿Dónde puedo encontrar/conseguir ...?**	doanday pwaydhoa aynkontrahr/konsaygeer
How far?	**¿A qué distancia?**	ah kay deestahnthyah
How long?	**¿Cuánto tiempo?**	kwahntoa tyaympoa
How much?	**¿Cuánto?**	kwahntoa
How many?	**¿Cuántos?**	kwahntoass
How much does it cost?	**¿Cuánto cuesta?**	kwahntoa kwaystah
How do I get to ...?	**¿Cómo puedo llegar a ...?**	koamoa pwaydhoa lyaygahr ah

When does ... open/ close?	**¿Cuándo abren/ cierran ...?**	**kwahn**doa ah**brayn**/ **thyayr**rahn
What do you call this/ that in Spanish?	**¿Cómo se llama esto/ eso en español?**	koamoa say **lyah**mah **ays**toa/ **ays**soa ayn ayspah**ñol**
What do you call these/those in Spanish?	**¿Cómo se llaman estos/esos en español?**	koamoa say **lyah**mahn **ays**toass/**ays**soass ayn ayspah**ñol**
What does this/ that mean?	**¿Qué quiere decir esto/eso?**	kay **kyay**ray day**theer ays**toa/ **ays**soa
Is that correct?	**¿Es correcto?**	ayss koar**rayk**toa
Why are you laughing?	**¿Por qué se ríe?**	poar kay say **ree**ay
Is my pronunciation that bad?	**¿Es mala mi pronunciación?**	ayss **mah**lah mee proanoonthyah**thyon**

Do you speak ...? *¿Habla usted ...?*

Do you speak English?	**¿Habla usted inglés?**	**ah**blah oos**taydh** een**glayss**
Is there anyone here who speaks ...?	**¿Hay alguien aquí que hable ...?**	igh **ahl**gyayn ah**kee** kay **ah**blay
I don't speak much Spanish.	**No hablo mucho español.**	noa **ah**bloa **moo**choa ayspah**ñol**
Could you speak more slowly?	**¿Puede usted hablar más despacio?**	**pway**dhay oos**taydh** ah**blahr** mahss days**pah**thyoa
Could you repeat that?	**¿Podría usted repetir eso?**	poa**dree**ah oos**taydh** raypay**teer ays**soa
Please write it down.	**Por favor, escríbalo.**	por fah**bhor** ays**kree**bhahloa
Can you translate this for me?	**¿Puede usted traducírmelo?**	**pway**dhay oos**taydh** trahdhoo**theer**mayloa
Can you translate this for us?	**¿Puede usted traducírnoslo?**	**pway**dhay oos**taydh** trahdhoo**theer**noasloa
Please point to the word/phrase/ sentence in the book.	**Por favor, señale la palabra/la expresión/la frase en el libro.**	por fah**bhor** say**ñah**lay lah pah**lah**brah/lah aykspray**syon**/lah **frah**ssay ayn ayl **lee**broa

Just a minute. I'll see if I can find it in this book.	**Un momento. Veré si lo puedo encontrar en este libro.**	oon moa**mayn**toa. bay**ray** see loa **pway**dhoa aynkoan**trahr** ayn **ays**tay **lee**broa
I understand.	**Comprendo/ Entiendo.**	koam**prayn**doa/ ayn**tyayn**doa
I don't understand.	**No comprendo.**	noa koam**prayn**doa
Do you understand?	**¿Comprende usted?**	koam**prayn**day oos**taydh**

Can/May ...? *¿Puede ...?*

Can I have ...?	**¿Puede darme ...?**	**pway**dhay **dahr**may
Can we have ...?	**¿Puede darnos ...?**	**pway**dhay **dahr**noass
Can you show me ...?	**¿Puede usted enseñarme ...?**	**pway**dhay oos**taydh** aynsay**ñahr**may
I can't.	**No puedo.**	noa **pway**dhoa
Can you tell me ...?	**¿Puede usted decirme ...?**	**pway**dhay oos**taydh** day**theer**may
Can you help me?	**¿Puede usted ayudarme?**	**pway**dhay oos**taydh** ahyoo**dhar**may
Can I help you?	**¿Puedo ayudarle?**	**pway**dhoa ahyoo**dhar**lay
Can you direct me to ...?	**¿Puede usted indicarmo la dirección a ...?**	**pway**dhay oos**taydh** eendee**kahr**may lah deerehk**thyon** ah

Wanting *Deseos*

I'd like ...	**Quisiera ...**	kee**ssyay**rah
We'd like ...	**Quisiéramos ...**	kee**ssyay**rahmoass
What do you want?	**¿Qué desea usted?**	kay day**ssehah** oos**taydh**
Please give me ...	**Por favor, déme ...**	por fah**bhor day**may
Give it to me, please.	**Démelo, por favor.**	daymayloa por fah**bhor**
Bring me ...	**Tráigame ...**	**trigh**gahmay
Bring it to me.	**Tráigamelo.**	**trigh**gahmayloa

Show me ...	**Enséñeme ...**	ayn**say**ñaymay
Show it to me.	**Enséñemelo.**	ayn**say**ñaymayloa
I'm hungry.	**Tengo hambre.**	**tayn**goa **ahm**bray
I'm thirsty.	**Tengo sed.**	**tayn**goa saydh
I'd like something to eat/drink.	**Quisiera algo para comer/beber.**	kee**ssyay**rah **ahl**goa **pah**rah koa**mayr**/bay**bhayr**
I'm tired.	**Estoy cansado(a).***	ay**stoy** kahn**sah**dhoa(ah)
I'm lost.	**Me he perdido.**	may ay payr**dee**dhoa
I'm looking for ...	**Estoy buscando ...**	ay**stoy** boos**kahn**doa
It's important.	**Es importante.**	ayss eempoar**tahn**tay
It's urgent.	**Es urgente.**	ayss oor**khayn**tay
Hurry up!	**¡Dése prisa!**	**day**ssay **pree**ssah

It is / There is ... *Es/Está/Hay ...*

It is/It's ...	**Es ...**	ayss
Is it ...?	**¿Es ...?**	ayss
It isn't ...	**No es ...**	noa ayss
Isn't it ...?	**¿No es ...?**	noa ayss
Here it is.	**Aquí está.**	ah**kee** ay**stah**
Here they are.	**Aquí están.**	ah**kee** ay**stahn**
There it is.	**Ahí está.**	ahee ay**stah**
There they are.	**Ahí están.**	ahee ay**stahn**
There is/There are ...	**Hay ...**	igh
Is there/Are there ...?	**¿Hay ...?**	igh
There isn't/There aren't ...	**No hay ...**	noa igh
Isn't there/Aren't there ...?	**¿No hay ...?**	noa igh
There isn't/There aren't any ...	**No hay ninguno(a)/ No hay ningunos(as) ...**	noa igh neen**goo**noa(ah)/noa igh neen**goo**noass(ahss)

* A woman would say *cansada*

It's ... *Es/Está ...*

big/small	**grande/pequeño***	**grahn**day/pay**kay**ñoa
quick/slow	**rápido/lento**	**rah**peedhoa/**layn**toa
early/late	**temprano/tarde**	taym**prah**noa/**tahr**day
cheap/expensive	**barato/caro**	bah**rah**toa/**kah**roa
near/far	**cerca/lejos**	**thehr**kah/**leh**khoss
hot/cold	**caliente/frío**	kah**lyayn**tay/**free**oa
full/empty	**lleno/vacío**	**lyay**noa/bah**thee**oa
easy/difficult	**fácil/difícil**	**fah**theel/dee**fee**theel
heavy/light	**pesado/ligero**	pay**ssah**dhoa/lee**khay**roa
open/shut	**abierto/cerrado**	ah**bhyehr**toa/thehr**rah**dhoa
free (vacant)/ occupied	**libre/ocupado**	**lee**bray/oakoo**pah**dhoa
right/wrong	**correcto/incorrecto**	koar**rehk**toa/eenkoar**rehk**toa
old/new	**viejo/nuevo**	**byay**khoa/**nway**bhoa
old/young	**viejo/joven**	**byay**khoa/**khoa**bhehn
next/last	**próximo/último**	**proak**seemoa/**ool**teemoa
beautiful/ugly	**bonito/feo**	boa**nee**toa/**feh**oa
good/bad	**bueno/malo**	**bway**noa/**mah**loa
better/worse	**mejor/peor**	meh**khor**/peh**or**

Quantities *Cantidades*

a little/a lot	**un poco/mucho**	oon **poa**koa/**moo**choa
few/a few	**pocos/(alg)unos**	**poa**koass/(ahl**g**)**oo**noass
much/many	**mucho/muchos**	**moo**choa/**moo**choass
more than/less than	**más que/menos que**	mahss kay/**may**noass kay
enough/too	**bastante/demasiado**	bahs**tahn**tay/daymah**ssyah**dhoa
some	**unos/unas**	**oo**noass/**oo**nahss
any	**alguno/alguna**	ahl**goo**noa/ahl**goo**nah

* For feminine and plural forms, see grammar section page 159 (adjectives).

Some more useful words *Algunas palabras útiles*

at	**a/en**	ah/ayn
on	**sobre/en**	**soa**bray/ayn
in	**en**	ayn
to	**a/para**	ah/**pah**rah
for	**por/para**	por/**pah**rah
from	**de/desde**	day/**days**day
inside	**dentro**	**dayn**troa
outside	**fuera**	**fway**rah
up/upstairs	**arriba**	ah**ree**bha
down/downstairs	**abajo**	ah**bhah**khoa
above	**encima**	ayn**thee**mah
below	**debajo**	day**bhah**khoa
under	**debajo**	day**bhah**khoa
next to	**junto a**	**khoon**toa ah
between	**entre**	**ayn**tray
with/without	**con/sin**	kon/seen
since	**desde**	**days**day
and	**y**	ee
or	**o**	oa
not	**no**	noa
nothing	**nada**	**nah**dhah
never	**nunca**	**noon**kah
none	**ninguno/ninguna**	neen**goo**noa/neen**goo**nah
very	**muy**	mwee
too (also)	**también**	tahm**byayn**
soon	**pronto**	**proan**toa
perhaps	**quizá/tal vez**	kee**thah**/tahl bayth
here	**aquí**	ah**kee**
there	**allí**	ah**lyee**
now	**ahora**	ah**oa**rah
then	**entonces**	ayn**toan**thayss
yet	**todavía**	toadhah**bhee**ah

Arrival

CONTROL DE PASAPORTES
PASSPORT CONTROL

Here's my passport.	**Aquí está mi pasaporte.**	ah**kee** ay**stah** mee pahssah**por**tay
I'll be staying ...	**Me quedaré ...**	may kaydah**ray**
a few days a week	**unos días** **una semana**	**oo**noas **dee**ahss **oo**nah say**mah**nah
I don't know yet.	**No lo sé todavía.**	noa loa say toadhah**bhee**ah
I'm here on holiday/ business.	**Estoy aquí de vacaciones/ negocios.**	ay**stoy** ah**kee** day bahkah**thyoa**nayss/ nay**go**thyoass
I'm just passing through.	**Estoy sólo de paso.**	ay**stoy** **soa**loa day **pah**ssoa

If things become difficult:

I'm sorry, I don't understand.	**Lo siento, no comprendo.**	loa **syayn**toa noa kom**prayn**doa
Is there anyone here who speaks English?	**¿Hay alguien aquí que hable inglés?**	igh **ahl**gyayn ah**kee** kay **ah**blay eeng**layss**

ADUANA
CUSTOMS

After collecting your baggage at the airport (*el aeropuerto* —ayl ahehroa**pwayr**toa) you have a choice: follow the green arrow if you have nothing to declare. Or leave via a doorway marked with a red arrow if you have items to declare (in excess of those allowed).

artículos para declarar goods to declare	**nada que declarar** nothing to declare

The chart below shows what you can bring in duty-free.*

	Cigarettes		Cigars		Tobacco	Spirits (Liquor)		Wine
1)	200	or	50	or	250 g.	1 l.	or	2 l.
2)	300	or	75	or	400 g.	1.5 l.	and	5 l.
3)	400	or	100	or	500 g.	1 l.	or	2 l.

1) Visitors arriving from EEC countries with tax-free items, and visitors from other European countries
2) Visitors arriving from EEC countries with non-tax-free items
3) Visitors arriving from countries outside Europe

I've nothing to declare.	**No tengo nada que declarar.**	noa **tayn**goa **nah**dhah kay dayklah**rahr**
I've a ...	**Tengo ...**	**tayn**goa
carton of cigarettes	**un cartón de cigarrillos**	oon kahr**ton** day theegahr**ree**lyoass
bottle of whisky	**una botella de whisky**	**oo**nah boa**tay**lyah day **wees**kee
bottle of wine	**una botella de vino**	**oo**nah boa**tay**lyah day **bee**noa
It's for my personal use.	**Es de mi uso personal.**	ayss day mee **oo**ssoa pehrsoa**nahl**
It's a gift.	**Es un regalo.**	ayss oon ray**gah**loa

Su pasaporte, por favor.	Your passport, please.
¿Tiene usted algo que declarar?	Do you have anything to declare?
Por favor, abra esta bolsa.	Please open this bag.
Tendrá que pagar impuestos por esto.	You'll have to pay duty on this.
¿Tiene usted más equipaje?	Do you have any more luggage?

Baggage—Porters *Equipaje—Mozos*

You'll find porters to carry your luggage to taxi ranks or bus stops. Major airports have self-service luggage carts which can be found in the baggage claim area.

Porter!	**¡Mozo!**	moathoa
Please take this luggage.	**Por favor, lleve este equipaje.**	por fahbhor lyaybhay aystay aykeepahkhay
That's mine.	**Eso es mío.**	ayssoa ayss meeoa
That's my bag/ suitcase.	**Esa es mi bolsa/ maleta.**	ayssay eyss mee bolsah/ mahlaytah
There is one piece missing.	**Falta un bulto.**	fahltah oon booltoa
Please take this/my luggage to the ...	**Por favor, lleve este/ mi equipaje ...**	por fahbhor lyaybhay aystay/mee aykeepahkhay
bus	**al autobús**	ahl owtoabhooss
luggage lockers	**a la consigna automática**	ah lah konseegnah owtoamahteekah
taxi	**al taxi**	ahl tahksee
How much is that?	**¿Cuánto es?**	kwahntoa ayss
Where are the baggage trolleys (carts)?	**¿Dónde están los carritos de equipaje?**	doanday aystahn los kahrreetoss day aykeepahkhay

Changing money *Cambio de moneda*

Where's the nearest currency exchange office?	**¿Dónde está la oficina de cambio más cercana?**	doanday aystah lah oafeetheenah day kahmbyoa mahss thayrkahnah
Can you change these traveller's cheques (checks)?	**¿Puede cambiarme estos cheques de viajero?**	pwaydhay kahmbyahrmay aystoass chaykayss day byahkhayroa
I want to change some ...	**Quiero cambiar ...**	kyayroa kahmbyahr
dollars	**dólares**	doalahrayss
pounds	**libras**	leebrahss
Can you change this into pesetas?	**¿Puede cambiarme esto en pesetas?**	pwaydhay kahmbyahrmay aystoa ayn payssaytahss
What's the exchange rate?	**¿A cuánto está el cambio?**	ah kwahntoa aystah ayl kahmbyoa

TIPPING, see inside back-cover

Where is ...? *¿Dónde está ...?*

Where is/are the ...?	**¿Dónde está/ están ...?**	**doan**day ays**tah**/ays**tahn**
booking office	**la oficina de reservas**	lah oafee**thee**nah day rays**sayr**bahss
car hire	**la agencia de alquiler de coches**	lah ah**khayn**thyah day ahl-kee**layr** day **koa**chayss
currency-exchange office	**la oficina de cambio de moneda**	lah oafee**thee**nah day **kahm**-byoa day moa**nay**dhah
duty-free shop	**la tienda libre de impuestos**	lah **tyayn**dah **lee**bray day eemp**wayss**toass
luggage lockers	**la consigna automatica**	lah kon**see**gnah owto-**mah**teekah
newsstand	**el quiosco de periódicos**	ayl **kyos**koa day pay**ryo**dheekoass
restaurant	**el restaurante**	ayl raystow**rahn**tay
toilets	**los servicios**	loss sehr**bee**thyoass
How do I get to ...?	**¿Como podria ir a ...?**	koamoa poa**dree**ah eer ah
Is there a bus into town?	**¿Hay un autobús que va al centro?**	igh oon owtoa**bhooss** kay bah ahl **thayn**troa
Where can I get a taxi?	**¿Dónde puedo coger un taxi?**	**doan**day **pway**dhoa koa**khayr** oon **tahk**see

Hotel reservation *Reserva de hotel*

Do you have a hotel guide?	**¿Tiene una guía de hoteles?**	**tyay**nay **oo**nah **gee**ah day oa**tehl**ayss
Could you please reserve a room for me at a hotel/ boarding-house?	**¿Podría reservarme una habitación en un hotel/una pensión, por favor?**	poa**dree**ah rayssayr**bahr**-may **oo**nah ahbheetah**thyon** ayn oon oa**tehl**/**oo**nah payn**syon** por fah**bor**
in the centre	**en el centro**	ayn ayl **thayn**troa
near the railway station	**cerca de la estación de ferrocarril**	**thayr**kah day lah aystah-**thyon** day fehrrokahr**reel**
a single room	**una habitación sencilla**	**oo**nah ahbheetah**thyon** sayn**thee**lyah
a double room	**una habitación doble**	**oo**nah ahbheetah**thyon** **doa**blay
not too expensive	**no muy cara**	noa mwee **kah**rah
Where is the hotel/ boarding-house?	**¿Dónde está el hotel/ la pensión?**	**doan**day ays**tah** ayl oa**tehl**/ lah payn**syon**

HOTEL, see page 22

Car hire (rental) *Alquiler de coches*

Normally you must be over 21 and hold an international driving licence. In practice, British, American and European licences are accepted in almost all situations.

I'd like to hire (rent) a ...	**Quisiera alquilar un ...**	kee**ssyay**rah ahlkee**lahr** oon
car	**coche**	**koa**chay
small car	**coche pequeño**	**koa**chay pay**kay**ñoa
medium-sized car	**coche no de lujo**	**koa**chay noa day **loo**khoa
large car	**coche grande**	**koa**chay **grahn**day
automatic car	**coche automático**	**koa**chay owtoa**mah**teekoa
I'd like it for ...	**Lo quisiera para ...**	loa kee**ssyay**rah **pah**rah
a day	**un día**	oon **dee**ah
a week	**una semana**	**oo**nah say**mah**nah
Are there any week-end arrangements?	**¿Hay condiciones especiales para los fines de semana?**	igh koandee**thyo**nayss ayspay**thyah**layss **pah**rah loas **fee**nayss day say**mah**nah
Do you have any special rates?	**¿Tienen tarifas especiales?**	**tyay**nayn tah**ree**fahss ayspay**thyah**layss
What's the charge per day/week?	**¿Cúanto cobran por día/semana?**	**kwahn**toa **koa**brahn por **dee**ah/say**mah**nah
Is mileage included?	**¿Está incluido el kilometraje?**	ays**tah** eenklo**oee**dhoa ayl keeloamay**trah**khay
Is petrol (gasoline) included?	**¿Está incluida la gasolina?**	ays**tah** eenkloo**ee**dhah lah gahssoa**lee**nah
What's the charge per kilometre?	**¿Cuánto cobran por kilómetro?**	**kwahn**toa **koa**brahn por kee**loa**maytroa
I want to hire the car here and leave it in ...	**Quiero alquilar un coche aquí y entregarlo en ...**	**kyay**roa ahlkee**lahr** oon **koa**chay ah**kee** ee ayntray**gahr**loa ayn
I want full insurance.	**Quiero un seguro a todo riesgo.**	**kyay**roa oon say**goo**roa ah **toa**dhoa **ryays**goa
What's the deposit?	**¿Cuál es el depósito?**	kwahl ayss ayl day**poa**sseetoa
I've a credit card.	**Tengo una tarjeta de crédito.**	**tayn**goa **oo**nah tahr**khay**tah day **kray**dheetoa
Here's my driving licence.	**Este es mi permiso de conducir.**	**ays**tay ayss mee pehr**mee**ssoa day kondoo**theer**

CAR, see page 75

Taxi *Taxi*

Taxis in major towns are fitted with meters. The figure displayed at the end of your trip may not be the full price. Legitimate added charges are compounded for night and holiday travel, pickups at railway stations, theatres or bullrings, and for baggage. It's usually best to ask the approximate fare beforehand.

Where can I get a taxi?	**¿Dónde puedo coger un taxi?**	**doan**day **pway**dhoa koa**khehr** oon **tahk**see
Please get me a taxi.	**Pídame un taxi, por favor.**	**pee**dhahmay oon **tahk**see por fah**bhor**
What's the fare to ...?	**¿Cuánto es la tarifa a ...?**	**kwahn**toa ayss lah tah**ree**fah ah
How far is it to ...?	**¿Cuánto se tarda a ...?**	**kwahn**toa say **tahr**dah ah
Take me to ...	**Lléveme ...**	**lyay**bhaymay
this address	**a estas señas**	ah **ay**stahss **say**ñahss
the airport	**al aeropuerto**	ahl ahehro**pwayr**to
the air terminal	**a la terminal aérea**	ah lah tehrmee**nahl** ahayrayah
the railway station	**a la estación de ferrocarril**	ah lah aystah**thyon** day fehrrokahr**reel**
the town centre	**al centro de la ciudad**	ahl **thayn**troa day lah thyoo**dhahdh**
the ... Hotel	**al hotel ...**	ahl oa**tehl**
Turn ... at the next corner.	**Doble ... en la próxima esquina.**	**doa**blay ... ayn lah **prok**seemah ays**kee**nah
left	**a la izquierda**	ah lah eeth**kyayr**dah
right	**a la derecha**	ah lah day**ray**chah
Go straight ahead.	**Siga derecho.**	**see**gah day**ray**choa
Please stop here.	**Pare aquí, por favor.**	**pah**ray ah**kee** por fah**bhor**
I'm in a hurry.	**Tengo mucha prisa.**	**tayn**goa **moo**chah **pree**ssah
Could you drive more slowly?	**¿Puede usted ir más despacio?**	**pway**dhay oos**taydh** eer mahss days**pah**thyoa
Could you help me carry my bags?	**¿Podría ayudarme a llevar mi equipaje?**	poa**dree**ah ahyoo**dhahr**may ah lyay**bhahr** mee aykee**pah**khay
Would you please wait for me?	**¿Puede esperarme, por favor?**	**pway**dhay ayspay**rahr**may por fah**bhor**

TIPPING, see inside back-cover

Hotel—Other accommodation

Early reservation (and confirmation) is essential in most major tourist centres in the high season. Most towns and arrival points have a tourist information office, and that's the place to go if you're stuck without a room.

Hotel (oa**tehl**) — There are five official categories of hotels: luxury, first class A, first class B, second class and third class. There may be price variations within any given category, depending on the location and the facilities offered. There are also, of course, plenty of unclassified hotels where you will find clean, simple accommodation and good food.

Hostal (oas**tahl**) — Modest hotels, often family concerns, graded one to three stars.

Residencia (raysseedaynthyah) — When referred to as *hostal-residencia* or *hotel-residencia,* this term indicates a hotel without a restaurant.

Pensión (payn**syon**) — This roughly corresponds to a boarding house. Usually divided into four categories, it offers *pensión completa* (full board) or *media pensión* (half board). Meals are likely to be from a set menu.

Albergue (ahl**behr**gay) — Modern country inns, catering especially to the motorist.

Parador (pahrah**dhor**) — Palaces, country houses or castles that have been converted into hotels and are under government supervision.

Refugio (reh**foo**khyoa) — Small inns in remote and mountainous regions. They're often closed in winter.

Apartamento amueblado (ahpahrtah**mayn**toa ahmway**blah**dhoa) — A furnished flat (apartment) mainly in resorts. Available from specialized travel agents or directly from the landlord (look for the sign *se alquila*—to let, for rent).

Albergue de juventud (ahl**behr**gay day khoobhehn**toodh**) — Youth hostel. Foreign tourists wishing to use them should be members of the international Youth Hostels Association.

CAMPING, see page 32

Checking in—Reception *Recepción*

My name is ...	**Mi nombre es ...**	mee **noam**bray ayss
I've a reservation.	**He hecho una reserva.**	eh **ay**choa **oo**nah ray**ssayr**bah
We've reserved two rooms.	**Hemos reservado dos habitaciones.**	**eh**moass rayssayr**bah**dhoa doss ahbheetah**thyo**nayss
Here's the confirmation.	**Aquí está la confirmación.**	ah**kee** ays**tah** lah konfeermah**thyon**
Do you have any vacancies?	**¿Tiene habitaciones libres?**	**tyay**nay ahbheetah**thyo**nayss **lee**bhrayss
I'd like a single/ double room.	**Quisiera una habitación sencilla/ doble.**	kee**ssyay**rah **oo**nah ahbheetah**thyon** sayn**thee**lyah/**doa**blay
I'd like a room ...	**Quisiera una habitación ...**	kee**ssyay**rah **oo**nah ahbheetah**thyon**
with twin beds	**con dos camas**	kon doss **kah**mahss
with a double bed	**con una cama matrimonial**	kon **oo**nah **kah**mah mahtreemoa**nyahl**
with a bath	**con baño**	kon **bah**ñoa
with a shower	**con ducha**	kon **doo**chah
with a balcony	**con balcón**	kon bahl**kon**
with a view	**con vista**	kon **bees**tah
in the front	**en la parte delantera**	ayn lah **pahr**tay daylahn**tay**rah
at the back	**en la parte trasera**	ayn lah **pahr**tay trah**ssay**rah
facing the sea	**con vista al mar**	kon **bees**tah ahl mahr
facing the courtyard	**con vista al patio**	kon **bees**tah ahl **pah**tyoa
It must be quiet.	**Tiene que ser tranquila.**	**tyay**nay kay sayr trahn**kee**lah
Is there ...?	**¿Hay ...?**	igh
air conditioning	**aire acondicionado**	**igh**ray ahkondeethyoa**nah**dhoa
heating	**calefacción**	kahlayfahk**thyon**
a radio/a television in the room	**radio/televisión en la habitación**	**rah**dhyoa/taylaybhee**ssyon** ayn lah ahbheetah**thyon**
laundry/room service	**servicio de lavado/ de habitación**	sehr**bee**thyoa day lah**bhah**dhoa/day ahbheetah**thyon**
hot water	**agua caliente**	**ahg**wah kah**lyayn**tay
running water	**agua corriente**	**ahg**wah kor**ryayn**tay
a private toilet	**water particular**	**wah**tayr pahrteekoo**lahr**

CHECKING OUT, see page 31

How much? *¿Cuánto cuesta?*

What's the price ...?	**¿Cuánto cuesta ...?**	kwahntoa kwaystah
per night/per week	**por noche/por semana**	por noachay/por saymahnah
for bed and breakfast	**por dormir y desayunar**	por dormeer ee dayssahyoonahr
excluding meals	**excluyendo las comidas**	aykslooyayndoa lahss koameedhahss
for full board (A.P.)	**por pensión completa**	por paynsyon komplaytah
for half board (M.A.P.)	**por media pensión**	por maydhyah paynsyon
Does that include service/breakfast?	**¿Está incluido el servicio/el desayuno?**	aystah eenklooeedhoa ayl sehrbeethyoa/ayl dayssahyoonoa
Is tax included?	**¿Están incluidos los impuestos?**	aystahn eenklooeedhoass loss eempwaystoass
Is there any reduction for children?	**¿Hay algún descuento para los niños?**	igh ahlgoon dayskwayntoa pahrah loss neeñoass
Do you charge for the baby?	**¿Cobran ustedes por el bebé?**	koabrahn oostaydhayss por ayl baybay
That's too expensive.	**Eso es demasiado caro.**	ayssoa ayss daymahssyahdhoa kahroa
Haven't you anything cheaper?	**¿No tiene usted nada más barato?**	noa tyaynay oostaydh nahdhah mahss bahrahtoa

Decision *Decisión*

May I see the room?	**¿Puedo ver la habitación?**	pwaydhoa behr lah ahbheetahthyon
No, I don't like it.	**No, no me gusta.**	noa noa may goostah
It's too ...	**Es demasiado ...**	ayss daymahssyahdhoa
cold/hot	**fría/caliente**	freeah/kahlyayntay
dark/small	**oscura/pequeña**	oskoorah/paykayñah
noisy	**ruidosa**	rweedhoassah
I asked for a room with a bath.	**Yo había pedido una habitación con baño.**	yoa ahbheeah paydheedhoa oonah ahbheetahthyon kon bahñoa

NUMBERS, see page 147

Do you have anything ...?	**¿Tiene usted algo ...?**	tyaynay oos**taydh ahl**goa
better/bigger	**mejor/más grande**	meh**khor**/mahss **grahn**day
cheaper	**más barato**	mahss bah**rah**toa
quieter	**más tranquilo**	mahss trahn**kee**loa
higher up/lower down	**más arriba/más abajo**	mahss ahr**ree**bhah/mahss ah**bhah**khoa
Do you have a room with a better view?	**¿Tiene usted una habitación con una vista mejor?**	**tyay**nay oos**taydh oo**nah ahbheetah**thyon** kon **oo**nah **bees**tah meh**khor**
That's fine, I'll take it.	**Muy bien, la tomaré.**	mwee byayn lah toamah**ray**

Registration *Inscripción*

Upon arrival at a hotel or boarding house you'll be asked to fill in a registration form *(una ficha)*.

Apellido/Nombre	Name/First name
Domicilio/Calle/nº	Home address/Street/No.
Nacionalidad/Profesión	Nationality/Profession
Fecha de nacimiento	Date of birth
Lugar	Place
Fecha	Date
Firma	Signature

What does this mean?	**¿Qué quiere decir esto?**	kay **kyay**ray day**theer ay**stoa

¿Me deja ver su pasaporte?	May I see your passport?
¿Le importa llenar esta ficha?	Would you mind filling in this registration form?
Firme aquí, por favor.	Please sign here.
¿Cuánto tiempo va a quedarse?	How long will you be staying?

We'll be staying ...	**Nos quedaremos ...**	noss kaydhah**ray**moass
overnight only	**sólo una noche**	**soa**loa **oo**nah **noa**chay
a few days	**algunos días**	ahl**goo**noass **dee**ahss
a week (at least)	**una semana (por lo menos)**	**oo**nah say**mah**nah (por loa **may**noass)
I don't know yet.	**No lo sé todavía.**	noa loa say toadhah**bhee**ah

Hotel staff *Personal del hotel*

hall porter	**el conserje**	ayl koan**sayr**khay
maid	**la camarera**	lah kahmah**ray**rah
manager	**el director**	ayl deerehk**toar**
page (bellboy)	**el botones**	ayl boa**toa**nayss
porter	**el mozo**	ayl **moa**thoa
receptionist	**el recepcionista**	ayl raythaypthyo**nees**tah
switchboard operator	**la telefonista**	lah taylayfoa**nees**tah
waiter	**el camarero**	ayl kahmah**ray**roa
waitress	**la camarera**	lah kahmah**ray**rah

General requirements *Peticiones generales*

What's my room number?	**¿Cuál es el número de mi habitación?**	kwahl ayss ayl **noo**mayroa day mee ahbheetah**thyon**
The key, please.	**La llave, por favor.**	lah **lyah**bhay por fah**bhor**
Where can I park my car?	**¿En dónde puedo aparcar mi coche?**	ayn **doan**day **pway**dhoa ahpahr**kahr** mee **koa**chay
Does the hotel have a garage?	**¿Tiene garaje el hotel?**	**tyay**nay gah**rah**khay ayl oa**tehl**
Will you have our luggage sent up?	**¿Puede usted encargarse de que suban nuestro equipaje?**	**pway**dhay oos**taydh** aynkahr**gahr**say day kay **soo**bhahn **nways**troa aykee**pah**khay
Is there a bath on this floor?	**¿Hay baño en este piso?**	igh **bah**ñoa ayn **ays**tay **pees**soa
Where's the socket (outlet) for the shaver?	**¿Dónde está el enchufe para la máquina de afeitar?**	**doan**day ays**tah** ayl ayn**choo**fay **pah**rah lah **mah**keenah day ahfay**tahr**

Can we have breakfast in our room?	**¿Podemos desayunar en nuestra habitación?**	poa**dhay**moass dayssahyoo**nahr** ayn **nways**strah ahbheetah**thyon**
I'd like to leave this in your safe.	**Me gustaría dejar esto en su caja fuerte.**	may goostah**ree**ah day**khahr ays**toa ayn soo **kah**khah **fwehr**tay
Can you find me a ...?	**¿Podría buscarme ...?**	poa**dree**ah boos**kahr**may
baby-sitter	**una niñera**	oonah nee**ñay**rah
secretary	**una secretaria**	oonah saykray**tahr**yah
typewriter	**una máquina de escribir**	oonah **mah**keenah day ayskree**bheer**
Will you please wake me up at ...	**Por favor, ¿puede despertarme a las ...?**	por fah**bhor pway**dhay dayspayr**tahr**may ah lahss
May I have a/an/some ...?	**¿Me puede dar ...?**	may **pway**dhay dahr
ashtray	**un cenicero**	oon thaynee**thay**roa
bath towel	**una toalla de baño**	oonah toa**ah**lyah day **bah**ñoa
(extra) blanket	**una manta (más)**	oonah **mahn**tah (mahss)
envelopes	**unos sobres**	oonoass **soa**brayss
hot-water bottle	**una botella de agua caliente**	oonah bhoa**tay**lyah day **ah**gwah kah**lyayn**tay
(more) hangers	**(más) perchas**	(mahss) **pehr**chahss
ice cubes	**cubitos de hielo**	koo**bhee**toass day **yay**loa
needle and thread	**una aguja e hilo**	oonah ah**goo**kha ay **ee**loa
(extra) pillow	**una almohada (más)**	oonah ahlmoa**ah**dhah (mahss)
reading-lamp	**una lámpara para leer**	oonah **lahm**pahrah **pah**rah lay**ehr**
soap	**jabón**	khah**bhon**
writing-paper	**papel de escribir**	pah**pehl** day ayskree**bheer**
Where's the ...?	**¿Dónde está ...?**	**doan**day ays**tah**
beauty salon	**el salón de belleza**	ayl sah**lon** day bay**lyay**thah
dining-room	**el comedor**	ayl koamay**dhor**
emergency exit	**la salida de emergencia**	lah sah**lee**dhah day aymayr**khayn**thyah
hairdresser's	**la peluquería**	lah paylookay**ree**ah
lift (elevator)	**el ascensor**	ayl ahsthayn**soar**
restaurant	**el restaurante**	ayl raystow**rahn**tay
television room	**la sala de televisión**	lah **sah**lah day taylaybhee**ssyon**
toilet	**el servicio**	ayl sayr**bee**thyoa

BREAKFAST, see page 38

Telephone—Post (mail) *Teléfono – Correo*

Can you get me Madrid 123-45-67?	**¿Puede comunicarme con el número 123-45-67 de Madrid?**	**pway**dhay komoonee-**kahr**may kon ayl **noo**mayroa 123-45-67 day mah**dreedh**
Do you have any stamps?	**¿Tiene usted sellos?**	**tyay**nay oos**taydh** **say**lyoass
Would you please mail this for me?	**Por favor, ¿mandaría usted esto por correo?**	por fah**bhor** mahndah**ree**ah oos**taydh** **ays**toa por kor**reh**oa
Are there any messages for me?	**¿Hay algún recado para mí?**	igh ahl**goon** ray**kah**dhoa **pah**rah mee
How much are my telephone charges?	**¿Cuánto debo de llamadas telefónicas?**	**kwahn**toa **day**boa day lyah**mah**dahss taylay**foa**-neekahss

Difficulties *Dificultades*

The ... doesn't work.	**... no funciona.**	... noa foon**thyoa**nah
air conditioner	**el acondicionador de aire**	ayl ahkondeethyoanah-**dhor** day **igh**ray
fan	**el ventilador**	ayl baynteelah**dhor**
heating	**la calefacción**	lah kahlayfahk**thyon**
light	**la luz**	lah **looth**
radio	**la radio**	lah **rah**dhyoa
toilet	**los servicios**	loss sehr**bee**thyoass
television	**el televisor**	ayl taylaybhee**ssoar**
The window is jammed.	**La ventana está atrancada.**	lah bayn**tah**nah ays**tah** ahtrahn**kah**dha
The curtain is stuck.	**La cortina está atrancada.**	lah koar**tee**nah ays**tah** ahtrahn**kah**dhah
There's no (hot) water.	**No hay agua (caliente).**	noa igh **ahg**wah (kah**lyayn**tay)
The wash-basin is clogged.	**El lavabo está atascado.**	ayl lah**bhah**bhoa ays**tah** ahtahs**kah**dhoa
The tap (faucet) is dripping.	**El grifo está goteando.**	ayl **gree**foa ays**tah** goatay**ahn**dhoa
My bed hasn't been made up yet.	**Aún no me han hecho la cama.**	ah**oon** noa may ahn **ay**choa lah **kah**mah

POST OFFICE AND TELEPHONE, see page 132–135

The bulb is burnt out.	**La bombilla está fundida.**	lah bom**bee**lyah ays**tah** foon**dee**dhah
The ... is broken.	**... está roto (rota).**	... ays**tah** **ro**toa (**ro**tah)
blind	**la persiana**	lah pehr**syah**nah
lamp	**la lámpara**	lah **lahm**pahrah
plug	**una clavija de enchufe**	**oo**nah klah**bhee**khah day ayn**choo**fay
shutter	**el postigo**	ayl pos**tee**goa
switch	**el interruptor**	ayl eentehrroop**tor**
Can you get it repaired?	**¿Puede usted arreglarlo(la)?**	**pway**dhay oos**taydh** ahrray**glahr**loa(lah)

Laundry—Dry cleaner's *Lavandería—Tintorería*

I want these clothes ...	**Quiero que ... esta ropa**	**kyay**roa kay ... **ays**tah **roa**pah
cleaned	**limpien**	**leem**pyayn
ironed/pressed	**planchen**	**plahn**chayn
washed	**laven**	**lah**bhayn
When will it be ready?	**¿Cuándo estará lista?**	**kwahn**doa aystah**rah** **lees**tah
I need it ...	**La necesito para ...**	lah naythay**ssee**toa **pah**rah
today	**hoy**	oy
tonight	**esta noche**	**ays**tah **noa**chay
tomorrow	**mañana**	mah**ñah**nah
before Friday	**antes del viernes**	**ahn**tayss dayl **byehr**nayss
Can you mend/sew this?	**¿Puede usted remendar/coser esto?**	**pway**dhay oos**taydh** rehmayn**dahr**/koa**ssayr** **ays**toa
Can you sew on this button?	**¿Puede usted coser este botón?**	**pway**dhay oos**taydh** koa**ssayr** **ays**tay boa**ton**
Can you get this stain out?	**¿Puede usted quitar esta mancha?**	**pway**dhay oos**taydh** kee**tahr** **ays**tah **mahn**chah
This isn't mine.	**Esto no es mío.**	**ays**toa noa ayss **mee**oa
There's one piece missing.	**Falta una prenda.**	**fahl**tah **oo**nah **prayn**dah
There's a hole in this.	**Hay un hoyo aquí.**	igh oon **oa**yoa ah**kee**
Is my laundry ready?	**¿Está lista mi ropa?**	ays**tah** **lees**tah mee **roa**pah

Hairdresser's—Barber's *Peluquería—Barbería*

Is there a hairdresser/ beauty salon in the hotel?	**¿Hay una peluquería/ un salón de belleza en el hotel?**	igh **oo**nah paylookay**ree**ah/ oon sah**lon** day bay**lyay**thah ayn ayl oa**tehl**
Can I make an appointment for this afternoon?	**¿Puedo pedir hora para esta tarde?**	**pway**dhoa pay**dheer oa**rah **pah**rah **ay**stah **tahr**dhay
I want a haircut, please.	**Quiero un corte de pelo, por favor.**	**kyay**roa oon **kor**tay day **peh**loa por fah**bhor**
I'd like a shave.	**Quisiera que me afeitaran.**	kee**ssyay**rah kay may ahfay**tah**rahn
I want (a) ...	**Quiero ...**	**kyay**roa
bleach	**un aclarado**	oon ahklah**rah**dhoa
blow dry	**un modelado**	oon moaday**lah**dhoa
colour rinse	**unos reflejos**	**oo**noass reh**flay**khoass
dye	**una tintura**	**oo**nah teen**too**rah
fringe (bangs)	**un flequillo**	oon flay**kee**lyoa
manicure	**una manicura**	**oo**nah mahnee**koo**rah
parting (part)	**una raya**	**oo**nah **rah**yah
left/right/ in the middle	**a la izquierda/ derecha/en medio**	a lah eeth**kyayr**dhah/ day**ray**chah/ayn **may**dhyoa
permanent wave	**una permanente**	**oo**nah pehrmah**nayn**tay
setting lotion	**un fijador**	oon feekha**dhoar**
shampoo and set	**lavado y marcado**	lah**bhah**dhoa ee mahr**kah**dhoa
I'd like a shampoo for ... hair.	**Quisiera un champú para cabello ...**	kee**syay**rah oon chahm**poo** **pah**rah kah**bhay**lyoa
dry	**seco**	**say**koa
greasy (oily)	**graso**	**grah**ssoa
normal	**normal**	nor**mahl**
Do you have a colour chart?	**¿Tiene usted un muestrario?**	**tyay**nay oo**staydh** oon mway**strah**ryoa
Don't cut it too short.	**No me lo corte mucho.**	noa may loa **koar**tay **moo**choa
That's enough off.	**Eso es bastante.**	**ay**ssoa ayss bahs**tahn**tay
A little more off the ...	**Un pocco más ...**	oon **poa**koa mahss
back	**por detrás**	por day**trahss**
neck	**en el cuello**	ayn ayl **kway**lyoa
sides	**en los lados**	ayn loss **lah**dhoass
top	**arriba**	ahr**ree**bhah

DAYS OF THE WEEK, see page 151

Please don't use any oil/hairspray.	**Por favor, no me dé ningún aceite/laca.**	por fah**bhor** noa may day neen**goon** ah**thay**tay/**lah**kah
Would you please trim my ...?	**¿Quiere usted recortarme ...?**	**kyay**ray oos**taydh** rehkor**tahr**may
beard	**la barba**	lah **bahr**bah
moustache	**al bigote**	ayl bee**goa**tay
sideboards (sideburns)	**las patillas**	lahss pah**tee**lyahss

Checking out *Al marcharse*

May I have my bill, please?	**Por favor, ¿puede darme mi cuenta?**	por fah**bhor** **pway**dhay **dahr**may mee **kwayn**tah
I'm leaving early in the morning. Please have my bill ready.	**Me marcho por la mañana, temprano. Por favor, tenga mi cuenta preparada.**	may **mahr**choa por lah mah**ñah**nah taym**prah**noa. por fah**bhor** **tayn**gah mee **kwayn**tah praypah**rah**dhah
What time must I check out?	**¿A qué hora debo desocupar la habitación?**	ah kay **oa**rah **day**bhoa dayssoakoo**pahr** lah ahbheetah**thyon**
Would you call a taxi, please?	**¿Quiere llamar un taxi, por favor?**	**kyay**ray lyah**mahr** oon **tahk**see por fah**bhor**
I must leave at once.	**Debo marcharme ahora mismo.**	**day**bhoa mahr**chahr**may ahorah **mees**moa
Is everything included?	**¿Está todo incluido?**	ay**stah** **toa**dhoa eenkloo**ee**dhoa
Do you accept credit cards?	**¿Acepta tarjetas de crédito?**	ah**thayp**tah tahr**khay**tahss day **kray**dheetoa
You've made a mistake in this bill, I think.	**Creo que se ha equivocado usted en esta cuenta.**	**kre**hoa kay say ah aykee-bhoa**kah**dhoa oos**taydh** ayn **ay**stah **kwayn**tah
Would you send someone to bring down our luggage?	**¿Quiere usted mandar a alguien para bajar nuestro equipaje?**	**kyay**ray oos**taydh** mahn**dahr** ah **ahl**gyayn **pah**rah bah**khahr** **nway**stroa aykee**pah**khay
Here's my forwarding address.	**Remita mis cartas a esta dirección.**	ray**mee**tah meess **kahr**tahss ah **ay**stah deerayk**thyon**
It's been a very enjoyable stay.	**Ha sido una estancia muy agradable.**	ah **see**dhoa **oo**nah ay**stahn**thyah mwee ahgrah**dhah**blay

TAXI, see page 21

Camping *Camping*

Camping facilities vary, but most sites have electricity and running water. Many have shops and children's playgrounds, and some even laundrettes and restaurants. For a complete list of camp sites consult any Spanish National Tourist Office.

Is there a camp site near here?	**¿Hay algún camping cerca de aquí?**	igh al**goon** **kahm**peeng **thehr**kah day ah**kee**
Can we camp here?	**¿Podemos acampar aquí?**	poa**dhay**moass ahkahm**pahr** ah**kee**
Have you room for a caravan (trailer)/tent?	**¿Tiene sitio para una tienda/caravana?**	**tyay**nay **see**tyo **pah**rah **oo**nah **tyayn**dah/kahrah**bhah**nah
What's the charge ...?	**¿Cuál es el precio ...?**	kwahl ayss ayl **pray**thyoa
per day/person	**por día/persona**	por **dee**ah/pehr**soa**nah
for a car/tent	**por coche/tienda**	por **koa**chay/**tyayn**dah
for a caravan (trailer)	**por caravana**	por kahrah**bhah**nah
May we light a fire?	**¿Podemos encender una hoguera?**	poa**dhay**moass aynthayn**dehr** **oo**nah oa**geh**rah
Is there/Are there (a) ...?	**¿Hay ...?**	igh
drinking water	**agua potable**	**ah**gwah poa**tah**blay
electricity	**electricidad**	aylayktreethee**dhahd**
playground	**un campo de juego**	oon **kahm**poa day **khway**goa
restaurant	**un restaurante**	oon raystow**rahn**tay
shopping facilities	**tiendas**	**tyayn**dahss
swimming pool	**una piscina**	**oo**nah pees**thee**nah
Where are the showers/toilets?	**¿Dónde están las duchas/los servicios?**	**doan**day ays**tahn** lahss **doo**chahss/loass sayr**bee**thyoass
Where can I get butane gas?	**¿Dónde puedo conseguir gas butano?**	**doan**day **pway**dhoa konsay**geer** gahss boo**tah**noa

PROHIBIDO ACAMPAR NO CAMPING	**PROHIBIDO ACAMPAR CON CARAVANA** NO CARAVANS (TRAILERS)

CAMPING EQUIPMENT, see page 106

Eating out

There are many different places where you can eat and drink in Spain.

Albergue de carretera (ahl**behr**gay day kahrreh**tay**rah) — Motel; strategically located on main roads; snacks and full meals offered, quick service

Bar (bahr) — Bar; drinks and *tapas* (see page 63) served, sometimes hot beverages, too

Café (kah**fay**) — As in all Mediterranean countries, *cafés* can be found on virtually every street corner. An indispensable part of everyday life, the *café* is where people get together for a chat over a coffee, soft drink or glass of wine.

Cafetería (kahfaytay**ree**ah) — Coffee shop; not to be confused with the English word cafeteria; there's counter service or —for a few pesetas extra—you can choose a table. The set menu is often very good.

Casa de comidas (**kah**ssah day koa**mee**dhahss) — Simple inn serving cheap meals

Fonda (**fon**dah) — Typical Spanish inn

Hostería (ostay**ree**ah) — Restaurant; often specializing in regional cooking

Merendero (mayrayn**day**roa) — Seaside fish restaurant; you can usually eat out-of-doors

Parador (pahrah**dhor**) — A government-supervised establishment located in a historic castle, palace or former monastery. A *parador* is usually noted for excellent regional dishes served in a dining room with handsome Spanish decor.

Pastelería/ Confitería (pahstaylay**ree**ah/ konfeetay**ree**ah) — Pastry shop; some serve coffee, tea and drinks

Posada (poa**ssah**dhah) — A humble version of a *fonda;* the food is usually simple but good

Refugio (rehfookhyoa)	Mountain lodge serving simple meals
Restaurante (raystow**rahn**tay)	Restaurant; these are classified by the government but the official rating has more to do with the decor than with the quality of cooking
Salón de té (sahlon day tay)	Tearoom; at bit exclusive
Taberna (tah**beh**rnah)	Similar to an English pub or American tavern in atmosphere; always a variety of *tapas* on hand as well as other snacks
Tasca (**tah**skah)	Similar to a *bar;* drinks and *tapas* are served at the counter; standing only

Meal times *Horas de comida*

Breakfast (*el desayuno*—ayl dayssah**yoo**noa) is generally served from 7 to 10 a.m.

Lunch (*el almuerzo*—ayl ahl**mwayr**thoa) is generally served from around 2 or 3 p.m.

Dinner (*la cena*—lah **thay**nah) is served far later than at home, from about 8 p.m. in tourist areas, elsewhere from about 9.

The Spaniards like to linger over a meal, so service may seem on the leisurely side.

Spanish Cuisine *Cocina española*

The history of Spain has had much to do with the wealth and variety of Spanish cuisine. The Celtic tribes which settled Galicia cooked with animal fats, in particular pork fat. The Romans introduced garlic, as well as olive oil, which is today the basic ingredient of Spanish cooking. The conquering Arabs brought lemons, oranges, saffron, dates and rice. And the discovery of America in 1492 further enriched Spanish cuisine with the potato, pimentos, pepper and cocoa.

In addition, Spain's 5,000 kilometres of coastline offer, at all seasons, a profusion of Atlantic and Mediterranean sea-food.

¿Qué desea?	What would you like?
Le recomiendo esto.	I recommend this.
¿Qué desea beber?	What would you like to drink?
No tenemos ...	We haven't got ...
¿Desea ...?	Do you want ...?

Hungry? *¿Hambre?*

I'm hungry/I'm thirsty.	**Tengo hambre/ Tengo sed.**	tayngoa ahmbray/ tayngoa saydh
Can you recommend a good restaurant?	**¿Puede recomendarme un buen restaurante?**	pwaydhay raykoamayndahrmay oon bwayn raystowrahntay
Where can we get a typical Spanish meal?	**¿Dónde podemos encontrar comidas típicas de España?**	doanday poadhaymoass aynkontrahr koameedhahss teepeekahss day ayspahñah
Are there any inexpensive restaurants around here?	**¿Hay restaurantes no muy caros cerca de aquí?**	igh raystowrahntayss noa mwee kahroass thehrkah day ahkee

If you want to be sure of getting a table in well-known restaurants, it may be better to telephone in advance. Some of them close one day a week (usually a Monday).

I'd like to reserve a table for 4.	**Quiero reservar una mesa para 4.**	kyayroa rehssayrbahr oonah mayssah pahrah 4
We'll come at 8.	**Vendremos a las 8.**	bayndraymoass ah lahss 8

TIPPING, see inside back-cover

Asking and ordering *Preguntando y pidiendo*

Good evening, I'd like a table for 3.	**Buenas tardes, quisiera una mesa para 3.**	**bway**nahss **tahr**dayss kee**ssyay**rah **oo**nah **may**ssah **pah**rah 3
Could we have a table ...?	**¿Nos puede dar una mesa ...?**	noss **pway**dhay dahr **oo**nah **may**ssah
in the corner	**en el rincón**	ayn ayl reen**kon**
by the window	**al lado de la ventana**	ahl **lah**dhoa day lah behn**tah**nah
in a non-smoking area	**en la sección de no fumadores**	ayn lah sek**thyon** day noa foomah**dho**rayss
outside/on the patio	**fuera/en el patio**	**fway**rah/ayn ayl **pah**tyoa
Waiter!/ Waitress!	**¡Camarero!/ ¡Camarera!**	kahmah**ray**roa/ kahmah**ray**rah
I'd like something to eat/drink.	**Quisiera algo de comer/beber.**	kee**ssyay**rah **ahl**goa day koa**mayr**/beh**bhayr**
What do you recommend?	**¿Qué me aconseja?**	kay may ahkoan**seh**khah
May I please have the menu?	**¿Puedo ver la carta, por favor?**	**pway**dhoa behr lah **kahr**tah por fah**bhor**
What's this?	**¿Qué es esto?**	kay ayss **ays**toa
Do you have ...?	**¿Tienen ...?**	**tyay**nayn
a set menu/local dishes	**platos combinados/ especialidades locales**	**plah**toass koambee**nah**dhoass/ayspaythyahlee**dhah**dhayss loa**kah**layss
I'd like a supplement.	**Quisiera otra ración.**	kee**ssyay**rah **oa**trah rah**thyon**
Nothing more, thanks.	**Nada más, gracias.**	**nah**dhah mahss **grah**thyahss
Can we have a/an ..., please?	**¿Puede darnos ..., por favor?**	**pway**dhay **dahr**noass ... por fah**bhor**
ashtray	**un cenicero**	oon thaynee**thay**roa
(extra) chair	**una silla (más)**	**oo**nah **see**lyah (mahss)
cup	**una taza**	**oo**nah **tah**thah
fork	**un tenedor**	oon taynay**dhoar**
glass	**un vaso**	oon **bah**ssoa
knife	**un cuchillo**	oon koo**chee**lyoa
napkin (serviette)	**una servilleta**	**oo**nah sehrbee**lyay**tah
plate	**un plato**	oon **plah**toa
spoon	**una cuchara**	**oo**nah koo**chah**rah

COMPLAINTS, see page 61

I'd like some ...	**Quisiera ...**	kee**ssyay**rah
bread	**pan**	pahn
butter	**mantequilla**	mahntay**kee**lyah
ketchup	**salsa de tomate**	**sahl**sah day toa**mah**tay
lemon	**limón**	lee**mon**
mustard	**mostaza**	moas**tah**thah
oil	**aceite**	**athay**tay
olive oil	**aceite de oliva**	a**thay**tay day oa**lee**bhah
pepper	**pimienta**	pee**myayn**tah
rolls	**panecillos**	pahnay**thee**lyoass
salt	**sal**	sahl
seasoning	**condimentos**	kondee**myayn**toass
sugar	**azúcar**	ah**thoo**kahr
vinegar	**vinagre**	bee**nah**gray

Some useful expressions if you have to follow a diet:

I have to live on a diet.	**Tengo que guardar dieta.**	**tayn**goa kay gwahr**dahr dyay**tah
I mustn't eat food containing ...	**No debo comer alimentos que contengan ...**	noa **day**bhoa koa**mayr** ahlee**mayn**toass kay koan**tayn**gahn
flour/fat	**harina/grasa**	ah**ree**nah/**grah**ssah
salt/sugar	**sal/azúcar**	sahl/ah**thoo**kahr
Do you have ... for diabetics?	**¿Tiene ... para diabéticos?**	**tyay**nay ... **pah**rah dyah**bhay**teekoass
cakes	**pasteles**	pahss**tay**layss
fruit juice	**jugo de frutas**	**khoo**goa day **froo**tahss
special menus	**menús especiales**	may**nooss** aysspay**thyah**layss
Do you have vegetarian dishes?	**¿Tiene platos vegetarianos?**	**tyay**nay **plah**toass baykhaytah**ryah**noass
Could I have ... instead of the dessert?	**¿Podría tomar ... en lugar del postre?**	poa**dhryah** toa**mahr** ... ayn loo**gahr** dayl **poass**tray
cheese	**queso**	**kay**ssoa
fruit	**fruta**	**froo**tah
Can I have an artificial sweetener?	**¿Puede darme un edulcorante?**	**pway**dhay **dahr**may oon aydhoolkoa**rahn**tay

Breakfast *Desayuno*

Most Spaniards eat continental breakfast: coffee, bread or rolls and jam. However, many of the larger hotels also provide a full breakfast (*el desayuno completo*—ayl dayssahy**oo**noa kom**play**toa) with fruit juice and eggs.

I'd like breakfast, please.	**Quisiera desayunar, por favor.**	kee**ssyay**rah dayssahyoo**nahr** por fah**bhor**
I'll have a/an/some ...	**Tomaré ...**	toamah**ray**
bacon and eggs	**huevos con tocino**	**way**bhoass kon toa**thee**noa
cereal	**cereales**	thayrayah**lay**ss
boiled egg	**huevo cocido**	**way**bhoa koa**thee**dhoa
soft	**pasado por agua**	pah**ssah**dhoa por **ah**gwah
medium	**blando (mollet)**	**blahn**doa (moa**lyayt**)
hard	**duro**	**doo**roa
fried eggs	**huevos fritos**	**way**bhoass **free**toass
fruit juice	**un jugo de fruta**	oon **khoo**goa day **froo**tah
grapefruit	**pomelo**	po**may**loa
orange	**naranja**	nah**rahn**khah
ham and eggs	**huevos con jamón**	**way**bhoass kon khah**mon**
jam	**mermelada**	mehrmay**lah**dhah
marmalade	**mermelada amarga de naranjas**	mehrmay**lah**dhah ah**mahr**gah day nah**rahn**khahss
scrambled eggs	**huevos revueltos**	**way**bhoass ray**bhwayl**toass
toast	**tostadas**	toas**tah**dhahss
May I have some ...?	**¿Podría darme ...?**	poa**dree**ah **dahr**may
bread	**pan**	pahn
butter	**mantequilla**	mahntay**kee**lyah
(hot) chocolate	**chocolate (caliente)**	choakoa**lah**tay (kah**lyayn**tay)
coffee	**café**	kah**fay**
caffein-free	**descafeinado**	dayskahfayee**nah**dhoa
black	**solo**	**soa**loa
with milk	**con leche**	kon **lay**chay
honey	**miel**	myehl
milk	**leche**	**lay**chay
cold/hot	**fría/caliente**	**free**ah/kah**lyayn**tay
pepper	**pimienta**	pee**myayn**tah
salt	**sal**	sahl
tea	**té**	tay
with milk	**con leche**	kon **lay**chay
with lemon	**con limón**	kon lee**mon**
(hot) water	**agua (caliente)**	**ah**gwah (kah**lyayn**tay)

What's on the menu? *¿Qué hay en el menú?*

Under the headings below you'll find alphabetical lists of dishes that might be offered on a Spanish menu with their English equivalent. You can simply show the book to the waiter. If you want some fruit, for instance, let *him* point to what's available on the appropriate list. Use pages 36 and 37 for ordering in general.

In addition to various à la carte dishes, restaurants usually offer one or more set menus *(platos combinados)* or a dish of the day *(plato del día)* which provide a good meal at a fair price.

Reading the menu *Leyendo la carta*

Especialidades de la casa	Specialities of the house
Especialidades locales	Local specialities
Plato del día	Dish of the day
Platos fríos	Cold dishes
Platos típicos	Specialities
Recomendamos	We recommend
Suplemento sobre ...	... extra

agua mineral	ah**g**wah meenay**rahl**	mineral water
aperitivos	ahpayree**tee**bhoass	apéritifs
arroces	ah**rro**thayss	rice
asados	ah**ssah**dhoass	roasts
aves	**ah**bhayss	poultry
bebidas	bay**bhee**dhahss	drinks
carnes	**kahr**nayss	meat
caza	**kah**thah	game
cerveza	thehr**bay**thah	beer
entremeses	ayntray**may**ssayss	starters (appetizers)
ensaladas	aynsah**lah**dhahss	salads
frutas	**froo**tahss	fruit
granizados	grahnee**thah**dhoass	iced drinks
helados	ay**lah**dhoass	ice-cream
huevos	**way**bhoass	egg dishes
jugo	**khoo**goa	fresh juice
legumbres	lay**goom**brayss	vegetables
mariscos	mah**rees**koass	seafood
parrilladas	pahrree**lyah**dhass	grills
pastas	**pahss**tahss	pastas
pastelería	pahsstaylay**ree**ah	pastries
patatas	pah**tah**tahss	potatoes
pescados	pays**kah**dhoass	fish
postres	**poas**trayss	dessert
quesos	**kay**ssoass	cheese
refrescos	ray**frayss**koass	cold drinks
sopas	**soa**pahss	soups
verduras	bayr**doo**rahss	vegetables
vinos	**bee**noass	wine
zumo	**thoo**moa	fresh juice

Starters (Appetizers) *Entremeses*

If you are planning to eat a three-course meal try not to tuck into too many of the great variety of *tapas* (see page 63) over your apéritif.

I'd like a starter (appetizer).	**Quisiera unos entremeses.**	kee**ssyay**rah **oo**noass ayntray**may**ssayss
What do you recommend?	**¿Qué me aconseja?**	kay may ahkon**say**khah
aceitunas (rellenas)	ahthay**too**nahss (ray**lyay**nahss)	(stuffed) olives
aguacate	ah wah**kah**tay	avocado
alcachofas	ahlkah**choa**fahss	artichoke
almejas	ahl**meh**khahss	clams
a la marinera	ah lah mahree**nay**rah	in paprika sauce
anchoas	[illegible]	anchovies
anguila ahumada	ahn**gee**lah ahoo**mah**dhah	smoked eel
arenque (ahumado)	ah**rehn**kay (ahoo**mah**dhoa)	(smoked) herring
atún	ah**toon**	tunny (tuna)
cabeza	kah**beh**thah	brawn (headcheese)
de cordero	day koar**day**roa	lamb's
de ternera	day tehr**nay**rah	calf's
calamares	kahlah**mah**rayss	squid
a la romana	ah lah roa**mah**nah	deep-fried
callos	**kah**lyoass	tripe (usually in hot paprika sauce)
caracoles	kahrah**koa**layss	snails
carne de cangrejo	**kahr**nay day kahn**greh**khoa	crabmeat
champiñones	chahmpee**ñoa**nayss	button mushrooms
chorizo	choa**ree**thoa	spicy sausage made of pork, garlic and paprika
cigalas	thee**gah**lahss	Dublin Bay prawns (sea crayfish)
entremeses variados	ayntray**may**ssayss bah**ryah**dhoass	assorted appetizers
espárragos (puntas de)	ay**spar**rahgoass (**poon**tahss day)	asparagus (tips)
fiambres	**fyahm**brayss	cold cuts
gambas	**gahm**bahss	prawns (shrimps)
al ajillo	ahl ah**khee**lyoa	with garlic
a la plancha	ah lah **plahn**chah	grilled
higaditos de pollo	eegah**dhee**toass day **poa**lyoa	chicken livers

huevos duros	**way**bhoass doo**roass**	hard-boiled eggs
jamón	khah**mon**	ham
en dulce	ayn **dool**thay	boiled
serrano	say**rrah**noa	cured
langosta	lahn**goas**tah	spiny lobster
langostinos	lahngoas**tee**noass	prawns (shrimps)
mejillones	mehkhee**lyoa**nayss	mussels
melón	may**lon**	melon
ostras	**oas**trahss	oysters
palitos de queso	pah**lee**toass day **kay**ssoa	cheese sticks (straws)
pepinillos	paypee**nee**lyoass	gherkins
pepino	pay**pee**noa	cucumber
percebes	pehr**thay**bhayss	goose barnacles
pimientos	pee**myayn**toass	peppers
quisquillas	kees**kee**lyahss	common prawns (shrimps)
rábanos	**rah**bhanoass	radishes
salchichón	sahlchee**chon**	salami
salmón (ahumado)	sahl**mon** (ahoo**mah**dhoa)	(smoked) salmon
sardinas	sahr**dee**nahss	sardines
zumo de fruta	**thoo**moa day **froo**tah	fruit juice
piña/tomate	**pee**ñah/toa**mah**tah	pineapple/tomato
pomelo/naranja	poa**may**loa/nah**rahn**khah	grapefruit/orange

If you feel like something more ambitious and are prepared to leave the gastronomic beaten track, some of these may tempt you:

albóndigas (ahl**bon**dee ahss)	spiced meatballs
banderillas (bahndayr**ee**lyahss)	similar to *palitos* but with gherkins
buñuelitos (booñway**lee**toass)	small fritters made with ham, fish, egg or a wide variety of other fillings
empanadillas (aympahnah**dhee**lyahss)	small savoury pasties stuffed with meat or fish
palitos (pah**lee**toass)	ham, cheese, pâté, smoked anchovy, trout or eel on a skewer
pinochos, pinchitos (pee**noa**choass, peen**chee**toass)	grilled skewered meat
tartaletas (tahrtah**lay**tahss)	small open tarts filled with fish, meat, vegetables or cheese

Salads *Ensaladas*

What salads do you have?	**¿Qué clase de ensaladas tienen?**	kay **klah**ssay day aynsah**lah**dhahss **tyay**nayn
Can you recommend a local speciality?	**¿Puede aconsejarnos una especialidad local?**	**pway**dhay ahkonsay**khahr**noass **oo**nah ayspaythyahlee**dhahdh** loa**kahl**

ensalada	aynsah**lah**dhah	salad
de gambas	day **gahm**bahss	shrimp
de lechuga	day lay**choo**gah	green
de patata	day pah**tah**tah	potato
de pepino	day pay**pee**noa	cucumber
del tiempo	dayl tyaympoa	(in) season
de tomate	day toa**mah**tay	tomato
valenciana	balayn**thyah**nah	with green peppers, lettuce and oranges

Soups *Sopas*

In Spain, soup is undoubtedly the most popular first course. There is a great variety of soups ranging from the simple *sopa de ajo* to the filling *sopa de mariscos*. Here are a few that you're sure to find on the menu during your trip.

consomé al jerez	konsoa**may** ahl khay**rayth**	chicken broth with sherry
sopa de ajo	**soa**pah day **ah**khoa	garlic soup
sopa de arroz	**soa**pah day ar**roth**	rice soup
sopa de cangrejos	**soa**pah day kahn**greh**khoass	crayfish soup
sopa de cebolla	**soa**pah day thay**boa**lyah	onion soup
sopa de cocido	**soa**pah day koa**thee**dhoa	a kind of broth
sopa de espárragos	**soa**pah day ays**pahr**rahgoass	asparagus soup
sopa de fideos	**soa**pah day fee**dhay**oass	noodle soup
sopa Juliana	**soa**pah joo**lyah**nah	bouillon of finely shredded vegetables
sopa de mariscos	**soa**pah day mah**rees**koass	seafood soup
sopa de patatas	**soa**pah day pah**tah**tahss	potato soup
sopa de pescado	**soa**pah day pays**kah**dhoa	fish soup
sopa de tomate	**soa**pah day toa**mah**tay	tomato soup
sopa de tortuga	**soa**pah day tor**too**gah	turtle soup
sopa de verduras	**soa**pah day bayr**doo**rahss	vegetable soup

caldo gallego (**kahl**doa gah**lyeh**goa) — meat and vegetable broth

gazpacho (gahth**pah**choa) — a cold soup of cucumber, tomato, green pepper, bread, onion and garlic

Omelets *Tortillas*

The Spanish omelet is more likely to be round rather than the rolled form of the classic French *omelette*. Here are the names of a few of the more common egg dishes you'll find on the menu:

tortilla	toar**tee**lyah	omelet
de alcachofa	day ahlkah**choa**fah	artichoke omelet
de cebolla	day thay**boa**lyah	onion omelet
de espárragos	day ays**pahr**rahgoass	asparagus omelet
gallega	gah**lyeh**gah	potato omelet with ham, chili peppers and peas
de jamón	day kha**mon**	ham omelet
paisana	paheess**ah**nah	omelet with potatoes, peas, prawns or ham
de patatas	day pah**tah**tahss	potato omelet
de queso	day **kay**ssoa	cheese omelet
al ron	ahl ron	rum omelet
de setas	day **say**tahss	mushroom omelet

... and other egg dishes:

huevos a la flamenca (**way**bhoass ah lah flah**mayn**kah) — eggs baked with tomato, onion and diced ham; often garnished with asparagus tips, red peppers or slices of spicy pork sausage

huevos al nido (**way**bhoass ahl **nee**dhoa) — "eggs in the nest"; egg yolks set in small, soft rolls; fried and then covered in egg white

huevos al trote (**way**bhoass ahl **troa**tay) — boiled eggs filled with tunny (tuna) fish and dressed with mayonnaise

huevos revueltos al pisto (**way**bhoass ray**wayl**toass ahl **pee**stoa) — scrambled eggs with vegetables

Paella

An immensely popular dish along Spain's Mediterranean coast, *paella* actually refers to the large metal pan traditionally used for making rice dishes in the Valencia region. Basically, the *paella* dish is made of golden saffron rice garnished with meat, fish, seafood and/or vegetables. Here are four of the most popular ways of preparing *paella* (pah**ay**lyah):

catalana (kahtah**lah**nah)	spicy pork sausages, pork, squid, tomato, chili pepper, peas; the same dish is sometimes referred to as *arroz a la catalana*
marinera (mahree**nay**rah)	fish and seafood only
valenciana (bahlayn**thyah**nah)	chicken, shrimp, mussels, prawns, squid, peas, tomato, chili pepper, garlic—it's the classic *paella*
zamorana (thamoa**rah**nah)	ham, pork loin, pig's trotters (feet), chili pepper

Another rice dish is called *arroz a la cubana* (ahr**roth** ah lah koo**bhah**nah) made with white rice, fried eggs and bananas and a savoury tomato sauce.

Fish and seafood *Pescado y mariscos*

Don't miss the opportunity to sample some of the wide variety of fresh fish and seafood in coastal areas.

I'd like some fish.	**Quisiera pescado.**	kee**ssyay**rah pays**kah**dhoa
What kind of seafood do you have?	**¿Qué tipo de mariscos tiene usted?**	kay **tee**poa day mah**rees**koass **tyay**nay oo**staydh**
almejas	ahl**meh**khahss	clams
arenques	ah**rehn**kayss	herring
atún	ah**toon**	tunny (tuna)
bacalao	bahkah**lah**oa	cod
besugo	bay**ssoo**goa	(sea) bream
bonito	boa**nee**toa	tunny (tuna)
boquerones	boakay**roa**nayss	whitebait
caballa	kah**bhah**lyah	mackerel

calamares	kahlah**mah**rayss	squid
cangrejo	kahn**greh**khoa	crab/crayfish
chipirones	cheepee**roa**nayss	baby squid
cigalas	thee**gah**lahss	Dublin Bay prawns (sea crayfish)
congrio	**koan**gryoa	conger eel
escarcho	ays**kahr**choa	roach
lampreas	lahm**preh**ahss	lamprey
langosta	lahn**goa**stah	spiny lobster
langostinos	lahngoas**tee**noass	prawns (shrimps)
lenguado	layn**gwah**dhoa	sole
merluza	mayr**loo**thah	hake
mero	**meh**roa	seabass
mújol	**moo**khoal	mullet
ostras	**os**trahss	oysters
perca	**pehr**kah	perch
percebes	pehr**thay**bhayss	goose barnacles
pescadilla	payskah**dhee**lyah	whiting
pez espada	payth ays**pah**dhah	swordfish
pulpitos	pool**pee**toass	baby octopus
pulpo	**pool**poa	octopus
quisquillas	kees**kee**lyahss	common prawns (shrimps)
rape	**rah**pay	monkfish
rodaballo	roadhah**bhah**lyoa	turbot
salmón	sahl**mon**	salmon
salmonetes	sahlmoa**nay**tayss	red mullet
sardinas	sahr**dee**nahss	sardines
pequeñas	pay**kay**ñahss	sprats
trucha	**troo**chah	trout
veneras	bay**nay**rah	scallops

You'll want to try the spicy fish and seafood stew called *zarzuela* (thahr**thway**lah)—the pride of Catalonia.

baked	**al horno**	ahl **oar**noa
cured	**en salazón**	ayn sahlah**thon**
deep fried	**a la romana**	ah lah roa**mah**nah
fried	**frito**	**free**toa
grilled	**a la parrilla**	ah lah pahr**ree**lyah
marinated	**en escabeche**	ayn ayskah**bhay**chay
poached	**hervido**	ayr**bee**dhoa
sautéed	**salteado**	sahlteh**ah**dhoa
smoked	**ahumado**	ahoo**mah**dhoa
steamed	**cocido al vapor**	koa**thee**dhoa ahl bah**por**

Meat *Carne*

Although fish and rice dishes predominate, meat also has a place in the cuisine of Spain—especially pork.

I'd like some ...	**Quisiera ...**	keessyayrah
beef	**carne de buey**	kahrnay day bway
lamb	**carne de cordero**	kahrnay day koardayroa
pork	**carne de cerdo**	kahrnay day thehrdoa
veal	**carne de ternera**	kahrnay day tehrnayrah

biftec	beeftayk	beef steak
cabrito	kahbreetoa	kid
carne picada	kahrnay peekahdhah	minced meat
carnero	kahrnayroa	mutton
chuletas	choolaytahss	chops
corazón	koarahthon	heart
criadillas	kreeahdheelyahss	sweetbreads
filete	feelaytay	steak
hígado	eegahdhoa	liver
jamón	khahmon	ham
lechón	laychon	suck(l)ing pig
morcilla	moartheelyah	black pudding (blood sausage)
paletilla	pahlayteelyah	shank
patas	pahtahss	trotters (feet)
pierna	pyehrnah	leg
rabo de buey	rahbhoa day bway	oxtail
riñones	reeñoanayss	kidneys
salchichas	sahlcheechahss	sausages
sesos	sayssoass	brains
solomillo de cerdo	soaloameelyoa day therdoa	tenderloin of pork
tocino	toatheenoa	bacon

callos a la madrileña (kahlyoass ah lah mahdreelayñah)	tripe in piquant sauce with spicy pork sausage and tomatoes
cochifrito de cordero (koacheefreetoa day koardayroa)	highly seasoned stew of lamb or kid
cochinillo asado (koacheeneelyoa ahssahdhoa)	crispy roasted Castillian suck(l)ing pig
empanada gallega (aympahnahdhah gahlyaygah)	tenderloin of pork, onions and chili peppers in a pie
magras al estilo de Aragón (mahgrahss ahl aysteeloa day ahrahgon)	cured ham in tomato sauce

pimientos a la riojana (peemyayntoass ah lah ryoakhahnah)	sweet peppers stuffed with minced meat
riñones al jerez (reeñyoanayss ahl khehrayth)	kidneys braised in sherry

baked	**al horno**	ahl oarnoa
boiled	**hervido**	ayrbheedhoa
braised	**estofado**	aystoafahdhhoa
braised in casserole	**en salsa**	ayn sahlssah
fried	**frito**	freetoa
grilled (broiled)	**a la parrilla**	ah lah pahrreelyah
pot roasted	**en su jugo**	ayn soo khoogoa
roast	**asado**	ahssahdhoa
sautéed	**salteado**	sahltehahdhoa
stewed	**estofado**	aystoafahdhoa
underdone (rare)	**poco hecho**	poakoa aychoa
medium	**regular**	rehgoolahr
well-done	**muy hecho**	mwee aychoa

Poultry and game *Aves y carne de caza*

Chicken is prepared in scores of ways in Spain. In the north, rabbit is a favourite dish—sometimes even prepared with chocolate!

I'd like some game.	**Quisiera carne de caza.**	keessyayrah kahrnay day kahthah
What poultry dishes do you have?	**¿Qué tipo de ave tiene usted?**	kay teepoa day ahbhay tyaynay oostaydh

becada	baykahdhah	woodcock
capón	kahpon	capon
codorniz	koadoarneeth	quail
conejo	koanaykhoa	rabbit
conejo de monte	koanaykhoa day moantay	wild rabbit
corzo	koarthoa	deer
faisán	fighssahn	pheasant
gallina	gahlyeenah	hen
ganso	gahnsoa	goose
higaditos de pollo	eegahdheetoass day poalyoa	chicken liver

jabalí	khahbhah**lee**	wild boar
lavanco	lah**bhahn**koa	wild duck
liebre	**lyeh**bray	hare
pato	**pah**toa	duck/duckling
pavo	**pah**bhoa	turkey
perdiz	pehr**deeth**	partridge
pichón	pee**chon**	pigeon
pollo	**poa**lyoa	chicken
muslo de pollo	**moos**loa day **poa**lyoa	chicken leg
pechuga de pollo	pay**choo**gah day **poa**lyoa	breast of chicken
pollo asado	**poa**lyoa ah**ssah**dhoa	roast chicken
pollo a la brasa	**poa**lyoa ah lah **brah**ssah	grilled chicken
venado	bay**nah**dhoa	venison

conejo al ajillo (koa**nay**khoa ahl ah**khee**lyoa) — rabbit with garlic

menestra de pollo (may**nay**strah day **poa**lyoa) — casserole of chicken and vegetables

perdices estofadas (pehr**dee**thayss aystoa**fah**dhahss) — partridges served in a white-wine sauce

Sauces *Salsas*

Many meat, fish or vegetable dishes are dressed or braised in a light, delicate sauce. Here are the names of some well-known preparations:

salsa allioli (**sahl**sah ahl**yoa**lee) — garlic sauce

a la catalana (ah lah kahtah**lah**nah) — sauce of tomatoes and green peppers

en escabeche (ayn ayskah**bhay**chay) — sweet and sour sauce

salsa romesco (**sahl**sah roa**mays**koa) — green peppers, pimentos, garlic; popular chilled dressing for fish on the east cost around Tarragona

a la vasca (ah lah **bahs**kah) — parsley, peas, garlic; a delicate green dressing for fish in the Basque country

Vegetables *Verduras*

What vegetables do you recommend?	**¿Qué verduras me aconseja?**	kay bayr**doo**rahss may ahkoan**say**khah
I'd prefer a salad.	**Prefiero una ensalada.**	pray**fyay**roa **oo**nah aynsah**lah**dah

achicoria	ahchee**koa**ryah	endive (Am. chicory)
alcachofas	ahlkah**choa**fahss	artichoke
apio	**ah**pyoa	celery
arroz	ahr**roth**	rice
berenjena	bayrayn**khay**nah	aubergine (eggplant)
berza	**bayr**thah	cabbage
calabacín	kahlahbha**theen**	courgette (zucchini)
cebolla	thay**boa**lyah	onion
champiñones	chahmpee**ñoa**nayss	button mushrooms
chirivías	cheeree**bhee**ahss	parsnips
coles de bruselas	**koa**layss day broo**ssay**lahss	Brussels sprouts
coliflor	koleef**lor**	cauliflower
espárragos	ays**pahr**rahgoass	asparagus
espinacas	ayspee**nah**kahss	spinach
garbanzos	gahr**bahn**thoass	chickpeas
guisantes	gee**ssahn**tayss	peas
habas	**ah**bhahss	broad beans
hinojo	ee**noa**khoa	fennel
judías blancas	khoo**dhee**ahss **blahn**kahss	white beans
judías verdes	khoo**dhee**ahss **behr**dayss	green beans
lechuga	lay**choo**gah	lettuce
lentejas	layn**tay**khahss	lentils
lombarda	loam**bahr**dah	red cabbage
macedonia de legumbres	mahthay**dhoa**neeah day lay**goom**brayss	mixed vegetables
maíz	mah**eeth**	sweet corn
patatas	pah**tah**tahss	potatoes
pepinillos	paypee**nee**lyoass	gherkins
pepino	pay**pee**noa	cucumber
pimientos morrones	pee**myayn**toass moar**roa**nayss	sweet red peppers
puerros	**pwayr**roass	leeks
rábanos	**rah**bhahnoass	radishes
remolacha	raymoa**lah**chah	beetroot
repollo	ray**poa**lyoa	cabbage
setas	**say**tahss	mushrooms
tomates	toa**mah**tayss	tomatoes
trufas	**troo**fahss	truffles
zanahorias	thahnah**oa**ryahss	carrots

Here's a savoury vegetable dish you're sure to like. It goes well with roast chicken or other roasted and grilled meats:

pisto (**pees**toa)	a stew of green peppers, onions, tomatoes and courgettes (zucchini); in Catalonia it's called *samfaina,* and you might also see it referred to as *frito de verduras.*

Herbs and spices *Condimentos y especias*

What is it flavoured with?	**¿Con qué está condimentado?**	kon kay ays**tah** kondeemayn**tah**dhoa
Is it very spicy?	**¿Tiene muchas especias?**	**tyay**nay **moo**chahss ays**pay**thyahss
ajo	**ah**khoa	garlic
albahaca	ahlbah**ah**kah	basil
alcaparra	ahlkah**pah**rrah	caper
anís	ah**neess**	aniseed
azafrán	ahthah**frahn**	saffron
berro	**bay**rroa	cress
canela	kah**nay**lah	cinnamon
cebolleta	thaybhoa**lyay**tah	chive
clavo	**klah**bhoa	clove
comino	koa**mee**noa	caraway
eneldo	ay**nayl**doa	dill
estragón	ehstrah**gon**	tarragon
guindilla	geen**dee**lyah	chili pepper
hierbas finas	**yayr**bahss **fee**nahss	mixture of herbs
hoja de laurel	**oa**khah day lahoo**rayl**	bay leaf
jengibre	khayn**khee**bray	ginger
menta	**mayn**tah	mint
mostaza	moas**tah**thah	mustard
nuez moscada	nwayth moas**kah**dah	nutmeg
orégano	oa**ray**gahnoa	oregano
perejil	payray**kheel**	parsley
perifollo	payree**foa**lyoa	chervil
pimentón	peemayn**ton**	chili pepper
pimienta	pee**myayn**tah	pepper
romero	roa**may**roa	rosemary
sal	sahl	salt
salvia	**sahl**byah	sage
tomillo	toa**mee**lyoa	thyme
vainilla	bigh**nee**lyah	vanilla

Cheese *Queso*

Spanish restaurants seldom have a cheeseboard. Some well-known Spanish cheeses are listed below. Be sure to specify the cheese you'd like, otherwise you might be given imported cheese.

What sort of cheese do you have?	**¿Qué clases de queso tiene?**	kay **klah**ssayss day **kay**ssoa **tyay**nay
A piece of that one, please.	**Un trozo de ése, por favor.**	oon **troa**thoa day **ay**ssay por fa**bhor**

burgos (**boor**goass) A soft, creamy cheese named after the province from which it originates

cabrales (kah**brah**layss) A tangy, veined goat cheese; its flavour varies, depending upon the mountain region in which it was produced.

mahón (mah**on**) A goat cheese from Menorca in the Balearic Islands

manchego (mahn**chay**goa) Produced from ewe's milk, this hard cheese from La Mancha can vary from milky white to golden yellow. The best *manchego* is said to come from Ciudad Real.

perilla (peh**ree**lyah) A firm, bland cheese made from cow's milk; sometimes known as *teta*

roncal (ron**kahl**) A sharp ewe's milk cheese from northern Spain; hand-pressed, salted and smoked, with leathery rind

san simón (sahn see**mon**) Similar to *perilla*

villalón (beelyah**lon**) A curd cheese made from ewe's milk

blue	**tipo roquefort**	teepoa rokeh**foart**
cream	**cremoso**	kray**moa**ssoa
hard	**duro**	**doo**roa
mild	**suave**	**swah**bhay
ripe	**añejo**	ah**ñay**khoa
soft	**blando**	**blahn**doa
strong	**fuerte**	**fwayr**tay

Fruit *Fruta*

Do you have fresh fruit?	**¿Tiene usted fruta fresca?**	**tyay**nay oos**taydh froo**tah **frehs**kah
I'd like a (fresh) fruit cocktail.	**Quisiera una ensalada de fruta (fresca).**	kee**ssyay**rah **oo**nah aynsah**lah**dhah day **froo**tah (**frehs**kah)
albaricoques	ahlbahree**koa**kayss	apricots
almendras	ahl**mayn**drahss	almonds
arándanos	ah**rahn**dahnoass	blueberries
avellanas	ahbhay**lyah**nahss	hazelnuts
brevas	**bray**bhahss	blue figs
cacahuetes	kahkah**way**tayss	peanuts
castañas	kahs**tah**ñahss	chestnuts
cerezas	thay**ray**thahss	cherries
ciruelas	theer**way**lahss	plums
ciruelas pasas	theer**way**lahss **pah**ssahss	prunes
coco	**koa**koa	coconut
dátiles	**dah**teelayss	dates
frambuesas	frahm**bway**ssahss	raspberries
fresas	**fray**ssahss	strawberries
granadas	grah**nah**dhahss	pomegranates
grosellas negras	groa**ssay**lyahss **nay**grahss	blackcurrants
grosellas rojas	groa**ssay**lyahss **roa**khahss	redcurrants
higos	**ee**goass	figs
lima	**lee**mah	lime
limón	lee**mon**	lemon
mandarina	mahndah**ree**nah	tangerine
manzana	mahn**thah**nah	apple
melocotón	mayloakoa**ton**	peach
melón	may**lon**	melon
naranja	nah**rahn**khah	orange
nueces	**nway**thayss	walnuts
nueces variadas	**nway**thayss bah**ryah**dhahss	assorted nuts
pasas	**pah**ssahss	raisins
pera	**peh**rah	pear
piña	**pee**ñah	pineapple
plátano	**plah**tahnoa	banana
pomelo	poa**may**loa	grapefruit
ruibarbo	rwoo**bhahr**boa	rhubarb
sandía	sahn**dee**ah	watermelon
uvas	**oo**bhahss	grapes
blancas	**blahn**kahss	green
negras	**nay**grahss	blue
zarzamoras	thahrthah**moa**rahss	blackberries

Dessert *Postre*

I'd like a dessert, please.	**Quisiera un postre, por favor.**	kee**ssyay**rah oon **poas**tray por fah**bhor**
Something light, please.	**Algo ligero, por favor.**	**ahl**goa lee**khay**roa por fah**bhor**
Just a small portion.	**Una ración pequeña.**	**oo**nah rah**thyon** pay**kay**ñah

If you aren't sure what to order, ask the waiter:

What do you have for dessert?	**¿Qué tiene de postre?**	kay **tyay**nay day **poas**tray
What do you recommend?	**¿Qué me aconseja?**	kay may ahkoan**seh**khah
arroz con leche	ahr**roth** kon **lay**chay	rice pudding
bizcocho	heeth**koa**choa	sponge cake
crema catalana	kraymah kahtah**lah**nah	caramel pudding
flan	flahn	caramel pudding
fritos	**free**toass	fritters
galletas	gah**lyay**tahss	biscuits (cookies)
helado	ay**lah**dhoa	ice-cream
de chocolate	day choakoa**lah**tay	chocolate
de fresa	day **fray**ssah	strawberry
de limón	day lee**mon**	lemon
de moka	day **moa**kah	mocha
de vainilla	day bigh**nee**lyah	vanilla
mantecado	mahnteh**kah**dhoa	enriched ice-cream
mazapán	mahthah**pahn**	marzipan
melocotón en almíbar	mayloakoa**ton** ayn ahl**mee**bhahr	peaches in syrup
membrillo	maym**bree**lyoa	quince paste
merengue	may**rayn**gay	meringue
nata batida	**nah**tah bah**tee**dhah	whipped cream
pastas	**pah**stahss	biscuits (cookies)
pastel	pah**stayl**	cake
pastel de queso	pah**stayl** day **kay**ssoa	cheesecake
tarta de almendras	**tahr**tah day ahl**mayn**drahss	almond tart
tarta de manzana	**tahr**tah day mahn**thah**nah	apple tart
tarta de moka	**tahr**tah day **moa**kah	mocha cake
tarta helada	**tahr**tah ay**lah**dhah	ice-cream cake
tarteletas	tahrtay**lay**tahss	small tarts
tortitas	tor**tee**tahss	waffles
turrón	too**rron**	nougat

Aperitifs *Aperitivos*

For most Spaniards, a before-dinner *vermut* (behr**moot**—vermouth) or *jerez* (kheh**rayss**—sherry) is just as important as our cocktail or highball. Vermouth is rarely drunk neat (straight) but usually on the rocks or with seltzer water. Some Spaniards, on the other hand, content themselves with a glass of the local wine. You'll probably be given a dish of olives or nuts to nibble on with your sherry or vermouth. Or in a bar specializing in *tapas* (see page 63), you can order various snacks.

Without question, the country's most renowned drink is its sherry. Like marsala, madeira and port wine, sherry has a bit of alcohol or brandy added to it—to "fortify" it—during the fermentation process.

Sherry was the first fortified wine to become popular in England. Back in Shakespeare's day it was called *sack* or *sherris sack*. *Sack* was derived from the Spanish *sacar* (to export) while the English wrote *Sherris* for the name of the town, *Jerez*, where sherry wine originated. Sherry can be divided into two groups:

fino (feenoa)	These are the pale, dry sherries which make good aperitifs. The Spaniards themselves are especially fond of *amontillado* and *manzanilla*. Some of the best *finos* are *Tío Pepe* and *La Ina*.
oloroso (oloarossoa)	These are the heavier, darker sherries which are sweetened before being bottled. They're fine after-dinner drinks. One exception is *amoroso* which is medium dry. Brown and cream sherries are full-bodied and slightly less fragrant than *finos*.

¡SALUD!
(sah**loodh**)
YOUR HEALTH/CHEERS!

Wine *Vino*

Though Spain is one of the world's principal producers of wine, the nation's *vino*—with the exception of sherry—is among the most unpredictable in terms of quality. Using outmoded techniques in both cultivating grapes and fermenting wine, the wine of a specific vineyard can vary considerably from one year to the next.

Some restaurants list their wine in a corner of the menu while others have them posted on a wall. As much of the country's wine doesn't travel well, don't expect an *hostería* to offer more than a few types of wine. Most of the wine must be drunk young so don't look too hard for vintage labels.

A government board permits some vintners to include *denominación de origen* on a bottle as an indication of the wine's quality. However, this designation is unreliable.

Uncontestably, Spain's best wine comes from Rioja, a region of Old Castile of which Logroño is the centre. Winemakers there add *garantía de origen* to wine they feel is of above average quality, and this term is a respected one. But other regions—notably Andalusia, Aragon, Catalonia, Navarre, New Castile, Toledo and Valdepeñas—produce quality wine, too. This is your opportunity to sample local wine, some of which is surprisingly good.

The Penedés region near Barcelona is a major source of the world's best selling white sparkling wine, unofficially called Spanish *champán.*

The general rule of thumb is that white wine goes well with fish and light meats while red wine is reserved for dark meats. A good rosé goes with almost anything. The chart on the following page will help you to choose your wine if you want to do some serious wine-tasting.

If you need help in choosing a wine, don't hesitate to ask the waiter. He'll often suggest a bottle of local renown, perhaps from the *patrón*'s own wine cellar.

Type of wine	Examples	Accompanies
sweet white wine	A *moscatel*	desserts, custards, cakes, rice puddings, biscuits (cookies)
light, dry white wine	Much local white wine falls into this category; much of the white wine of Rioja, like *Monopole*	fish, seafood, *tapas,* cold meat, boiled meat, egg dishes like *tortillas*
rosé	*López de Heredia, Marqués de Murrieta*	goes with almost anything but especially cold dishes, eggs, pork, lamb, *paella*
light-bodied red wine	Many local wines come into this group; much of the Rioja red wine classifies, including *Viña Pomal* or the Catalonian *Priorato Reserva especial*	roast chicken, turkey, veal, lamb, beef fillet, ham, liver, quail, pheasant, stews, steaks, *zarzuela, paella, tortillas*
full-bodied red wine	sometimes a red wine of Tarragone, Alicante or Rioja can be classed in this category	duck, goose, kidneys, most game, tangy cheese like *cabrales*—in short, any strong-flavoured preparations
sparkling wine	*Champán* or *Cordoniu*	goes well with desserts and custards; if it's really dry you might try some as an aperitif or with shellfish, nuts, dried fruit

May I please have the wine list?	**¿Puedo ver la carta de vinos, por favor?**	pwaydhoa behr lah kahrtah day beenoass por fahbhor
I'd like ... of ...	**Quisiera ... de ...**	keessyayrah ... day
a carafe	**una garrafa**	oonah gahrrahfah
a bottle	**una botella**	oonah boataylyah
half bottle	**media botella**	maydhyah boataylyah
a glass	**un vaso**	oon bahssoa
a small glass	**un chato**	oon chahtoa
a litre	**un litro**	oon leetroa
I want a bottle of white/red wine.	**Quiero una botella de vino blanco/ vino tinto.**	kyayroa oonah boataylyah day beenoa blahnkoa/ beenoa teentoa

If you enjoyed the wine, you may want to say:

Please bring me another ...	**Tráigame otro/ otra ..., por favor.**	trighgahmay oatroa/oatrah ... por fahbhor
Where does this wine come from?	**¿De dónde viene este vino?**	day doanday byaynay aystay beenoa

red	**tinto**	teentoa
white	**blanco**	blahnkoa
rosé	**rosé**	rosay
dry	**seco**	saykoa
full-bodied	**de cuerpo**	day kwehrpoa
light	**livlano**	leebhyahnoa
sparkling	**espumoso**	ayspoomoassoa
sweet	**dulce**	doolthay
very dry	**muy seco**	mwee saykoa

Sangria

Sangría (sahn**gree**ah) is an iced, hot-weather drink that combines red wine, brandy and mineral water, with fruit juice, sliced oranges and other fruit and sugar to taste. Beware: it can pack a punch, especially when laced with rough brandy, but you can always dilute *sangría* with soda water and plenty of ice.

Beer *Cerveza*

Spanish beer, generally served cool, is good and cheap. Try *Aguila especial* or *San Miguel especial.*

A beer, please.	**Una cerveza, por favor.**	oonah thayr**bhay**thah por fah**bhor**
light beer	**cerveza rubia**	thayr**bhay**thah **roo**bhyah
dark beer	**cerveza negra**	thayr**bhay**than **nay**grah
foreign beer	**cerveza extranjera**	thayr**bhay**thah aykstrahn**khay**rah

Spirits and liqueurs *Licores*

If you'd like to sip a brandy after dinner, try a Spanish *coñac* like *Fundador* (foondah**dhor**) or *Carlos III* (**kahr**loass tehr**thay**roa). The Spaniards are also noted for their delicious liqueurs such as *Licor 43, Calisay,* or *Aromas de Montserrat.*

glass	**un vaso**	oon **bah**ssoa
bottle	**una botella**	**oo**nah boa**tay**lyah
double (a double shot)	**doble**	**doa**blay
neat (straight)	**solo**	**soa**loa
on the rocks	**con hielo**	kon **yay**loa

I'd like a glass of ..., please.	**Quisiera un vaso de ..., por favor.**	kee**ssyay**rah oon **bah**ssoa day ... por fah**bhor**
Are there any local specialities?	**¿Tiene alguna especialidad local?**	**tyay**nay ahl**goo**nah ayspaythyahlee**dhadh** loa**kahl**
Please bring me a ... of ...	**Tráigame un/una ... de ..., por favor.**	**trigh**gahmay oon/**oo**nah ... day ... por fah**bhor**
aniseed liqueur	**anís**	ah**neess**
bourbon	**whisky americano**	**wees**kee ahmayree**kah**noa
brandy	**coñac**	koa**ñahk**
gin	**ginebra**	**khee**nay**b**rah
gin-fizz	**ginebra con limón**	khee**nay**brah kon lee**mon**

gin and tonic	**ginebra con tónica**	khee**nay**brah kon **toa**neekah
liqueur	**licor**	lee**kor**
port	**oporto**	oa**por**toa
rum	**ron**	ron
rum coke	**Cuba libre**	koobhah **lee**bray
Scotch	**whisky escocés**	**wees**kee ayskoa**thayss**
sherry	**jerez**	kheh**rayss**
vermouth	**vermut**	behr**moot**
vodka	**vodka**	**bod**kah
whisky	**whisky**	**wees**kee
whisky and soda	**whisky con soda**	**wees**kee kon **soa**dhah

Nonalcoholic drinks *Bebidas sin alcohol*

I'd like a/an ...	**Quisiera ...**	kee**ssyay**rah
(hot) chocolate	**un chocolate (caliente)**	oon choakoa**lah**tay (kah-**lyayn**tay)
coffee	**un café**	oon kah**fay**
cup of coffee	**una taza de café**	**oo**nah **tah**thah day kah**fay**
black coffee	**café solo**	kah**fay** **soa**loa
white coffee	**café con leche**	kah**fay** kon **lay**chay
coffee with cream	**café con crema**	kah**fay** kon **kray**mah
espresso coffee	**café exprés**	kah**fay** ayks**prayss**
strong coffee	**un corto**	oon **koar**toa
caffein-free coffee	**café descafeinado**	kah**fay** dayskahfayee-**nah**dhoa
fruit juice	**un jugo de fruta**	oon **khoo**goa day **froo**tah
apple/grapefruit	**manzana/pomelo**	mahn**thah**nah/poa**meh**loa
lemon/orange	**limón/naranja**	lee**mon**/nah**rahn**khah
pineapple/tomato	**piña/tomate**	**pee**ñah/toa**mah**tay
lemonade	**una limonada**	**oo**nah leemoa**nah**dhah
milk	**leche**	**lay**chay
milkshake	**un batido**	oon bah**tee**dhoa
mineral water	**agua mineral**	**ah**gwah meenay**rahl**
orangeade	**una naranjada**	**oo**nah nahrahn**khah**dhah
soda water	**una soda**	**oo**nah **soa**dhah
tea	**un té**	oon tay
with milk/lemon	**con leche/con limón**	kon **lay**chay/kon lee**mon**
iced tea	**un té helado**	oon tay ay**lah**dhoa
tonic water	**una tónica**	**oo**nah **toa**neekah
(iced) water	**agua (helada)**	**ah**gwah (ay**lah**dhah)

Complaints *Reclamaciones*

That's not what I ordered.	**Esto no es lo que he pedido.**	aystoa noa ayss loa kay ay pehdheedhoa
I asked for ...	**He pedido ...**	ay pehdheedhoa
I asked for a small portion (for the child).	**He pedido una porción pequeña (para el niño).**	ay pehdheedhoa oonah porthyon paykayñah (pahrah ayl neeñoa)
There must be some mistake.	**Debe haber algún error.**	daybhay ahbhayr ahlgoon ayrroar
May I change this?	**¿Puede cambiarme eso?**	pwaydhay kahmbyahrmay ayssoa
The meat is ...	**Esta carne está ...**	aystah kahrnay aystah
overdone	**demasiado hecha**	daymahssyahdhoa ehchah
underdone	**poco hecha**	poakoa ehchah
too rare	**demasiado cruda**	daymahssyahdhoa kroodhah
too tough	**demasiado dura**	daymahssyahdhoa doorah
This is too ...	**Esto está ...**	aystoa aystah
bitter/salty/sweet	**amargo/salado/dulce**	ahmahrgoa/sahlahdhoa/ doolthay
The food is cold.	**La comida está fría.**	lah koameedhah aystah freeah
This isn't fresh.	**Esto no está fresco.**	aystoa noa aystah frayskoa
What's taking you so long?	**¿Por qué se demora tanto?**	por kay say daymoarah tahntoa
Where are our drinks?	**¿Dónde están nuestras bebidas?**	doanday aystahn nwaystrahss baybheedhahss
There's a plate/ glass missing.	**Falta un plato/ vaso.**	fahltah oon plahtoa/ bahssoa
The wine is too cold.	**El vino está demasiado frío.**	ayl beenoa aystah daymahssyahdhoa freeoa
The wine is corked.	**El vino sabe al corcho.**	ayl beenoa sahbhay ahl korchoa
This isn't clean.	**Esto no está limpio.**	aystoa noa aystah leempyoa
Would you ask the head waiter to come over?	**¿Quiere usted decirle al jefe que venga?**	kyayray oostaydh daytheerlay ahl khehfay kay bayngah

The bill (check) *La cuenta*

The service charge (*el servicio*—ayl sehr**bee**thyoa) is generally included. On some set menus you'll notice that wine is included in the price *(vino incluido)*.

I'd like to pay.	**Quisiera pagar.**	kee**ssyay**rah pah**gahr**
We'd like to pay separately.	**Quisiéramos pagar separadamente.**	kee**ssyay**rahmoass pah**gahr** saypahrahdhah**mayn**tay
I think you made a mistake in this bill.	**Creo que se ha equivocado usted en esta cuenta.**	**kreh**oa kay say ah aykeebhoa**kah**dhoa oos**taydh** ayn **ays**tah **kwayn**tah
What's this amount for?	**¿Para qué es esta cantidad?**	**pah**rah kay ayss **ays**tah kahntee**dhahdh**
Is service included?	**¿Está el servicio incluido?**	ays**tah** ayl sehr**bee**thyoa eenkloo**ee**dhoa
Is the cover charge included?	**¿Está el cubierto incluido?**	ays**tah** ayl koo**byehr**toa eenklooe**e**dhoa
Is everything included?	**¿Está todo incluido?**	ays**tah** **toa**dhoa eenkloo**ee**dhoa
Do you accept traveller's cheques?	**¿Acepta usted cheques de viajero?**	ah**thayp**tah oos**taydh** **chay**kayss day byah**khay**roa
Do you accept this credit card?	**¿Acepta esta tarjeta de crédito?**	ah**thayp**tah **ays**tah tahr**khay**tah day **kray**dheetoa
Thank you, this is for you.	**Gracias, esto es para usted.**	**grah**thyahss **ays**toa ayss **pah**rah oos**taydh**
That was a very good meal.	**Ha sido una comida excelente.**	ah **see**dhoa **oo**nah koa**mee**dhah aykthay**layn**tay
We enjoyed it, thank you.	**Nos ha gustado, gracias.**	noss ah goos**tah**dhoa **grah**thyahss

SERVICIO INCLUIDO
SERVICE INCLUDED

TIPPING, see inside back-cover

Snacks – Picnic *Tentempiés – Meriendas*

Tapas (**tah**pahss) are snacks, served with drinks in cafés and *tapa* bars. The variety is enormous. A *tapa* can be anything that tastes good and fits on a cocktail stick: smoked mountain ham, spicy sausages, cheese, olives, sardines, mushrooms, mussels, squid, octopus, meat balls, fried fish, plus sauces and exotic-looking specialities of the house. *Una tapa* is a mouthful, *una ración* is half a plateful, and *una porción* a generous amount.

I'll have one of those, please.	**Déme uno de ésos, por favor.**	**day**may **oo**noa day **ay**ssoass por fah**bhor**
Give me two of these and one of those.	**Déme dos de éstos y uno de ésos, por favor.**	**day**may doss day **ays**toass ee **oo**noa day **ay**ssoass por fah**bhor**
to the left	**a la izquierda**	ah lah eethkyayrdah
to the right	**a la derecha**	ah lah day**ray**chah
above	**encima**	ayn**thee**mah
below	**debajo**	day**bhah**khoa
Please give me a/an/some ...	**Déme ... por favor.**	**day**may ... por fah**bhor**
It's to take away.	**Es para llevar.**	ayss **pah**rah lyay**bhahr**
How much is that?	**¿Cuánto es?**	**kwahn**toa ayss

Here's a basic list of food and drinks that might come in useful for a light meal or when shopping for a picnic.

apples	**manzanas**	mahn**thah**nahss
bananas	**unos plátanos**	**oo**noass **plah**tahnoass
biscuits (Br.)	**unas galletas**	**oo**nahss gah**lyay**tahss
bread	**pan**	pahn
butter	**mantequilla**	mahntay**kee**lyah
cake	**unos bollos/ pasteles**	**oo**noass **boa**lyoass/ pahs**tay**layss
candy	**unos caramelos**	**oo**noass kahrah**may**loass
cheese	**queso**	**kay**ssoa
chicken	**pollo**	**poa**lyoa
half a roasted chicken	**medio pollo asado**	**may**dhyoa **poa**lyoa ah**ssah**dhoa
chips (Am.)	**patatas fritas/chips**	pah**tah**tahss **free**tahss
chips (Br.)	**patatas fritas**	pah**tah**tahss **free**tahss
chocolate	**chocolate**	choakoa**lah**tay

coffee	**café**	kah**fay**
cold cuts	**unos fiambres**	**oo**noass **fyahm**brayss
cookies	**unas galletas**	**oo**nahss gah**lyay**tahss
crackers	**unas galletas saladas**	**oo**nahss gah**lyay**tahss sah**lah**dhahss
cream	**nata**	**nah**tah
crisps (Br.)	**patatas fritas/chips**	pah**tah**tahss **free**tahss
cucumber	**un pepino**	oon pay**pee**noa
eggs	**huevos**	**way**bhoass
french fries	**patatas fritas**	pah**tah**tahss **free**tahss
fried eggs	**huevos fritos**	**way**bhoass **free**toass
fried fish	**pescado frito**	pays**kah**dhoa **free**toa
gherkins	**unos cohombrillos**	**oo**noass kom**bree**lyoass
grapes	**unas uvas**	**oo**nahss **oo**bhahss
ham	**jamón**	khah**mon**
ham and eggs	**jamón y huevos**	khah**mon** ee **way**bhoass
ham sandwich	**un bocadillo de jamón**	oon boakah**dhee**lyoa day khah**mon**
ketchup	**salsa de tomate**	**sahl**sah day toa**mah**tay
hamburger	**una hamburguesa**	**oo**nah ahmboor**gay**ssah
ice-cream	**helado**	ay**lah**dhoa
lemons	**unos limones**	**oo**noass lee**moa**nayss
lettuce	**una lechuga**	**oo**nah lay**choo**gah
melon	**melón**	may**lon**
milk	**leche**	**lay**chay
mustard	**mostaza**	moas**tah**thah
oranges	**naranjas**	nah**rahn**khahss
pastry	**pasteles**	pahs**tay**layss
pâté	**paté**	pah**tay**
pepper	**pimienta**	pee**myayn**tah
pickles	**unos pepinillos**	**oo**noass paypee**nee**lyoass
potatoes	**unas patatas**	**oo**nahss pah**tah**tahss
rolls	**unos panecillos**	**oo**noass pahnay**thee**lyoass
salad	**una ensalada**	**oo**nah aynsah**lah**dhah
salami	**salchichón**	sahlchee**chon**
salt	**sal**	sahl
sandwich	**un bocadillo**	oon boakah**dhee**lyoa
sausages	**unas salchichas**	**oo**nahss sahl**chee**chahss
spaghetti	**espaguetis**	ayspah**gay**teess
sugar	**azúcar**	ah**thoo**kahr
sweetener	**un edulcorante**	oon aydoolkoa**rahn**tay
sweets	**unos caramelos**	**oo**noass kahrah**may**loass
tea	**té**	tay
tomatoes	**unos tomates**	**oo**noass toa**mah**tayss
toast	**unas tostadas**	**oo**nahss toas**tah**dhahss
yoghurt	**un yogur**	oon **yoa**goor

Travelling around

Plane *Avión*

Is there a flight to Madrid?	**¿Hay algún vuelo a Madrid?**	igh ahl**goon bway**loa ah mah**dreedh**
Is it a nonstop flight?	**¿Es un vuelo sin escalas?**	ayss oon **bway**loa seen ays**kah**lahss
Do I have to change planes?	**¿Tengo que cambiar de avión?**	**tayn**goa kay kahm**byahr** day ah**bhyon**
Can I make a connection to Alicante?	**¿Puedo hacer conexión con un vuelo a Alicante?**	**pway**dhoa ah**thayr** koanayk**syon** kon oon **bway**loa ah ahlee**kahn**tay
I'd like a ticket to London.	**Quisiera un billete para Londres.**	kee**ssay**rah oon bee**lyay**-tay **pah**rah **loan**drayss
What's the fare to París?	**¿Cuál es la tarifa a París?**	kwahl ayss lah tah**ree**fah ah pah**reess**
single (one-way)	**ida**	**ee**dhah
return (roundtrip)	**ida y vuelta**	**ee**dhah ee **bwehl**tah
What time does the plane take off?	**¿A qué hora despega el avión?**	ah kay **oa**rah days**pay**gah ayl ah**bhyon**
What time do I have to check in?	**¿A qué hora debo presentarme?**	ah kay **oa**rah **day**bhoa prayssayn**tahr**may
Is there a bus to the airport?	**¿Hay un autobús que va al aeropuerto?**	igh oon owtoa**bhooss** kay bah ahl ahehroa**pwayr**toa
What's the flight number?	**¿Cuál es el número del vuelo?**	kwahl ayss ayl **noo**mayroa day **bway**loa
At what time do we arrive?	**¿A qué hora llegaremos?**	ah kay **oa**rah lyaygah**ray**moass
I'd like to ... my reservation.	**Quisiera ... mi reserva.**	kee**ssyay**rah ... mee ray**ssayr**bah
cancel	**anular**	ahnoo**lahr**
change	**cambiar**	kahm**byahr**
confirm	**confirmar**	konfeer**mahr**

LLEGADA ARRIVAL	**SALIDA** DEPARTURE

Train *Tren*

A nationalized company, the Red Nacional de los Ferrocarriles Españoles (R.E.N.F.E.—**rayn**fay) handles all rail services. While local trains are very slow, stopping at almost all stations, long-distance services are fast and reasonably punctual. First-class coaches are comfortable; second-class, adequate. Tickets can be purchased at travel agencies as well as at railway stations. Seat reservations are recommended.

EuroCity (ayooroa**thee**tee)	International express, first and second classes
Talgo, Ter, Intercity, Electrotren, Tren Estrella (**tahl**goa, tehr, "intercity", aylayktroatrayn, trayn ays**tray**lyah)	Luxury diesel, first and second classes; supplementary charge over regular fare
Expreso, Rápido (ayks**pray**ssoa, **rah**peedhoa)	Direct trains; stop at all main towns
Omnibus, Tranvía, Automotor (omneebhooss, trahn**wee**ah, owtoamoa**tor**)	Local trains (frequent stops)
Auto Expreso (owtoa ayks**pray**ssoa)	Car train

PRIMERA CLASE	**SEGUNDA CLASE**
FIRST CLASS	SECOND CLASS

Coche comedor (koachay koamay**dhor**)	Dining-car
Coche cama (koachay **kah**mah)	Sleeping-car; compartments with wash basins and 1, 2 or 3 berths.
Litera (lee**tay**rah)	Berths (with sheets, blankets and pillows)
Furgón de equipajes (foor**gon** day aykee**pah**khayss)	Luggage van (baggage car); only registered luggage permitted

To the railway station *A la estación*

Where's the railway station?	**¿Dónde está la estación de ferrocarril?**	**doan**day ay**stah** lah aystah**thyon** day fehrrokahr**reel**
Taxi, please!	**¡Taxi! por favor.**	**tah**ksee por fah**bhor**
Take me to the railway station.	**Lléveme a la estación de ferrocarril.**	**lyay**bhaymay ah lah aystah**thyon** day fehrrokahr**reel**
What's the fare?	**¿Cuál es la tarifa?**	kwahl ayss lah tah**ree**fah

INFORMACION TURISTICA	TOURIST INFORMATION
CAMBIO DE MONEDA	CURRENCY EXCHANGE

Where's ...? *¿Dónde está ...?*

Where is/are the ...?	**¿Dónde está/ están ...?**	**doan**day ay**stah**/ay**stahn**
booking office	**la oficina de reservas**	lah oafee**thee**nah day ray**ssayr**bahss
buffet	**el buffet**	ayl boo**fay**
currency-exchange office	**la oficina de cambio de moneda**	lah oafee**thee**nah day **kahm**byoa day moa**nay**dhah
information office	**la oficina de información**	lah oafee**thee**nah day eenformah**thyon**
left-luggage office (baggage check)	**la oficina de equipaje**	lah oafee**thee**nah day aykee**pah**khay
lost property (lost and found) office	**la oficina de objetos perdidos**	lah oafee**thee**nah day ob**khay**toass pehr**deed**hoass
luggage lockers	**la consigna automatica**	lah kon**seeg**nah owtoa**mah**teekah
newsstand	**el quiosco de periódicos**	ayl **kyos**koa day pay**ryo**dheekoass
platform 7	**el andén 7**	ayl ahn**dayn** 7
restaurant	**el restaurante**	ayl raystow**rahn**tay
ticket office	**la taquilla**	lah tah**kee**lyah
toilets	**los servicios**	loss sehr**bee**thyoass
waiting room	**la sala de espera**	lah **sah**lah day ays**pay**rah

TAXI, see page 21

Inquiries *Información*

What time does the ... train for Granada leave?	**¿A qué hora sale el ... tren para Granada?**	ah kay **oa**rah **sah**lay ayl ... trayn **pah**rah grah**nah**dhah
first/last/next	**primer/último/ próximo**	pree**mayr**/**ool**teemoa/ **prok**seemoa
Is it a direct train?	**¿Es un tren directo?**	ayss oon trayn dee**rehk**toa
Is there a connection to ...?	**¿Hay transbordo en ...?**	igh trahns**bor**doa ayn
Do I have to change trains?	**¿Tengo que cambiar de tren?**	**tayn**goa kay kahm**byahr** day trayn
Is there sufficient time to change?	**¿Hay tiempo suficiente para transbordar?**	igh **tyaym**poa soofee**thyayn**tay **pah**rah trahnsbor**dahr**
Will the train leave on time?	**¿Saldrá el tren a su hora?**	sahl**drah** ayl trayn ah soo **oa**rah
What time does the train arrive at Santander?	**¿A qué lora llega el tren a Santander?**	ah kay **oa**rah **lyay**gah ayl trayn ah sahntahn**dayr**
Is there a sleeping-car/dining-car on the train?	**¿Hay coche cama/ coche restaurante en el tren?**	igh **koa**chay **kah**mah/ **koa**chay raystow**rahn**tay ayn ayl trayn
Does the train stop at Gerona?	**¿Para el tren en Gerona?**	**pah**rah ayl trayn ayn khay**roa**nah
What platform does the train for Barcelona leave from?	**¿De qué andén sale el tren para Barcelona?**	day kay ahn**dayn sah**lay ayl trayn **pah**rah bahrthay**loa**nah
What platform does the train from ... arrive at?	**¿A qué andén llega el tren de ...?**	ah kay ahn**dayn lyay**gah ayl trayn day
I'd like to buy a timetable.	**Quisiera comprar una guía de ferrocarriles.**	kee**ssyay**rah kom**prahr** **oo**nah **gee**ah day fehrrokahr**ree**layss

ENTRADA	ENTRANCE
SALIDA	EXIT
A LOS ANDENES	TO THE PLATFORMS

Es un tren directo.	It's a through train.
Usted tiene que cambiar de tren en ...	You have to change at ...
Cambie de tren en ... y tome un tren de cercanías.	Change at ... and get a local train.
El andén ... está ...	Platform ... is ...
allí/arriba **a la izquierda/a la derecha**	over there/upstairs on the left/on the right
Hay un tren para Barcelona a las ...	There's a train to Barcelona at ...
Su tren sale del andén ...	Your train will leave from platform ...
Habrá una demora de ... minutos.	There'll be a delay of ... minutes.
Primera clase está al frente/ en medio/al final.	First class is in the front/ in the middle/at the end.

Tickets *Billetes*

I want a ticket to Bilbao.	**Quiero un billete para Bilbao.**	kyayroa oon beelyaytay pahrah beelbahoa
single (one-way)	**ida**	eedhah
return (roundtrip)	**ida y vuelta**	eedhah ee bwehltah
first class	**primera clase**	preemayrah klahssay
second class	**segunda clase**	saygoondah klahssay
half price	**media tarifa**	maydyah tahreefah
with surcharge for Talgo/Ter	**con suplemento para el Talgo/Ter**	kon sooplaymayntoa pahrah ayl tahlgoa/tehr

Reservation *Reserva*

I want to book a ...	**Quiero reservar ...**	kyayroa rayssayrbahr
seat	**un asiento**	oon ahssyayntoa
by the window	**al lado de la ventana**	ahl lahdhoa day lah bayntahnah
smoking/ non-smoking	**fumadores/ no fumadores**	foomahdhorayss/ noa foomahdhorayss

berth	**una litera**	**oonah leetayrah**
upper	**superior**	soopayr**yor**
middle	**media**	**may**dhyah
lower	**inferior**	eenfay**ryor**
berth in the sleeping car	**una litera en el coche cama**	**oonah leetayrah** ayn ayl **koa**chay **kah**mah
How much does it cost?	**¿Cuánto cuesta?**	**kwahn**toa **kways**tah

All aboard *¡Al tren!*

Is this the right platform for the train to Paris?	**¿Es éste el andén del tren para París?**	ayss **ays**tay ayl ahn**dayn** dayl trayn **pah**rah pah**reess**
Is this the train to Madrid?	**¿Es éste el tren para Madrid?**	ayss **ays**tay ayl trayn **pah**rah mah**dreedh**
Excuse me. May I get by?	**Perdóneme. ¿Puedo pasar?**	pehr**doa**naymay. **pway**dhoa pah**ssahr**
Is this seat taken?	**¿Está occupado este asiento?**	ays**tah** oakoo**pah**dhoa **ays**tay ah**ssyayn**toa
Do you mind if I smoke?	**¿Le importa si fumo?**	lay eem**poar**tah see **foo**moa

FUMADORES SMOKER	**NO FUMADORES** NONSMOKER

I think that's my seat.	**Creo que ése es mi asiento.**	**kray**oa kay **ay**ssay ayss mee ah**ssyayn**toa
Would you let me know before we get to Valencia?	**¿Me avisaría antes de llegar a Valencia?**	may ahbheessah**ree**ah **ahn**tayss day lyay**gahr** ah bah**layn**thyah
What station is this?	**¿Qué estación es ésta?**	kay aystah**thyon** ayss **ays**tah
How long does the train stop here?	**¿Cuánto tiempo para el tren aquí?**	**kwahn**toa **tyaym**poa **pah**rah ayl trayn ah**kee**
When do we get to Barcelona?	**¿Cuándo llegamos a Barcelona?**	**kwahn**doa lyay**gah**moass ah bahrthay**loa**nah

Sleeping *Durmiendo*

Are there any free compartments in the sleeping-car?	**¿Hay un departamento libre en el coche cama?**	igh oon daypahrtah**mayn**to **lee**bray ayn ayl **koa**chay **kah**mah
Where's the sleeping-car?	**¿Dónde está el coche cama?**	**doan**day ay**stah** ayl **koa**chay **kah**mah
Where's my berth?	**¿Dónde está mi litera?**	**doan**day ay**stah** mee lee**tay**rah
Would you make up our berths?	**¿Nos podrá hacer usted la litera?**	noss poa**drah** ah**thayr** oos**taydh** lah lee**tay**rah
Would you call me at 7 o'clock?	**¿Me podrá llamar usted a las 7?**	may poa**drah** lyah**mahr** oos**taydh** ah lahss 7
Would you bring me some coffee in the morning?	**¿Me podrá traer usted café por la mañana?**	may poa**drah** trah**ehr** oos**taydh** kah**fay** por lah mah**ñah**nah

FACTURACION

REGISTERING (CHECKING) BAGGAGE

Baggage and porters *Equipaje y mozos*

Where's the left-luggage office (baggage check)?	**¿Dónde está la oficina de equipaje?**	**doan**day ay**stah** lah oafee**thee**nah day aykee**pah**khay
Where are the luggage lockers?	**¿Dónde está la consigna automática?**	**doan**day ay**stah** la kon**seeg**nah owtoa**mah**teekah
I'd like to leave my luggage, please.	**Quisiera dejar mi equipaje, por favor.**	kee**ssyay**rah day**khahr** mee aykee**pah**khay por fah**bhor**
I'd like to register (check) my luggage, please.	**Quisiera facturar mi equipaje, por favor.**	kee**ssyay**rah fahktoo**rahr** mee aykee**pah**khay por fah**bhor**
Where are the luggage trolleys (carts)?	**¿Dónde están los carritos de equipaje?**	**doan**day ay**stahn** loss kahr**ree**toss day aykee**pah**khay
Porter!	**¡Mozo!**	**moa**thoa
Can you help me with my luggage?	**¿Puede usted ayudarme con mi equipaje?**	**pway**dhay oos**taydh** ahyoo**dhahr**may kon mee aykee**pah**khay

PORTERS, see also page 18

Coach (long-distance bus) *Autocar*

Travel by coach is good if you want to visit out-of-the-way places. There's no cross-country bus line. Most buses only serve towns and villages within a region or province, or they link the provincial capital with Madrid if there's no rail service.

Note: Most of the phrases on the previous pages can be used or adapted for bus travel.

Bus *Autobús*

In most buses, you pay as you enter. In some rural buses, you may find the driver also acting as the conductor. In major cities it may be worthwhile to get a pass or a booklet of tickets.

I'd like a pass/ booklets of tickets.	**Quisiera un pase/ taco de billetes.**	keessyayrah oon pahssay/ tahkoa day beelyaytayss
Where can I get a bus to the beach?	**¿Dónde puedo tomar un autobús para la playa?**	doanday pwaydhoa toamahr oon owtoabhooss pahrah lah plahyah
Which bus do I take for the university?	**¿Qué autobús debo tomar para la Universidad?**	kay owtoabhooss daybhoa toamahr pahrah lah ooneebhehrseedhahdh
Where's the ...?	**¿Dónde está ...?**	doanday aystah
bus stop	**la parada de autobuses**	lah pahrahdhah day owtoabhoossayss
terminus	**la terminal**	lah tehrmeenahl
When is the ... bus to the Prado?	**¿A qué hora sale el ... autobús para El Prado?**	ah kay oarah sahlay ayl ... owtoabhooss pahrah ayl prahdhoa
first/last/next	**primer/último/ próximo**	preemayr/oolteemoa/ prokseemoa
How often do the buses to the town centre run?	**¿Cada cuánto pasan los autobuses para el centro?**	kahdhah kwahntoa pahssahn loss owtoa-bhoossayss pahrah ayl thayntroa
How much is the fare to ...?	**¿Cuánto es la tarifa para ...?**	kwahntoa ayss lah tahreefah pahrah

How many bus stops are there to ...?	**¿Cuántas paradas de autobús hay hasta ...?**	**kwahn**tahss pah**rah**dhahss day owtoa**bhooss** igh **ahs**tah
Do I have to change buses?	**¿Tengo que cambiar de autobús?**	**tayn**goa kay kahm**byahr** day owtoa**bhooss**
How long does the journey (trip) take?	**¿Cuánto dura el viaje?**	**kwahn**toa **doo**rah ayl **byah**khay
Will you tell me when to get off?	**¿Me diría usted cuándo tengo que apearme?**	may dee**ree**ah oos**taydh** **kwahn**doa **tayn**goa kay ahpay**ahr**may
I want to get off at the cathedral.	**Quiero apearme en la Catedral.**	**kyay**roa ahpay**ahr**may ayn lah kahtay**drahl**
Please let me off at the next stop.	**Por favor, pare en la próxima parada.**	por fah**bhor** **pah**ray ayn lah **prok**seemah pah**rah**dhah

PARADA DE AUTOBUS	REGULAR BUS STOP
SOLO PARA A PETICION	STOPS ON REQUEST

Underground (subway) *Estación de metro*

Madrid and Barcelona have extensive underground (subway) networks. The fare is the same irrespective of the distance. The underground is open from 5 a.m. to 11 p.m.

Where's the nearest underground station?	**¿Dónde está la estación de metro más cercana?**	**doan**day ays**tah** lah aystah**thyon** day **may**troa mahss thehr**kah**nah
Does this train go to ...?	**¿Va este tren a ...?**	bah **ays**tay trayn ah
Where do I change for ...?	**¿Dónde tengo que hacer transbordo para ...?**	**doan**day **tayn**goa kay ah**thayr** trahns**bor**dao **pah**rah
Which line do I take?	**¿Qué línea tengo que coger?**	kay **lee**nayah **tayn**goa kay koa**khayr**
Is the next station ...?	**¿Es ... la próxima estación?**	ayss ... lah **prok**seemah aystah**thyon**

Boat service *Barcos*

When does the next/last boat for ... leave?	**¿Cuándo sale el próximo/último barco para ...?**	**kwahn**doa **sah**lay ayl **prok**seemoa/**ool**teemoa **bahr**koa **pah**rah
Where's the embarkation point?	**¿Dónde está el lugar de embarco?**	**doan**day ay**stah** ayl loo**gahr** day aym**bahr**koa
How long does the crossing take?	**¿Cuánto dura la travesía?**	**kwahn**toa **doo**rah lah trahbhay**see**ah
At which ports do we stop?	**¿En qué puertos nos detenemos?**	ayn kay **pwayr**toass noass daytay**nay**moass
I'd like to take a cruise.	**Quisiera tomar un crucero.**	kee**ssyay**rah toa**mahr** oon kroo**thay**roa
boat	**el barco**	ayl **bahr**koa
cabin	**el camarote**	ayl kahmah**roa**tay
single/double	**sencillo/doble**	sayn**thee**lyoa/**doa**blay
cruise	**el crucero**	ayl kroo**thay**roa
deck	**la cubierta**	lah koo**bhyayr**tah
ferry	**el transbordador**	ayl trahnsboardah**dhoar**
hovercraft	**el aerodeslizador**	ayl ahayroadhayslee-thah**dhoar**
hydrofoil	**el hidroplano**	ayl eedroa**plah**noa
life belt/boat	**el cinturón/bote salvavidas**	ayl theentoo**ron**/**boa**tay sahlbah**bhee**dhahss
port	**el puerto**	ayl **pwayr**toa
ship	**la embarcación**	lah aymbahrkah**thyon**

Other means of transport *Otros medios de transporte*

bicycle	**la bicicleta**	lah beetheek**lay**tah
cable car	**el funicular**	ayl fooneekoo**lahr**
car	**el coche**	ayl **koa**chay
helicopter	**el helicóptero**	ayl aylee**kop**tayroa
moped	**el velomotor**	ayl bayloamoa**toar**
motorbike	**la motocicleta**	lah moatoatheek**lay**tah
scooter	**el escúter**	ayl ays**koo**tayr

Or perhaps you prefer:

to hitchhike	**hacer auto-stop**	ah**thayr** **ow**toa-stop
to ride	**montar a caballo**	moan**tahr** ah kah**bhah**lyoa
to walk	**caminar**	kahmee**nahr**

Car *El coche*

Spain's expanding motorway (expressway) network is excellently engineered, but rather expensive tolls are charged. Main roads are adequate to very good. Unclassified country roads can be in a poor driving condition. Wearing of the seat belt *(el cinturón de seguridad)* is compulsory.

Filling station *Gasolinera*

Give me ... litres of petrol (gasoline).	**Déme ... litros de gasolina.**	**day**may ... **lee**troass day gahssoa**lee**nah
Full tank, please.	**Llénelo, por favor.**	**lyay**nayloa por fah**bhor**
super (premium)/ normal/unleaded petrol/diesel	**super/normal/ gasolina sin plomo/diesel**	**soo**payr/nor**mahl**/ gahssoa**lee**nah seen **ploa**moa/**dee**sayl
Please check the ...	**Controle ...**	kon**tro**lay
battery	**la batería**	lah bahtay**ree**ah
brake fluid	**el líquido de frenos**	ayl **lee**keedhoa day **fray**noass
oil/water	**el aceite/el agua**	ayl ah**thay**tay/ayl **ah**gwah
Would you check the tyre pressure, please?	**¿Puede controlar la presión de los neumáticos, por favor?**	**pway**dhay kontro**lahr** lah pray**ssyon** day loass nayoo**mah**teekoass por fah**bhor**
1.6 front, 1.8 rear.	**1,6 delanteras, 1,8 traseras.**	1 **koa**mah 6 daylahn**tay**rahss 1 **koa**mah 8 trah**ssay**rahss
Please check the spare tyre, too.	**Mire la rueda de repuesto también, por favor.**	**mee**ray lah **rway**dhah day ray**pway**stoa tahm**byayn** por fah**bhor**
Can you mend this puncture (fix this flat)?	**¿Puede arreglar este pinchazo?**	**pway**dhay ahrray**glahr** **ay**stay peen**chah**thoa
Would you please change the ...?	**¿Puede cambiar ..., por favor?**	**pway**dhay kahm**byahr** ... por fah**bhor**
bulb	**la bombilla**	lah boam**bee**lyah
fan belt	**la correa del ventilador**	lah kor**ray**ah dayl bayntee**lah**dhor
spark(ing) plug	**la bujía**	lah boo**khee**ah
tyre	**el neumático**	ayl nayoo**mah**teekoa
wipers	**los limpiaparabrisas**	loass leempyahpahrah**bree**ssahss

CAR HIRE, see page 20/CONVERSION CHARTS, see page 158

Would you clean the windscreen (windshield)?	**¿Quiere limpiar el parabrisas?**	**kyay**ray leem**pyahr** ayl pahrah**bree**ssahss
Do you have a road map of this district?	**¿Tiene un mapa de carreteras de esta comarca?**	**tyay**nay oon **mah**pah day kahrray**tay**rahss day **ay**stah koa**mahr**kah

Asking the way—Street directions *Preguntas – Direcciones*

Can you tell me the way to ...?	**¿Me puede decir cómo se va a ...?**	may **pway**dhay day**theer** **koa**moa say bah ah
How do I get to ...?	**¿Cómo se va a ...?**	**koa**moa say bah ah
Where does this street lead to?	**¿Adónde lleva esta calle?**	ah**dhoan**day **lyay**bhah **ay**stah **kah**lyay
Is the road good?	**¿Está la carretera en buen estado?**	ay**stah** la kahrray**tay**rah ayn bwayn ay**stah**dhoa
Is there a motorway (expressway)?	**¿Hay una autopista?**	igh **oo**nah owtoa**pees**stah
Is there a road with little traffic?	**¿Hay una carretera con poco tráfico?**	igh **oo**nah kahrray**tay**rah kon **poa**koa **trah**feekoa
How long does it take by car/on foot?	**¿Cuánto se tarda en coche/a pie?**	**kwahn**toa say **tahr**dah ayn **koa**chay/ah pyay
Are we on the right road for ...?	**¿Es ésta la carretera hacia ...?**	ayss **ay**stah lah kahrray**tay**rah **ah**thyah
How far is the next village?	**¿Qué distancia hay hasta el próximo pueblo?**	kay dee**stahn**thyah igh **ah**stah ayl **proak**seemoa **pway**bloa
How far is it to ... from here?	**¿Qué distancia hay desde aquí hasta ...?**	kay dee**stahn**thyah igh **days**day ah**kee** **ah**stah
Can you tell me where ... is?	**¿Puede decirme dónde está ...?**	**pway**dhay day**theer**may **doan**day ay**stah**
How do I get to this address?	**¿Cómo puedo llegar a esta dirección?**	**koa**moa **pway**dhoa lyay**gahr** ah **ay**stah deerayk**thyon**
Can I drive to the centre of town?	**¿Puedo conducir hasta el centro de la ciudad?**	**pway**dhoa kondoo**theer** **ah**stah ayl **thayn**troa day lah thyoo**dhahdh**
Can you show me on the map where I am?	**¿Puede enseñarme en el mapa dónde estoy?**	**pway**dhay aynsay**ñahr**may ayn ayl **mah**pah **doan**day ay**stoy**

Se ha equivocado usted de carretera.	You're on the wrong road.
Siga todo derecho.	Go straight ahead.
norte/sur/este/oeste	north/south/east/west
Es hacia allí ...	It's down there ...
a la izquierda/derecha **enfrente/atrás ...** **junto a/después de ...**	on the left/right opposite/behind ... next to/after ...
Tome la carretera para ...	Take the road for ...
Tiene que regresar hasta ...	You have to go back to ...
Vaya al primer/segundo cruce.	Go to the first/second crossroads (intersection).
Doble a la izquierda en el semáforo.	Turn left at the traffic lights.
Doble a la derecha en la próxima esquina.	Turn right at the next corner.

Parking *Aparcamiento*

Where can I park?	**¿Dónde puedo aparcar?**	**doan**day **pway**dhoa ahpahr**kahr**
Is there a car park nearby?	**¿Hay un estacionamiento cerca de aquí?**	igh oon aystahthyonah**myayn**toa **thayr**kah day ah**kee**
How long can I park here?	**¿Cuánto tiempo puedo aparcar aquí?**	**kwahn**toa **tyaym**poa **pway**dhoa ahpahr**kahr** ah**kee**
What's the charge per hour?	**¿Cuánto cuesta por hora?**	**kwahn**toa **kways**tah por **oa**rah
Do you have some change for the parking meter?	**¿Tiene suelto para el parquímetro?**	**tyay**nay **swayl**toa **pah**rah ayl pahr**kee**mehtroa
Where can I get a parking disc?	**¿Dónde puedo conseguir un disco de aparcamiento?**	**doan**day **pway**dhoa konsay**geer** oon **dees**koa day ahpahrkah**myayn**toa

Breakdown *Averías*

Where's the nearest garage?	**¿Dónde está el garaje más cercano?**	**doan**day ay**stah** ayl gah**rah**khay mahss thehr**kah**noa
What's the telephone number of the nearest garage?	**¿Cuál es el número de teléfono del garaje más cercano?**	kwahl ayss ayl **noo**mayroa day tay**lay**foanoa dayl gah**rah**khay mahss thehr**kah**noa
My car won't start.	**Mi coche no quiere arrancar.**	mee **koa**chay noa **kyay**ray ahrrahn**kahr**
The battery is dead.	**La batería está descargada.**	lah bahtay**ree**ah ay**stah** dayskahr**gah**dhah
I've run out of petrol (gasoline).	**Se ha terminado la gasolina.**	say ah tayrmee**nah**dhoa lah gahssoa**lee**nah
I have a flat tyre.	**Tengo un pinchazo**	**tayn**goa oon peen**chah**thoa
The engine is overheating.	**El motor está demasiado caliente.**	ayl moa**tor** ay**stah** daymah**ssyah**dhoa kah**lyayn**tay
There is something wrong with the ...	**Hay algo estropeado en ...**	igh **ahl**goa aystroapay**ah**dhoa ayn
brakes	**los frenos**	loass **fray**noass
carburetor	**el carburador**	ayl kahrboorah**dhoar**
exhaust pipe	**el tubo de escape**	ayl **too**boa day ays**kah**pay
radiator	**el radiador**	ayl rahdhyah**dhoar**
wheel	**la rueda**	lah **rway**dhah
I've had a breakdown at ...	**Tengo un coche estropeado en ...**	**tayn**goa oon **koa**chay aystroapay**ah**dhoa ayn
Can you send a mechanic?	**¿Puede usted mandar un mecánico?**	**pway**dhay oos**taydh** mahn**dahr** oon may**kah**neekoa
Can you send a breakdown van (tow-truck)?	**¿Puede usted mandar un coche grúa?**	**pway**dhay oos**taydh** mahn**dahr** oon **koa**chay **groo**ah
How long will you be?	**¿Cuánto tardarán?**	**kwahn**toa tahrdah**rahn**

Accident—Police *Accidentes – Policía*

Please call the police.	**Llamen a la policía, por favor.**	**lyah**mayn ah lah poalee**thee**ah por fah**bhor**
There's been an accident.	**Ha habido un accidente.**	ah ah**bhee**dhoa oon ahktheed**hayn**tay

It's about 2 km. from ...	**Está a unos 2 kilómetros de ...**	ay**stah** ah **oo**noass 2 kee**loa**maytroass day
There are people injured.	**Hay gente herida.**	igh **khayn**tay ay**ree**dhah
Call a doctor/an ambulance.	**Llamen a un doctor/una ambulancia.**	**lyah**mayn ah oon doak**tor**/oonah ahmboo**lahn**thyah
Here's my driving licence.	**Aquí está mi permiso de conducir.**	ah**kee** ay**stah** mee payr**mee**ssoa day kondoo**theer**
What's your name and address?	**¿Cuál es su nombre y dirección?**	kwahl ayss soo **nom**bray ee deerayk**thyon**
What's your insurance company?	**¿Cuál es su compañía de seguros?**	kwahl ayss soo kompah**ñee**ah day say**goo**roass

Road signs *Señales de circulación*

ADUANA	Customs
¡ALTO!	Stop
ATENCION	Caution
AUTOPISTA (DE PEAJE)	Motorway/Turnpike (with toll)
CALZADA DETERIORADA	Bad road surface
CARRETERA CORTADA	No through road
CEDA EL PASO	Give way (yield)
CRUCE PELIGROSO	Dangerous crossroads
CUIDADO	Caution
CURVA PELIGROSA	Dangerous bend (curve)
DESPACIO	Drive slowly
DESVIACION	Diversion (detour)
DIRECCION UNICA	One-way street
ENCENDER LAS LUCES	Switch on headlights
ESCUELA	School
ESTACIONAMIENTO PROHIBIDO	No parking
ESTACIONAMIENTO REGLAMENTADO	Limited parking zone
FUERTE DECLIVE	Steep incline
OBRAS	Road works (men working)
PASO A NIVEL	Level (railroad) crossing
PASO PROHIBIDO	No entry
PEATONES	Pedestrians
PELIGRO	Danger
PROHIBIDO ADELANTAR	No overtaking (passing)
PUESTO DE SOCORRO	First-aid
SALIDA DE FABRICA	Factory exit

Sightseeing

Where's the tourist office/information centre?	**¿Dónde está la oficina de turismo/ la información?**	**doan**day ay**stah** lah oafee**thee**nah day too**rees**moa/ lah eenformah**thyon**
What are the main points of interest?	**¿Cuáles son los principales puntos de interés?**	**kwah**layss son loss preentheep**ah**layss **poon**toass day eentay**rayss**
We're here for only a few hours/a day.	**Estamos aquí sólo unas pocas horas/ un día.**	ay**stah**moass ah**kee soa**loa **oo**nahss **poa**kahss **oa**rahss/ oon **dee**ah
Can you recommend a ...?	**¿Puede usted recomendarme ...?**	**pway**dhay oos**taydh** raykoamayn**dahr**may
sightseeing tour	**un recorrido turístico**	oon rehkor**ree**dhoa too**rees**teekoa
popular excursion	**una excursión popular**	**oo**nah aykskoor**syon** poapoo**lahr**
What's the point of departure?	**¿Cuál es el lugar de salida?**	kwahl ayss ayl loo**gahr** day sah**lee**dhah
Will the coach pick us up at the hotel?	**¿Nos recogerá el autocar en el hotel?**	noss rehkoakhay**rah** ayl owtoa**kahr** ayn ayl oa**tehl**
How much does the tour cost?	**¿Cuánto cuesta el recorrido?**	**kwahn**toa **kway**stah ayl rehkor**ree**dhoa
What time does the tour start?	**¿A qué hora empieza el recorrido?**	ah kay **oa**rah aym**pyay**thah ayl rehkor**ree**dhoa
Is lunch included?	**¿Está incluido el almuerzo?**	ay**stah** eenkloo**ee**dhoa ayl ahl**mwayr**thoa
What time do we get back?	**¿A qué hora volvemos?**	ah kay **oa**rah bol**bay**moass
Do we have free time in ...?	**¿Tenemos tiempo libre en ...?**	tay**nay**moass **tyaym**poa **lee**bray ayn
Is there an English-speaking guide?	**¿Hay algún guía que hable inglés?**	igh ahl**goon gee**ah kay **ah**blay een**glayss**
I'd like to hire a private guide for ...	**Quisiera un guía particular para ...**	kee**ssyay**rah oon **gee**ah pahrteekoo**lahr pah**rah
half a day	**medio día**	**may**dhyoa **dee**ah
a full day	**todo el día**	**toa**dhoa ayl **dee**ah

TIME OF THE DAY, see page 153

Where is ...? *¿Dónde está ...?*

Where is/are the ...?	**¿Dónde está/ están ...?**	**doan**day ays**tah**/ays**tahn**
abbey	**la abadía**	lah ahbhad**hee**ah
art gallery	**la galería de arte**	lah gahlay**ree**ah day **ahr**tay
artist's quarter	**el barrio de los artistas**	ayl **bahr**reeoa day loss ahr**tees**tahss
botanical gardens	**el jardín botánico**	ayl khahr**deen** boa**tah**neekoa
bullring	**la plaza de toros**	lah **plah**thah day **to**roass
castle	**el castillo**	ayl kahs**tee**lyoa
cathedral	**la catedral**	lah kahtay**drahl**
caves	**las cuevas**	lahss **kway**bhahss
cemetery	**el cementerio**	ayl thaymayn**tay**ryoa
chapel	**la capilla**	lah kah**pee**lyah
church	**la iglesia**	lah ee**glay**ssyah
city centre	**el centro de la ciudad**	ayl **thayn**troa day lah thyoo**dhahdh**
concert hall	**la sala de conciertos**	lah **sah**lah day kon**thyehr**toass
convent	**el convento**	ayl kon**bayn**toa
convention hall	**el palacio de convenciones**	ayl pah**lah**thyoa day konbayn**thyo**nayss
court house	**el palacio de justicia**	ayl pah**lah**thyoa day khoos**tee**thyah
downtown area	**el centro de la ciudad**	ayl **thayn**troa day lah thyoo**dhahdh**
exhibition	**la exhibición**	lah ehkseebhee**thyon**
factory	**la fábrica**	lah **fah**breekah
fair	**la feria**	lah **fay**ryah
flea market	**el mercado de cosas viejas**	ayl mehr**kah**dhoa day **ko**ssahss **byay**khahss
fortress	**la fortaleza/el alcázar**	lah fortah**lay**thah/ayl ahl**kah**thahr
fountain	**la fuente**	lah **fwayn**tay
gardens	**los jardines públicos**	loss khahr**dee**nayss **poob**leekoss
harbour	**el puerto**	ayl **pwayr**toa
library	**la biblioteca**	lah beeblyoa**tay**kah
market	**el mercado**	ayl mehr**kah**dhoa
monastery	**el monasterio**	ayl moanahs**tay**ryoa
monument	**el monumento**	ayl moanoo**mayn**toa
museum	**el museo**	ayl moo**ssay**oa
old town	**la ciudad vieja**	lah thyoo**dhahdh byay**khah
palace	**el palacio**	ayl pah**lah**thyoa
park	**el parque**	ayl **pahr**kay

ASKING THE WAY, see page 76

parliament building	**el edificio de las Cortes**	ayl aydhee**fee**thyoa day lahss **kor**tayss
royal palace	**el palacio real**	ayl pah**lah**thyoa ray**ahl**
ruins	**las ruinas**	lahss **rwee**nahss
shopping area	**la zona de tiendas**	lah **thoa**nah day **tyayn**dahss
square	**la plaza**	lah **plah**thah
stadium	**el estadio**	ayl ays**tah**dhyoa
statue	**la estatua**	lah ays**tah**twah
stock exchange	**la bolsa**	lah **bol**sah
tomb	**la tumba**	lah **toom**bah
tower	**la torre**	lah **tor**ray
town hall	**el ayuntamiento**	ayl ahyoontah**myayn**toa
town walls	**las murallas**	lahss moo**rah**lyahss
university	**la universidad**	lah ooneebhehrsee**dhahdh**
zoo	**el zoológico**	ayl thoa**lo**kheekoa

Admission *Entrada*

Is ... open on Sundays?	**¿Está ... abierto los domingos?**	ays**tah** ... ah**bhyayr**toa loss doa**meen**goass
When does it open/close?	**¿A qué hora abren/cierran?**	ah kay **oa**rah **ah**brayn/**thyayr**rahn
How much is the entrance fee?	**¿Cuánto vale la entrada?**	**kwahn**toa **bah**lay lah ayn**trah**dhah
Is there any reduction for (the) ...?	**¿Hay algún descuento para ...?**	igh ahl**goon** days**kwayn**toa **pah**rah
disabled	**incapacitados**	eenkahpahthee**tah**doass
groups	**grupos**	**groo**poass
pensioners	**jubilados**	khoobhee**lah**dhoass
students	**estudiantes**	aystoo**dhyahn**tayss
Have you a guidebook (in English)?	**¿Tiene usted una guía (en inglés)?**	**tyay**nay oos**taydh oo**nah **gee**ah (ayn een**glayss**)
Can I buy a catalogue?	**¿Puedo comprar un catálogo?**	**pway**dhoa kom**prahr** oon kah**tah**loagoa
Is it all right to take pictures?	**¿Se pueden tomar fotografías?**	say **pway**dhayn toa**mahr** foatoagrah**fee**ahss

ENTRADA LIBRE	ADMISSION FREE
PROHIBIDO TOMAR FOTOGRAFIAS	NO CAMERAS ALLOWED

Who—What—When? *¿Quién – Qué – Cuándo?*

What's that building?	**¿Qué es ese edificio?**	kay ayss **ay**ssay aydhee**fee**thyoa
Who was the ...?	**¿Quién fue ...?**	kyayn fweh
architect	**el arquitecto**	ayl ahrkee**tehk**toa
artist	**el artista**	ayl ahr**tee**stah
painter	**el pintor**	ayl peen**tor**
sculptor	**el escultor**	ayl ayskool**tor**
Who painted that picture?	**¿Quién pintó ese cuadro?**	kyayn peen**toa ay**ssay **kwah**droa
When did he live?	**¿En qué época vivió?**	ayn kay **ay**poakah bee**bhyoa**
When was it built?	**¿Cuándo se construyó?**	**kwahn**doa say konstroo**yoa**
Where's the house where ... lived?	**¿Dónde está la casa en que vivió ...?**	**doan**day ay**stah** lah **kah**ssah ayn kay beebhyoa
We're interested in ...	**Nos interesa(n) ...**	noss eentay**ray**ssah(n)
antiques	**las antigüedades**	lahss ahnteegwee**dhah**dhayss
archaeology	**la arqueología**	lah ahrkayoalo**khee**ah
art	**el arte**	ayl **ahr**tay
botany	**la botánica**	lah boa**tah**neekah
ceramics	**la cerámica**	lah thay**rah**meekah
coins	**las monedas**	lahss moa**nay**dhahss
fine arts	**las bellas artes**	lahss **bay**lyahss **ahr**tayss
furniture	**los muebles**	loss **mway**blayss
geology	**la geología**	lah khayoaloa**khee**ah
handicrafts	**la artesanía**	lah ahrtayssah**nee**ah
history	**la historia**	lah ees**toa**ryah
medicine	**la medicina**	lah maydee**thee**nah
music	**la música**	lah **moo**sseekah
natural history	**la historia natural**	lah ees**toa**ryah nahtoo**rahl**
ornithology	**la ornitologia**	lah oarneetoaloa**khee**ah
painting	**la pintura**	lah peen**too**rah
pottery	**la alfarería**	lah ahlfahray**ree**ah
religion	**la religión**	lah raylee**khyon**
sculpture	**la escultura**	lah ayskool**too**rah
zoology	**la zoología**	lah thoalo**khee**ah
Where's the ... department?	**¿Dónde está el departamento de ...?**	**doan**day ay**stah** ayl daypahrtah**mayn**toa day

It's ...	**Es ...**	ayss
amazing	**asombroso***	ahssoam**broa**ssoa
awful	**horrible**	or**ree**blay
beautiful	**hermoso**	ayr**moa**ssoa
gloomy	**lúgubre**	**loo**goobray
impressive	**impresionante**	eemprayssyoa**nahn**tay
interesting	**interesante**	eentayray**ssahn**tay
magnificent	**magnífico**	mah**gnee**feekoa
overwhelming	**abrumador**	ahbroomah**dhor**
strange	**extraño**	**aykstrah**ñoa
superb	**soberbio**	soa**bhehr**byoa
terrible	**terrible**	tehr**ree**blay
terrifying	**aterrador**	ahtehrrah**dhor**
tremendous	**tremendo**	tray**mayn**doa
ugly	**feo**	**feh**oa

Churches—Religious services *Iglesias – Servicios religiosos*

Predominantly Roman Catholic, Spain is rich in cathedrals and churches worth visiting. Most are open to the public except, of course, during mass. If you're interested in taking pictures, you should obtain permission first. Shorts and backless dresses are definitely out when visiting churches.

Is there a/an ... near here?	**¿Hay una ... cerca de aquí?**	igh **oo**nah ... **ther**kah day ah**kee**
Catholic/Protestant church	**iglesia católica/ protestante**	ee**glay**ssyah kah**toa**leekah/ proatay**stahn**tay
synagogue	**sinagoga**	seenah**goa**gah
mosque	**mezquita**	mayth**kee**tah
At what time is ...?	**¿A qué hora es ...?**	ah kay **oa**rah ayss
mass	**la misa**	lah **mee**ssah
the service	**el servicio**	ayl sehr**bee**thyoa
Where can I find a ... who speaks English?	**¿Dónde puedo encontrar un ... que hable inglés?**	**doan**day **pway**dhoa aynkon**trahr** oon ... kay **ah**blay een**glayss**
priest/minister/ rabbi	**sacerdote/ministro/ rabino**	sahthehr**doa**tay/mee**nee**stroa/rah**bhee**noa
I'd like to visit the church.	**Quisiera visitar la iglesia.**	kee**ssyay**rah beessee**tahr** lah ee**glay**ssyah

*For feminine and plural forms, see grammar section page 159 (adjectives).

Countryside *En el campo*

How high is that mountain?	**¿Qué altura tiene esa montaña?**	kay ahl**too**rah **tyay**nay **ay**ssah moan**tah**ñah
How far is it to ...?	**¿Qué distancia hay hasta ...?**	kay dees**tahn**thyah igh **ahs**tah
Can we walk?	**¿Podemos ir a pie?**	poa**day**moass eer ah pyay
Is there a scenic route to ...?	**¿Hay una carretera panorámica a ...?**	igh **oo**nah kahrray**tay**rah pahno**rah**meekah ah
How do we get back to ...?	**¿Cómo regresamos a ...?**	**koa**moa raygray**ssah**moass ah
What's the name of that ...?	**¿Cómo se llama ...?**	**koa**moa say **lyah**mah
animal/bird/ flower/tree	**ese animal/pájaro/ esa flor/ese árbol**	**ay**ssay ahnee**mahl**/ **pah**khahroa/**ay**ssah floar/ **ay**ssay **ahr**boal

Landmarks *Puntos de referencia*

bridge	**el puente**	ayl **pwayn**tay
building	**el edificio**	ayl aydhee**fee**thyoa
church	**la iglesia**	lah eeg**lay**ssyah
cliff	**el acantilado**	ayl ahkahntee**lah**dhoa
farm	**la granja**	lah **grahn**khah
field	**el campo**	ayl **kahm**poa
footpath	**el sendero**	ayl sayn**day**roa
forest	**el bosque**	ayl **boas**kay
fortress	**la fortaleza**	lah fortah**lay**thah
garden	**el jardín**	ayl khahr**deen**
hill	**la colina**	lah koa**lee**nah
house	**la casa**	lah **kah**ssah
hut	**la cabaña**	lah kah**bhah**ñah
lake	**el lago**	ayl **lah** oa
meadow	**el prado**	ayl **prah**dhoa
river	**el río**	ayl **ree**oa
road	**la carretera**	lah kahrray**tay**rah
sea	**el mar**	ayl mahr
valley	**el valle**	ayl **bah**lyay
village	**el pueblo**	ayl **pway**bloa
vineyard	**el viñedo**	ayl bee**ñay**dhoa
wall	**el muro**	ayl **moo**roa
waterfall	**la cascada**	lah kahs**kah**dhah
windmill	**el molino de viento**	ayl moa**lee**noa day **byayn**toa

ASKING THE WAY, see page 76

Relaxing

Cinema (Movies) – Theatre *Cine - Teatro*

Most films are dubbed in Spanish. The first showing usually starts around 2 p.m. in cities, but at 4 elsewhere. Sometimes there are only two showings in the evening—at 7 and 10.30 or 11 p.m.; for these advance booking is advisable. Curtain time at the theatre is at 7 and 10.30 or 11 p.m. There are daily performances but a few theatres close one day a week.

You can find out what's playing from the newspapers and billboards or from magazines like "This Week in ...".

What's on at the cinema tonight?	**¿Qué ponen en el cine esta noche?**	kay **poa**nehn ayn ayl **thee**nay **ays**tah **noa**chay
What's playing at the ... theatre?	**¿Qué ponen en el teatro ...?**	kay **poa**nehn ayn ayl tay**ah**troa
Can you recommend a ...?	**¿Puede recomendarme ...?**	**pway**dhay rehkoamayn**dahr**may
comedy	**una comedia**	**oo**nah koa**may**dhyah
drama	**un drama**	oon **drah**mah
film	**una película**	**oo**nah pay**lee**koolah
musical	**una comedia musical**	**oo**nah koa**may**dhyah moossee**kahl**
revue	**una revista**	**oo**nah reh**bhees**tah
thriller	**una película de suspense**	**oo**nah pay**lee**koolah day soos**payn**say
western	**una película del Oeste**	**oo**nah pay**lee**koolah dayl oa**ays**tay
What time does the first evening performance begin?	**¿A qué hora empieza la primera función de noche?**	ah kay **oa**rah aym**pyay**thah lah pree**may**rah foon**thyon** day **noa**chay
Are there any seats for ...?	**¿Quedan localidades para ...?**	**kay**dhahn loakahlee**dhah**dhayss **pah**rah
How much are the seats?	**¿Cuánto valen las localidades?**	**kwahn**toa **bah**layn lahss loakahlee**dhah**dhayss
I want to reserve 2 seats for the show on Friday evening.	**Quiero reservar 2 localidades para la función del viernes por la noche.**	**kyay**roa rayssayr**bahr** 2 loakahlee**dhah**dhayss **pah**rah lah foon**thyon** dayl **byayr**nayss por lah **noa**chay

DAYS, see page 151

Can I have a seat for the matinée on Tuesday?	**¿Me puede dar una localidad para la sesión de tarde del martes?**	may **pway**dhay dahr **oo**nah loakahlee**dhahdh pah**rah lah say**ssyon** day **tahr**day dayl **mahr**tayss
I want a seat in the stalls (orchestra).	**Quiero una localidad de platea.**	**kyay**roa **oo**nah loakahlee**dhahdh** day plah**tay**ah
Not too far back.	**No muy atrás.**	noa mwee ah**trahss**
Somewhere in the middle.	**En algún lugar en el medio.**	ayn ahl**goon** loo**gar** ayn ayl **may**dhyoa
How much are the seats in the circle (mezzanine)?	**¿Cuánto valen las localidades de anfiteatro?**	**kwahn**toa **bah**layn lahss loakahlee**dhah**dhayss day ahnfeetay**ah**troa
May I please have a programme?	**¿Me da un programa, por favor?**	may dah oon proa**grah**mah por fah**bhor**

Lo siento, las localidades están agotadas.	I'm sorry, we're sold out.
Sólo quedan algunos asientos en el anfiteatro.	There are only a few seats left in the circle (mezzanine).
¿Puedo ver su entrada?	May I see your ticket?
Este es su sitio.	This is your seat.

Opera—Ballet—Concert *Opera – Ballet – Concierto*

Where's the opera house?	**¿Dónde está el Teatro de la Opera?**	**doan**day ay**stah** ayl tay**ah**troa day lah **oa**payrah
Where's the concert hall?	**¿Dónde está la Sala de Conciertos?**	**doan**day ay**stah** lah **sah**lah day kon**thyayr**toass
Can you recommend a ...?	**¿Puede recomendarme ...?**	**pway**dhay raykoamayn**dahr**may
ballet	**un ballet**	oon bah**layt**
concert	**un concierto**	oon kon**thyayr**toa
opera	**una ópera**	**oo**nah **oa**payrah
operetta	**una opereta**	**oo**nah oapay**ray**tah
What's on at the opera tonight?	**¿Qué ópera ponen esta noche?**	kay **oa**payrah **poa**nehn ay**stah noa**chay

Who's singing/ dancing?	**¿Quién canta/baila?**	kyayn **kahn**tah/**bigh**lah
What time does the programme start?	**¿A qué hora empieza el programa?**	ah kay **oa**rah aym**pyay**thah ayl proa**grah**mah
Which orchestra is playing?	**¿Qué orquesta toca?**	kay oar**kay**stah **toa**kah
What are they playing?	**¿Qué tocan?**	kay **toa**kahn
Who's the conductor?	**¿Quién es el director?**	kyayn ayss ayl deerehk**tor**

Nightclubs *Centros nocturnos*

Nightclubs—with dinner, dancing and a floor show—are found only in major cities and popular resorts. But you'll certainly want to experience the informal atmosphere of a *bodega* or *taberna*. Some of them are found in candlelit cellars or in bars where a tiny space has been set aside for entertainment. While sipping a sherry or Spanish brandy, you might watch fiery flamenco dancing or listen to melancholy guitar music.

Can you recommend a good nightclub?	**¿Puede recomendarme un buen centro nocturno?**	**pway**dhay raykoamayn**dahr**may oon bwayn **thayn**troa noak**toor**noa
Is there a floor show?	**¿Hay atracciones?**	igh ahtrahk**thyo**nayss
What time does the floor show start?	**¿A qué hora empiezan las atracciones?**	ah kay **oa**rah aym**pyay**thahn lahss ahtrahk**thyo**nayss
Is evening attire necessary?	**¿Se necesita traje de noche?**	say naythay**ssee**tah **trah**khay day **noa**chay

Disco *Discoteca*

Where can we go dancing?	**¿Dónde podemos ir a bailar?**	**doan**day poa**dhay**moass eer ah bigh**lahr**
Is there a discotheque in town?	**¿Hay alguna discoteca en la ciudad?**	igh ahl**goo**nah deeskoa**tay**kah ayn lah thyoo**dhahdh**
May I have this dance?	**¿Me permite este baile?**	may payr**mee**tay **ay**stay **bigh**lay

Bullfight *La corrida*

The *corrida* (literally "running of the bulls") will either fascinate you or appal you. To a Spaniard, a bullfight is not a choice of life and death for the bull. It is simply an opportunity for it to die heroically.

In some ways the spectacle resembles a ballet. There are colourful moments when the procession *(paseo)* arrives. The entry of the bull into the arena is a moment of high suspense. The movements of cape and bullfighter are graceful and precise.

The *matador* and his team of assistants goad the bull so as to assess its reactions to the cape. A *picador* weakens the bull by piercing its neck muscles with a lance.

A *banderillero* then confronts the animal. At great peril, he thrusts three sets of barbed sticks between its shoulder blades. Throughout each stage of the performance, the Spanish crowd will be watching critically for the finer points—weighing the fearlessness of bull and man, and the *matador's* skill as he executes a series of dangerous passes, leading up to the final climax of the kill.

You may well find the whole performance cruel. Should death be a public spectacle? Disturbing, too, is the treatment of the *picador*'s horse. Although protected by padding, he catches the repeated fury of the bull's charge and horns. The horse takes this in silence, incidentally, because his vocal cords have been cut.

You'll be asked whether you want a seat in the sun or shade *(sol o sombra)*. Be sure to specify *sombra,* for the Spanish sun is hot. Rent a cushion for the hard concrete stands.

I'd like to see a bullfight.	**Quisiera ver una corrida.**	keessyayrah behr oonah korreedhah
I want a seat in the shade/in the sun.	**Quisiera una localidad de sombra/de sol.**	keessyayrah oonah loakahleedhahdh day soambrah/day sol
I'd like to rent a cushion.	**Quisiera alquilar una almohadilla.**	keessyayrah ahlkeelahr oonah ahlmoaahdheelyah

Sports *Deportes*

Football (soccer) and *pelota* are as popular in Spain as bullfighting. *Pelota* is similar to handball but instead of a glove, the players wear a curved wicker basket *(cesta)*. The ball *(pelota)* is hard and covered with goatskin. It can be played off the back and side walls as well as the front. Caught in the *cesta,* and hurled at the wall with great force, it bounces with extraordinary speed. Usually played in the late afternoon or evening, *pelota* is well worth watching. In Latin America, the game is known as *jai alai* (the Basque word for the sport).

In spring and fall, there's good horse racing in Madrid, San Sebastián and Sevilla. Besides, facilities abound to go fishing—even deep-sea fishing hunting, golfing, swimming, sailing, windsurfing or play tennis.

Though one wouldn't think of going to Spain to ski, you can don your ski togs from December to April in the Catalonian Pyrenees, near Madrid and in the Sierra Nevada near Granada.

Is there a football (soccer) match anywhere today?	**¿Hay algún partido de fútbol hoy?**	igh ahl**goon** pahr**tee**dhoa day **foot**bol oy
Who's playing?	**¿Quiénes juegan?**	**kyay**nayss **khway**gahn
Can you get me 2 tickets?	**¿Puede conseguirme 2 entradas?**	**pway**dhay konsay**geer**may 2 ayn**trah**dhahss

basketball	**el baloncesto**	ayl bahloan**thays**toa
boxing	**el boxeo**	ayl boak**say**oa
cycling	**el ciclismo**	ayl thee**klees**moa
dog racing	**las carreras de galgos**	lahs kahr**ray**rahss day **gahl**goass
horse riding	**la equitación**	lah aykeetah**thyon**
skiing	**el esquí**	ayl ays**kee**
swimming	**la natación**	lah nahtah**thyon**
volleyball	**el balonvolea**	ayl bahloanboa**lay**ah

I'd like to see a pelota match.	**Quisiera ver un partido de pelota.**	kee**ssyay**rah behr oon pahr**tee**dhoa day pay**loa**tah
Where's the nearest golf course?	**¿Dónde está el campo de golf más cercano?**	**doan**day ays**tah** ayl **kahm**poa day goalf mahss thehr**kah**noa
Can we hire (rent) clubs?	**¿Podemos alquilar los palos?**	poa**dhay**moass ahlkee**lahr** loss **pah**loass
Where are the tennis courts?	**¿Dónde están las pistas de tenis?**	**doan**day ays**tahn** lahss **pees**tahss day **tay**neess
Can I hire rackets?	**¿Puedo alquilar raquetas?**	**pway**dhoa ahlkee**lahr** rah**kay**tahss
What's the charge per ...?	**¿Cuánto cuesta por ...?**	**kwahn**toa **kways**tah por
day/round/hour	**día/juego/hora**	**dee**ah/**khway**goa/**oa**rah
Where's the nearest race course (track)?	**¿Dónde está la pista de carreras más cercana?**	**doan**day ays**tah** lah **pees**tah day kahr**ray**rahss mahss thehr**kah**nah
What's the admission charge?	**¿Cuánto vale la entrada?**	**kwahn**toa **bah**lay lah ayn**trah**dhah
Is there a swimming pool here?	**¿Hay una piscina aquí?**	igh **oo**nah pees**thee**nah ah**kee**
Is it open-air/ indoors?	**¿Está al aire libre/ Es cubierta?**	ays**tah** ahl **igh**ray **lee**bray/ ayss koo**bhyayr**tah
Can one swim in the lake/river?	**¿Se puede nadar en el lago/río?**	say **pway**dhay nah**dhahr** ayn ayl **lah**goa/**ree**oa
Is there a sandy beach?	**¿Hay una playa de arena?**	igh **oo**nah **plah**yah day ah**ray**nah
Is there any good fishing/hunting around here?	**¿Hay un buen lugar para pescar/cazar en los alrededores?**	igh oon bwayn loo**gahr** **pah**rah pays**kahr**/kah**thahr** ayn loass ahlraydhay**dhoa**rayss
Do I need a permit?	**¿Se requiere permiso?**	say ray**kyay**ray payr**mee**ssoa
Where can I get one?	**¿Dónde puedo conseguir uno?**	**doan**day **pway**dhoa konsay**geer** **oo**noa
What are the skiing conditions like at ...?	**¿Cómo están las condiciones para esquiar en ...?**	**koa**moa ays**tahn** lahss kondee**thyo**nayss **pah**rah ays**kyahr** ayn
Are there ski lifts?	**¿Hay telesquís?**	igh taylays**keess**

On the beach *En la playa*

Is it safe for swimming?	**¿Se puede nadar sin peligro?**	say **pway**dhay nah**dhahr** seen peh**lee**groa
Is there a lifeguard?	**¿Hay vigilante?**	igh beekhee**lahn**tay
There are some big waves.	**Hay algunas olas muy grandes.**	igh ahl**goo**nahss **oa**lahss mwee **grahn**dayss
Are there any dangerous currents?	**¿Hay alguna corriente peligrosa?**	igh ahl**goo**nah kor**ryayn**tay pehlee**groa**ssah
Is it safe for children?	**¿Es seguro para los niños?**	ayss seh**goo**roa **pah**rah loos **nee**ñoass
What time is high/ low tide?	**¿A qué hora es la marea alta/baja?**	ah kay **oa**rah ayss lah mah**reh**ah **ahl**tah/**bah**khah
What's the temperature of the water?	**¿Cuál es la temperatura del agua?**	kwahl ayss lah taympayrah**too**rah dayl **ah**gwah
I want to hire a/an/ some ...	**Quiero alquilar ...**	**kyay**roa ahlkee**lahr**
air mattress (raft)	**un colchón neumático**	oon koal**chon** nayoo**mah**teekoa
bathing hut (cabana)	**una cabina**	**oo**nah kah**bhee**nah
deck-chair	**una silla de lona**	**oo**nah **see**lyah day **loa**nah
skin-diving equipment	**un equipo para natación submarina**	oon ay**kee**poa **pah**rah nahtah**thyon** soobmah**ree**nah
sunshade (umbrella)	**una sombrilla**	**oo**nah soam**bree**lyah
surfboard	**una plancha de deslizamiento**	**oo**nah **plahn**chah day daysleethah**myayn**toa
water skis	**unos esquís acuáticos**	**oo**noass ays**keess** ah**kwah**teekoass
Where can I rent a ...?	**¿Dónde puedo alquilar ...?**	**doan**day **pway**dhoa ahlkee**lahr**
canoe	**una canoa**	**oo**nah kah**noa**ah
motorboat	**una motora**	**oo**nah moa**toa**rah
rowing-boat	**una barca**	**oo**nah **bahr**kah
sailing-boat	**un velero**	oon bay**leh**roa
What's the charge per hour?	**¿Cuánto cobran por hora?**	**kwahn**toa **koa**brahn por **oa**rah

PLAYA PARTICULAR	PRIVATE BEACH
PROHIBIDO BAÑARSE	NO SWIMMING

Making friends

Introductions *Presentaciones*

How do you do? (Pleased to meet you.)	**Encantado(a)* de conocerle.**	aynkahn**tah**dhoa(ah) day koanoa**thayr**lay
How are you?	**¿Cómo está usted?**	**koa**moa ays**tah** oos**taydh**
Fine, thanks. And you?	**Bien, gracias. ¿Y usted?**	byayn **grah**thyahss. ee oos**taydh**
May I introduce ...	**Quiero presentarle a ...**	**kyay**roa prayssayn**tahr**lay ah
My name's ...	**Me llamo ...**	may **lyah**moa
What's your name?	**¿Cómo se llama?**	**koa**moa say **lyah**mah
Glad to know you.	**Tanto gusto.**	**tahn**toa **goos**toa

Follow-up *Continuación ...*

How long have you been here?	**¿Cuánto tiempo lleva usted aquí?**	**kwahn**toa **tyaym**poa **lyay**bhah oos**taydh** ah**kee**
We've been here a week.	**Llevamos aquí una semana.**	lyay**bhah**moass ah**kee** **oo**nah say**mah**nah
Is this your first visit?	**¿Es la primera vez que viene?**	ayss lah pree**may**rah behth kay **byay**nay
No, we came here last year.	**No, vinimos el año pasado.**	noa bee**nee**moass ayl **ah**ñoa pah**ssah**dhoa
Are you enjoying your stay?	**¿Está disfrutando de su estancia?**	ays**tah** deesfroo**tahn**doa day soo ays**tahn**thyah
Yes, I like ... very much.	**Sí, me gusta mucho ...**	see may **goos**tah **moo**choa
Where do you come from?	**¿De dónde es usted?**	day **doan**day ayss oos**taydh**
I'm from ...	**Soy de ...**	soy day
Where are you staying?	**¿Dónde se hospeda?**	**doan**day say os**peh**dhah

*A woman would say *encantada*

COUNTRIES, see page 146

Are you on your own?	**¿Ha venido usted solo/sola?**	ah bay**nee**dhoa oos**taydh** **soa**loa/**soa**lah
I'm with my ...	**Estoy con ...**	ays**toy** kon
husband	**mi marido**	mee mah**ree**dhoa
wife	**mi mujer**	mee moo**khehr**
family	**mi familia**	mee fah**mee**lyah
parents	**mis padres**	meess **pah**drayss
boyfriend	**mi amigo**	mee ahmeegoa
girlfriend	**mi amiga**	mee ahmeegah

father/mother	**el padre/la madre**	ayl **pah**dray/lah **mah**dray
son/daughter	**el hijo/la hija**	ayl **ee**khoa/lah **ee**khah
brother/sister	**el hermano/ la hermana**	ayl ayr**mah**noa/ lah ayr**mah**nah
uncle/aunt	**el tío/la tía**	ayl **tee**oa/lah **tee**ah
nephew/niece	**el sobrino/la sobrina**	ayl soa**bree**noa/ lah soa**bree**nah
cousin	**el primo/la prima**	ayl **pree**moa/lah **pree**mah

Are you married/ single?	**¿Está casado(a)/ soltero(a)*?**	ays**tah** kah**ssah**dhoa(ah) soal**tay**roa(ah)
Do you have children?	**¿Tiene niños?**	**tyay**nay **nee**ñoass
What's your occupation?	**¿Cuál es su ocupación?**	kwahl ays soo oakoopah**thyon**
I'm a student.	**Soy estudiante.**	soy aystoo**dhyahn**tay
I'm here on a business trip.	**Estoy aquí en viaje de negocios.**	ays**toy** ah**kee** ayn **byah**khay day nay**goa**thyoass
We hope to see you again soon.	**Esperamos verle pronto por aquí.**	ayspay**rah**moass **bayr**lay **proan**toa por ah**kee**
See you later/See you tomorrow.	**Hasta luego/Hasta mañana.**	**ah**stah **lway**goa/**ah**stah mah**ñah**nah

The weather *El tiempo*

What a lovely day!	**¡Qué día tan bueno!**	kay **dee**ah tahn **bway**noa
What awful weather!	**¡Qué tiempo más malo!**	kay **tyaym**poa mahss **mah**loa

* If addressing a woman *casada/soltera*

Is it usually as cold/ warm as this?	**¿Hace normalmente este frío/calor?**	**ah**thay noarmahl**mayn**tay **ay**stay **free**oa/kah**lor**
Do you think it'll ... tomorrow?	**¿Cree usted que ... mañana?**	**kray**eh oos**taydh** kay ... mah**ñah**nah
rain/snow	**lloverá/nevará**	lyoabhay**rah**/naybhah**rah**
clear up/be sunny	**hará mejor/hará sol**	ah**rah** meh**khor**/ah**rah** sol
be windy/cloudy	**hará viento/estará nublado**	ah**rah** **byayn**toa/aystah**rah** noo**blah**dhoa

Invitations *Invitaciones*

Would you like to have dinner with us on ...?	**¿Quiere acompañar-nos a cenar en ...?**	**kyay**ray ahkoampah**ñahr**-noass ah thay**nahr** ayn
May I invite you for lunch?	**¿Puedo invitarlo/la a almorzar?**	**pway**dhoa eenbee**tahr**-loa/lah ah ahlmoar**thahr**
Can you come over for a drink this evening?	**¿Puede usted venir a tomar una copa esta noche?**	**pway**dhay oos**taydh** bay**neer** ah toa**mahr** **oo**nah **koa**pah **ay**stah **noa**chay
That's very kind of you.	**Es usted muy amable.**	ayss oos**taydh** mwee ah**mah**blay
What time shall we come?	**¿A qué hora vamos?**	ah kay **oa**rah **bah**moass
May I bring a friend?	**¿Puedo llevar a un amigo/una amiga?**	**pway**dhoa lyay**bhar** ah oon ah**mee**goa/**oo**nah ah**mee**gah
I'm afraid we've got to leave now.	**Me temo que debemos marchar-nos ahora.**	may **tay**moa kay day**bhay**-moass mahr**chahr**noass ahoarah
Next time you must come to visit us.	**Otro día tienen que venir ustedes a vernos.**	**oa**troa **dee**ah **tyay**nayn kay bay**neer** oos**tay**dhayss ah **bayr**noass
Thanks for the evening. It was great.	**Muchas gracias por la velada. Ha sido estupenda.**	**moo**chahss **grah**thyahss por lah bay**lah**dhah. ah **see**dhoa aystoo**payn**dah

Dating *Citas*

Would you like a cigarette?	**¿Quiere usted un cigarrillo?**	**kyay**ray oos**taydh** oon theegahr**ree**lyoa
Do you have a light, please?	**¿Tiene usted lumbre, por favor?**	**tyay**nay oos**taydh** **loom**bray por fah**bhor**

DAYS, see page 151

Can I get you a drink?	**¿Quiere usted beber algo?**	kyayray oostaydh baybhayr ahlgoa
Are you waiting for someone?	**¿Está usted esperando a alguien?**	aystah oostaydh ayspayrahndoa ah ahlgyayn
Do you mind if I sit down here?	**¿Le importa si me siento aquí?**	lay eempoartah see may syayntoa ahkee
Are you free this evening?	**¿Está usted libre esta tarde?**	aystah oostaydh leebray aystah tahrday
Would you like to go out with me tonight?	**¿Quisiera usted salir conmigo esta noche?**	keessyayrah oostaydh sahleer konmeegoa aystah noachay
Would you like to go dancing?	**¿Quisiera usted ir a bailar?**	keessyayrah oostaydh eer ah bighlahr
Shall we go to the cinema (movies)?	**¿Quiere que vayamos al cine?**	kyayray kay bahyahmoass ahl theenay
Would you like to go for a drive?	**¿Quiere usted dar un paseo en coche?**	kyayray oostaydh dahr oon pahssayoa ayn koachay
Where shall we meet?	**¿Dónde nos encontramos?**	doanday noss aynkontrahmoass
What's your address/ telephone number?	**¿Cuál es su dirección/ número de teléfono?**	kwahl ayss soo deeraykthyon/noomayroa day taylayfoanoa
I'll call for you at 8 o'clock.	**Iré a recogerla a las 8.**	eeray ah rehkohkhayrlah ah lahss 8
May I take you home?	**¿Puedo acompañarla hasta su casa?**	pwaydhoa ahkoampahñahrlah ahstah soo kahssah
Can I see you again tomorrow?	**¿Puedo verla mañana?**	pwaydhoa bayrlah mahñahnah

. . . and you might answer:

I'd love to, thank you.	**Me encantaría, gracias.**	may aynkahntahreeah grahthyahss
I've enjoyed myself.	**Lo he pasado muy bien.**	loa ay pahssahdhoa mwee byayn
Thank you, but I'am busy.	**Gracias, pero estoy ocupado(a).**	grathyahss payroa aystoy oakoopahdhoa(ah)
No, thank you, I'd rather not.	**No gracias, mejor no.**	noa grathyahss maykhoar noa

Shopping guide

This shopping guide is designed to help you find what you want with ease, accuracy and speed. It features:

1. A list of all major shops, stores and services (p. 98)
2. Some general expressions required when shopping to allow you to be specific and selective (p. 100)
3. Full details of the shops and services most likely to concern you, grouped under the headings below.

LAUNDRY, see page 29/HAIRDRESSER'S, see page 30

Shops and services *Comercios y servicios*

Shopping hours: 9.30 a.m. to 1.30 p.m. and 4 to 8 p.m. Monday to Friday, 9.30 a.m. to 2 p.m. on Saturdays; department stores are generally open from 10 a.m. to 8 p.m. without a break, Monday to Saturday.

Where's the nearest ...?	**¿Dónde está ... más cercano/cercana?**	doanday ay**stah** ... mahss thayr**kah**noa/thayr**kah**nah
antique shop	**la tienda de antigüedades**	lah **tyayn**dah day ahnteegway**dhah**dhayss
art gallery	**la galería de arte**	lah gahlay**ree**ah day **ahr**tay
baker's	**la panadería**	lah pahnahdhay**ree**ah
bank	**el banco**	ayl **bahn**koa
barber's	**la barbería**	lah bahrbay**ree**ah
beauty salon	**el salón de belleza**	ayl sah**lon** day bay**lyay**thah
bookshop	**la librería**	lah leebray**ree**ah
butcher's	**la carnicería**	lah kahrneethay**ree**ah
cake shop	**la pastelería**	lah pahstaylay**ree**ah
camera shop	**la tienda de fotografía**	lah **tyayn**dah day foatoagrah**fee**ah
candy store	**la bombonería**	lah boamboanay**ree**ah
chemist's	**la farmacia**	lah fahr**mah**thyah
confectioner's	**la confitería**	lah konfeethay**ree**ah
dairy	**la lechería**	lah laychay**ree**ah
delicatessen	**la mantequería**	lah mahntaykay**ree**ah
dentist	**el dentista**	ayl dayn**tee**stah
department store	**los grandes almacenes**	loss **grahn**dayss ahlmah**thay**nayss
doctor	**el médico**	ayl **may**deekoa
drugstore	**la farmacia**	lah fahr**mah**thyah
dry cleaner's	**la tintorería**	lah teentoaray**ree**ah
electrician	**el electricista**	ayl aylayktree**thee**stah
fishmonger's	**la pescadería**	lah payskahdhay**ree**ah
flower shop	**la florería**	lah floaray**ree**ah
fruit stand	**la frutería**	lah frootay**ree**ah
furrier's	**la peletería**	lah paylaytay**ree**ah
greengrocer's	**la verdulería**	lah bayrdoolay**ree**ah
grocery	**la tienda de comestibles**	lah **tyayn**dah day koamay**stee**blayss
hairdresser's (ladies)	**la peluquería**	lah paylookay**ree**ah
hardware store	**la ferretería**	lah fehrraytay**ree**ah
health food shop	**la tienda de alimentos dietéticos**	lah **tyayn**dah day ahleemayntoass dyay**tay**teekoass
hospital	**el hospital**	ayl oaspee**tahl**
ironmonger's	**la ferretería**	lah fehrraytay**ree**ah

jeweller's	**la joyería**	lah khoyay**ree**ah
launderette	**la launderama**	lah lahoondayr**ah**mah
laundry	**la lavandería**	lah lahbhahndayr**ee**ah
leather goods store	**la tienda de artículos de cuero**	lah **tyayn**dah day ahr**tee**kooloass day **kway**roa
library	**la biblioteca**	lah beeblyo**tay**kah
market	**el mercado**	ayl mehr**kah**dhoa
newsstand	**el quiosco de periódicos**	ayl **kyos**koa day payr**yo**dheekoass
optician	**el óptico**	ayl **op**teekoa
pastry shop	**la pastelería**	lah pahstaylay**ree**ah
photographer	**el fotógrafo**	ayl foat**oa**grahfoa
police station	**la comisaría**	lah koameessah**ree**ah
post office	**la oficina de correos**	lah oafee**thee**nah day kor**reh**oass
shirt-maker's	**la camisería**	lah kahmeesseh**ree**ah
shoemaker's (repairs)	**el zapatero**	ayl thahpah**tay**roa
shoe shop	**la zapatería**	lah thahpahtay**ree**ah
shopping centre	**el centro comercial**	ayl **thayn**troa koamayr**thyahl**
souvenir shop	**la tienda de objetos de regalo**	lay **tyayn**dah day oab**khay**toass day ray**gah**loa
sporting goods shop	**la tienda de artículos de deportes**	lah **tyayn**dah day ahr**tee**kooloass day day**por**tayss
stationer's	**la papelería**	lah pahpaylay**ree**ah
supermarket	**el supermercado**	ayl soopayrmayr**kah**dhoa
sweet shop	**la bombonería**	lah boamboanay**ree**ah
tailor's	**el sastre**	ayl **sahs**tray
telephone office	**la oficina de teléfonos**	lah oafee**thee**nah day tay**lay**foanoass
tobacconist's	**el estanco/los tabacos**	ayl ehs**tahn**koa/loss tah**bhah**koass
toy shop	**la juguetería**	lah khoogaytay**ree**ah
travel agency	**la agencia de viajes**	lah ah**khayn**thyah day **byah**khayss
vegetable store	**la verdulería**	lah bayrdoolay**ree**ah
veterinarian	**el veterinario**	ayl baytayree**nah**ryoa
watchmaker's	**la relojería**	lah rehlokhay**ree**ah
wine merchant's	**la tienda de vinos/la bodega**	lah **tyayn**dah day **bee**noass/lah boa**dhay**gah

ENTRADA	ENTRANCE
SALIDA	EXIT
SALIDA DE EMERGENCIA	EMERGENCY EXIT

Where? *¿Dónde?*

Where's a good ...?	**¿Dónde hay un buen/una buena ...?**	**doan**day igh oon bwayn/ **oo**nah **bway**nah
Where can I find a ...?	**¿Dónde puedo encontrar un/una ...?**	**doan**day **pway**dhoa aynkoan**trahr** oon/**oo**nah
Where do they sell ...?	**¿Dónde venden ...?**	**doan**day **bayn**dayn
Where's the main shopping area?	**¿Dónde está la zona de tiendas más importante?**	**doan**day ay**stah** lah **thoa**nah day **tyayn**dahss mahss eempoar**tahn**tay
Is it far from here?	**¿Está muy lejos de aquí?**	ay**stah** mwee **leh**khoass day ah**kee**
How do I get there?	**¿Cómo puedo llegar allí?**	**koa**moa **pway**dhoa lyay**gahr** ah**lyee**

Service *Servicio*

Can you help me?	**¿Puede usted atenderme?**	**pway**dhay oos**taydh** ahtayn**dayr**may
I'm just looking.	**Estoy sólo mirando.**	ay**stoy** **soa**loa mee**rahn**doa
I want ...	**Quiero ...**	**kyay**roa
Do you have any ...?	**¿Tiene usted ...?**	**tyay**nay oos**taydh**
Where is the ... department?	**¿Dónde está el departamento de ...?**	**doan**day ay**stah** ayl daypahrtah**mayn**toa day
Where's the lift (elevator)/escalator?	**¿Dónde está el ascensor/la escalera mecánica?**	**doan**day ay**stah** ayl ahsthayn**soar**/lah ayskah**lay**rah may**kah**neekah
Where do I pay?	**¿Dónde pago?**	**doan**day **pah**goa

That one *Ese*

Can you show me ...?	**¿Puede usted enseñarme ...?**	**pway**dhay oos**taydh** aynsay**ñahr**may
that/those	**ése/ésos**	**ay**ssay/**ay**ssoass
the one in the window/in the display case	**el del escaparate/ de la vitrina**	ayl dayl ehskahpah**rah**tay/ day lah bee**tree**nah
It's over there.	**Está allí.**	ay**stah** ah**lyee**

Preference *Preferencias*

Can you show me some more?	**¿Puede usted enseñarme algo más?**	**pway**dhay oos**taydh** ayn-sayñ**ahr**may **ahl**goa mahss
Haven't you anything ...?	**¿No tiene usted algo ...?**	noa **tyay**nay oos**taydh** **ahl**goa
cheaper/better	**más barato/mejor**	mahss bah**rah**toa/meh**khor**
larger/smaller	**más grande/más pequeño**	mahss **grahn**day/mahss pay**kay**ñoa
more/less colourful	**más/menos colorido**	mahss/**may**noass koaloa**ree**dhoa

big	**grande***	**grahn**day
cheap	**barato**	bah**rah**toa
dark	**oscuro**	os**koo**roa
good	**bueno**	**bway**noa
heavy	**pesado**	pay**ssah**dhoa
large	**grande**	**grahn**day
light (weight)	**ligero**	lee**khay**roa
light (colour)	**claro**	**klah**roa
rectangular	**rectangular**	rehktahngoo**lahr**
round	**redondo**	ray**dhon**doa
small	**pequeño**	pay**kay**ñoa
square	**cuadrado**	kwah**drah**dhoa

How much? *¿Cuánto cuesta?*

How much is this?	**¿Cuánto cuesta esto?**	**kwahn**toa **kways**tah **ays**toa
I don't understand.	**No entiendo.**	noa ayn**tyayn**doa
Please write it down.	**Escríbamelo, por favor.**	ays**kree**bhahmayloa por fah**bhor**
I don't want anything too expensive.	**No quiero algo muy caro.**	noa **kay**roa **ahl**goa mwee **kah**roa
I don't want to spend more than ...	**No quiero gastar más de ...**	noa **kyay**roa gahs**tahr** mahss day ...

REBAJAS SALE

* For feminine and plural forms, see grammar section page 159 (adjectives).

COLOURS, see page 113

Decision *Decisión*

It's not quite what I want.	**No es realmente lo que quiero.**	noa ayss rehahl**mayn**tay loa kay **kyay**roa
No, I don't like it.	**No, no me gusta.**	noa noa may **goos**tah
I'll take it.	**Me lo llevo.**	may loa **lyay**bhoa

Anything else? *¿Algo más?*

No, thanks, that's all.	**No gracias, eso es todo.**	noa **grah**thyahss **ay**ssoa ayss **toa**dhoa
Yes, I want ...	**Sí, quiero ...**	see **kyay**roa

Ordering *Encargar*

Can you order it for me?	**¿Puede usted encargarlo para mí?**	**pway**dhay oos**taydh** aynkahr**gahr**loa **pah**rah mee
How long will it take?	**¿Cuánto tardará?**	**kwahn**toa tahrdah**rah**

Delivery *Enviar*

Deliver it to the ... Hotel.	**Envíelo al hotel ...**	ayn**bee**ayloa ahl oa**tehl**
Please send it to this address.	**Por favor, mándelo a estas señas.**	por fah**bhor mahn**dayloa ah **ay**stahss **say**ñahss
Do I have to pay the sales tax?	**¿Tengo que pagar el impuesto?**	**tayn**goa kay pah**gahr** ayl eem**pwayss**toa
Will I have any difficulty with the customs?	**¿Tendré alguna dificultad con la aduana?**	tayn**dray** ahl**goo**nah deefeekool**tahdh** kon lah ah**dwah**nah

Paying *Pagar*

How much is it?	**¿Cuánto es?**	**kwahn**toa ayss
Can I pay by traveller's cheque?	**¿Puedo pagar con cheque de viajero?**	**pway**dhoa pah**gahr** kon **chay**kay day byah**khay**roa
Do you accept dollars/ pounds/credit cards?	**¿Acepta usted dólares/libras/ tarjetas de crédito?**	ah**thayp**tah oos**taydh doa**lahrayss/**lee**brahss/tahr**khay**tahss day **kray**dheetoa

Haven't you made a mistake in the bill?	**¿No se ha equivocado usted en la cuenta?**	noa say ah aykeebhoa**kah**dhoa oos**taydh** ayn lah **kwayn**tah
Will you please wrap it?	**¿Me hace el favor de envolverlo?**	may **ah**thay ayl fah**bhor** day aynboal**behr**loa
May I have a bag, please?	**¿Puede darme una bolsa, por favor?**	**pway**day **dahr**may **oo**nah **boal**sah por fah**bhor**

Dissatisfied *Descontento*

Can you please exchange this?	**¿Podría usted cambiarme esto, por favor?**	poa**dree**ah oos**taydh** kahm**byahr**may **ays**toa por fah**bhor**
I want to return this.	**Quiero devolver esto.**	**kyay**roa daybhol**behr** **ays**toa
I'd like a refund. Here's the receipt.	**Quisiera que me devolviesen el dinero. Aquí está el recibo.**	kee**ssyay**rah kay may daybhol**byays**sayn ayl dee**nay**roa. ah**kee** ays**tah** ayl ray**thee**bhoa

¿En qué puedo ayudarle?	Can I help you?
¿Qué desea?	What would you like?
¿Qué ... desea?	What ... would you like?
color/forma calidad/cantidad	colour/shape quality/quantity
Lo siento, no lo tenemos.	I'm sorry, we haven't any.
Se nos ha agotado.	We're out of stock.
¿Quiere que se lo encarguemos?	Shall we order it for you?
¿Lo llevará consigo o se lo enviamos?	Will you take it with you or shall we send it?
¿Algo más?	Anything else?
Son ... pesetas, por favor.	That's ... pesetas, please.
La caja está allí.	The cashier's over there.

Bookshop—Stationer's *Librería – Papelería*

In Spain, bookshops and stationer's are usually separate shops, though the latter will often sell paperbacks. Newspapers and magazines are sold at newsstands.

Where's the nearest ...?	**¿Dónde está ... más cercano/cercana?**	**doan**day ay**stah** ... mahss thehr**kah**noa/thehr**kah**nah
bookshop	**la librería**	lah leebray**ree**ah
stationer's	**la papelería**	lah pahpaylay**ree**ah
newsstand	**el quiosco de periódicos**	ayl **kyos**koa day pay**ryo**dheekoass
Where can I buy an English newspaper?	**¿Dónde puedo comprar un periódico inglés?**	**doan**day **pway**dhoa kom**prahr** oon pay**ryo**dheekoa een**glayss**
Where's the guide-book section?	**¿Dónde está la sección de libros-guía?**	**doan**day ay**stah** lah sayk**thyon** day **lee**broass **gee**ah
Where do you keep the English/second-hand books?	**¿Dónde están los libros ingleses/ de segunda mano?**	**doan**day ay**stahn** loss **lee**broass een**glays**sayss/ day say**goon**doa mahnoa
Where can I make photocopies?	**¿Dónde puedo hacer fotocopias?**	**doan**day **pway**dhoa ah**thayr** foatoa**koa**pyahss
I want to buy a/an/ some ...	**Quiero ...**	**kyay**roa
address book	**un librito de direcciones**	oon lee**bree**toa day deerehk**thyo**nayss
ball-point pen	**un bolígrafo**	oon boa**lee**grahfoa
book	**un libro**	oon **lee**broa
calendar	**un calendario**	oon kahlayn**dah**ryoa
carbon paper	**papel carbón**	pah**pehl** kahr**bon**
cellophane tape	**cinta adhesiva**	**theen**tah ahday**ssee**bhah
crayons	**unos lápices de color**	**oo**noas lah**pee**thayss day koa**loar**
dictionary	**un diccionario**	oon deekthyoa**nah**ryoa
Spanish-English	**Español-Inglés**	ayspah**ñoal**-een**glayss**
drawing paper	**papel de dibujo**	pah**pehl** day dee**bhoo**khoa
drawing pins	**chinchetas**	cheen**chay**tahss
envelopes	**unos sobres**	**oo**noas **soa**brayss
eraser	**una goma de borrar**	**oo**nah **goa**mah day bor**rahr**
exercise book	**un cuaderno**	oon kwah**dher**noa
felt-tip pen	**un rotulador**	oon roatoolah**dhoar**
file	**una carpeta**	**oo**nah kahr**pay**tah
fountain pen	**una pluma estilográfica**	**oo**nah **ploo**mah aysteeloa**grah**feekah

glue	**cola de pegar**	**koa**lah day pay**gahr**
grammar book	**un libro de gramática**	con **lee**broa day grah**mah**teekah
guidebook	**una guía**	**oo**nah **gee**ah
ink	**tinta**	**tee**ntah
black/red/blue	**negra/roja/azul**	**nay**grah/**roa**khah/ah**thool**
(adhesive) labels	**unas etiquetas (adhesivas)**	**oo**nahss aytee**kay**tahss (ahday**ssee**bhahss)
magazine	**una revista**	**oo**nah ray**bhee**s**tah**
map	**un mapa**	oon **mah**pah
of the town	**de la ciudad**	day lay thyoo**dhahdh**
road map of ...	**de carreteras de ...**	day kahrray**tay**rahss day
newspaper	**un periódico**	oon pay**ryo**dheekoa
American/English	**americano/inglés**	ahmayree**kah**noa/een**glayss**
notebook	**un cuaderno**	oon kwah**dhehr**noa
note paper	**papel de cartas**	pah**pehl** day **kahr**tahss
paperback	**una rústica**	**oo**nah **roos**teekah
paper napkins	**unas servilletas de papel**	**oo**nahss sayrbee**lyay**tahss day pah**pehl**
paintbox	**una caja de pinturas**	**oo**nah **kah**khah day peen**too**rahss
paste	**engrudo**	ayn**groo**dhoa
pen	**una pluma**	**oo**nah **ploo**mah
pencil	**un lápiz**	oon **lah**peeth
pencil sharpener	**un sacapuntas**	oon sahkah**poon**tahss
playing cards	**unas naipes**	**oo**nahss **nigh**payss
pocket calculator	**una calculadora de bolsillo**	**oo**nah kahlkoolah**dhoa**rah day boal**see**lyoa
post cards	**unas tarjetas postales**	**oo**nahss tahr**khay**tahss poas**tah**layss
refill (for a pen)	**un recambio (para pluma)**	oon ray**kahm**byoa (**pah**rah **ploo**mah)
rubber	**una goma de borrar**	**oo**nah **goa**mah day boar**rahr**
ruler	**una regla**	**oo**nah **reh**glah
sketching block	**un bloc de dibujo**	oon bloak day dee**bhoo**khoa
staples	**unas grapas**	**oo**nahs **grah**pahss
string	**una cuerda**	**oo**nah **kwayr**dah
thumbtacks	**chinchetas**	cheen**chay**tahss
tissue paper	**papel de seda**	pah**pehl** day **say**dhah
tracing paper	**papel transparente**	pah**pehl** trahnspah**rayn**tay
typewriter ribbon	**una cinta para máquina**	**oo**nah **theen**tah **pah**rah **mah**keenah
typing paper	**papel de máquina**	pah**pehl** day **mah**keenah
wrapping paper	**papel de envolver**	pah**pehl** day aynboal**behr**
writing pad	**un bloc de papel**	oon bloak day pah**pehl**

Camping equipment *Equipo de camping*

I'd like a/an/some ...	**Quisiera ...**	kee**ssyay**rah
bottle-opener	**un abridor de botellas**	oon ahbree**dhor** day boa**tay**lyahss
bucket	**un cubo**	oon **koo**bhoa
butane gas	**gas butano**	gahss boo**tah**noa
campbed	**una cama de campaña**	oonah **kah**mah day kahm**pah**ñah
can opener	**un abrelatas**	oon ahbray**lah**tahss
candles	**unas velas**	oonahss **bay**lahss
chair	**una silla**	oonah **see**lyah
folding chair	**silla plegable**	**see**lyah play**gah**blay
charcoal	**carbón**	kahr**bon**
clothes pegs	**unas perchas**	oonahss **payr**chahss
compass	**una brújula**	oonah **brookhoo**lah
cool box	**una nevera portátil**	oonah nay**bhay**rah poar**tah**teel
corkscrew	**un sacacorchos**	oon sahkah**koar**choass
crockery	**una vajilla**	oonah bah**khee**lyah
cutlery	**unos cubiertos**	oonoass koob**hyayr**toass
deckchair	**una silla de lona**	oonah **see**lyah day **loa**nah
dishwashing detergent	**detergente para la vajilla**	daytayr**khayn**tay **pah**rah lah bah**khee**lyah
first-aid kit	**un botiquín**	oon boatee**keen**
fishing tackle	**un aparejo de pesca**	oon ahpah**reh**khoa day **pays**kah
flashlight	**una linterna**	oonah leen**tehr**nah
food box	**una fiambrera**	oonah fyahm**bray**rah
frying pan	**una sartén**	oonah sahr**tayn**
groundsheet	**una alfombra (de hule)**	oonah ahl**foam**brah (day **oo**lay)
hammer	**un martillo**	oon mahr**tee**lyoa
ice pack	**un elemento congelable**	oon aylay**mayn**toa koan-khay**lah**blay
kerosene	**petróleo**	pay**troa**lehoa
lamp	**una lámpara**	oonah **lahm**pahrah
matches	**unas cerillas**	oonahss thay**ree**lyahss
mattress	**un colchón**	oon koal**chon**
methylated spirits	**alcohol de quemar**	ahlkoa**ol** day kay**mahr**
mosquito net	**una red para mosquitos**	oonah **raydh** **pah**rah moas**kee**toass
paraffin	**petróleo**	pay**troa**lehoa
penknife	**un cortaplumas**	oon koartah**ploo**mahss
picnic basket	**una bolsa para merienda**	oonah **boal**sah **pah**rah may**ryayn**dah

English	Spanish	Pronunciation
plastic bags	**unas bolsas de plástico**	**oo**nahss **boal**sahss day **plahs**teekoa
rope	**una cuerda**	**oo**nah **kwayr**dah
rucksack	**una mochila**	**oo**nah moa**chee**lah
saucepan	**un cazo**	oon **kah**thoa
scissors	**unas tijeras**	**oo**nahss tee**khay**rahss
screwdriver	**un destornillador**	oon daystoarneelyah**dhor**
sleeping bag	**un saco de dormir**	oon **sah**koa day doar**meer**
stew pot	**una cacerola**	**oo**nah kahthay**roa**lah
table	**una mesa**	**oo**nah **may**ssah
folding table	**mesa plegable**	**may**ssah play**gah**blay
tent	**una tienda de campaña**	**oo**nah **tyayn**dah day kahm**pah**ñah
tent peg	**una estaca**	**oo**nah ehs**tah**kah
tent pole	**un mástil**	oon **mahs**teel
tinfoil	**papel de estaño**	pah**pehl** day ays**tah**ñoa
tin opener	**un abrelatas**	oon ahbray**lah**tahss
tool kit	**una caja de herramientas**	**oo**nah **kah**khah day ehrrah**myayn**tahss
torch	**una linterna**	**oo**nah leen**tehr**nah
vacuum flask	**un termo**	oon **tayr**moa
washing powder	**jabón en polvo**	khah**bhoan** ayn **poal**boa
washing-up liquid	**detergente para la vajilla**	daytayr**khayn**tay **pah**rah lah bah**khee**lyah
water flask	**una cantimplora**	**oo**nah kahnteem**ploa**rah
wood alcohol	**alcohol de quemar**	ahlkoa**ol** day kay**mahr**

Crockery *Vajilla*

English	Spanish	Pronunciation
cups	**unas tazas**	**oo**nahss **tah**thahss
mugs	**unas tazas altas sin plato**	**oo**nahss **tah**thahss **ahl**tahss seen **plah**toa
plates	**unos platos**	**oo**noass **plah**toass
saucers	**unos platillos**	**oo**noass plah**tee**lyoass

Cutlery *Cubiertos*

English	Spanish	Pronunciation
forks	**unos tenedores**	**oo**noass taynay**dhoa**rayss
knives	**unos cuchillos**	**oo**noass koo**chee**lyoass
spoons	**unas cucharas**	**oo**nahss koo**chah**rahss
teaspoons	**unas cucharillas**	**oo**nahss koochah**ree**lyahss
(made of) plastic	**(de) plástico**	(day) **plahs**teekoa
(made of) stainless steel	**(de) acero inoxidable**	(day) ah**thay**roa eenoakseed**hah**blay

Chemist's (drugstore) *Farmacia*

A Spanish chemist's normally doesn't stock the range of items that you'll find in England or in the U.S. For example, he doesn't sell photographic equipment or books. And for perfume, make-up, etc., you must go to a *perfumería* (payrfoomay**ree**ah).

This section has been divided into two parts:

1. Pharmaceutical—medicine, first-aid, etc.
2. Toiletry—toilet articles, cosmetics

Where's the nearest (all-night) chemist's?	**¿Dónde está la farmacia (de guardia) más cercana?**	**doan**day ay**stah** lah fahr**mah**thyah (day **gwahr**dyah) mahss thehr**kah**nah
What time does the chemist's open/ close?	**¿A qué hora abren/ cierran la farmacia?**	ah kay **oa**rah **ah**brayn/ **thye**rrahn lah fahr**mah**thyah

1—Pharmaceutical *Productos farmacéuticos*

I want something for ...	**Quiero algo para ...**	**kyay**roa **ahl**goa **pah**rah
a cold/a cough	**un resfriado/una tos**	oon rays**fryah**dhoa/**oo**nah toss
hay fever	**la fiebre del heno**	lah **fyeh**bray dayl **ay**noa
a hangover	**la resaca**	lah ray**ssah**kah
insect bites	**las picaduras de insecto**	lahss peekah**dhoo**rahss day een**sayk**toa
sunburn	**las quemaduras del sol**	lahss kaymah**dhoo**rahss dayl sol
travel sickness	**el mareo**	ayl mah**reh**oa
an upset stomach	**las molestias de estómago**	lahss moa**lays**tyahss day ay**stoa**mahgoa
How many do I take?	**¿Cuántos(as) debo tomar?**	**kwanh**toass(ahss) **day**bhoa toa**mahr**
Can you make up this prescription for me?	**¿Puede usted prepararme esta receta?**	**pway**dhay oos**taydh** praypah**rahr**may **ay**stah ray**thay**tah
Shall I wait?	**¿Espero?**	ay**spay**roa
Can I get it without a prescription?	**¿Puede dármelo sin receta?**	**pway**dhay **dahr**mayloa seen ray**thay**tah

DOCTOR, see page 137

Can I have a/an/ some ...?	¿Puede darme ...?	**pway**dhay **dahr**may
antiseptic cream	una crema antiséptica	oonah **kray**mah ahntee-**ssayp**teekah
aspirins	unas aspirinas	**oo**nahss ahspee**ree**nahss
bandage	una venda	oonah **bayn**dah
elastic bandage	vendas elásticas	**bayn**dahss ay**lahs**teekahss
Band Aids	esparadrapo	ehspahrah**drah**poa
contraceptives	unos anticonceptivos	**oo**noass ahnteekoanthayp-**tee**bhoass
corn plasters	unos callicidas	**oo**noass kahlyee**thee**-dhahss
cotton wool (absorbent cotton)	algodón	ahlgoa**don**
cough drops	unas gotas para la tos	**oo**nahss **goa**tahss **pah**rah lah toss
disinfectant	un desinfectante	oon daysseenfehk**tahn**tay
ear drops	gotas para los oídos	**goa**tahss **pah**rah loss oa**ee**dhoass
Elastoplast	esparadrapo	ehspahrah**drah**poa
eye drops	unas gotas para los ojos	**oo**nahss **goa**tahss **pah**rah loss **okh**oass
gauze	gasa	**gah**ssah
insect repellent/ spray	un repelente/spray para insectos	oon raypay**layn**tay/**ay**sprehy **pah**rah een**sehk**toass
iodine	yodo	**yoa**dhoa
laxative	un laxante	oon lahk**sahn**tay
mouthwash	unos gargarismos	**oo**noass gahrgah**rees**moass
sanitary towels (napkins)	unos paños higiénicos	**oo**noass **pah**ñoass ee**khyay**neekoass
sleeping pills	un somnífero	oon soam**nee**fayroa
suppositories	unos supositorios	**oo**noass soopoassee**toa**ryoass
surgical dressing	unas hilas	**oo**nahss **ee**lahss
... tablets	unas tabletas para ...	**oo**nahs tah**blay**tahss **pah**rah
tampons	unos tampones higiénicos	**oo**noass tahm**poa**nayss ee**khyay**neekoass
thermometer	un termómetro	oon tayr**moa**maytroa
throat lozenges	unas pastillas para la garganta	**oo**nahss pahs**tee**lyahss **pah**rah lah gahr**gahn**tah
tranquillizer	un sedante	oon say**dhahn**tay

¡VENENO!	POISON!
SOLO PARA USO EXTERNO	FOR EXTERNAL USE ONLY

2—Toiletry *Artículos de tocador*

I'd like a/an/some ...	**Quisiera ...**	keessyayrah
acne cream	**una crema para el acné**	oonah kraymah pahrah ayl ahknay
after-shave lotion	**una loción para después del afeitado**	oonah loathyon pahrah dayspwayss dayl ahfaytahdhoa
astringent	**un astringente**	oon ahstreenkhayntay
bath salts	**sales de baño**	sahlayss day bahñoa
cologne	**agua de colonia**	ahgwah day koaloanyah
cream	**una crema**	oonah kraymah
cleansing cream	**limpiadora**	leempyahdhoarah
cold cream	**nutritiva**	nootreeteebhah
foundation cream	**maquillaje**	mahkeelyahkhay
moisturizing cream	**hidratante**	eedrahtahntay
night cream	**de noche**	day noachay
cuticle remover	**un quitacutículas**	oon keetahkooteekoolahss
deodorant	**un desodorante**	oon dayssoadhoarahntay
emery boards	**unas limas de papel**	oonahss leemahss day pahpehl
eye liner	**un perfilador de ojos**	oon pehrfeelahdhor day okhoss
eye pencil	**un lápiz de ojos**	oon lahpeeth day okhoss
eye shadow	**una sombra de ojos**	oonah soambrah day okhoss
face powder	**polvos de la cara**	poalboass day lah kahrah
foot cream	**una crema para los pies**	oonah kraymah pahrah loss pyayss
hand cream/lotion	**una crema/loción para las manos**	oonah kraymah/loathyon pahrah lahss mahnoass
lipsalve	**cacao para los labios**	kahkahoa pahrah loss lahbhyoass
lipstick	**un lápiz de labios**	oon lahpeeth day lahbhyoass
make-up remover pads	**unas toallitas de maquillage**	oonahss toaahlyeetahss day mahkeelyahkhay
mascara	**pintura de pestañas**	peentoorah day pehstahñahss
nail clippers	**alicates de uñas**	ahleekahtayss day ooñahss
nail file	**una lima de uñas**	oonah leemah day ooñahss
nail polish	**un esmalte de uñas**	oon ehsmahltay day ooñahss
nail polish remover	**acetona quita-esmalte de uñas**	ahthaytoanah keetahehsmahltay day ooñahss
nail scissors	**tijeras de uñas**	teekhayrahss day ooñahss
perfume	**perfume**	pehrfoomay

owder	**polvos**	poalboass
azor	**una máquina (navaja) de afeitar**	oonah mahkeenah (nahbhahkhah) day ahfaytahr
azor blades	**unas hojas de afeitar**	oonahss oakhahss day ahfaytahr
ouge (blusher)	**colorete**	koaloaraytay
afety pins	**unos imperdibles**	oonoass eempehrdeeblayss
having cream	**crema de afeitar**	kraymah day afaytahr
oap	**jabón**	khahbhon
ponge	**una esponja**	oonah ehsponkhah
un-tan cream	**una crema solar**	oonah kraymah soalahr
alcum powder	**polvos de talco**	poalboass day tahlkoa
issues	**unos pañuelos de papel**	oonoass pahñwayloass day pahpehl
oilet paper	**papel higiénico**	pahpehl eekhyayneekoa
oothbrush	**un cepillo de dientes**	oon thaypeelyoa day dyayntayss
oothpaste	**pasta de dientes**	pahstah day dyayntayss
weezers	**unas pinzas**	oonahss peenthahss

or your hair *Para su cabello*

colour shampoo	**un champú colorante**	oon champoo koaloarahntay
comb	**un peine**	oon paynay
dye	**una tintura**	oonah teentoorah
hairbrush	**un cepillo para el pelo**	oon thaypeelyoa pahrah ayl pehloa
hairgrips (bobby pins)	**unas horquillas de pinza**	oonahss orkeelyahss day peenthah
hair lotion	**un loción capilar**	oonah loathyon kahpeelahr
hair spray	**una laca para el pelo**	oonah lahkah pahrah ayl payloa
hairpins	**unas horquillas**	oonahss oarkeelyahss
ollers	**unos rulos**	oonoass rooloass
setting lotion	**un fijador**	oon feekhahdhoar
dry) shampoo for dry/greasy (oily) hair	**un champú (seco) para cabellos secos/grasos**	oon chahmpoo (saykoa) pahrah kahbhaylyoass saykoass/grahssoass
int	**un tinte**	oon teentay

or the baby *Para el bebé*

baby food	**alimento para bebé**	ahleemayntoa pahrah baybhay
bib	**un babero**	oon bahbhayroa
dummy (pacifier)	**un chupete**	oon choopaytay
eeding bottle	**un biberón**	oon beebhayroan
nappies (diapers)	**pañales**	pahñahlayss
eat (nipple)	**una tetina**	oonah tayteenah

Clothing *Prendas de vestir*

If you want to buy something specific, prepare yourself in advance. Look at the list of clothing on page 117. Get some idea of the colour, material and size you want. They're all listed on the next few pages.

I'd like ...	**Quisiera ...**	kee**ss**yayrah
I want ... for a 10 year-old boy/girl.	**Quiero ... para un niño/una niña de 10 años.**	**kyay**roa ... **pah**rah oon **nee**ñoa/oonah **nee**ñah day 10 **ah**ñoass
I want something like this.	**Quiero algo como esto.**	**kyay**roa **ahl**goa **koa**moa **ays**toa
I like the one in the window.	**Me gusta el que está en el escaparate.**	may **goos**tah ayl kay ays**tah** ayn ayl eskahpah**rah**tay
How much is that per metre?	**¿Cuánto cuesta el metro?**	**kwahn**toa **kways**tah ayl **may**troa

1 centimetre (cm.)	= 0.39 in.	1 inch	= 2.54 cm.
1 metre (m.)	= 39.37 in.	1 foot	= 30.5 cm.
10 metres (m.)	= 32.81 ft.	1 yard	= 0.91 m.

Colour *Color*

I want something in ...	**Quiero algo en ...**	**kyay**roa **ahl**goa ayn
I want a darker/ lighter shade.	**Quiero un tono más oscuro/claro.**	**kyay**roa oon **toa**noa mahss oas**koo**roa/**klah**roa
I want something to match this.	**Quiero algo que haga juego con esto.**	**kyay**roa **ahl**goa kay **ah**gah **khway**goa kon **ays**toa
I don't like the colour.	**No me gusta el color.**	noa may **goos**tah ayl koa**loar**

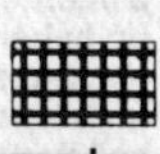

liso (**lee**soa) **rayas** (**rah**yahss) **lunares** (loona**h**rayss) **cuadros** (**kwah**droass) **estampado** (ehstahm**pah**dhoa)

beige	**beige***	"behzh"
black	**negro**	**neh**groa
blue	**azul**	ah**thool**
brown	**marrón**	mahr**ron**
cream	**crema**	**kray**mah
golden	**dorado**	doa**rah**dhoa
green	**verde**	**behr**day
grey	**gris**	greess
mauve	**malva**	**mahl**bah
orange	**naranja**	nah**rahn**khah
pink	**rosa**	**ro**ssah
purple	**purpúreo**	poor**poo**rehoa
red	**rojo**	**roa**khoa
scarlet	**escarlata**	ayskahr**lah**tah
silver	**plateado**	plahtay**ah**dhoa
turquoise	**turquesa**	toor**kay**ssah
white	**blanco**	**blahn**koa
yellow	**amarillo**	ahmah**ree**lyoa
light ...	**... claro**	**klah**roa
dark ...	**... oscuro**	oas**koo**roa

Material *Tejidos*

Do you have anything in ...?	**¿Tiene usted algo en ...?**	**tyay**nay oos**taydh ahl**goa ayn
I want a cotton blouse.	**Quisiera una blusa de algodón.**	kee**ssyay**rah **oo**nah **bloo**sah day ahlgoa**don**
Is that handmade/ made here?	**¿Está hecho a mano/ aquí?**	ays**tah ay**choa ah **mah**noa/ah**kee**
Is it ...?	**¿Es ...?**	ayss
pure cotton/wool	**puro algodón/ pura lana**	**poo**roa ahlgoa**dhon**/**poo**rah **lah**nah
colour fast	**color fijo**	koa**loar fee**khoa
machine/hand washable	**lavable en máquina/ a mano**	lah**bhah**blay ayn **mah**keenah/ah **mah**noa
Can it be dry-cleaned?	**¿Puede limpiarse en seco?**	**pway**dhay leem**pyahr**say ayn **say**koa
Will it shrink?	**¿Encogerá?**	aynkoakhay**rah**

* For feminine and plural forms, see grammar section page 159 (adjectives).

I want something thinner.	**Quiero algo más tenue.**	**kyay**roa **ahl**goa mahss **tay**nooay
Do you have any better quality?	**¿Tiene usted una calidad mejor?**	**tyay**nah oos**taydh oo**nah kahlee**dhadh** meh**khor**
What's it made of?	**¿De qué está hecho?**	day kay ays**tah ay**choa

cambric	**batista**	bah**tees**tah
camel hair	**pelo de camello**	**peh**loa day kah**may**lyoa
chiffon	**gasa**	**gah**ssah
corduroy	**pana**	**pah**nah
cotton	**algodón**	ahlgoa**don**
crepe	**crepé**	kray**pay**
denim	**algodón asargado**	ahlgoa**don** ahssahr**gah**dhoa
felt	**fieltro**	**fyayl**troa
flannel	**franela**	frah**nay**lah
gabardine	**gabardina**	gahbhahr**dee**nah
lace	**encaje**	ayn**kah**khay
leather	**cuero**	**kway**roa
linen	**hilo**	**ee**loa
pique	**piqué**	pee**kay**
poplin	**popelín**	poapay**leen**
satin	**raso**	**rah**ssoa
serge	**estameña**	aystah**may**ñah
silk	**seda**	**say**dhah
suede	**ante**	**ahn**tay
taffeta	**tafetán**	tahfay**tahn**
terrycloth	**tela de toalla**	**tay**lah day toa**ahl**yah
tulle	**tul**	tool
tweed	**cheviot**	chay**bhyoat**
velvet	**terciopelo**	tehrthyoa**peh**loa
wool	**lana**	**lah**nah
worsted	**estambre**	ays**tahm**bray
artificial	**artificial**	ahrteefee**thyahl**
synthetic	**sintético**	seen**tay**teekoa

Size *Talla*

My size is 38.	**Mi talla es la 38.**	mee **tah**lyah ayss lah 38
Could you measure me?	**¿Puede usted medirme?**	**pway**dhay oos**taydh** may**dheer**may
I don't know Spanish sizes.	**No conozco las tallas españolas.**	noa koa**noath**koa lahss **tah**lyahss ayspah**ño**lahss

This is your size *Esta es su talla*

Sizes can vary somewhat from country to country and from one manufacturer to another, so be sure to try on shoes and clothing before you buy.

Women *Señoras*

Dresses/Suits						
American	8	10	12	14	16	18
British	10	12	14	16	18	20
Continental	36	38	40	42	44	46

Stockings						
American / British	8	8½	9	9½	10	10½
Continental	0	1	2	3	4	5

Shoes				
American	6	7	8	9
British	4½	5½	6½	7½
Continental	37	39	40	41

Men *Caballeros*

Suits/Overcoats						
American / British	36	38	40	42	44	46
Continental	46	48	50	52	54	56

Shirts				
American / British	15	16	17	18
Continental	38	41	43	45

Shoes									
American / British	5	6	7	8	8½	9	9½	10	11
Continental	38	39	41	42	43	43	44	44	45

A good fit? *Una buena caída*

Can I try it on?	**¿Puedo probármelo?**	pway**dhoa** prob**hahr**-mayloa
Where's the fitting room?	**¿Dónde está el probador?**	**doan**day ays**tah** ayl probhah**dhor**
Is there a mirror?	**¿Tiene usted un espejo?**	**tyay**nay oos**taydh** oon ays**pay**khoa
It fits very well.	**Me queda muy bien.**	may **kay**dhah mwee byayn

NUMBERS, see page 147

It doesn't fit.	**No me queda bien.**	noa may **kay**dhah byayn
It's too ...	**Es demasiado ...**	ayss daymah**ssyah**dhoa
short/long tight/loose	**corto/largo** **ajustado/ancho**	**koar**toa/**lahr**goa ahkhoos**tah**doa/**ahn**choa
How long will it take to alter?	**¿Cuánto tardarán en arreglarlo?**	**kwahn**toa tahrdah**rahn** ayn ahrray**glahr**loa

Shoes *Zapatos*

I'd like a pair of ...	**Quisiera un par de ...**	kee**ssyay**rah oon pahr day
(rain) boots	**botas (par la lluvia)**	**boa**tahss **pah**rah lah **lyoo**bhyah
plimsolls (sneakers) sandals shoes flat/with a heel leather/suede slippers	**zapatos de lona** **sandalias** **zapatos** **planos/con tacón** **de cuero/de ante** **zapatillas**	thah**pah**toass day **loa**nah sahn**dah**lyahss thah**pah**toass **plah**noass/kon tah**kon** day **kway**roa/day **ahn**tay tahpahtee**l**yahss
These are too ...	**Estos son demasiado ...**	**ays**toass son daymah**ssyah**dhoa
narrow/wide large/small	**estrechos/anchos** **grandes/pequeños**	ays**tray**choass/**ahn**choass **grahn**dayss/pay**kay**ñoass
Do you have a smaller/larger size?	**¿Tiene una talla más pequeña/grande?**	**tyay**nay **oo**nah **tah**lyah mahss/pay**kay**ñah/**grahn**day
Do you have the same in brown/ black?	**¿Tiene usted lo mismo en marrón/ negro?**	**tyay**nay oos**taydh** loa **mees**moa ayn mah**rron**/ **neh**groa
I need some shoe polish/shoelaces.	**Necesito crema/ cordones para zapatos.**	naythay**ssee**toa **kray**mah/ koar**doa**nayss **pah**rah thah**pah**toass

Shoes worn out? Here's the key to getting them fixed again:

Can you repair these shoes?	**¿Puede usted reparar estos zapatos?**	**pway**dhay oos**taydh** raypah**rahr** **ays**toass tha**pah**toass
I want new soles and heels.	**Quiero nuevas suelas y tacones.**	**kyay**roa **nway**bhahss **sway**lahss ee tah**koa**nayss
When will they be ready?	**¿Cuándo estarán listos?**	**kwahn**doa aystah**rahn** **lees**toass

COLOURS, see page 113

Clothes and accessories *Ropa y accessorios*

I'd like a/an/some ...	**Quisiera ...**	keessyayrah
bathing cap	**un gorro de baño**	oon gorroa day bahñoa
bathing suit	**un traje de baño**	oon trahkhay day bahñoa
bathrobe	**un albornoz**	oon ahlboarnoth
blazer	**un blázer**	oon blahther
blouse	**una blusa**	oonah bloossah
bow tie	**una corbata de lazo**	oonah korbahtah day lahthoa
bra	**un sostén**	oon soastayn
braces	**unos tirantes**	oonoass teerahntayss
briefs	**unos calzoncillos**	oonoass kahlthontheelyoass
cap	**una gorra**	oonah gorrah
cardigan	**una chaqueta de punto**	oonah chakaytah day poontoa
coat (woman's)	**un abrigo**	oon ahbreegoa
coat (man's)	**un gabán**	oon gahbhahn
dinner jacket	**un smoking**	oon smoakeeng
dress	**un vestido**	oon baysteedhoa
dressing gown	**una bata**	oonah bahtah
evening dress (woman's)	**un traje de noche**	oon trahkhay day noachay
garter belt	**un portaligas**	oon poartahleegahss
garters	**unas ligas**	oonahss leegahss
girdle	**una faja**	oonah fahkhah
gloves	**unos guantes**	oonoass gwahntayss
handbag	**un bolso de mano**	oon boalsoa day mahnoa
handkerchief	**un pañuelo**	oon pahñwayloa
hat	**un sombrero**	oon soambrayroa
jacket	**una chaqueta**	oonah chahkaytah
jeans	**unos tejanos**	oonoass tehkhahnoass
jersey	**un jersey**	oon khayrsay
nightdress	**un camisón**	oon kahmeesson
panties	**unas bragas**	oonahss brahgahss
pants (Am.)	**unos pantalones**	oonoass pahntahloanayss
panty girdle	**una faja braga**	oonah fahkhah brahgah
panty hose	**unos leotardos**	oonoass layoatahrdoass
pullover	**un pullover**	oon pooloabhehr
roll-neck (turtleneck)/round-neck/ V-neck	**cuello vuelto/ redondo/en forma de V**	kwaylyoa bwehltoa/ raydoandoa/ayn foarmah day bayeh
with long/short sleeves	**con mangas largas/ cortas**	kon mahngahss lahrgahss/ koartahss
without sleeves	**sin mangas**	seen mahngahss

pyjamas	**un pijama**	oon pee**khah**mah
raincoat	**un impermeable**	oon eempehrmay**ah**blay
scarf	**una bufanda**	**oo**nah boo**fahn**dah
shirt	**una camisa**	**oo**nah kah**mee**ssah
shorts	**unos pantalones cortos**	**oo**noass pahntah**loa**nayss **koar**toass
skirt	**una falda**	**oo**nah **fahl**dah
slip	**una combinación**	**oo**nah koambeenah**thyon**
socks	**unos calcetines**	**oo**noass kahlthay**tee**nayss.
stockings	**unas medias**	**oo**nahss **may**dhyahss
suit (man's)	**un traje**	oon **trah**khay
suit (woman's)	**un vestido**	oon bays**tee**dhoa
suspenders	**unos tirantes**	**oo**noass tee**rahn**tayss
sweater	**un suéter**	oon **sway**tehr
sweatshirt	**un suéter de tela de punto**	oon **sway**tehr day **tay**lah day **poon**toa
swimming trunks	**un bañador**	oon bahñah**doar**
swimsuit	**un traje de baño**	oon **trah**khay day **bah**ñoa
T-shirt	**una camiseta**	**oo**nah kahmee**ssay**tah
tie	**una corbata**	**oo**nah kor**bah**tah
tights	**unos leotardos**	**oo**noass layoa**tahr**doass
tracksuit	**un chandal de entrenamiento**	oon chahn**dahl** day ehntraynah**myayn**toa
trousers	**unos pantalones**	**oo**noass pahntah**loa**nayss
tuxedo	**un smoking**	oon **smoa**keeng
twin set	**un conjunto de lana**	oon koan**khoon**toa day **lah**nah
umbrella	**un paraguas**	oon pah**rah**gwahss
underpants	**unos calzoncillos**	**oo**noass kahlthon**thee**lyoass
undershirt	**una camiseta**	**oo**nah kahmee**ssay**tah
vest (Am.)	**un chaleco**	oon chah**lay**koa
vest (Br.)	**una camiseta**	**oo**nah kahmee**ssay**tah
waistcoat	**un chaleco**	oon chah**lay**koa

belt	**un cinturón**	oon theentoo**ron**
buckle	**una hebilla**	**oo**nah ay**bhee**lyah
button	**un botón**	oon boa**ton**
collar	**un cuello**	oon **kway**lyoa
elastic	**un elástico**	oon ay**lah**steekoa
pocket	**un bolsillo**	oon boal**see**lyoa
press stud (snap fastener)	**un broche de presión**	oon **broa**chay day pray**ssyon**
zip (zipper)	**una cremallera**	**oo**nah kraymah**lyay**rah

Electrical appliances *Aparatos eléctricos*

Today 220-volt A.C. 50 cycles is becoming standard, but older installations of 125 volts can still be found. So check the voltage before you plug your appliance in. Don't forget to take along a plug adaptor: two-pin (prong) continental plugs are used in Spain.

What's the voltage?	**¿Cuál es el voltaje?**	kwahl ayss ayl boal**tah**khay
This is broken. Can you repair it?	**Esto está roto. ¿Puede usted arreglarlo?**	**ays**toa ays**tah roa**toa. **pway**dhay oos**taydh** ahrray**glahr**loa
I'd like (to hire) a video cassette/ video recorder.	**Quisiera (alquilar) una video-cassette/ video-grabadora.**	kee**ssyay**rah (ahlkee**lahr**) **oo**nah **bee**dhayoa-kah**ssayt**tay/**bee**dhayoa-grahbhah**dhoa**rah
Can you show me how it works?	**¿Puede mostrarme cómo funciona?**	**pway**dhay moas**trahr**may **koa**moa foon**thyo**nah
I'd like a/an/some ...	**Quisiera ...**	kee**ssyay**rah
adaptor	**un adaptador**	oon ahdhahptah**dhor**
amplifier	**un amplificador**	oon ahmpleefeekah**dhor**
battery	**una pila**	**oo**nah **pee**lah
bulb	**una bombilla**	**oo**nah boam**bee**lyah
electric toothbrush	**un cepillo de dientes eléctrico**	oon thay**pee**lyoa day **dyayn**tayss ay**layk**treekoa
hair dryer	**un secador de pelo**	oon saykahdhor day **peh**loa
headphones	**un casco con auriculares**	oon **kahs**koa kon owreekoo**lah**rayss
(travelling) iron	**una plancha (de viaje)**	**oo**nah **plahn**chah day **byah**khay
lamp	**una lámpara**	**oo**nah **lahm**pahrah
plug	**una clavija de enchufe**	**oo**nah klah**bhee**khah day ayn**choo**fay
portable ...	**... portátil**	... por**tah**teel
radio	**una radio**	**oo**nah **rah**dhyoa
car radio	**una radio para coche**	**oo**nah **rah**dhyoa **pah**rah **koa**chay
record player	**un tocadiscos**	oon toakah**dhees**koass
shaver	**una máquina de afeitar eléctrica**	**oo**nah **mah**keenah day ahfay**tahr** ay**layk**treekah
speakers	**unos altavoces**	**oo**noass ahltah**bhoa**thayss
(cassette) tape recorder	**un magnetófono (cassette)**	oon mahgnay**to**foanoa (kah**ssayt**tay)
transformer	**un transformador**	oon trahnsformah**dhor**

Grocery *Tienda de comestibles*

I want some bread, please.	**Quiero pan, por favor.**	kyayroa pahn por fabhor
What sort of cheese do you have?	**¿Qué clases de queso tiene?**	kay klahssayss day kayssoa tyaynay
A piece of ...	**Un trozo ...**	oon troathoa
that one	**de ése**	day ayssay
the one on the shelf	**del que está en el estante**	dayl kay aystah ayn ayl aystahntay
I'd like one of these and two of those.	**Quisiera uno de éstos y dos de ésos.**	keessyayrah oonoa day aystoass ee oonoa day ayssoass
May I help myself?	**¿Puedo servirme yo mismo?**	pwaydhoa sehrbeermay yoa meesmoa
I'd like ...	**Quisiera ...**	keessyayrah
a kilo of apples	**un kilo de manzanas**	oon keeloa day mahnthahnahss
half a kilo of tomatoes	**medio kilo de tomates**	maydhyoa keeloa day toamahtayss
100 g of butter	**100 gr. de mantequilla**	100 grahmoass day mahntaykeelyah
a litre of milk	**un litro de leche**	oon leetroa day laychay
4 slices of ham	**4 rebanadas de jamón**	4 raybhahnahdhahss day khahmon
a packet of tea	**un paquete de té**	oon pahkaytay day tay
a jar of honey	**un tarro de miel**	oon tahrroa day myehl
a tin (can) of pears	**una lata de peras**	oonah lahtah day pehrahss
a tube of mustard	**un tubo de mostaza**	oon toobhoa day moastahthah

1 kilogram or kilo (kg.) = 1000 grams (g.)

100 g. = 3.5 oz.	½ kg. = 1.1 lbs.
200 g. = 7.0 oz.	1 kg. = 2.2 lbs.

1 oz. = 28.35 g.
1 lb. = 453.60 g.

1 litre (l.) = 0.88 imp. quarts = 1.06 U.S. quarts

1 imp. quart = 1.14 l.	1 U.S. quart = 0.95 l.
1 imp. gallon = 4.55 l.	1 U.S. gallon = 3.8 l.

FOOD, see also page 63

Jeweller's—Watchmaker's *Joyería – Relojería*

I'd like a small present for ...	**Quisiera un regalito para ...**	kee**syay**rah oon raygah**lee**toa **pah**rah
Is this real silver?	**¿Es esto de plata auténtica?**	ayss **ays**toa day **plah**tah ow**tayn**teekah
Do you have anything in gold?	**¿Tiene usted algo de oro?**	**tyay**nay oos**taydh ahl**goa day **oa**roa
How many carats is this?	**¿De cuántos quilates es esto?**	day **kwahn**toass kee**lah**tayss ayss **ays**toa
Can you repair this watch?	**¿Puede arreglar este reloj?**	**pway**dhay ahrray**glahr ays**tay reh**lokh**
I'd like a/an/some ...	**Quisiera ...**	kees**syay**rah
alarm clock	**un despertador**	oon dayspayrtah**dhor**
bangle	**una esclava**	**oo**nah ays**klah**bhah
battery	**una pila**	**oo**nah **pee**lah
bracelet	**una pulsera**	**oo**nah pool**say**rah
charm bracelet	**pulsera de fetiches**	pool**say**rah day fay**tee**chayss
brooch	**un broche**	oon **bro**chay
chain	**una cadena**	**oo**nah kah**dhay**nah
charm	**un amuleto**	oon ahmoo**lay**toa
cigarette case	**una pitillera**	**oo**nah peeteel**yay**rah
cigarette lighter	**un encendedor**	oon aynthaynday**dhor**
clip	**un clip**	oon kleep
clock	**un reloj**	oon reh**lokh**
cross	**una cruz**	**oo**nah krooth
cuff links	**unos gemelos**	**oo**noass khay**may**loass
cutlery	**unos cubiertos**	**oo**noass koo**bhyehr**toass
earrings	**unos pendientes**	**oo**noass payn**dyayn**tayss
jewel box	**un joyero**	oon kho**yay**roa
mechanical pencil	**un lapicero**	oon lahpee**thay**roa
necklace	**un collar**	oon koa**lyahr**
pendant	**un medallón**	oon maydhah**lyon**
pin	**un alfiler**	oon ahlfee**lehr**
pocket watch	**un reloj de bolsillo**	oon reh**lokh** day boal**see**lyoa
powder compact	**una polvera**	**oo**nah poal**bay**rah
propelling pencil	**un lapicero**	oon lahpee**thay**roa
ring	**una sortija**	**oo**nah sor**tee**khah
engagement ring	**sortija de pedida**	sor**tee**khah day pay**dhee**dhah
signet ring	**sortija de sello**	sor**tee**khah day **say**lyoa
wedding ring	**un anillo de boda**	oon ah**nee**lyoa day **boa**dhah

rosary	**un rosario de cuentas**	oon roa**ssah**ryoa day **kwayn**tahss
silverware	**unos objetos de plata**	**oo**noass ob**khay**toass day **plah**tah
tie clip	**un sujetador de corbata**	oon sookhaytah**dhor** day kor**bah**tah
tie pin	**un alfiler de corbata**	oon ahlfee**lehr** day kor**bah**tah
watch (wristwatch)	**un reloj (de pulsera)**	oon reh**lokh** (day pool**say**rah)
automatic	**automático**	aotoa**mah**teekoa
with a second hand	**con segundero manecilla**	kon say**goon**dayroa mahnay**thee**lyah
with quartz movement	**con mecanismo de cuarzo**	kon maykah**nees**moa day **kwahr**thoa
watchstrap (watchband)	**una correa de reloj**	oonah korr**eh**ah day reh**lokh**

amber	**ámbar**	**ahm**bahr
amethyst	**amatista**	ahmah**tees**tah
copper	**cobre**	**koa**bray
coral	**coral**	ko**rahl**
crystal	**cristal**	krees**tahl**
cut glass	**cristal tallado**	krees**tahl** tah**lyah**dhoa
diamond	**diamante**	dyah**mahn**tay
emerald	**esmeralda**	aysmay**rahl**dah
enamel	**esmalte**	ays**mahl**tay
gold	**oro**	**oa**roa
gold plate	**lámina de oro**	**lah**meenah day **oa**roa
ivory	**marfil**	mahr**feel**
jade	**jade**	**khah**dheh
onyx	**ónix**	**o**neekss
pearl	**perla**	**pehr**lah
pewter	**peltre**	**pehl**tray
platinum	**platino**	plah**tee**noa
ruby	**rubí**	roo**bhee**
sapphire	**zafiro**	thah**fee**roa
silver	**plata**	**plah**tah
silver plate	**plata chapada**	**plah**tah chah**pah**dhah
stainless steel	**acero inoxidable**	ah**thay**roa eenoksee**dhah**blay
topaz	**topacio**	to**pah**thyoa
turquoise	**turquesa**	toor**kay**ssah

Optician *El óptico*

Where can I find an optician?	**¿Dónde puedo encontrar un óptico?**	**doan**day **pway**dhoa aynkoan**trahr** oon **oap**teekoa
I've broken my glasses.	**Se me han roto las gafas.**	say may ahn **roa**toa lahss **gah**fahss
Can you repair them for me?	**¿Me las puede usted arreglar?**	may lahss **pway**dhay oos**taydh** ahrray**glahr**
When will they be ready?	**¿Cuándo estarán listas?**	**kwahn**dhoa aystah**rahn** **lees**tahss
Can you change the lenses?	**¿Puede cambiar los lentes?**	**pway**dhay kahm**byahr** loss **layn**tayss
I want tinted lenses.	**Quiero cristales ahumados.**	**kyay**roa krees**tah**layss ow**mah**dhoass
I'd like to have my eyes checked.	**Quisiera que me controlara los ojos.**	kee**ssyay**rah kay may koantroa**lah**rah loass **oa**khoass
I'm short-sighted/ long-sighted.	**Soy miope/présbite.**	soy **myoa**pay/**prays**beetay
I want some contact lenses.	**Quiero lentes de contacto.**	**kyay**roa **layn**tayss day kon**tahk**toa
I've lost a contact lens.	**He perdido un lente de contacto.**	ay payr**dhee**dhoa oon **layn**tay day koan**tahk**toa
I have hard/soft lenses.	**Tengo lentes duros/ suaves.**	**tayn**goa **layn**tays **doo**roas/ **swah**bhayss
Do you have some solution for contact lenses?	**¿Tiene una solución para lentes de contacto?**	**tyay**nay **oo**nah soaloo**thyon** **pah**rah **layn**tayss day koan**tahk**toa
May I look in a mirror?	**¿Puedo verme en un espejo?**	**pway**dhoa **bayr**may ayn oon ays**pay**khoa
I'd like a spectacle case.	**Quisiera un estuche para gafas.**	kee**ssyay**rah oon ays**too**chay **pah**rah **gah**fahss
I'd like to buy a pair of binoculars.	**Quisiera comprar unos binoculares.**	kee**ssyay**rah kom**prahr** **oo**noass beenoakoo**lah**rayss
I'd like to buy a pair of sunglasses.	**Quisiera comprar unas gafas de sol.**	kee**ssyay**rah kom**prahr** **oo**nahss **gah**fass day sol
How much do I owe you?	**¿Cuánto le debo?**	**kwahn**toa lay **day**bhoa

NUMBERS, see page 147

Photography *Fotografía*

I want a camera.	**Quisiera una cámara.**	kee**ssyay**rah **oo**nah **kah**mahrah
automatic/inexpensive/simple	**automática/ barata/sencilla**	owtoa**mah**teekah/ bah**rah**tah/saynt**hee**lyah
Show me a cine (movie) camera, please.	**Enséñeme una cámara de filmar, por favor.**	ayn**say**ñaymay **oo**nah **kah**mahrah day feel**mahr** por fah**bhor**
I'd like to have some passport photos taken.	**Quisiera que me haga unas fotos para pasaporte.**	kee**ssyay**rah kay may **ah**gah **oo**nahss **foa**toass **pah**rah pahssah**poar**tay

Film *Rollos/Películas*

I'd like a film for thic camera.	**Quisiera un rollo para esta cámara.**	kee**ssyay**rah oon **roa**lyoa **pah**rah **ays**tah **kah**mahrah
black and white	**en blanco y negro**	ayn **blahn**koa ee **nay**groa
colour	**en color**	ayn koa**loar**
colour negative	**negativo de color**	naygah**tee**bhoa day koa**loar**
colour slide	**diapositivas**	dyahposse**tee**bhahss
cartridge	**un cartucho**	oon kahr**too**choa
disc film	**un disco-película**	oon **dees**koa pay**lee**koolah
roll film	**un carrete/rollo**	oon kahr**ray**tay/**roa**lyoa
cine (movie) film	**una película**	oonah pay**lee**koolah
super eight	**super ocho**	**soo**pehr **oa**choa
video tape	**una cinta video**	**oo**nah **theen**tah **bee**dhayoa
24/36 exposures	**24/36 exposiciones**	baynteek**wah**troa/**trayn**tah ee sayss aykspoassee**thyon**ayss
this ASA/DIN number	**este número de ASA/DIN**	**ays**tay **noo**mayroa day **ah**ssah/deen
this size	**de este tamaño**	day **ays**tay tah**mah**ñoa
artificial light/ daylight type	**para luz artificial/ del dia**	**pah**rah looth ahrteefee**thyahl**/dayl **dee**ah
fast (high-speed)	**rápido**	**rah**peedhoa
fine grain	**de grano fino**	day **grah**noa **fee**noa

Processing *Revelado*

How much do you charge for developing/printing?	**¿Qué cobra por el revelado/la impresión?**	kay **koa**brah por ayl raybhay**lah**dhoa/lah eempray**ssyon**

NUMBERS, see page 147

I want ... prints of each negative.	**Quiero ... copias de cada negativo.**	**kyay**roa ... **koa**pyahss day **kah**dhah nayghah**tee**bhoa
with a mat/glossy finish	**con acabado mate/ de brillo**	kon ahkah**bhah**dhoa mahtay/day **breel**yoa
Will you please enlarge this?	**¿Haría usted una ampliación de ésta, por favor?**	ah**ree**ah oos**taydh oo**nah ahmplyah**thyon** day **ays**tah por fah**bhor**
When will the photos be ready?	**¿Cuándo estarán listas las fotos?**	**kwahn**doa aystah**rahn lees**tahss lahss **foa**toas

Accessories and repairs *Accesorios y reparaciones*

I want a/an ...	**Quisiera ...**	kee**ssyay**rah
battery	**una pila**	**oo**nah **pee**lah
cable release	**un cable del dispa-rador**	oon **kah**blay dayl dees-pahrah**dhoar**
camera case	**una funda**	**oo**nah **foon**dah
(electronic) flash	**un flash (electrónico)**	oon flash (aylayk**troa**-neekoa)
filter	**un filtro**	oon **feel**troa
for black and white	**para blanco y negro**	**pah**rah **blahn**koa ee **nay**groa
for colour	**para color**	**pah**rah koa**loar**
lens	**un objetivo**	oon obkhay**tee**bhoa
telephoto lens	**de acercamiento**	day ahthayrkah**myayn**toa
wide-angle lens	**gran angular**	grahn ahngoo**lahr**
lens cap	**un capuchón para el objetivo**	oon kapoo**chon pah**rah ayl obkhay**tee**bhoa
This camera doesn't work. Can you repair it?	**Esta cámara está estropeada. ¿Puede usted repararla?**	**ays**tah **kah**mahrah ays**tah** aystroapeh**ahd**hah. **pway**dhay oos**taydh** raypah**rahr**lah
The film is jammed.	**La película está atrancada.**	lah pay**lee**koolah ays**tah** ahtrahn**kah**dhah
There's something wrong with the ...	**Hay algo que va mal en ...**	igh **ahl**goa kay bah mahl ayn
exposure counter	**la escala de expo-sición**	lah ays**kah**lah day aykspoassee**thyon**
film winder	**el enrollador**	ayl aynroalyah**dhor**
light meter	**el exposímetro**	ayl aykspoa**ssee**mehtroa
rangefinder	**el telémetro**	ayl tay**lay**maytroa
shutter	**el obturador**	ayl obtoorah**dhor**

Tobacconist's *Tabacos*

Most Spanish cigarettes are made of strong, black tobacco. Nearly all major foreign brands are available in Spain at two to three times the price of local cigarettes.

A packet/carton of cigarettes, please.	**Una cajetilla/un cartón de cigarrillos, por favor.**	oonah kahkhayteelyah/oon kahrton day theegahr-reelyoass por fahbhor
I'd like a box of ...	**Quisiera una caja de ...**	keessyayrah oonah kahkhah day
May I have a/an/ some ..., please?	**¿Puede darme ..., por favor?**	pwayday dahrmay por fahbhor
candy	**unos caramelos**	oonoass kahrahmayloass
chewing gum	**un chicle**	oon cheeklay
chocolate	**un chocolate**	oon choakoalahtay
cigarettes	**unos cigarrillos**	oonoass theegahrreelyoass
American	**americanos**	ahmayreekahnoass
English	**ingleses**	eenglayssayss
menthol	**mentolados**	mayntoalahdhoass
mild/strong	**suaves/fuertes**	swahbhayss/fwehrtayss
cigarette lighter	**un encendedor**	oon aynthayndaydhor
cigarette paper	**papel para cigarrillos**	pahpehl pahrah theegahrreelyoass
cigars	**unos puros**	oonoass pooroass
flints	**unas piedras de mechero**	oonahss pyaydrahss day maychayroa
lighter fluid/gas	**gasolina/gas para encendedor**	gahssoaleenah/gahss pahrah aynthayndaydhor
matches	**unas cerillas**	oonahss thayreelyahss
pipe	**una pipa**	oonah peepah
pipe cleaners	**unas limpiapipas**	oonahss leempyahpeepahss
pipe tobacco	**tabaco para pipa**	tahbhahkoa pahrah peepah
pipe tool	**utensilios para pipa**	ootaynseelyoass pahrah peepah
post cards	**unas tarjetas postales**	oonahss tahrkhaytahss poastahlayss
snuff	**rapé**	rahpay
stamps	**unos sellos**	oonoass saylyoass
sweets	**unos caramelos**	oonoass kahrahmayloass
wick	**una mecha**	oonah maychah

filter tipped	**con filtro**	kon feeltroa
without filter	**sin filtro**	seen feeltroa

Miscellaneous *Diversos*

Souvenirs *Recuerdos*

Spain's souvenir industry churns out everything from personalized bull-fighting posters to plastic castanets. Kitsch aside, you will also find a selection of fine hand-crafted articles: shawls, embroidered linen, lace-work, painted fans, hand-woven shopping baskets, wicker-work and carved wood.

You may come across special outlets for handicrafts *(artesanía)*, some of them government sponsored.

bullfight poster	**el cartel de toros**	ayl kahrtayl day toaroass
bullfighter's cap	**la montera**	lah moantayrah
castanets	**las castañuelas**	lahss kahstahñwaylahss
copperware	**objetos de cobre**	oabkhaytoass day koabray
doll	**la muñeca**	lah mooñaykah
earrings	**los pendientes**	loss payndyayntayss
earthenware	**la loza de barro**	lah loathah day bahrroa
embossed leather	**el cuero repujado**	ayl kwayroa raypookhahdhoa
embroidery	**el bordado**	ayl boardahdhoa (day
fan	**el abanico**	ayl ahbhahneekoa
guitar	**la guitarra**	lah geetahrrah
jewellery	**las joyas**	lahss khoyahss
lace	**los encajes**	loss aynkahkhayss
mantilla	**la mantilla**	lah mahnteelyah
pitcher	**el botijo**	ayl boateekhoa
poncho	**el poncho**	ayl ponchoa
rosary	**el rosario**	ayl roassahryoa
tambourine	**la pandereta**	lah pahndayraytah
wineskin	**la bota**	lah boatah
woodcarving	**la talla en madera**	lah tahlyah ayn mahdhayrah

Records—Cassettes *Discos – Cassettes*

I'd like a ...	**Quisiera ...**	keessyayrah
cassette	**una cassette**	oonah kahssayttay
compact disc	**un disco compacto**	oon deeskoa koampahktoa
record	**un disco**	oon deeskoa
video cassette	**una video-cassette**	oonah beedhayoa-kahssayttay

Can I listen to this record?	**¿Puedo escuchar este disco?**	pwaydhoa aysskoochahr aystay deeskoa

L.P. (33 rmp)	**33 revoluciones**	trayntah ee trayss raybhoaloothyonayss
E.P. (45 rmp)	**maxi 45**	maxi kwahrayntah ee theenkoa
single	**45 revoluciones**	kwahrayntah ee theenkoa raybhoaloothyonayss

chamber music	**música de cámara**	moosseekah day kahmahrah
classical music	**música clásica**	moosseekah klahsseekah
folk music	**música folklórica**	moosseekah folkloareekah
instrumental music	**música instrumental**	moosseekah eenstroomayntahl
light music	**música ligera**	moosseekah leekhayrah
orchestral music	**música de orquesta**	moosseekah day orkaystah
pop music	**música pop**	moosseekah pop

Toys *Juguetes*

I'd like a toy for a boy/a 5-year-old-girl.	**Quisiera un juguete para un niño/una niña de 5 años.**	keessyayrah oon khoogaytay pahrah oon neeñoa/oonah neeñah day 5 ahñoass
I'd like a/an/some ...	**Quisiera ...**	keessyayrah
beach ball	**una pelota de playa**	oonah payloatah day plahyah
bucket and spade (pail and shovel)	**un cubo y una pala**	oon koobhoa ee oonah pahlah
building blocks	**unos cubos de construcción**	oonoass koobhoass day koanstrookthyon
card game	**un juego de cartas**	oon khwaygoa day kahrtahss
chess set	**un ajedrez**	oon ahkhaydrayth
dice	**unos dados**	oonoass dahdhoass
electronic game	**un juego electrónico**	oon khwaygoa aylayktroaneekoa
flippers	**unas aletas para nadar**	oonahss ahlaytahss pahrah nahdhahr
roller skates	**unos patines de ruedas**	oonoass pahteenayss day rwaydhahss
snorkel	**unos espantasuegras**	oonoass ayspahntahswaygrahss

Your money: banks—currency

The normal banking hours in Spain are from 9 a.m. to 2 p.m. Monday to Friday (Saturday 9 a.m. to 1 p.m.). Outside normal banking hours, many travel agencies, major hotels and other businesses displaying a *cambio* sign will change foreign currency into pesetas. Always take your passport with you for identification when you go to change money.

Credit cards *Tarjetas de crédito*

All the internationally recognized credit cards are accepted by hotels, restaurants and businesses in Spain.

Traveller's cheques *Cheques de viajero*

In tourist areas, shops and all banks, hotels and travel agencies accept traveller's cheques, though you are likely to get a better rate of exchange at a national or regional bank. You'll have no problem settling bills or paying for purchases with Eurocheques.

Monetary unit *La unidad monetaria*

The basic unit of currency is the *peseta* (pay**ssay**tah), abbreviated *pta*. There are coins of 1, 2, 5, 10, 25, 50, 100 and 200 pesetas and banknotes of 100, 200 (rare), 500, 1,000, 2,000 and 5,000 pesetas.

Where's the nearest bank?	**¿Dónde está el banco más cercano?**	**doan**day ay**stah** ayl **bahn**koa mahss thehr**kah**noa
Where's the nearest currency exchange office?	**¿Dónde está la oficina de cambio más cercana?**	**doan**day ay**stah** lah oafee**thee**nah day **kahm**byoa mahss thehr**kah**nah
What time does the bank open/close?	**¿A qué hora abren/cierran el banco?**	ah kay **oa**rah **ah**brayn/ **thyay**rrahn ayl **bahn**koa
Where can I cash a traveller's cheque (check)?	**¿Dónde puedo cobrar un cheque de viajero?**	**doan**day **pway**dhoa koa**brahr** oon **chay**kay day byah**khay**roa

At the bank *En el banco*

I want to change some dollars/ pounds.	**Quiero cambiar unos dólares/unas libras esterlinas.**	**kyay**roa kahm**byahr** oonoass **doa**lahrayss/ oonahss **lee**brahss aystayr**lee**nahss
I want to cash a traveller's cheque.	**Quiero cobrar un cheque de viajero.**	**kyay**roa koa**brahr** oon **chay**kay day byah**khay**roa
Here's my passport.	**Aquí está mi pasaporte.**	ah**kee** ay**stah** mee passah**por**tay
What's the exchange rate?	**¿A cómo está el cambio?**	ah **koa**moa ay**stah** ayl **kahm**byoa
How much of commission do you charge?	**¿Qué comisión cargan?**	kay koamee**ssyon** **kahr**gahn
Can you cash a personal cheque?	**¿Puede hacer efectivo un cheque personal?**	**pway**dhay ah**thayr** ayfayk**tee**bhoa oon **chay**kay pehrsoa**nahl**
How long will it take to clear?	**¿Cuánto tardará en tramitarlo?**	**kwahn**toa tahrdah**rah** ayn trahmee**tahr**loa
Can you telex my bank in London?	**¿Puede mandar un télex a mi banco en Londres?**	**pway**dhay mahn**dahr** oon **tay**layks ah mee **bahn**koa ayn **lon**drayss
I have a/an/some ...	**Tengo ...**	**tayn**goa
credit card	**una tarjeta de crédito**	**oo**nah tahr**khay**tah day **kray**deetoa
Eurocheques	**unos eurocheques**	**oo**noass ayooroa**chay**kayss
introduction from ...	**un formulario de presentación de ...**	oon foarmoo**lah**ryoa day prayssayntah**thyon** day
letter of credit	**una carta de crédito**	**oo**nah **kahr**tah day **kray**deetoa
I'm expecting some money from Chicago. Has it arrived yet?	**Espero una transferencia de Chicago. ¿Ha llegado ya?**	ay**spay**roa **oo**nah trahnsfay**rayn**thyah day chee**kah**goa ah lyay**gah**dhoa yah
Please give me ... notes (bills) and some small change.	**Por favor, déme ... billetes y algo en moneda.**	por fah**bhor** **day**may ... beel**yay**tayss ee **ahl**goa ayn moa**nay**dhah
Give me ... large notes and the rest in small notes.	**Déme ... en los billetes de más valor que tenga y el resto en billetes de menor valor.**	**day**may ... ayn loss bee**lyay**tayss day mahss bah**lor** kay **tayn**gah ee ayl **ray**stoa ayn bee**lyay**tayss day may**nor** bah**lor**

NUMBERS, see page 146

Depositing *Depósitos*

I want to credit this to my account.	**Quiero acreditar esto a mi cuenta.**	**kyay**roa ahkraydhee**tahr** **ays**toa ah mee **kwayn**tah
I want to credit this to Mr ... 's account.	**Quiero acreditar esto a la cuenta del Señor ...**	**kyay**roa ahkraydhee**tahr** **ays**toa ah lah **kwayn**tah dayl say**ñor**
I want to open an account/withdraw ... pesetas.	**Quiero abrir una cuenta/retirar ... pesetas.**	**kyay**roa ah**breer oo**nah **kwayn**tah/raytee**rahr** ... pay**ssay**tahss

Business terms *Expresiones de negocios*

My name is ...	**Me llamo ...**	may **lyah**moa
Here's my card.	**Aquí está mi tarjeta.**	ah**kee** ays**tah** mee tahr**khay**tah
I have an appointment with ...	**Tengo una cita con ...**	**tayn**goa **oo**nah **thee**tah kon
Can you give me an estimate of the cost?	**¿Puede darme una estimación del precio?**	**pway**dhay **dahr**may **oo**nah aysteemah**thyon** dayl **pray**thyoa
What's the rate of inflation?	**¿Cuál es la tasa de inflación?**	kwahl ayss lah **tah**ssah day eenfla**thyon**
Can you provide me with an interpreter/ a secretary?	**¿Puede conseguirme un intérprete/una secretaria?**	**pway**dhay konsay**geer**may oon een**tayr**praytay/ **oo**nah saykray**tah**ryah

amount	**la suma**	lah **soo**mah
balance	**el balance**	ayl bah**lahn**thay
capital	**el capital**	ayl kahpee**tahl**
cheque book	**la chequera**	lah chay**kay**rah
interest	**el interés**	ayl eentay**rayss**
investment	**la inversión**	lah eenbayr**syon**
invoice	**la factura**	lah fahk**too**rah
loss	**la pérdida**	lah **payr**deedhah
mortgage	**la hipoteca**	lah eepoa**tay**kah
payment	**el pago**	ayl **pah**goa
profit	**la ganancia**	lah gah**nahn**thyah
purchase	**la compra**	lah **koam**prah
sale	**la venta**	lah **bayn**tah
transfer	**la transferencia**	lah trahnsfay**rayn**thyah
value	**el valor**	ayl bah**loar**

At the post office

Post offices are for mail and telegrams only; normally you can't make telephone calls from them. Hours vary slightly from town to town, but routine postal business is generally transacted from 9 a.m. to 1 or 1.30 p.m. and 4 to 6 or 7 p.m., Monday to Saturday except for Saturday afternoons.

Stamps are also on sale at tobacconists' *(tabacos)* and often at hotels. Letter boxes (mailboxes) are yellow with a red insignia.

Where's the nearest post office?	**¿Dónde está la oficina de correos más cercana?**	**doan**day ay**stah** lah oafee**thee**nah day ko**rreh**oass mahss thehr**kah**nah
What time does the post office open/ close?	**¿A qué hora abren/ cierran correos?**	ah kay **oa**rah **ah**brayn/ **thyayr**rahn ko**rreh**oass
Which window do I go to for stamps?	**¿A qué ventanilla debo ir para comprar sellos?**	ah kay bayntah**nee**lyah **day**bhoa eer **pah**rah koam**prahr say**lyoass
At which counter can I cash an international money order?	**¿En qué mostrador puedo hacer efectivo un giro postal internacional?**	ayn kay moastrah**dhor pway**dhoa ah**thayr** ayfayk**tee**bhoa oon **khee**roa pos**tahl** eentehrnahthyo**nahl**
I want some stamps, please.	**Quiero unos sellos, por favor.**	**kyay**roa **oo**noass **say**lyoass por fah**bhor**
A stamp for this letter/postcard, please.	**Un sello para esta carta/tarjeta, por favor.**	oon **say**lyoa **pah**rah **ay**stah **kahr**tah/tahr**khay**tah por fah**bhor**
What's the postage for a letter/postcard to London?	**¿Cuál es el franqueo para una carta/tarjeta para Londres?**	kwahl ayss ayl **frahn**kayoa **pah**rah **oo**nah **kahr**tah/ tahr**khay**tah **pah**rah **lon**drayss
Do all letters go airmail?	**¿Van todas las cartas por correo aéreo?**	bahn **toa**dhahss lahss **kahr**tahss por ko**rreh**oa ah**ay**rehoa
I want to send this parcel.	**Quiero mandar este paquete.**	**kyay**roa mahn**dahr ay**stay pah**kay**tay

Do I need to fill in a customs declaration?	**¿Es necesario que cumplimente una declaración para la aduana?**	ayss naythay**ssahr**yoa kay koomplee**mayn**tay **oo**nah dayklahrah**thyon pah**rah lah ah**dwah**nah
Where's the letter box (mailbox)?	**¿Dónde está el buzón?**	**doan**day ays**tah** ayl boo**thon**
I want to send this ...	**Quiero mandar esto ...**	**kyay**roa mahn**dahr ays**toa
airmail	**por correo aéreo**	por kor**re**hoa ah**ay**rehoa
express (special delivery)	**urgente**	oor**khayn**tay
registered mail	**por correo certificado**	por kor**re**hoa thayrteefee**kah**dhoa
Where's the poste restante (general delivery)?	**¿Dónde está la Lista de Correos?**	**doan**day ays**tah** lah **lees**tah day kor**re**hoass
Is there any mail for me? My name is ...	**¿Hay correo para mí? Me llamo ...**	igh kor**re**hoa **pah**rah mee. may **lyah**moa

SELLOS	STAMPS
PAQUETES	PARCELS
GIROS POSTALES	MONEY ORDERS

Telegrams *Telegramas*

In Spain telegrams are dispatched by the post office.

I want to send a telegram/telex.	**Quiero mandar un telegrama/télex.**	**kyay**roa mahn**dahr** oon taylay**grah**mah/**tay**layks
May I please have a form?	**¿Me da un impreso, por favor?**	may dah oon eem**pray**ssoa por fah**bhor**
How much is it per word?	**¿Cuánto cuesta por palabra?**	**kwahn**toa **kways**tah por pah**lah**brah
How long will a cable to Boston take?	**¿Cuánto tardará un telegrama a Boston?**	**kwahn**toa tahrdah**rah** oon taylay**grah**mah ah **bos**ton
I'd like to reverse the charges.	**Quisiera que fuera por cobro revertido.**	kee**ssyay**rah kay **fway**rah por **koa**broa raybhayr**tee**dhoa

Telephoning *Teléfonos*

Local and international calls can be made from call boxes (phone booths). Area codes for different countries are displayed in booths. In main towns, long-distance calls can also be placed from telephone offices (usually distinct from post offices).

Where's the telephone?	**¿Dónde está el teléfono?**	**doan**day ay**stah** ayl tay**lay**foanoa
Where's the nearest call box (phone booth)?	**¿Dónde está la cabina de teléfonos más cercana?**	**doan**day ay**stah** lah kah**bhee**nah day tay**lay**foanoass mahss thehr**kah**nah
May I use your phone?	**¿Puedo usar su teléfono?**	**pway**dhoa oo**ssahr** soo tay**lay**foanoa
Do you have a telephone directory for Valladolid?	**¿Tiene usted una guía de teléfonos de Valladolid?**	**tyay**nay oos**taydh oo**nah **gee**ah day tay**lay**foanoass day bahlyahdhoa**leedh**
Can you help me get this number?	**¿Me puede usted obtener este número?**	may **pway**dhay oos**taydh** obteh**nayr ays**tay **noo**mayroa
Can I dial direct?	**¿Puedo marcar directamente?**	**pway**dhoa mahr**kahr** deerayktah**mayn**tay
What's the dialing (area) code for ...?	**¿Cuál es el indicativo para ...?**	kwahl ayss ayl eendeekah**tee**bhoa **pah**rah
How do I get the (international) operator?	**¿Cómo puedo conseguir la telefonista (internacional)?**	**koa**moa **pway**dhoa konsay**geer** lah taylayfoa**nees**tah (eentayrnahthyoa**nahl**)

Operator *La telefonista*

Do you speak English?	**¿Habla usted inglés?**	**ah**blah oos**taydh** een**glayss**
Good morning, I want Madrid 123 45 67.	**Buenos días, quiero hablar con Madrid, número 123 45 67.**	**bway**noass **dee**ahss **kyay**roa ah**blahr** kon mah**dreedh noo**mayroa 123 45 67
I want to place a personal (person-to-person) call.	**Quiero una llamada personal.**	**kyay**roa **oo**nah lyah**mah**dhah pehrsoa**nahl**

I want to reverse the charges.	**Quiero que sea con cobro revertido.**	**kyay**roa kay **seh**ah kon **koa**broa raybhayr**tee**dhoa
Will you tell me the cost of the call afterwards?	**¿Puede decirme el coste de la llamada después?**	**pway**dhay day**theer**may ayl **koas**tay day lah lyah**mah**dhah days**pwayss**

Telephone alphabet

A	**Antonio**	an**toa**nyoa	N	**Navarra**	nah**bhahr**rah
B	**Barcelona**	bahrtheh**loa**nah	Ñ	**Ñoño**	**ñoa**ñoa
C	**Carmen**	**kahr**mayn	O	**Oviedo**	oa**bhyay**dhoa
CH	**Chocolate**	choakoa**lah**tay	P	**París**	pah**reess**
D	**Dolores**	doa**loa**rayss	Q	**Querido**	kay**ree**dhoa
E	**Enrique**	ayn**ree**kay	R	**Ramón**	rah**mon**
F	**Francia**	**frahn**thyah	S	**Sábado**	**sah**bhahdhoa
G	**Gerona**	kheh**roa**nah	T	**Tarragona**	tahrrah**goa**nah
H	**Historia**	ees**toa**ryah	U	**Ulises**	oo**lee**ssayss
I	**Inés**	ee**nayss**	V	**Valencia**	bah**layn**thyah
J	**José**	khoa**ssay**	W	**Washington**	**wah**sheenton
K	**Kilo**	**kee**loa	X	**Xiquena**	ksee**kay**nah
L	**Lorenzo**	loa**rayn**thoa	Y	**Yegua**	**yeh**gwah
LL	**Llobregat**	lyoabray**gaht**	Z	**Zaragoza**	thahrah**go**thah
M	**Madrid**	mah**dreedh**			

Speaking *Hablando*

Hello. This is ... speaking.	**Oiga. Aquí habla con ...**	**oy**gah. ah**kee ah**blah kon
I want to speak to ...	**Quiero hablar con ...**	**kyay**roa ah**blahr** kon
I want extension ...	**Quisiera la extensión ...?**	kee**ssyay**rah lah aykstayn**ssyon**
Is this ...?	**¿Es ...?**	ayss
Speak louder/more slowly, please.	**Hable más fuerte/ más despacio, por favor.**	**ah**blay mahss **fwayr**tay/ mahss days**pah**thyoa por fa**bhor**

Bad luck *Mala suerte*

Would you please try again later?	**¿Querría intentarlo de nuevo más tarde?**	kehr**ree**ah eentayn**tahr**loa day **nway**bhoa mahss **tahr**day

Operator, you gave me the wrong number.	**Señorita, me ha dado el número equivocado.**	sayñoa**ree**tah may ah **dah**dhoa ayl **noo**mayroa aykeebhoa**kah**dhoa
Operator, we were cut off.	**Señorita, se nos ha cortado la línea.**	sayñoa**ree**tah say noas ah koar**tah**dhoa lah **lee**nayah

Not there *Está ausente*

When will he/she be back?	**¿Cuándo estará de vuelta?**	**kwahn**doa aystah**rah** day **bwayl**tah
Will you tell him/her I called? My name is ...	**Dígale que lo/la he llamado. Mi nombre es ...**	**de**gahlay kay loa/lah ay lyah**mah**dhoa. mee **noam**bray ayss
Would you ask him/her to call me?	**¿Querría pedirle que me llame?**	kehr**ree**ah peh**dheer**lay kay may **lyah**may
Would you please take a message?	**¿Por favor, quiere tomar un recado?**	por fah**bhor kyay**ray toa**mahr** oon ray**kah**dhoa

Charges *Tarifas*

What was the cost of that call?	**¿Cuál ha sido el coste de esa llamada?**	kwahl ah **see**dhoa ayl **koas**tay day **ays**sah lyah**mah**dhah
I want to pay for the call.	**Quiero pagar la llamada.**	**kyay**roa pah**gahr** lah lyah**mah**dhah

Hay una llamada para usted.	There's a telephone call for you.
¿A qué número llama?	What number are you calling?
Comunica.	The line's engaged.
No contestan.	There's no answer.
Tiene el número equivocado.	You've got the wrong number.
No está ahora.	He's/She's out at the moment.
Un momento.	Just a moment.
Espere, por favor.	Hold on, please.

Doctor

To be at ease, make sure your health insurance policy covers any illness or accident while on holiday. If not, ask your insurance representative, automobile association or travel agent for details of special health insurance.

General *Locuciones básicas*

Can you get me a doctor?	**¿Puede llamar a un médico?**	**pway**dhay lyah**mahr** ah oon **meh**dheekoa
Is there a doctor here?	**¿Hay un médico aquí?**	igh oon **meh**dheekoa ah**kee**
I need a doctor quickly.	**Necesito un médico —rápidamente.**	naythayseetoa oon meh dheekoa **rah**peedhahmayntay
Where can I find a doctor who speaks English?	**¿Dónde puedo encontrar un médico que hable inglés?**	**doan**day **pway**dhoa aynkon**trahr** oon **meh**dheekoa kay **ah**blay eeng**layss**
Where's the surgery (doctor's office)?	**¿Dónde es la consulta?**	**doan**day ayss lah koan**sool**tah
What are the surgery (office) hours?	**¿Cuáles son las horas de consulta?**	**kwah**layss son lahss **oa**rahss day koan**sool**tah
Could the doctor come to see me here?	**¿Podría venir el médico a reconocerme?**	poa**dree**ah bay**neer** ayl **meh**deekoa ah raykoanoa**thayr**may
What time can the doctor come?	**¿A qué hora puede venir el doctor?**	ah kay **oa**rah **pway**dhay bay**neer** ayl doak**toar**
Can you recommend a/an ...?	**¿Me puede recomendar a un ...?**	may **pway**dhay raykoamayn**dahr** ah oon
general practitioner	**generalista**	khaynayrah**lees**tah
children's doctor	**pediatra**	pay**dhyah**trah
eye specialist	**oculista**	oakoo**lees**tah
gynaecologist	**ginecólogo**	kheenay**koa**loagoa
Can I have an appointment ...?	**¿Me puede dar una cita ...?**	may **pway**dhay dahr **oo**nah **thee**tah
right now	**inmediatamente**	eenmaydhyahtah**mayn**tay
tomorrow	**mañana**	mah**ñah**nah
as soon as possible	**tan pronto como sea posible**	tahn **proan**toa **koa**moa **say**ah poa**ssee**blay

CHEMIST'S, see page 108

Parts of the body *Partes del cuerpo*

arm	**el brazo**	ayl **brah**thoa
artery	**la arteria**	lah ahr**tay**ryah
back	**la espalda**	lah ay**spahl**dah
bladder	**la vesícula**	lah bay**ssee**koolah
bone	**el hueso**	ayl **way**ssoa
bowels	**los intestinos**	loass eentay**stee**noass
breast	**el seno**	ayl **say**noa
chest	**el pecho**	ayl **pay**choa
ear	**la oreja**	lah oa**ray**khah
eye	**el ojo**	ayl **oa**khoa
face	**la cara**	lah **kah**rah
finger	**el dedo**	ayl **day**dhoa
foot	**el pie**	ayl pyay
gland	**la glándula**	lah **glahn**doolah
hand	**la mano**	lah **mah**noa
head	**la cabeza**	lah kah**bhay**thah
heart	**el corazón**	ayl koarah**thon**
jaw	**la mandíbula**	lah mahn**dee**bhoolah
joint	**la articulación**	lah ahrteekoolah**thyon**
kidney	**el riñón**	ayl ree**ñon**
knee	**la rodilla**	lah roa**dhee**lyah
leg	**la pierna**	lah **pyehr**nah
lip	**el labio**	ayl **lah**bhyoa
liver	**el hígado**	ayl **ee**gahdhoa
lung	**el pulmón**	ayl pool**mon**
mouth	**la boca**	lah **boa**kah
muscle	**el músculo**	ayl **moos**kooloa
neck	**el cuello**	ayl **kway**lyoa
nerve	**el nervio**	ayl **nehr**byoa
nervous system	**el sistema nervioso**	ayl seestaymah nehr**byoa**ssoa
nose	**la nariz**	lah nah**reeth**
rib	**la costilla**	lah koas**tee**lyah
shoulder	**la espalda**	lah ay**spahl**dah
skin	**la piel**	lah pyayl
spine	**la espina dorsal**	lah ay**spee**nah doar**sahl**
stomach	**el estómago**	ayl ay**stoa**mahgoa
tendon	**el tendón**	ayl tayn**don**
thigh	**el muslo**	ayl **moos**loa
throat	**la garganta**	lah gahr**gahn**tah
thumb	**el pulgar**	ayl pool**gahr**
toe	**el dedo del pie**	ayl **day**dhoa dayl pyay
tongue	**la lengua**	lah **layn**gwah
tonsils	**las amígdalas**	lahss ah**meeg**dahlahss
vein	**la vena**	lah **bay**nah

Accident—Injury *Accidente – Herida*

There has been an accident.	**Ha habido un accidente.**	ah ahb**hee**dhoa oon akthee**dayn**tay
My child has had a fall.	**Se ha caído el niño/la niña.**	say ah ka**hee**dhoa ayl **nee**ñoa/lah **nee**ñah
He/She has hurt his/her head.	**Se ha dado un golpe en la cabeza.**	say ah **dah**dhoa oon **goal**pay ayn lah kah**bhay**thah
He's/She's unconscious.	**Está inconsciente.**	ay**stah** eenkoans**thyayn**tay
He's/She's bleeding heavily.	**Está sangrando mucho.**	ay**stah** sahn**grahn**doa **moo**choa
He's/She's (seriously) injured.	**Tiene una herida (muy seria).**	**tyay**nay **oo**nah ay**ree**dhah (mwee **say**ryah)
His/Her arm is broken.	**Su brazo está roto.**	soo **brah**thoa ay**stah roa**toa
His/Her ankle is swollen.	**Su tobillo está hinchado.**	soo toa**bhee**lyoa ay**stah** een**chah**dhoa
I've cut myself.	**Me he cortado.**	may ay koar**tah**dhoa
I've pulled a muscle.	**Tengo un músculo distendido.**	**tayn**goa oon **moos**kooloa deestayn**dee**dhoa
I've got something in my eye.	**Me ha entrado algo en el ojo.**	may ah ayn**trah**dhoa **ahl**goa ayn ayl **oa**khoa
I've got a/an ...	**Tengo ...**	**tayn**goa
blister	**una ampolla**	**oo**nah ahm**poa**lyah
boil	**un forúnculo**	oon foa**roon**kooloa
bruise	**un cardenal**	oon kahrday**nahl**
burn	**una quemadura**	**oo**nah kaymah**dhoo**rah
cut	**una cortadura**	**oo**nah koartah**dhoo**rah
graze	**un arañazo**	oon ahrah**ñah**thoa
insect bite	**una picadura de insecto**	**oo**nah peekah**dhoo**rah day eensehktoa
lump	**un chichón**	oon chee**choan**
rash	**un sarpullido**	oon sahrpoo**lyee**dhoa
sting	**una picadura**	**oo**nah peekah**dhoo**rah
swelling	**una hinchazón**	**oo**nah eenchah**thon**
wound	**una herida**	**oo**nah ay**ree**dhah
Could you have a look at it?	**¿Podría mirarlo?**	poa**dree**ah mee**rahr**loa
I can't move my ... It hurts.	**No puedo mover el/la ... Me duele.**	noa **pway**dhoa moa**bher ayl/lah** ... may **dway**lay

No se mueva.	Don't move.
¿Dónde le duele?	Where does it hurt?
¿Qué clase de dolor es?	What kind of pain is it?
apagado/agudo **palpitante/constante** **intermitente**	dull/sharp throbbing/constant on and off
Está roto/torcido/ dislocado/desgarrado.	It's broken/sprained/ dislocated/torn.
Quiero que le hagan una radiografía.	I want you to have an X-ray taken.
Lo van a enyesar.	You'll get a plaster.
Está infectado.	It's infected.
¿Lo han vacunado contra el tétanos?	Have you been vaccinated against tetanus?
Le daré un antiséptico/ un analgésico.	I'll give you an antiseptic/ a painkiller.
Quiero que venga a verme dentro de ... días.	I'd like you to come back in ... days.

Illness *Enfermedad*

I'm not feeling well.	**No me siento bien.**	noa may **syayn**toa byayn
I'm ill.	**Estoy enfermo(a).**	ays**toy** ayn**fehr**moa(ah)
I feel ...	**Me siento ...**	may **syayn**toa
dizzy nauseous shivery	**mareado(a)** **con náuseas** **con escalofríos**	mahray**ah**dhoa(ah) kon **now**ssayahss kon ayskahloa**free**oass
I've got a fever.	**Tengo fiebre.**	**tayn**goa **fyeh**bray
My temperature is 38 degrees.	**Tengo 38 grados de temperatura.**	**tayn**goa 38 **grah**dhoass day taympayrah**too**rah
I've been vomiting.	**He tenido vómitos.**	ay tay**nee**dhoa **boa**meetoass
I'm constipated.	**Estoy estreñido(a).**	ays**toy** aystreh**ñee**dhoa(ah)
I've got diarrhoea.	**Tengo diarrea.**	**tayn**goa dyahr**ray**ah
My ... hurts.	**Me duele ...**	may **dway**lay

NUMBERS, see page 147

I've got (a/an) ...	**Tengo ...**	**tayn**goa
asthma	**asma**	**ahs**mah
backache	**dolor de espalda**	doa**lor** day ays**pahl**dah
cold	**un resfriado**	oon rays**fryah**dhoa
cough	**tos**	toass
cramps	**calambres**	kah**lahm**brayss
earache	**dolor de oídos**	doa**lor** day oa**ee**dhoass
headache	**dolor de cabeza**	doa**lor** day kah**bhay**thah
indigestion	**una indigestión**	**oo**nah eendeekhays**tyon**
nosebleed	**una hemorragia nasal**	**oo**nah aymoar**rah**khyah nah**ssahl**
palpitations	**palpitaciones**	pahlpeetah**thyo**nayss
rheumatism	**reumatismo**	rayoomah**tees**moa
sore throat	**anginas**	ahn**khee**nahss
stiff neck	**tortícolis**	tor**tee**koaleess
stomach ache	**dolor de estómago**	doa**lor** day ays**toa**mahgoa
sunstroke	**una insolación**	**oo**nah eensoalah**thyon**
I have difficulties breathing.	**Tengo dificultades respiratorias.**	**tayn**goa deefeekoolltah**dhay**ss rayspeerah**toa**ryahss
I have a pain in my chest.	**Tengo un dolor en el pecho.**	**tayn**goa oon doa**lor** ayn ayl **pay**choa
I had a heart attack ... years ago.	**Tuve un ataque al corazón hace ... años.**	**too**bhay oon ah**tah**kay ahl koarah**thon ah**thay ... **ah**ñoass
My blood pressure is too high/too low.	**Mi presión sanguínea es demasiado alta/baja.**	mee pray**ssyon** sahn**gee**nayah ayss daymah**ssyah**dhoa **ahl**tah/**bah**khah
I'm allergic to ...	**Soy alérgico(a) a ...**	soy ah**lehr**kheekoa(ah) ah
I'm a diabetic.	**Soy diabético(a).**	soy dyah**bhay**teekoa(ah)

Women's section *Asuntos de la mujer*

I have period pains.	**Tengo dolores menstruales.**	**tayn**goa doa**loa**rayss mayns**trooahl**ayss
I have a vaginal infection.	**Tengo una infección vaginal.**	**tayn**goa **oo**nah eenfayk**thyon** bahkhee**nahl**
I'm on the pill.	**Tomo la píldora.**	**toa**moa lah **peel**doarah
I haven't had my period for 2 months.	**Hace dos meses que no tengo reglas.**	**ah**thay doass **may**ssayss kay noa **tayn**goa **ray**glahss
I'm pregnant.	**Estoy embarazada.**	ays**toy** aymbahrah**thah**dhah

¿Cuánto tiempo hace que se siente así?	How long have you been feeling like this?
¿Es la primera vez que ha tenido esto?	Is this the first time you've had this?
Le voy a tomar la presión/ la temperatura.	I'll take your blood pressure/ temperature.
Súbase la manga, por favor.	Roll up your sleeve, please.
Desvístase (hasta la cintura), por favor.	Please undress (down to the waist).
Acuéstese ahí, por favor.	Please lie down over there.
Abra la boca.	Open your mouth.
Respire profundo.	Breathe deeply.
Toca, por favor.	Cough, ploooo.
¿Dónde le duele?	Where do you feel the pain?
Tiene (un/una) . . .	You've got (a/an) . . .
apendicitis	appendicitis
cistitis	cystitis
enfermedad venérea	venereal disease
gastritis	gastritis
gripe	flu
ictericia	jaundice
inflamación de . . .	inflammation of . . .
intoxicación	food poisoning
neumonía	pneumonia
sarampión	measles
Le pondré una inyección.	I'll give you an injection.
Necesito una muestra de sangre/heces/orina.	I want a specimen of your blood/stools/urine.
Debe quedarse en cama durante . . . días.	You must stay in bed for . . . days.
Quiero que consulte a un especialista.	I want you to see a specialist.
Quiero que vaya al hospital para un reconocimiento general.	I want you to go to the hospital for a general check-up.
Tendrán que operarlo.	You'll have to have an operation.

Prescription—Treatment *Prescripción – Tratamiento*

This is my usual medicine.	**Esta es la medicina que tomo normalmente.**	**ay**stah ayss lah maydheet**hee**nah kay **toa**moa noarmahl**mayn**tay
Can you give me a prescription for this?	**¿Puede darme una receta para esto?**	**pway**dhay **dahr**may **oo**nah ray**thay**tah **pah**rah **ays**toa
Can you prescribe an antidepressant/ some sleeping pills?	**¿Puede recetarme un antidepresivo/ un somnífero?**	**pway**dhay raythay**tahr**may oon ahnteedaypray**ssee**bhoa oon soam**nee**fayroa
I'm allergic to antibiotics/penicilline.	**Soy alérgico(a) a los antibióticos/ la penicilina.**	soy ah**lehr**kheekoa(ah) ah loass ahntee**bhyoa**teekoass/ lah payneethee**lee**nah
I don't want anything too strong.	**No quiero nada demasiado fuerte.**	noa **kyay**roa **nah**dhah daymah**ssyah**dhoa **fwayr**tay
How many times a day should I take it?	**¿Cuántas veces al día tengo que tomarlo?**	**kwahn**tahss **bay**thayss ahl **deeah tayn**goa kay toa**mahr**loa

¿Qué tratamiento está siguiendo?	What treatment are you having?
¿Qué medicina está tomando?	What medicine are you taking?
¿Qué dosis utiliza normalmente?	What's your normal dose?
En inyección u oral?	Injection or oral?
Tome .. cucharillas de esta medicina ... cucharillas de esta medicina ...	Take ... teaspoons of this medicine ...
Tome una píldora con un vaso de agua ...	Take one pill with a glass of water ...
cada ... horas **... veces por día** **antes/después de cada comida** **por la mañana/por la noche** **en caso de dolor** **durante ... días**	every ... hours ... times a day before/after each meal in the morning/at night in case of pain for ... days

CHEMIST'S, see p. 108

Fee *Honorarios*

How much do I owe you?	**¿Cuánto le debo?**	**kwahn**toa lay **day**bhoa
May I have a receipt for my health insurance?	**¿Puede darme un recibo para mi seguro?**	**pway**dhay **dahr**may oon ray**thee**bhoa **pah**rah mee say**goo**roa
Can I have a medical certificate?	**¿Me puede dar un certificado médico?**	may **pway**dhay dahr oon thayrteefee**kah**dhoa **may**dheekoa
Would you fill in this health insurance form, please?	**¿Quiere llenar esta hoja de seguro, por favor?**	**kyay**ray lyay**nahr ays**tah **oa**khah day say**goo**roa por fah**bhor**

Hospital *Hospital*

What are the visiting hours?	**¿Cuáles son las horas de visita?**	**kwah**layss son lahss **oa**rahss day bee**see**tah
When can I get up?	**¿Cuándo puedo levantarme?**	**kwahn**doa **pway**dhoa laybhahn**tahr**may
When will the doctor come?	**¿Cuándo viene el médico?**	**kwahn**doa **byay**nay ayl **may**dheekoa
I can't eat/sleep.	**No puedo comer/dormir.**	noa **pway**dhoa koa**mayr**/dor**meer**
I'm in pain.	**Me duele.**	may **dway**lay
Can I have a painkiller?	**¿Me puede dar un analgésico?**	may **pway**dhay **dahr** oon ahnahl**khay**sseekoa

doctor/surgeon	**el médico/cirujano**	ayl **may**dheekoa/theeroo**khah**noa
nurse	**la enfermera**	lah aynfayr**may**rah
patient	**el/la paciente**	ayl/lah pah**thyayn**tay
anaesthetic	**el anestésico**	ayl ahnays**tay**sseekoa
blood transfusion	**la transfusión de sangre**	lah trahnsfoo**ssyon** day **sahn**gray
injection	**la inyección**	lah eenyayk**thyon**
operation	**la operación**	lah oapayrah**thyon**
bed	**la cama**	lah **kah**mah
bedpan	**la silleta**	lah see**lyay**tah
thermometer	**el termómetro**	ayl tayr**moa**maytroa

Dentist *Dentista*

Can you recommend a good dentist?	**¿Puede recomendarme un buen dentista?**	pwaydhay raykoamayndahrmay oon bwayn daynteestah
Can I make an (urgent) appointment to see Dr ...?	**¿Puedo pedir cita (urgente) para ver al Doctor ...?**	pwaydhoa paydheer theetah (oorkhayntay) pahrah behr ahl doaktor
Can't you possibly make it earlier than that?	**¿No sería posible antes?**	noa sayreeah poasseeblay ahntayss
I have a broken tooth.	**Me he roto un diente.**	may ay roatoa oon dyayntay
I have a toothache.	**Tengo dolor de muelas.**	tayngoa doalor day mwaylahss
I have an abscess.	**Tengo un flemón.**	tayngoa oon flaymon
This tooth hurts.	**Me duele este diente.**	may dwaylay aystay dyayntay
at the top	**arriba**	ahrreebhah
at the bottom	**abajo**	ahbhahkhoa
in the front	**delante**	daylahntay
at the back	**detrás**	daytrahss
Can you fix it temporarily?	**¿Puede usted arreglarlo temporalmente?**	pwaydhay oostaydh ahrrayglahrloa taympoarahlmayntay
I don't want it extracted.	**No quiero que me la saque.**	noa kyayroa kay may lah sahkay
Could you give me an anaesthetic?	**¿Puede ponerme anestesia local?**	pwaydhay poanayrmay ahnaystayssyah loakahl
I've lost a filling.	**He perdido un empaste.**	ay pehrdeedhoa oon aympahstay
The gum is very sore/bleeding.	**La encía está muy inflamada/sangra.**	lah ayntheeah aystah mwee eenflahmahdhah/sahngrah
I've broken this denture.	**Se me ha roto la dentadura.**	say may ah roatoa lah dayntahdhoorah
Can you repair this denture?	**¿Puede usted arreglar esta dentadura?**	pwaydhay oostaydh ahrrayglahr aystah dayntahdhoorah
When will it be ready?	**¿Cuándo estará lista?**	kwahndoa aystahrah leestah

Reference section

Where do you come from? *¿De dónde viene usted?*

Africa	**Africa**	**ah**freekah
Asia	**Asia**	**ah**ssyah
Australia	**Australia**	ow**strah**lyah
Europe	**Europa**	ayoo**roa**pah
North/South/ Central America	**América del Norte/ del Sur/Central**	ah**may**reekah dayl **nor**tay/ dayl soor/thayn**trahl**
Algeria	**Argelia**	ahr**khay**lyah
Austria	**Austria**	**ow**stryah
Belgium	**Bélgica**	**bayl**kheekah
Canada	**Canadá**	kahnah**dhah**
China	**China**	**chee**nah
Denmark	**Dinamarca**	deenah**mahr**ka
England	**Inglaterra**	eenglah**tay**rrah
Finland	**Finlandia**	feen**lahn**dyah
France	**Francia**	**frahn**thyah
Germany	**Alemania**	ahlay**mah**nyah
Gibraltar	**Gibraltar**	kheebrahl**tahr**
Great Britain	**Gran Bretaña**	grahn bray**tah**ñah
Greece	**Grecia**	**gray**thyah
India	**India**	**een**dyah
Ireland	**Irlanda**	eer**lahn**dah
Israel	**Israel**	eesrah**ayl**
Italy	**Italia**	ee**tah**lyah
Japan	**Japón**	khah**pon**
Luxembourg	**Luxemburgo**	looksaym**boor**goa
Morocco	**Marruecos**	mahr**rway**koass
Netherlands	**Países Bajos**	pah**ee**ssayss **bah**khoass
New Zealand	**Nueva Zelandia**	**nway**bhah thay**lahn**dyah
Norway	**Noruega**	noar**way**gah
Portugal	**Portugal**	portoo**gahl**
Scotland	**Escocia**	ay**skoa**thyah
South Africa	**Africa del Sur**	**ah**freekah dayl soor
Soviet Union	**Unión Soviética**	oo**nyon** soa**bhyay**teekah
Spain	**España**	ay**spah**ñah
Sweden	**Suecia**	**sway**thyah
Switzerland	**Suiza**	**swee**thah
Tunisia	**Túnez**	**too**nayth
Turkey	**Turquía**	toor**kee**ah
United States	**Estados Unidos**	ay**stahd**hoass oo**need**hoass
Wales	**País de Gales**	pah**eess** day **gah**layss
Yugoslavia	**Yugoslavia**	yogoas**lah**bhyah

Numbers *Números*

0	**cero**	**thay**roa
1	**uno**	**oo**noa
2	**dos**	doss
3	**tres**	trayss
4	**cuatro**	**kwah**troa
5	**cinco**	**theen**koa
6	**seis**	sayss
7	**siete**	**syay**tay
8	**ocho**	**oa**choa
9	**nueve**	**nway**bhay
10	**diez**	dyayth
11	**once**	**on**thay
12	**doce**	**doa**thay
13	**trece**	**tray**thay
14	**catorce**	kah**tor**thay
15	**quince**	**keen**thay
16	**dieciséis**	dyaythee**ssayss**
17	**diecisiete**	dyaythee**ssyay**tay
18	**dieciocho**	dyaythee**oa**choa
19	**diecinueve**	dyaythee**nway**bhay
20	**veinte**	**bayn**tay
21	**veintiuno**	baynteeoonoa
22	**veintidós**	bayntee**doss**
23	**veintitrés**	bayntee**trayss**
24	**veinticuatro**	bayntee**kwah**troa
25	**veinticinco**	bayntee**theen**koa
26	**veintiséis**	bayntee**ssayss**
27	**veintisiete**	bayntee**ssyay**tay
28	**veintiocho**	bayntee**oa**choa
29	**veintinueve**	bayntee**nway**bhay
30	**treinta**	**trayn**tah
31	**treinta y uno**	**trayn**tah ee **oo**noa
32	**treinta y dos**	**trayn**tah ee doss
33	**treinta y tres**	trayntah ee trayss
40	**cuarenta**	kwah**rayn**tah
50	**cincuenta**	theen**kwayn**tah
60	**sesenta**	say**ssayn**tah
70	**setenta**	say**tayn**tah
80	**ochenta**	oa**chayn**tah
90	**noventa**	noa**bhayn**tah
100	**cien/ciento***	thyayn/**thyayn**toa
101	**ciento uno**	**thyayn**toa **oo**noa
102	**ciento dos**	**thyayn**toa doss

* *cien* is used before nouns and adjectives.

110	**ciento diez**	**thyayn**toa dyayth
120	**ciento veinte**	**thyayn**toa **bayn**tay
200	**doscientos**	dos**thyayn**toass
300	**trescientos**	trays**thyayn**toass
400	**cuatrocientos**	kwahtroa**thyayn**toass
500	**quinientos**	kee**nyayn**toass
600	**seiscientos**	says**thyayn**toass
700	**setecientos**	saytay**thyayn**toass
800	**ochocientos**	oachoa**thyayn**toass
900	**novecientos**	noabhay**thyayn**toass
1,000	**mil**	meel
1,100	**mil cien**	meel thyayn
2,000	**dos mil**	dos meel
10,000	**diez mil**	dyayth meel
100,000	**cien mil**	thyayn meel
1,000,000	**un millón**	oon mee**lyon**

1981	**mil novecientos ochenta y uno**	meel noabhay**thyayn**toass oa**chayn**tah ee **oo**noa
1992	**mil novecientos noventa y dos**	meel noabhay**thyan**toass noa**bhayn**tah ee doss
2003	**dos mil tres**	dos meel trayss
first	**primero**	pree**may**roa
second	**segundo**	say**goon**doa
third	**tercero**	tehr**thay**roa
fourth	**cuarto**	**kwahr**toa
fifth	**quinto**	**keen**toa
sixth	**sexto**	**sayks**toa
seventh	**séptimo**	**sayp**teemoa
eighth	**octavo**	oak**tah**bhoa
ninth	**noveno**	noa**bhay**noa
tenth	**décimo**	**day**theemoa
once	**una vez**	**oo**nah behth
twice	**dos veces**	doss **bay**thayss
three times	**tres veces**	trayss **bay**thayss
a half	**una mitad**	**oo**nah mee**tahdh**
half a ...	**medio ...**	**may**dhyoa
half of ...	**la mitad de ...**	lah mee**tahdh** day
half (adj.)	**medio**	**may**dhyoa
a quarter	**un cuarto**	oon **kwahr**toa
one third	**un tercio**	oon **tehr**thyoa
a dozen	**una docena**	**oo**nah do**thay**nah
3.4%	**3,4 por ciento**	trayss **koa**mah cuatro por **thyayn**toa

Year and age *Año y edad*

year	**el año**	ayl **ah**ñoa
leap year	**el año bisiesto**	ayl **ah**ñoa bee**ssyays**toa
decade	**la década**	lah **day**kahdah
century	**el siglo**	ayl **see**gloa
this year	**este año**	**ays**tay **ah**ñoa
last year	**el año pasado**	ayl **ah**ñoa pah**ssah**dhoa
next year	**el año próximo**	ayl **ah**ñoa **proak**seemoa
each year	**cada año**	**kah**dhah **ah**ñoa
Which year?	**¿Qué año?**	kay **ah**ñoa
two years ago	**hace dos años**	**ah**thay doss **ah**ñoass
in one year	**dentro de un año**	**dayn**troa day oon **ah**ñoa
in the eighties	**en los años ochenta**	ayn loass **ah**ñoass oa**chayn**tah
from the fifties	**desde los años cincuenta**	**days**day loass **ah**ñoass theen**kwayn**tah
the 16th century	**el siglo XVI**	ayl **see**gloa dyaytheessayss
from the 19th century	**desde el siglo XIX**	**days**day ayl **see**gloa dyaythee**nway**bhay
in the 20th century	**en el siglo XX**	ayn ayl **see**gloa **bayn**tay
old/young	**viejo/joven**	**byay**khoa/**khoa**bhehn
old/new	**viejo/nuevo**	**byay**khoa/**nway**bhoa
recent	**reciente**	ray**thyayn**tay
How old are you?	**¿Cuántos años tiene?**	**kwahn**toass **ah**ñoass **tyay**nay
I'm 30 years old.	**Tengo 30 años.**	**tayn**goa 30 **ah**ñoass
What's his/her age?	**¿Cuál es su edad?**	kwahl ays soo ay**dhahdh**
He/She was born in 1977.	**Nació en 1977.**	nah**thyoa** ayn 1977
Children under 16 are not admitted.	**No se admiten niños menores de 16 años.**	noa say ahd**mee**tayn **nee**ñoass **may**noarayss day 16 **ah**ñoass

Seasons *Estaciones*

spring	**la primavera**	lah preemah**bhay**rah
summer	**el verano**	ayl bay**rah**noa
autumn	**el otoño**	ayl o**toa**ñoa
winter	**el invierno**	ayl een**byayr**noa
in spring	**en primavera**	ayn preemah**bhay**rah
during the summer	**durante el verano**	doo**rahn**tay ayl bay**rah**noa
high season	**alta estación**	**ahl**tah aystah**thyon**
low season	**baja estación**	**bah**khah aystah**thyon**

Months *Meses*

January	**enero***	ay**nay**roa
February	**febrero**	feh**breh**roa
March	**marzo**	**mahr**thoa
April	**abril**	ah**breel**
May	**mayo**	**mah**yoa
June	**junio**	**khoo**nyoa
July	**julio**	**khoo**lyoa
August	**agosto**	ah**goas**toa
September	**septiembre**	sehp**tyaym**bray
October	**octubre**	ok**too**bray
November	**noviembre**	noa**bhyaym**bray
December	**diciembre**	dee**thyaym**bray
after June	**después de junio**	days**pwayss** day **khoo**nyoa
before July	**antes de julio**	**ahn**tays day **khoo**lyoa
during the month of August	**durante el mes de agosto**	doo**rahn**tay ayl mayss day ah**goas**toa
in September	**en septiembre**	ayn sehp**tyaym**bray
until November	**hasta noviembre**	**ahs**tah noa**bhyaym**bray
since December	**desde diciembre**	**days**day dee**thyaym**bray
last month	**el mes pasado**	ayl mayss pah**ssah**dhoa
next month	**el mes próximo**	ayl mayss **prok**seemoa
the month before	**el mes anterior**	ayl mayss ahnteh**ryor**
the month after	**el mes siguiente**	ayl mayss see**gyayn**tay
the beginning of January	**a principios de enero**	ah preen**thee**pyoass day ay**nay**roa
the middle of February	**a mediados de febrero**	ah may**dhyah**dhoass day feh**breh**roa
the end of March	**a finales de marzo**	ah fee**nah**layss day **mahr**thoa

Dates *Fechas*

What's the date today?	**¿En qué fecha estamos?**	ayn kay **fay**chah ay**stah**moass
When's your birthday?	**¿Cuándo es su cumpleaños?**	**kwahn**doa ayss soo koomplay**ah**ñoass
July 1	**el primero de julio**	ayl pree**may**roa day **khoo**lyoa
March 10	**el diez de marzo**	ayl dyayth day **mahr**thoa

* The names of months aren't capitalized in Spanish.

Days *Días de la semana*

What day is it today?	**¿Qué día es hoy?**	kay **dee**ah ayss oy
Sunday	**domingo***	doa**meen**goa
Monday	**lunes**	**loo**nayss
Tuesday	**martes**	**mahr**tayss
Wednesday	**miércoles**	**myayr**koalayss
Thursday	**jueves**	**khway**bhayss
Friday	**viernes**	**byayr**nayss
Saturday	**sábado**	**sah**bhadhoa
in the morning	**por la mañana**	por lah mah**ñah**nah
during the day	**durante el día**	doo**rahn**tay ayl **dee**ah
in the afternoon	**por la tarde**	por lah **tahr**day
in the evening	**por la tarde**	por lah **tahr**day
at night	**por la noche**	por lah **noa**chay
at dawn	**al amanecer**	ahl ahmahnay**thayr**
at dusk	**al anochecer**	ahl ahnoachay**thayr**
yesterday	**ayer**	ah**yehr**
today	**hoy**	oy
tomorrow	**mañana**	mah**ñah**nah
the day before	**el día anterior**	ayl **dee**ah ahnteh**ryor**
the next day	**el día siguiente**	ayl **dee**ah see**gyayn**tay
two days ago	**hace dos días**	**ah**thay doss **dee**ahss
in three days' time	**en tres días**	ayn trayss **dee**ahss
last week	**la semana pasada**	lah say**mah**nah pah**ssah**dhah
next week	**la semana próxima**	lah say**mah**nah **prok**seemah
in two weeks	**por una quincena**	por **oo**nah keen**theh**nah
birthday	**el cumpleaños**	ayl koomplay**ah**ñoass
day	**el día**	ayl **dee**ah
day off	**el día libre**	ayl **dee**ah **lee**bray
holiday	**el día festivo**	ayl **dee**ah fays**tee**bhoa
holidays	**las vacaciones**	lahss bahkah**thyo**nayss
school holidays	**las vacaciones del colegio**	lahss bahkah**thyo**nayss dayl koa**leh**khyoa
vacation	**las vacaciones**	lahss bahkah**thyo**nayss
week	**la semana**	lah say**mah**nah
weekday	**el día de la semana**	ayl **dee**ah day lah say**mah**nah
weekend	**el fin de semana**	ayl feen day say**mah**nah
working day	**el día laborable**	ayl **dee**ah lahbhoa**rah**blay

* The names of days aren't capitalized in Spanish.

Public holidays *Días festivos*

These are the main public holidays in Spain when banks, offices and shops are closed. In addition, there are various regional holidays.

January 1	**Año Nuevo**	New Year's Day
January 6	**Epifanía**	Epiphany
March 19	**San José**	St Joseph's Day
	Viernes Santo	Good Friday
	Lunes de Pascua	Easter Monday (Catalonia only)
May 1	**Día del Trabajo**	Labour Day
	Corpus Christi	Corpus Christi Day
July 25	**Santiago Apóstol**	St James's Day
August 15	**Asunción**	Assumption Day
October 12	**Día de la Hispanidad**	Columbus Day
November 1	**Todos los Santos**	All Saints' Day
December 6	**Día de la Constitución Española**	Constitution Day
December 8	**Inmaculada Concepción**	Immaculate Conception Day
December 25	**Navidad**	Christmas Day

Greetings *Saludos*

Merry Christmas!	**¡Feliz Navidad!**	fay**leeth** nahbhee**dhahdh**
Happy New Year!	**¡Feliz Año Nuevo!**	fay**leeth ah**ñoa **nway**bhoa
Happy Easter!	**¡Felices Pascuas!**	fay**lee**thayss **pahs**kwahss
Happy birthday!	**¡Feliz cumpleaños!**	fay**leeth** koomplay**ah**ñoass
Best wishes!	**¡Mejores deseos!**	may**khoa**rayss day**ssay**oass
Congratulations!	**¡Enhorabuena!**	aynoarah**bway**nah
Good luck!	**¡Buena suerte!**	**bway**nah **swayr**tay
Have a nice trip!	**¡Buen viaje!**	bwayn **byah**khay
All the best!	**¡Qué todo salga bien!**	kay **toa**dhoa **sahl**gah byayn
Best regards from/to ...	**Recuerdos de/a ...**	ray**kwayr**doass day/ah
Give my love to ...	**Saludos cariñosos a ...**	sah**loo**dhoass kahree**ñoa**ssoass ah

What time is it? *¿Qué hora es?*

Excuse me. Can you tell me the time?	**Perdone. ¿Puede decirme la hora?**	payr**doa**nay. **pway**dhay day**theer**may lah **oa**rah
It's ...	**Es/Son ...**	ayss/son
five past one	**la una y cinco**	lah **oo**nah ee **theen**koa
ten past two	**las dos y diez**	lahss doss ee dyayth
a quarter past three	**las tres y cuarto**	lahss trayss ee **kwahr**toa
twenty past four	**las cuatro y veinte**	lahss **kwah**troa ee **bayn**tay
twenty-five past five	**las cinco y veinticinco**	lahss **theen**koa ee bayntee**theen**koa
half past six	**las seis y media**	lahss sayss ee **may**dhyay
twenty-five to seven	**las siete menos veinticinco**	lahss **say**tay **may**noass baynte**etheen**koa
twenty to eight	**las ocho menos veinte**	lahss **oa**choa **may**noass **bayn**tay
a quarter to nine	**las nueve menos cuarto**	lahss **nway**bhay **may**noass **kwahr**toa
ten to ten	**las diez menos diez**	lahss dyayth **may**noass dyayth
five to eleven	**las once menos cinco**	lahss **on**thay **may**noass **theen**koa
twelve o'clock	**las doce**	lahss **doa**thay
a.m.	**de la mañana**	de lah mah**ñah**nah
p.m.	**de la tarde**	de lah **tahr**day
The train leaves at ...	**El tren sale a ...**	ayl trayn **sah**lay ah
13.04 (1.04 p.m.)	**las trece y cuatro**	lahss **tray**thay ee **kwah**troa
0.45 (0.45 a.m.)	**las cero horas y cuarenta y cinco**	lahss **thay**roa **oa**rahss ee kwah**rayn**tah ee **theen**koa
in five minutes	**en cinco minutos**	ayn **theen**koa mee**noo**toass
in a quarter of an hour	**en un cuarto de hora**	ayn oon **kwahr**toa day **oa**rah
half an hour ago	**hace media hora**	**ah**thay **may**dhyah **oa**rah
about two hours	**aproximadamente dos horas**	ahproakseemahdhah**mayn**tay doss **oa**rahss
more than ten minutes	**más de diez minutos**	mahss day dyayth mee**noo**toass
less than thirty seconds	**menos de treinta segundos**	**may**noass day **trayn**tah say**goon**doass
noon	**mediodía**	maydhyoa**dhee**ah
midnight	**medianoche**	maydhyah**noa**chay
early	**temprano**	taym**prah**noa
late	**tarde**	**tahr**day
in time	**a tiempo**	ah **tyaym**poa

Abbreviations *Abreviaturas*

A.C.	**año de Cristo**	A.D.
a/c	**al cuidado de**	c/o
a. de J.C.	**antes de Jesucristo**	B.C.
admón.	**administración**	administration
apdo.	**apartado de correos**	post office box
Av., Avda.	**Avenida**	avenue
C., Cía.	**Compañía**	company
C/	**Calle**	street
cta.	**cuenta**	account
cte.	**corriente**	of the present month
C.V.	**caballos de vapor**	horsepower
D.	**Don**	courtesy title (gentleman)
Da., Dª	**Doña**	courtesy title (lady)
EE.UU.	**Estados Unidos**	United States
f.c.	**ferrocarril**	railway
G.C.	**Guardia Civil**	police
h.	**hora**	hour
hab.	**habitantes**	population
M.I.T.	**Ministerio de Información y Turismo**	Ministry of Information and Tourism
Nª Sª	**Nuestra Señora**	Our Lady, the Virgin
Nº, núm.	**número**	number
p. ej.	**por ejemplo**	for example
P.P.	**porte pagado**	postage paid
pta., ptas.	**peseta(s)**	peseta(s)
P.V.P.	**precio de venta al público**	retail price
R.A.C.E.	**Real Automóvil Club de España**	Royal Automobile Club of Spain
R.C.	**Real Club ...**	Royal ... Club
RENFE	**Red Nacional de Ferrocarriles Españoles**	Spanish National Railway
R.N.E.	**Radio Nacional de España**	Spanish National Broadcasting Company
S., Sta.	**San, Santa**	Saint
S.A.	**Sociedad Anónima**	Ltd., Inc.
Sr.	**Señor**	Mr.
Sra.	**Señora**	Mrs.
Sres., Srs.	**Señores**	gentlemen
Srta.	**Señorita**	Miss
TVE	**Televisión Española**	Spanish Television
Ud., Vd.	**Usted**	you (singular)
Uds., Vds.	**Ustedes**	you (plural)
v.g., v.gr.	**verbigracia**	viz., namely

Signs and notices *Letreros e indicaciones*

Abajo	Down
Abierto	Open
Arriba	Up
Ascensor	Lift (elevator)
Averiado	Out of order
Caballeros	Gentlemen
Caja	Cash desk
Caliente	Hot
Carretera particular	Private road
Cerrado	Closed
Cierre la puerta	Close the door
Completo	No vacancy
Cuidado	Caution
Cuidado con el perro	Beware of the dog
Empujar	Push
Entrada	Entrance
Entrada libre	Admission free
Entre sin llamar	Enter without knocking
Frío	Cold
Libre	Vacant
No molestar	Do not disturb
No obstruya la entrada	Do not block entrance
No tocar	Do not touch
Ocupado	Occupied
Peligro	Danger
Peligro de muerte	Danger of death
Pintura fresca	Wet paint
Privado	Private
Prohibido arrojar basuras	No littering
Prohibido entrar	No entry
Prohibido fumar	No smoking
Prohibida la entrada a personas no autorizadas	No trespassing
Rebajas	Sale
Reservado	Reserved
Sala de espera	Waiting room
Salida	Exit
Salida de emergencia	Emergency exit
Se alquila	To let (for rent)
Se vende	For sale
Sendero para bicicletas	Bicycle path
Señoras	Ladies
Servicios	Toilets
Tirar	Pull
Toque el timbre, por favor	Please ring

Emergency *Urgencia*

Call the police	**Llama a la policía**	**lyah**mah ah lah poalee**theeah**
DANGER	**PELIGRO**	pay**lee**groa
FIRE	**FUEGO**	**fway** oa
Gas	**Gas**	gahss
Get a doctor	**Busque un doctor**	**boos**kay oon doak**tor**
Go away	**Váyase**	**bah**yahssay
HELP	**SOCORRO**	soko**arr**oa
Get help quickly	**Busque ayuda rápido**	**boos**kay ah**yoo**dhah **rah**peedhoa
I'm ill	**Estoy enfermo(a)**	ays**toy** ayn**fehr**moa(ah)
I'm lost	**Me he perdido**	may ay payr**dee**dhoa
Leave me alone	**Déjeme en paz**	**day**khaymay ayn pahth
LOOK OUT	**CUIDADO**	kwee**dhah**dhoa
POLICE	**POLICIA**	poalee**thee**ah
Quick	**Rápido**	**rah**peedhoa
STOP	**DETENGASE**	day**tayn**gahssay
Stop that man/woman	**Detenga a ese(a) hombre/mujer**	day**tayn**gah ah **ays**say(ah) **oam**bray/moo**khehr**
STOP THIEF	**AL LADRÓN**	ahl lah**dron**

Lost! *¡Perdido!*

Where's the ...?	**¿Dónde está la ...?**	**doan**day ays**tah** lah
lost property (lost and found) office	**oficina de objetos perdidos**	oafee**thee**nah day oab**khay**toass pehr**dee**dhoass
police station	**comisaría de policía**	koameessah**ree**ah day poalee**thee**ah
I want to report a theft.	**Quiero denunciar un robo.**	**kyay**roa daynoon**thyahr** oon **roa**bhoa
My ... has been stolen.	**Me han robado mi ...**	may ahn roa**bhah**dhoa mee
handbag	**bolso**	**boal**soa
money	**dinero**	dee**nay**roa
passport	**pasaporte**	passah**por**tay
ticket	**billete**	bee**lyay**tay
wallet	**cartera**	kahr**tay**rah
I've lost my ...	**He perdido mi ...**	ay pehr**dee**dhoa mee
I lost it in ...	**Lo perdí en ...**	loa pehr**dee** ayn
this morning	**esta mañana**	**ays**tah mah**ñah**nah
yesterday	**ayer**	ah**yehr**

CAR ACCIDENTS, see page 78

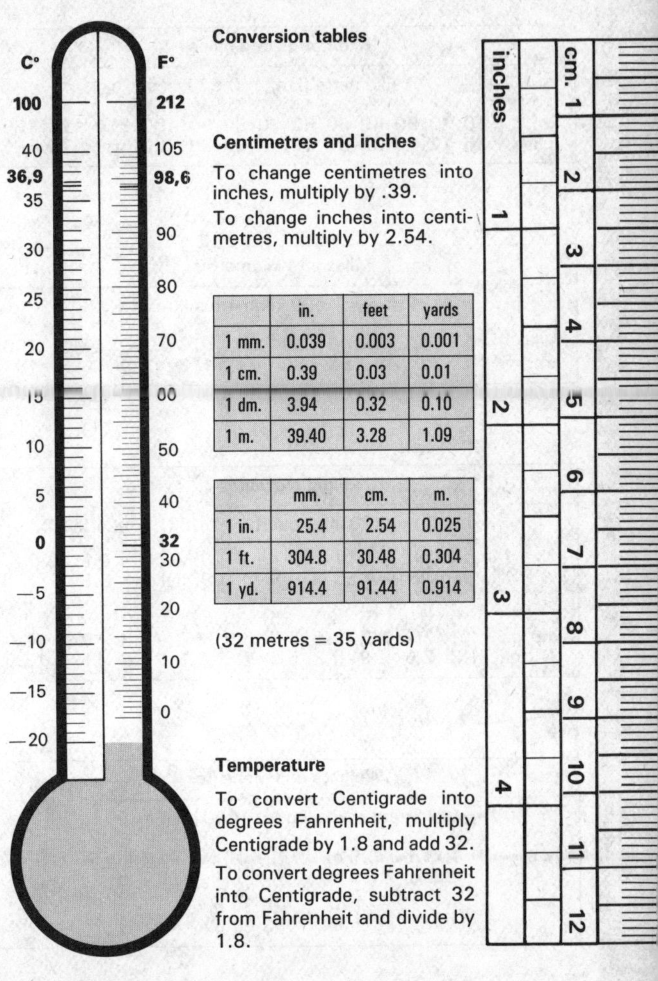

Conversion tables

Centimetres and inches

To change centimetres into inches, multiply by .39.

To change inches into centimetres, multiply by 2.54.

	in.	feet	yards
1 mm.	0.039	0.003	0.001
1 cm.	0.39	0.03	0.01
1 dm.	3.94	0.32	0.10
1 m.	39.40	3.28	1.09

	mm.	cm.	m.
1 in.	25.4	2.54	0.025
1 ft.	304.8	30.48	0.304
1 yd.	914.4	91.44	0.914

(32 metres = 35 yards)

Temperature

To convert Centigrade into degrees Fahrenheit, multiply Centigrade by 1.8 and add 32.

To convert degrees Fahrenheit into Centigrade, subtract 32 from Fahrenheit and divide by 1.8.

Kilometres into miles

1 kilometre (km.) = 0.62 miles

km.	10	20	30	40	50	60	70	80	90	100	110	120	130
miles	6	12	19	25	31	37	44	50	56	62	68	75	81

Miles into kilometres

1 mile = 1.609 kilometres (km.)

miles	10	20	30	40	50	60	70	80	90	100
km.	16	32	48	64	80	97	113	129	145	161

Fluid measures

1 litre (l.) = 0.88 imp. quarts = 1.06 U.S. quarts

1 imp. quart = 1.14 l.
1 imp. gallon = 4.55 l.

1 U.S. quart = 0.95 l.
1 U.S. gallon = 3.8 l.

l.	5	10	15	20	25	30	35	40	45	50
imp. gal.	1.1	2.2	3.3	4.4	5.5	6.6	7.7	8.8	9.9	11.0
U.S. gal.	1.3	2.6	3.9	5.2	6.5	7.8	9.1	10.4	11.7	13.0

Weights and measures

1 kilogram or kilo (kg.) = 1000 grams (g.)

100 g. = 3.5 oz.
200 g. = 7.0 oz.

½ kg. = 1.1 lb.
1 kg. = 2.2 lb.

1 oz. = 28.35 g.
1 lb. = 453.60 g.

Basic Grammar

Articles

Nouns in Spanish are either masculine or feminine. Articles agree in gender and number with the noun.

1. Definite article (the):

	singular		plural
masc.	**el tren**	the train	**los trenes**
fem.	**la casa**	the house	**las casas**

2. Indefinite article (a/an):

masc.	**un lápiz**	a pencil	**unos lápices**
fem.	**una carta**	a letter	**unas cartas**

Nouns

1. Most nouns which end in **o** are masculine. Those ending in **a** are generally feminine.
2. Normally, nouns which end in a vowel add **s** to form the plural; nouns ending in a consonant add **es**.
3. To show possession, use the preposition **de** (of).

el fin de la fiesta	the end of the party
el principio del* mes	the beginning of the month
las maletas de los viajeros	the travellers' suitcases
los ojos de las niñas	the girls' eyes
la habitación de Roberto	Robert's room

* (**del** is the contraction of **de + el**)

Adjectives

1. Adjectives agree with the noun in gender and number. If the masculine form ends in **o** the feminine ends in **a**. As a rule, the adjective comes after the noun.

el niño pequeño	the small boy
la niña pequeña	the small girl

If the masculine form ends in **e** or with a consonant, the feminine keeps in general the same form.

el muro/la casa grande	the big wall/house
el mar/la flor azul	the blue sea/flower

2. Most adjectives form their plurals in the same way as nouns.

un coche inglés	an English car
dos coches ingleses	two English cars

3. Possessive adjectives: They agree with the thing possessed, not with the possessor.

	sing.	plur.
my	**mi**	**mis**
your (fam.)	**tu**	**tus**
your (polite form)	**su**	**sus**
his/her/its	**su**	**sus**
our	**nuestro(a)**	**nuestros(as)**
your	**vuestro(a)**	**vuestros(as)**
their	**su**	**sus**

su hijo	*his* or *her* son
su habitación	*his* or *her* or *their* room
sus maletas	*his* or *her* or *their* suitcases

4. Comparative and superlative: These are formed by adding **más** (more) or **menos** (less) and **lo más** or **lo menos,** respectively, before the adjective.

alto	high	**más alto**	**lo más alto**

Adverbs

These are generally formed by adding **-mente** to the feminine form of the adjective (if it differs from the masculine); otherwise to the masculine.

cierto(a)	sure	**fácil**	easy
ciertamente	surely	**fácilmente**	easily

Possessive pronouns

	sing.	plur.
mine	**mío(a)**	**míos(as)**
yours (fam. sing.)	**tuyo(a)**	**tuyos(as)**
yours (polite form)	**suyo(a)**	**suyos(as)**
his/hers/its	**suyo(a)**	**suyos(as)**
ours	**nuestro(a)**	**nuestros(as)**
yours (fam. pl.)	**vuestro(a)**	**vuestros(as)**
theirs	**suyo(a)**	**suyos(as)**

Demonstrative pronouns

	masc.	fem.	neut.
this	**éste**	**ésta**	**esto**
these	**éstos**	**éstas**	**estos**
that	**ése/aquél**	**ésa/aquélla**	**eso/aquello**
those	**ésos/aquéllos**	**ésas/aquéllas**	**esos/aquellos**

The above masculine and feminine forms are also used as demonstrative adjectives, but accents are dropped. The two forms for "that" designate difference in place; **ése** means "that one", **aquél** "that one over there".

Esos libros no me gustan. I don't like those books.

Eso no me gusta. I don't like that.

Personal pronouns

	subject	direct object	indirect object
I	**yo**	**me**	**me**
you	**tú**	**te**	**te**
you	**usted**	**lo**	**le**
he	**él**	**lo**	**le**
she	**ella**	**la**	**le**
it	**él/ella**	**lo/la**	**le**
we	**nosotros(as)**	**nos**	**nos**
you	**vosotros(as)**	**os**	**os**
	ustedes	**los**	**les**
they	**ellos(as)**	**los**	**les**

Subject pronouns are generally omitted, except in the polite form **(usted, ustedes)** which corresponds to "you". **Tú** (sing.) and **vosotros** (plur.) are used when talking to relatives, close friends and children and between young people; **usted** and the plural **ustedes** (often abbreviated to **Vd./Vds.**) are used in all other cases.

Verbs

Here we are concerned only with the infinitive and the present tense.

	ser* (to be)	**estar*** (to be)	**haber*** (to have)
yo	**soy**	**estoy**	**he**
tú	**eres**	**estás**	**has**
usted	**es**	**está**	**ha**
él/ella	**es**	**está**	**ha**
nosotros(as)	**somos**	**estamos**	**hemos**
vosotros(as)	**sois**	**estáis**	**habéis**
ustedes	**son**	**están**	**han**
ellos(as)	**son**	**están**	**han**

*There are two verbs in Spanish for "to be". **Ser** is used to describe a permanent condition. **Estar** is used to describe location or a temporary condition.

** **haber** is used *only* in compound tenses.

Here are three of the main categories of regular verbs in the present tense:

	ends in **ar** **hablar** (to speak)	ends in **er** **comer** (to eat)	ends in **ir** **reír** (to laugh)
yo	**hablo**	**como**	**río**
tú	**hablas**	**comes**	**ríes**
usted	**habla**	**come**	**ríe**
él/ella	**habla**	**come**	**ríe**
nosotros(as)	**hablamos**	**comemos**	**reímos**
vosotros(as)	**habláis**	**coméis**	**reís**
ustedes	**hablan**	**comen**	**ríen**
ellos(as)	**hablan**	**comen**	**ríen**

Irregular verbs: As in all languages, these have to be learned. Here are four you will find useful.

	poder (to be able)	**ir** (to go)	**ver** (to see)	**tener** (to have)
yo	**puedo**	**voy**	**veo**	**tengo**
tú	**puedes**	**vas**	**ves**	**tienes**
usted	**puede**	**va**	**ve**	**tiene**
él/ella	**puede**	**va**	**ve**	**tiene**
nosotros(as)	**podemos**	**vamos**	**vemos**	**tenemos**
vosotros(as)	**podéis**	**vais**	**veis**	**tenéis**
ustedes	**pueden**	**van**	**ven**	**tienen**
ellos(as)	**pueden**	**van**	**ven**	**tienen**

Negatives

Negatives are formed by placing **no** before the verb.

Es nuevo. It's new. **No es nuevo.** It's not new.

Questions

In Spanish, questions are often formed by changing the intonation of your voice. Very often, the personal pronoun is left out, both in affirmative sentences and in questions.

Hablo español. I speak Spanish.
¿Habla español? Do you speak Spanish?

Note the double question mark used in Spanish.
The same is true of exclamation marks.

¡Qué tarde se hace! How late it's getting!

DICTIONARY

Dictionary
and alphabetical index

English–Spanish

f feminine *m* masculine *pl* plural

a un, una 159
abbey abadía *f* 81
abbreviation abreviatura *f* 154
able, to be poder 163
about *(approximately)* aproximadamente 153
above encima 15, 63
abscess flemón *m* 145
absent ausente 136
absorbent cotton algodón *m* 109
accept, to aceptar, 31, 62, 102
accessories accesorios *m/pl* 117, 125
accident accidente *m* 78, 139
accommodation alojamiento *m* 22
account cuenta *f* 131
ache dolor *m* 141
acne cream crema para el acné *f* 110
adaptor adaptador *m* 119
address señas *f/pl* 21, 102; dirección *f* 31, 76, 79
address book librito de direcciones *m* 104
adhesive adhesivo(a) 105
admission entrada *f* 82, 91, 155
admit, to admitir 149
Africa Africa *f* 146
after después de 77, 150; siguiente 150
afternoon tarde *f* 151
after-shave lotion loción para después del afeitado *f* 110
age edad *f* 149
ago hace 149, 151
air conditioner acondicionador de aire *m* 28
air conditioning aire acondicionado *m* 23
airmail por correo aéreo 133
air mattress colchón neumático *m* 92
airplane avión *m* 65
airport aeropuerto *m* 16, 21, 65
air terminal terminal aérea *f* 21
alarm clock despertador *m* 121
alcohol alcohol *m* 106
Algeria Argelia *f* 146
allergic alérgico(a) 141, 143
almond almendra *f* 53, 54
alphabet alfabeto *m* 9
alter, to *(garment)* arreglar 116
a.m. de la mañana 153
amazing asombroso(a) 84
amber ámbar *m* 122
ambulance ambulancia *f* 79
American americano(a) 105, 126
American plan pensión completa *f* 24
amethyst amatista *f* 122
amount cantidad *f* 62; suma *f* 131
amplifier amplificador *m* 119
anaesthetic anestésico *m* 144, 145
anchovy anchoa *f* 44
and y 15
animal animal *m* 85
aniseed anís *m* 51, 59
ankle tobillo *m* 139
another otro(a) 58
answer respuesta *f* 136
antibiotic antibiótico *m* 143
antidepressant antidepresivo 143
antiques antigüedades *f/pl* 83
antique shop tienda de antigüedades *f* 98

Diccionario

antiseptic antiséptico(a) 109
antiseptic antiséptico *m* 140
any alguno(a) 14
anyone alguien 11
anything algo 17, 25, 113
apartment *(flat)* apartamento *m* 22
aperitif aperitivo *m* 55
appendicitis apendicitis *f* 142
appetizer entremés *m* 41; tapa *f* 63
apple manzana *f* 54, 63
apple juice jugo de manzana *m* 60
appliance aparato *m* 119
appointment cita *f* 30, 131, 137, 145
apricot albaricoque *m* 54
April abril *m* 150
archaeology arqueología *f* 83
architect arquitecto *m* 83
area code indicativo *m* 134
arm brazo *m* 138, 139
arrival llegada *f* 16, 65
arrive, to llegar 65, 68, 130
art arte *m* 83
artery arteria *f* 138
art gallery galería de arte *f* 81, 98
artichoke alcachofa *f* 41, 44, 50
artificial artificial 114, 124
artist artista *m/f* 81, 83
ashtray cenicero *m* 36
Asia Asia *f* 146
ask for, to preguntar 36; pedir 24, 61, 136
asparagus espárrago *m* 41, 50
aspirin aspirina *f* 109
assorted variado(a) 41
asthma asma *m* 141
astringent astringente *m* 110
at a, en 15
at least por lo menos 24
at once ahora mismo 31
aubergine berenjena *f* 50
August agosto *m* 150
aunt tía *f* 94
Australia Australia *f* 146
automatic automático(a) 20, 122, 124
autumn otoño *m* 149
avocado aguacata *m* 41
awful horrible 84

B

baby bebé *m* 24, 111
baby food alimento para bebé *m* 111
babysitter niñera *f* 27
back espalda *f* 138
backache dolor de espalda *m* 141
bacon tocino *m* 38, 47
bacon and eggs huevos con tocino *m/pl* 38
bad malo(a) 11, 14
bag bolsa *f* 103
baggage equipaje *m* 18, 26, 31, 71
baggage car furgón de equipajes *m* 66
baggage cart carrito de equipaje *m* 18, 71
baggage check oficina de equipaje *f* 67, 71
baggage locker consigna automática *f* 18, 67, 71
baked al horno 46, 48
baker's panadería *f* 98
balance *(account)* balance *m* 131
balcony balcón *m* 23
ball *(inflated)* pelota *f* 128
ballet ballet *m* 87
ball-point pen bolígrafo *m* 101
banana plátano *m* 53, 63
bandage venda *f* 109
Band-Aid esparadrapo *m* 109
bangle esclava *f* 121
bangs flequillo *m* 30
bank *(finance)* banco *m* 98, 129, 130
banknote billete *m* 130
barber's barbería *f* 30, 98
basil albahaca *f* 51
basketball baloncesto *m* 90
bath *(hotel)* baño *m* 23, 25, 26
bathing cap gorro de baño *m* 117
bathing hut cabina *f* 92
bathing suit traje de baño *m* 117
bathrobe albornoz *m* 117
bath salts sales de baño *f/pl* 110
bath towel toalla de baño *f* 27
battery pila *f* 119, 121, 125; *(car)* batería *f* 75, 78
be, to ser, estar 13, 162
beach playa *f* 92
bean judía *f* 50
beard barba *f* 31
beautiful bonito(a) 14; hermoso(a) 84
beauty salon salón de belleza *m* 27, 30, 98
bed cama *f* 144
bed and breakfast habitación y desayuno *f* 24
bedpan silleta *f* 144

beef carne de buey *f* 47
beef steak biftec *m* 47
beer cerveza *f* 59
beet(root) remolacha *f* 50
before antes de 150; anterior 150, 151
begin, to empezar 80, 86, 88
beginning principio *m* 150
behind atrás 77
bellboy botones *m* 26
below debajo 14, 63
belt cinturón *m* 118
bend *(road)* curva *f* 79
berth litera *f* 66, 70, 71
best mejor 152
better mejor 14, 25, 101, 114
between entre 15
bicycle bicicleta *f* 74
big grande 14, 101
bill cuenta *f* 31, 62, 102; *(banknote)* billete *m* 130
binoculars binoculares *m/pl* 123
bird pájaro *m* 85
birth nacimiento *m* 25
birthday cumpleaños *m* 151, 152
biscuit *(Br.)* galleta *f* 54, 63; pasta *f* 54
bitter amargo(a) 61
black negro(a) 113
blackberry zarzamora *f* 53
blackcurrant grosella negra *f* 53
bladder vesícula *f* 138
blanket manta *f* 27
blazer blázer *m* 117
bleach aclarado *m* 30
bleed, to sangrar 139, 145
blind *(window)* persiana *f* 29
blister ampolla *f* 139
block *(paper)* bloc *m* 105
blood sangre *f* 142
blood pressure presión *f* 141, 142
blood transfusion transfusión de sangre *f* 144
blouse blusa *f* 113, 117
blow-dry modelado *m* 30
blue azul 113
blueberry arándano *m* 53
blusher colorete *m* 111
boar *(wild)* jabalí *m* 48
boarding house pensión *f* 19, 22
boat barco *m* 74
bobby pin horquilla de pinza *f* 111
body cuerpo *m* 138
boil furúnculo *m* 139
boiled cocido(a) 38; hervido(a) 48; en dulce 42
boiled egg huevo cocido *m* 38
bone hueso *m* 138
bonfire hoguera *f* 32
book libro *m* 11, 104
book, to reservar 69
booking office oficina de reservas *f* 19, 67
booklet taco *m* 72
bookshop librería *f* 98, 104
boot bota *f* 116
born nacido(a) 149
botanical gardens jardín botánico *m* 81
botany botánica *f* 83
bottle botella *f* 17, 58, 59
bottle-opener abridor de botellas *m* 106
bourbon whisky americano *m* 59
bowels intestinos *m/pl* 138
bow tie corbata de lazo *f* 117
box caja *f* 126
boxing boxeo *m* 90
boy niño *m* 112, 128
boyfriend amigo *m* 94
bra sostén *m* 117
bracelet pulsera *f* 121
braces *(suspenders)* tirantes *m/pl* 117
braised estofado(a) 48
brake freno *m* 78
brake fluid líquido de frenos *m* 75
brandy coñac *m* 59
brawn cabeza *f* 41
bread pan *m* 37, 38, 63
break, to romper 29, 119, 123, 139, 140, 145
break down, to estropear 78
breakdown avería *f* 78
breakdown van coche grúa *m* 78
breakfast desayuno *m* 24, 27, 34, 38
breast seno *m* 138
breathe, to respirar 141, 142
bridge puente *m* 85
briefs calzoncillos *m/pl* 117
bring, to traer 12
bring down, to bajar 31
broken roto(a) 29, 119, 139, 140, 145
brooch broche *m* 121
brother hermano *m* 94
brown marrón 113

bruise cardenal *m* 139
brush cepillo *m* 111
Brussels sprouts coles de bruselas *f/pl* 50
bucket cubo *m* 106, 128
buckle hebilla *f* 118
build, to construir 83
building edificio *m* 83, 85
building blocks cubos de construcción *m/pl* 128
bulb bombilla *f* 28, 75, 119
bullfight corrida *f* 89
bullfighter's cap montera *f* 127
bullfight poster cartel de toros *m* 127
bullring plaza de toros *f* 81
burn quemadura *f* 139
burn out, to *(bulb)* fundir 29
bus autobús *m* 18, 19, 65, 72, 73
business negocios *m/pl* 16, 131
business trip viaje de negocios *m* 94
bus stop parada de autobús *f* 72, 73
busy ocupado(a) 96
butane gas gas butano *m* 32, 106
butcher's carnicería *f* 98
butter mantequilla *f* 37, 38, 63
button botón *m* 29, 118
buy, to comprar 82, 104

C

cabbage berza *f*, repollo *m* 50
cabin *(ship)* camarote *m* 74
cable telegrama *m* 133
cable car funicular *m* 74
cable release cable del disparador *m* 125
caffein-free descafeinado(a) 38, 60
cake pastel *m* 54, 63; bollo *m* 63
cake shop pastelería *f* 98
calculator calculadora *f* 105
calendar calendario *m* 104
call *(phone)* llamada *f* 135, 136
call, to llamar 10, 31, 71, 78, 136, 156
cambric batista *f* 114
camel-hair pelo de camello *m* 114
camera cámara *f* 124, 125
camera shop tienda de fotografía *f* 98
camp, to acampar 32
campbed cama de campaña *f* 106
camping camping *m* 32
camping equipment equipo de camping *m* 106
camp site camping *m* 32
can *(of peaches)* lata *f* 120
can *(to be able)* poder 12, 163
Canada Canadá *m* 146
cancel, to anular 65
candle vela *f* 106
candy caramelo *m* 63, 126
candy store bombonería *f* 98
can opener abrelatas *m* 106
cap gorra *f* 116
caper alcaparra *f* 51
capital *(finance)* capital *m* 131
car coche *m* 20, 75, 76, 78
carafe garrafa *f* 58
carat quilate *m* 121
caravan caravana *f* 32
caraway comino *m* 51
carbon paper papel carbón *m* 104
carburetor carburador *m* 78
card tarjeta *f* 131
card game juego de cartas *m* 128
cardigan chaqueta de punto *f* 117
car hire alquiler de coches *m* 20
car park estacionamiento *m* 77
car radio radio para coche *f* 119
car rental alquiler de automóviles *m* 20
carrot zanahoria *f* 50
carry, to llevar 21
cart carrito *m* 18
carton *(cigarettes)* cartón (de cigarrillos) *m* 17
cartridge *(camera)* cartucho *m* 124
case *(instance)* caso *m* 143; *(glasses etc.)* estuche *m* 123; funda *f* 125
cash, to cobrar 129, 130
cash desk caja *f* 155
cashier cajero(a) *m/f* 103
cassette casette *f* 119, 127
castanets castañuelas *f/pl* 127
castle castillo *m* 81
catalogue catálogo *m* 82
cathedral catedral *f* 81
Catholic católico(a) 84
cauliflower coliflor *f* 50
caution cuidado *m* 79, 155; atención *f* 79
cave cueva *f* 81
celery apio *m* 50
cellophane tape cinta adhesiva *f* 104
cemetery cementerio *m* 81
centimetre centímetro *m* 112
centre centro *m* 19, 21, 72, 76, 81
century siglo *m* 149

ceramics cerámica *f* 83
cereal cereales *m/pl* 38
certificate certificado *m* 144
chain *(jewellery)* cadena *f* 121
chair silla *f* 36, 106
chamber music música de cámara *f* 128
champagne champán *m* 56
change *(money)* suelto *m* 77; moneda *f* 130
change, to cambiar 18, 61, 65, 68, 73, 75, 123, 130; hacer transbordo 73
chapel capilla *f* 81
charcoal carbón *m* 106
charge precio *m* 32; tarifa *f* 136
charge, to cobrar 24, 124; *(commission)* cargar 130
charm *(trinket)* amuleto *m* 121
charm bracelet pulsera de fetiches *f* 121
cheap barato(a) 14, 24, 25, 101
check cheque *m* 129; *(restaurant)* cuenta *f* 62
check, to controlar 75, 123; *(luggage)* facturar 71
check book chequera *f* 131
check in, to *(airport)* presentarse 65
check out, to marcharse 31
checkup *(medical)* reconocimiento general *m* 142
cheers! ¡salud! 55
cheese queso *m* 52, 63
cheesecake pastel de queso *m* 54
chemist's farmacia *f* 98, 108
cheque cheque *m* 130
cheque book chequera *f* 131
cherry cereza *f* 53
chervil perifollo *m* 51
chess ajedrez *m* 128
chest pecho *m* 138, 141
chestnut castaña *f* 53
chewing gum chicle *m* 126
chicken pollo *m* 49, 63
chicken breast pechuga de pollo *f* 49
chicken liver higadito de pollo *m* 41, 48
chickpea garbanzo *m* 50
chicory *(Am.)* achicoria *f* 50
chiffon gasa *f* 114
child niño(a) *m/f* 24, 61, 92, 139, 149
children's doctor pediatra *m/f* 137
chips patatas fritas *f/pl* 63; (Am.) patatas fritas *f/pl,* chips *m/pl* 63
chives cebolleta *f* 51
chocolate chocolate *m* 54, 63, 126; *(hot)* chocolate (caliente) *m* 38, 60
chop chuleta *f* 47
Christmas Navidad *f* 152
church iglesia *f* 81, 84, 85
cigar puro *m* 126
cigarette cigarrillo *m* 17, 95, 126
cigarette case pitillera *f* 121
cigarette lighter encendedor *m* 121, 126
cigarette paper papel para cigarrillos *m* 126
cine camera cámara de filmar *f* 124
cinema cine *m* 86, 96
cinnamon canela *f* 51
circle *(theatre)* anfiteatro *m* 87
city ciudad *f* 81
clam almeja *f* 41, 45
classical clásico(a) 128
clean limpio(a) 61
clean, to limpiar 29, 76
cleansing cream crema limpiadora *f* 110
cliff acantilado *m* 85
clip clip m 121
clock reloj *m* 121, 153
clog, to atascar 28
close *(near)* cercano(a) 78, 98
close, to cerrar 11, 82, 108, 129, 132, 155
closed cerrado(a) 155
clothes ropa *f* 29, 117
clothes peg percha *f* 106
clothing prendas de vestir *f/pl* 112
cloud nube *f* 95
clove clavo *m* 50
coach *(bus)* autocar *m* 72, 80
coat abrigo *m* 117
coconut coco *m* 53
cod bacalao *m* 45
coffee café *m* 38, 60, 64
coin moneda *f* 83
cold frío(a) 14, 25, 38, 61, 95
cold *(illness)* resfriado *m* 108, 141
cold cuts fiambres *m/pl* 41, 64
collar cuello *m* 118
collect call llamada a cobro revertido *f* 135
cologne agua de colonia *f* 110
colour color *m* 103, 112, 124, 125
colour chart muestrario *m* 30
colour fast color fijo 113
colourful colorido(a) 101

colour negative negativo de color *m* 124
colour rinse reflejos *m/pl* 30
colour shampoo champú colorante *m* 111
colour slide diapositiva *f* 124
comb peine *m* 111
come, to venir 34, 61, 93, 95, 137, 146
comedy comedia *f* 86
commission comisión *f* 130
compact disc disco compacto *m* 127
compartment departamento *m* 71
compass brújula *f* 106
complaint reclamación *f* 61
concert concierto *m* 87
concert hall sala de conciertos *f* 81, 87
condition condición *f* 91
conductor *(orchestra)* director *m* 88
confectioner's confitería *f* 98
confirm, to confirmar 65
confirmation confirmación *f* 23
congratulation enhorabuena *f* 152
connection *(plane)* conexión *f* 65; *(train)* transbordo *m* 68
constipated estreñido(a) 140
contact lens lente de contacto *m* 123
contain, to contener 37
contraceptive contraceptivo *m* 109
control control *m* 16
convent convento *m* 81
convention hall palacio de convenciones *m* 81
cookie galleta *f* 54, 64; pasta *f* 54
cool box nevera portátil *f* 106
copper cobre *m* 122
copperware objetos de cobre *m/pl* 127
coral coral *m* 122
corduroy pana *f* 114
cork corcho *m* 61
corkscrew sacacorchos *m* 106
corn *(Am.)* maíz *m* 50
corner rincón *m* 36; *(street)* esquina *f* 21, 77
corn plaster callicida *m* 109
correct correcto(a) 11
cost precio *m* 131; coste *m* 135, 136
cost, to costar 10, 80
cotton algodón *m* 114
cotton wool algodón *m* 109
cough tos *f* 108, 141
cough, to toser 142
cough drops gotas para la tos *f/pl* 109
counter mostrador *m* 132
countryside campo *m* 85
court house palacio de justicia *m* 81
courtyard patio *m* 23, 36
cousin primo(a) *m/f* 94
cover charge cubierto *m* 62
crab cangrejo *m* 46
cracker galleta salada *f* 64
cramp calambre *m* 141
crayfish cangrejo *m* 46
crayon lápiz de color *m* 104
cream crema 113
cream nata *f* 54, 64; crema *f* 60, 110
creamy cremoso(a) 52
credit crédito *m* 130
credit, to acreditar 131
credit card tarjeta de crédito *f* 20, 31, 62, 102, 129, 130
crepe crepé *m* 114
crisps patatas fritas *f/pl*, chips *m/pl* 64
crockery vajilla *f* 106, 107
cross cruz *f* 121
crossing *(by sea)* travesía *f* 74
crossroads cruce *m* 77, 79
cruise crucero *m* 74
crystal cristal m 122
cucumber pepino *m* 42, 50, 64
cuff link gemelo *m* 121
cuisine cocina *f* 34
cup taza *f* 36, 60, 107
cured en salazón 46; serrano 42
currency moneda *f* 129
currency exchange office oficina de cambio *f* 18, 67, 129
current corriente *f* 92
curtain cortina *f* 28
curve *(road)* curva *f* 79
customs aduana *f* 16, 79, 102
cut *(wound)* cortadura *f* 139
cut, to cortar 139
cut glass cristal tallado *m* 122
cuticle remover quitacutículas *m* 110
cutlery cubiertos *m/pl* 106, 107, 121
cycling ciclismo *m* 90
cystitis cistitis *f* 142

D

dairy lechería *f* 98
dance baile *m* 88
dance, to bailar 88, 96
danger peligro *m* 79, 155, 156
dangerous peligroso(a) 79, 92
dark oscuro(a) 25, 101, 112, 113
date fecha *f* 25, 150; *(fruit)* dátil *m* 53
daughter hija *f* 94
day día *m* 16, 20, 24, 32, 80, 151
daylight luz del día *f* 124
day off día libre *m* 151
death muerte *f* 155
decade década *f* 149
December diciembre *m* 150
decision decisión *f* 24, 102
deck *(ship)* cubierta *f* 74
deck-chair silla de lona *f* 92, 106
declare, to declarar 16, 17
deer corzo *m* 48
delay demora *f* 69
delicatessen mantequería *f* 98
deliver, to enviar 102
delivery envío *m* 102
denim algodón asargado *m* 114
dentist dentista *m/f* 98, 145
denture dentadura *f* 145
deodorant desodorante *m* 110
department departamento *m* 83, 100
department store grandes almacenes *m/pl* 98
departure salida *f* 65, 80
deposit depósito *m* 20, 131
deposit, to *(bank)* depositar 131
dessert postre *m* 37, 54
detour *(traffic)* desviación *f* 79
develop, to revelar 124
diabetic diabético(a) 141
diabetic diabético(a) *m/f* 37
dialling code indicativo *m* 134
diamond diamante *m* 122
diaper pañal *m* 111
diarrhoea diarrea *f* 140
dice dado *m* 128
dictionary diccionario *m* 104
diet dieta *f* 37
difficult difícil 14
difficulty dificultad *f* 28, 102, 141
dill eneldo *m* 51
dining-car coche restaurante *m* 66, 68
dining-room comedor *m* 27
dinner cena *f* 34, 95
dinner jacket smoking *m* 117
direct directo(a) 68, 134
direct, to indicar 12
direction dirección *f* 76
directory *(phone)* guía de teléfonos *f* 134
disabled minusválido(a) 82
disc disco *m* 77, 127, 128
disc film disco-película *m* 124
discotheque discoteca *f* 88
disease enfermedad *f* 142
dish plato *m* 37
dishwashing detergent detergente para vajilla *m* 106
disinfectant desinfectante *m* 109
dislocate, to dislocar 140
display case vitrina *f* 100
dissatisfied descontento(a) 103
district *(country)* comarca *f* 76
disturb, to molestar 155
diversion *(traffic)* desviación *f* 79
dizzy mareado(a) 140
doctor doctor(a) *m/f* 79, 137, 145; médico(a) *m/f* 137, 144
doctor's office consultorio *m* 137
dog perro *m* 155
doll muñeca *f* 127
dollar dólar *m* 18, 102, 130
door puerta *f* 155
dose dosis *f* 143
double doble 59, 74
double bed cama matrimonial *f* 23
double room habitación doble *f* 19, 23
down abajo 15
downstairs abajo 15
downtown centro de la ciudad *m* 81
dozen docena *f* 148
drawing paper papel de dibujo *m* 104
drawing pin chincheta *f* 104
dress vestido *m* 117
dressing gown bata *f* 117
drink bebida *f* 60, 61; copa *f* 95
drink, to beber 13, 35, 36
drinking water agua potable *f* 32
drip, to *(tap)* gotear 28
drive, to conducir 76
driving licence permiso de conducir *m* 20, 79
drop *(liquid)* gota *f* 109
drugstore farmacia *f* 98, 108
dry seco(a) 30, 58, 111
dry cleaner's tintorería *f* 29, 98

dry shampoo champú seco *m* 111
Dublin bay prawn cigala *f* 41, 46
duck pato *m* 49
dummy chupete *m* 111
during durante 150, 151
duty *(customs)* impuestos *m/pl* 17
duty-free shop tienda libre de impuestos *f* 19
dye tintura *f* 30, 111

E

each cada 149
ear oreja *f* 138
earache dolor de oídos *m* 141
ear drops gotas para los oídos *f/pl* 109
early temprano 14
earring pendiente *m* 121, 127
earthenware loza de barro *f* 127
east este *m* 77
Easter Pascua *f* 152
easy fácil 14
eat, to comer 13, 36, 144, 162
eel anguila *f* 41
egg huevo *m* 38, 42, 44, 64
eggplant berenjena *f* 50
eight ocho 147
eighteen dieciocho 147
eighth octavo(a) 148
eighty ochenta 147
elastic elástico(a) 109
elastic elástico *m* 118
Elastoplast esparadrapo m 109
electrical eléctrico(a) 119
electrical appliance aparato eléctrico *m* 119
electrician electricista *m* 98
electricity electricidad *f* 32
electronic electrónico(a) 125, 128
elevator ascensor *m* 27, 100
eleven once 147
embarkation embarco *m* 74
embroidery bordado *m* 127
emerald esmeralda *f* 122
emergency urgencia *f* 156
emergency exit salida de emergencia *f* 27, 99, 155
emery board lima de papel *f* 110
empty vacío(a) 14
enamel esmalte *m* 122
end final *m* 150
endive *(Br.)* achicoria *f* 50
engagement ring sortija de pedida *f* 121
engine *(car)* motor *m* 78
England Inglaterra *f* 146
English inglés(esa) 11, 80, 82, 84, 104, 105, 126
enjoy, to gustar 62
enjoyable agradable 31
enjoy oneself, to divertirse 96
enlarge, to amplificar 125
enough bastante 14
enquiry información *f* 68
enter, to entrar 155
entrance entrada *f* 68, 99, 155
entrance fee entrada *f* 82
envelope sobre *m* 27, 104
equipment equipo *m* 92, 106
eraser goma de borrar *f* 104
escalator escalera mecánica *f* 100
espresso coffee café exprés *m* 60
estimate estimación *f* 131
Europe Europa *f* 146
evening tarde *f* 9, 96, 151; noche *f* 86, 95
evening dress traje de noche *m* 88, 117
everything todo 31
excellent excelente 62
exchange, to cambiar 103
exchange rate cambio *m* 18, 130
exclude, to excluir 24
excursion excursión *f* 80
excuse, to perdonar 10
exercise book cuaderno *m* 104
exhaust pipe tubo de escape *m* 78
exhibition exhibición *f* 81
exit salida *f* 68, 79, 99, 155
expect, to esperar 130
expensive caro(a) 14, 19, 23, 101
exposure *(photography)* exposición *f* 124
exposure counter escala de exposición *f* 125
express urgente 133
expression expresión *f* 10
expressway autopista *f* 76, 79
external externo(a) 109
extra más 27, 36
extract, to *(tooth)* sacar 145
eye ojo *m* 123, 138, 139
eye drops gotas para los ojos *f/pl* 109
eye liner perfilador de ojos *m* 110
eye pencil lápiz de ojos *m* 110
eye shadow sombra de ojos *f* 110
eye specialist oculista *m/f* 137

F

face cara *f* 138
face powder polvo de la cara *m* 110
factory fábrica *f* 79, 81
fair feria *f* 81
fall caída *f* 139; *(autumn)* otoño *m* 149
family familia *f* 94
fan ventilador *m* 28; *(folding)* abanico *m* 127
fan belt correa de ventilador *f* 75
far lejos 14, 100
fare tarifa *f* 21, 65, 67, 72
farm granja *f* 85
fast rápido(a) 124
fat *(meat)* grasa *f* 37
father padre *m* 94
faucet grifo *m* 28
February febrero *m* 150
fee *(doctor)* honorarios *m/pl* 144
feeding bottle biberón *m* 111
feel, to *(physical state)* sentirse 140
felt fieltro *m* 114
felt-tip pen rotulador *m* 114
ferry transbordador *m* 74
fever fiebre *f* 140
few pocos(as) 14; *(a)* (alg)unos(as) 14
field campo *m* 85
fifteen quince 147
fifth quinto(a) 148
fig higo *m* 53
file *(tool)* lima *f* 110
fill in, to llenar 25, 144
filling *(tooth)* empaste *m* 145
filling station gasolinera *f* 75
film película *f* 86, 124, 125; rollo *m* 124
film winder enrollador *m* 125
filter filtro *m* 125
filter-tipped con filtro 126
find, to encontrar 10, 12, 100, 137
fine *(OK)* muy bien 25
fine arts bellas artes *f/pl* 83
finger dedo *m* 138
fire fuego *m* 156
first primero(a) 68, 72, 148
first class primera clase *f* 66, 69
first name nombre (de pila) *m* 25
fish pescado *m* 45
fish, to pescar 91
fishing pesca *f* 91
fishing tackle aparejo de pesca *m* 106
fishmonger's pescadería *f* 98
fit, to quedar bien 115, 116
fitting room probador *m* 115
five cinco 147
fix, to arreglar 75, 145
flannel franela *f* 114
flash *(photography)* flash *m* 125
flashlight linterna *f* 106
flat plano(a) 116
flat *(apartment)* apartamento *m* 22
flat tyre pinchazo *m* 75, 78
flea market mercado de cosas viejas *m* 81
flight vuelo *m* 65
flint piedra de mechero *f* 126
flippers aletas para nadar *f/pl* 128
floor piso *m* 26
floor show atracciones *m/pl* 88
flour harina *f* 37
flower flor *f* 85
flower shop florería *f* 98
flu gripe *f* 142
fluid líquido *m* 75
folding chair silla plegable *f* 107
folding table mesa plegable *f* 107
folk music música folklórica *f* 128
food alimento *m* 37, 111; comida *f* 61
food box fiambrera *f* 106
food poisoning intoxicación *f* 142
foot pie *m* 138
football fútbol *m* 90
foot cream crema para los pies *f* 110
footpath sendero *m* 85
for por, para 15
forbid, to prohibir 155
foreign extranjero(a) 59
forest bosque *m* 85
fork tenedor *m* 36, 107
form *(document)* impreso *m* 133; ficha *f* 25
fortnight quincena *f* 151
fortress fortaleza *f* 81, 85
forty cuarenta 147
foundation cream maquillaje *m* 110
fountain fuente *f* 81
fountain pen pluma estilográfica *f* 104
four cuatro 147
fourteen catorce 147
fourth cuarto(a) 148
France Francia *f* 146
free libre 14, 71, 82, 96, 155
french fries patatas fritas *f/pl* 64
fresh fresco(a) 53, 61

Friday viernes *m* 151
fried frito(a) 46, 48
fried egg huevo frito *m* 38, 64
friend amigo(a) *m/f* 93, 95
fringe flequillo *m* 30
frock vestido *m* 117
from de, desde 15
front delantero(a) 23, 75
fruit fruta *f* 53
fruit cocktail ensalada de fruta *f* 53
fruit juice jugo de fruta *m* 38, 60; zumo de fruta *m* 42
fruit stand frutería *f* 98
frying-pan sartén *f* 106
full lleno(a) 14
full board pensión completa *f* 24
full insurance seguro a todo riesgo *m* 20
furnished amueblado(a) 22
furniture muebles *m/pl* 83
furrier's peletería *f* 98

G

gabardine gabardina *f* 114
gallery galería *f* 81, 98
game juego *m* 128; *(food)* caza *f* 48
garage garaje *m* 26, 78
garden jardín *m* 85
gardens jardines públicos *m/pl* 81
garlic ajo *m* 51
garment prenda *f* 29
gas gas *m* 156
gasoline gasolina *f* 75, 78
gastritis gastritis *f* 142
gauze gasa *f* 109
general general 26
general delivery lista de correos *f* 133
general practitioner generalista *m/f* 137
gentleman caballero *m* 155
geology geología *f* 83
Germany Alemania *f* 146
get, to *(find, call)* conseguir 10, 32, 90, 134; coger 19, 21; llamar 137; buscar 156; *(go)* llegar 100
get back, to volver 80; regresar 85
get by, to pasar 70
get off, to apear 73
get to, to llegar a 10, 70; ir a 19
get up, to levantarse 144
gherkin pepinillo *m* 42, 50, 64
gift *(present)* regalo *m* 120
gin ginebra *f* 59
gin and tonic ginebra con tónica *f* 60
ginger jengibre *m* 51
girdle faja *f* 117
girl niña *f* 112, 128
girlfriend amiga *f* 94
give, to dar 12, 136, 140
give way, to *(traffic)* ceder el paso 79
glad *(to know you)* tanto gusto 93
gland glándula *f* 138
glass vaso *m* 36, 58, 59, 61, 143
glasses gafas *f/pl* 123
gloomy lúgubre 84
glossy *(finish)* acabado de brillo 125
glove guante *m* 117
glue cola de pegar *f* 104
go, to ir 77, 96, 163
go away, to irse 156
go back, to regresar 77
gold oro *m* 121, 122
golden dorado(a) 113
gold plate lámina de oro *f* 122
golf golf *m* 91
golf club palo de golf *m* 91
golf course campo de golf *m* 91
good bueno(a) 14, 101
good-bye adiós 9
Good Friday Viernes Santo *m* 152
goods artículos *m/pl* 16
goose ganso *m* 48
go out, to salir 96
gram gramo *m* 120
grammar book libro de gramática *m* 105
grape uva *f* 53, 64
grapefruit pomelo *m* 53
grapefruit juice jugo de pomelo *m* 38, 60; zumo de pomelo *m* 42
gray gris 113
graze arañazo *m* 139
greasy graso(a) 30, 111
great *(excellent)* estupendo(a) 95
Great Britain Gran Bretaña *f* 146
green verde 113
green bean judía verde *m* 50
greengrocer's verdulería *f* 98
green salad ensalada de lechuga *f* 43
greeting saludo *m* 9
grey gris 113
grilled a la parrilla 46, 48; a la plancha 41
grocery tienda de comestibles *f* 98, 120
groundsheet alfombra (de hule) *f* 106
group grupo *m* 82
guide guía *m/f* 80

guidebook guía *f* 82, 104, 105
guitar guitarra *f* 127
gum *(teeth)* encía 145
gynaecologist ginecólogo *m/f* 137

H

hair cabello *m* 30, 111
hairbrush cepillo para el pelo *m* 111
haircut corte de pelo *m* 30
hairdresser's peluquería *f* 27, 30, 98
hair dryer secador de pelo *m* 119
hairgrip horquilla de pinza *f* 111
hair lotion loción capilar *f* 111
hairpin horquilla *f* 111
hairspray laca para el pelo *f* 30, 111
hake merluza *f* 46
half mitad *f* 148
half a day medio día *m* 80
half an hour media hora *f* 153
half board media pensión *f* 24
half price *(ticket)* media tarifa *f* 69
hall *(large room)* sala *f* 81, 87
hall porter conserje *m* 26
ham jamón *m* 38, 42, 44, 47, 64
ham and eggs huevos con jamón *m/pl* 38
hamburger hamburguesa *f* 64
hammer martillo *m* 106
hand mano *f* 138
handbag bolso de mano *m* 117, 156
hand cream crema para las manos *f* 110
handicrafts artesanía *f* 83
handkerchief pañuelo *m* 117
hand lotion loción para las manos *f* 110
handmade hecho(a) a mano 113
hanger percha *f* 27
hangover resaca *f* 108
happy feliz 152
harbour puerto *m* 81
hard duro(a) 52, 123
hard-boiled *(egg)* duro 38, 42
hardware shop ferretería *f* 98
hare liebre *f* 49
hat sombrero *m* 117
have, to haber 162; tener 163
hay fever fiebre del heno *f* 108
hazelnut avellana *f* 53
él 161
cabeza *f* 138, 139
che dolor de cabeza *m* 141
eese cabeza *f* 41
luz *f* 79

headphones casco con auriculares *m* 119
head waiter jefe *m* 61
health salud *f* 55
health food shop tienda de alimentos dietéticos *f* 98
health insurance seguro *m* 144
health insurance form hoja de seguro *f* 144
heart corazón *m* 47, 138
heart attack ataque al corazón *m* 141
heating calefacción *f* 23, 28
heavy pesado(a) 14, 101
heel tacón *m* 116
height altura *f* 85
helicopter helicóptero *m* 74
hello! *(phone)* oiga 135
help ayuda *f* 156
help! ¡socorro! 156
help, to ayudar 12, 21, 71; atender 100; *(oneself)* servirse 120
hen gallina *f* 48
her su 160
herbs hierbas finas *f/pl* 51
here aquí 13, 15
herring arenque *m* 41, 45
high alto(a) 92, 141
high season alta estación *f* 149
high-speed rápido(a) 124
high tide marea alta *f* 92
hill colina *f* 85
hire alquiler *m* 20
hire, to alquilar 20, 91, 92, 119, 155
his su 160
history historia *f* 83
hitchhike, to hacer auto-stop 74
hold on! *(phone)* espere 136
hole hoyo *m* 29
holiday día festivo *m* 151
holidays vacaciones *f/pl* 16, 151
home address domicilio *m* 25
honey miel *f* 38
hope, to esperar 94
hors d'œuvre entremés *m* 41
horse riding equitación *f* 90
hospital hospital *m* 98, 144
hot caliente 14, 24, 38, 60, 95
hotel hotel *m* 19, 21, 22, 80
hotel guide guía de hoteles *f* 19
hotel reservation reserva de hotel *f* 19
hot water agua caliente *f* 23, 28

hot-water bottle botella de agua caliente *f* 27
hour hora *f* 153
house casa *f* 83, 85
hovercraft aerodeslizador *m* 74
how cómo 10
how far a qué distancia 10, 76
how long cuánto tiempo 10
how many cuántos(as) 10
how much cuánto 10
hundred cien, ciento 147
hungry, to be tener hambre 13, 35
hunt, to cazar 91
hurry *(to be in a)* tener prisa 21
hurry up! ¡dése prisa! 13
hurt, to doler 139, 140, 145
husband marido *m* 94
hut cabaña *f* 85
hydrofoil hidroplano *m* 74

I

I yo 161
ice cream helado *m* 54, 64
ice cube cubito de hielo *m* 27
ice pack elemento congelable *m* 106
iced tea té helado *m* 60
ill enfermo(a) 140, 156
illness enfermedad *f* 140
immediately inmediatamente 137
important importante 13
in en 15
include, to incluir 20, 24, 31, 62, 80
indigestion indigestión *f* 141
indoor *(swimming pool)* cubierto(a) 91
inexpensive barato(a) 35, 124
infect, to infectar 140
infection infección *f* 141
inflammation inflamación *f* 142
inflation inflación *f* 131
inflation rate tasa de inflación *f* 131
influenza gripe *f* 142
information información *f* 67, 80
injection inyección *f* 142, 144
injure, to herir 139
injured herido(a) 79, 139
injury herida *f* 139
ink tinta *f* 105
inn fonda *f*, posada *f* 33
inquiry información *f* 68
insect bite picadura de insecto *f* 108, 139
insect repellent repelente para insectos *m* 109
insect spray spray para insectos *m* 109
inside dentro 15
instead en lugar de 37
insurance seguro *m* 20, 79, 144
insurance company compañía de seguros *f* 79
interest interés *m* 80, 131
interested, to be interesarse 83
interesting interesante 84
international internacional 132, 134
interpreter intérprete *m* 131
intersection cruce *m* 77, 79
introduce, to presentar 93
introduction presentación *f* 93; formulario de presentación *m* 130
investment inversión *f* 131
invitation invitación *f* 94
invite, to invitar 94
invoice factura *f* 131
iodine yodo *f* 109
Ireland Irlanda *f* 146
iron *(laundry)* plancha *f* 119
iron, to planchar 29
ironmonger's ferretería *f* 99
Italy Italia *f* 146
its su 160
ivory marfil *m* 122

J

jacket chaqueta *f* 117
jade jade *m* 122
jam mermelada *f* 38
jam, to atrancar 28, 125
January enero *m* 150
jar tarro *m* 120
jaundice ictericia *f* 142
jaw mandíbula *f* 138
jeans tejanos *m/pl* 117
jersey jersey *m* 117
jewel box joyero *m* 121
jeweller's joyería *f* 99, 121
jewellery joyas *f/pl* 127
joint articulación *f* 138
journey viaje *m* 73
juice jugo *m* 38, 40, 60; zumo *m* 42
July julio *m* 150
June junio *m* 150
just *(only)* sólo 16, 100

K

kerosene petróleo *m* 106
ketchup salsa de tomate *f* 37, 64

key llave *f* 26
kid *(goat)* cabrito *m* 47
kidney riñón *m* 47, 48, 138
kilogram kilogramo *m* 120
kilometre kilómetro *m* 20, 79
kind amable 95
kind *(type)* clase *f* 140
knee rodilla *f* 138
knife cuchillo *m* 36, 107
knock, to llamar 155
know, to saber 16, 24; conocer 114

L

label etiqueta *f* 105
lace encaje *m* 114, 127
lady señora *f* 155
lake lago *m* 85, 91
lamb cordero *m* 47
lamp lámpara *f* 29, 106, 119
lamprey lamprea *f* 46
landmark punto de referencia *m* 85
large grande 101, 116
last último(a) 14, 68, 72, 74; pasado(a) 149, 150
late tarde 14
later más tarde 135
laugh, to reír 11, 162
launderette launderama *f* 99
laundry *(place)* lavandería *f* 29, 99; *(clothes)* ropa *f* 29
laundry service servicio de lavado *m* 23
laxative laxante *m* 109
lead, to llevar 76
leap year año bisiesto *m* 149
leather cuero *m* 114, 116
leather goods store tienda de artículos de cuero *f* 99
leave, to marcharse 31, 95; salir 68, 74; *(deposit)* dejar 27, 71
leek puerro *m* 50
left izquierdo(a) 21, 63, 69, 77
left-luggage office oficina de equipaje *f* 67, 71
leg pierna *f* 47, 138
lemon limón *m* 37, 38, 53, 60, 64
lemonade limonada *f* 60
lemon juice jugo de limón *m* 60
lens *(glasses)* lente *m* 123; *(camera)* objetivo *m* 125
lens cap capuchón para el objetivo *m* 125
lentil lenteja *f* 50
less menos 14
let, to *(hire out)* alquilar 155
letter carta *f* 132
letter box buzón *m* 133
letter of credit carta de crédito *f* 130
lettuce lechuga *f* 50, 64
level crossing paso a nivel *m* 79
library biblioteca *f* 81, 99
licence *(permit)* permiso *m* 20, 79
lie down, to acostarse 142
life belt cinturón salvavidas *m* 74
life boat bote salvavidas *m* 74
lifeguard vigilante *m* 92
lift ascensor *m* 27, 100
light luz *f* 28, 124; *(cigarette)* lumbre *f* 95
light ligero(a) 14, 54, 101, 128; liviano(a) 58; *(colour)* claro(a) 101, 112, 113
light, to *(fire)* encender 32
lighter encendedor *m* 126
lighter fluid gasolina para encendedor *m* 126
lighter gas gas para encendedor *m* 126
light meter exposímetro *m* 125
like, to querer 12, 20, 23; gustar 24, 27, 93, 102, 112
lime *(fruit)* lima *f* 53
line línea *f* 73
linen *(cloth)* hilo *m* 114
lip labio *m* 138
lipsalve cacao para los labios *m* 110
lipstick lápiz de labios *m* 110
liqueur licor *m* 59, 60
listen, to escuchar 128
litre litro *m* 58, 75, 120
little *(a)* un poco 14
live, to vivir 83
liver hígado *m* 47, 138
lobster *(spiny)* langosta *f* 42, 46
local local 36, 43, 59
long largo(a) 30, 116, 117
long-sighted présbite 123
look, to mirar 100; ver 123
look for, to buscar 13
look out! ¡cuidado! 156
lose, to perder 123, 156
loss pérdida *f* 131
lost perdido(a) 13, 156
lost and found office oficina de objetos perdidos *f* 67, 156
lost property office oficina de objetos perdidos *f* 67, 156

lot *(a)* mucho 14
lotion loción *f* 110
lovely bonito(a) 94
low bajo(a) 92,
lower inferior 70
low season baja estación *f* 149
low tide marea baja *f* 92
luck suerte *f* 135, 152
luggage equipaje *m* 18, 26, 31, 71
luggage locker consigna automática *f* 18, 67, 71
luggage trolley carrito de equipaje *m* 18, 71
luggage van furgón de equipajes *m* 66
lump *(bump)* chichón *m* 139
lunch almuerzo *m* 34, 80
lunch, to almorzar 95
lung pulmón *m* 138

M

machine máquina *f* 113
mackerel caballa *f* 45
magazine revista *f* 105
magnificent magnífico(a) 84
maid camarera *f* 26
mail, to mandar por correo 28
mail correo *m* 28, 133
mailbox buzón *m* 133
main principal 80
make, to hacer 104
make up, to hacer 28, 71; preparar 108
make-up remover pad toallita de maquillaje *f* 110
man caballero *m* 115; hombre *m* 156
manager director *m* 26
manicure manicura *f* 30
many muchos(as) 14
map mapa *m* 76, 105
March marzo *m* 150
marinated en escabeche 46
market mercado *m* 81, 99
marmalade mermelada amarga de naranjas *f* 38
married casado(a) 94
mascara pintura de pestañas *f* 110
mass *(church)* misa *f* 84
mat *(finish)* mate 125
match cerilla *f* 106, 126; *(sport)* partido *m* 90
match, to *(colour)* hacer juego 112
material *(cloth)* tejido *m* 113
matinée sesión de la tarde *f* 87
mattress colchón *m* 106
mauve malva 113
May mayo *m* 150
may *(can)* poder 12, 163
meadow prado *m* 85
meal comida *f* 24, 34, 35, 62, 143
mean, to querer decir 11, 25
means medio *m* 74
measles sarampión *m* 142
measure, to medir 114
meat carne *f* 47, 61
mechanic mecánico *m* 78
mechanical pencil lapicero *m* 121
medical médico(a) 144
medicine medicina *f* 83, 143
medium *(meat)* regular 48
meet, to encontrar 96
melon melón *m* 42, 53, 64
mend, to arreglar 75; *(clothes)* remendar 29
menthol *(cigarettes)* mentolado(a) 126
menu menú *m* 37, 39; *(printed)* carta *f* 36, 40
message recado *m* 28, 136
methylated spirits alcohol de quemar *m* 106
metre metro *m* 112
mezzanine *(theatre)* anfiteatro *m* 87
middle medio *m* 69, 87, 150
midnight medianoche *f* 153
mild suave 52
mileage kilometraje *m* 20
milk leche *f* 38, 60, 64
milkshake batido *m* 60
million millón *m* 148
minced meat carne picada *f* 47
mineral water agua mineral *f* 60
minister *(religion)* ministro *m* 84
mint menta *f* 51
minute minuto *m* 153
mirror espejo *m* 115, 123
miscellaneous diverso(a) 127
Miss señorita *f* 9
miss, to faltar 18, 29, 61
mistake error *m* 61; *(to make a mistake)* equivocarse 31, 62, 103
modified American plan media pensión *f* 24
moisturizing cream crema hidratante *f* 110
moment momento *m* 136
monastery monasterio *m* 81
Monday lunes *m* 151

money dinero *m* 129, 156
money order giro postal *m* 132
month mes *m* 150
monument monumento *m* 81
moped velomotor *m* 74
more más 14
morning mañana *f* 151
Morocco Marruecos *m* 146
mortgage hipoteca *f* 131
mosque mezquita *f* 81
mosquito net red para mosquitos *f* 106
mother madre *f* 94
motorbike motocicleta *f* 74
motorboat motora *f* 92
motorway autopista *f* 76, 79
mountain montaña *f* 85
moustache bigote *m* 31
mouth boca *f* 138
mouthwash gargarismo *m* 109
move, to mover 139, 140
movie película *f* 86
movie camera cámara de filmar *f* 124
movies cine *m* 86, 96
Mr. Señor *m* 9
Mrs. Señora *f* 9
much mucho 14
mug taza alta *f* 107
muscle músculo *m* 138, 139
museum museo *m* 81
mushroom seta *f* 44, 50; champiñon *m* 41, 50
music música *f* 83, 128
mussel mejillón *m* 42
must, to deber 31, 37, 61; tener que 23, 95
mustard mostaza *f* 37, 51, 64
mutton carnero *m* 47
my mi 160
myself mismo(a) 120

N

nail *(human)* uña *f* 110
nail clippers alicates de uñas *m/pl* 110
nail file lima de uñas *f* 110
nail polish esmalte de uñas *m* 110
nail polish remover acetona quita-esmalte de uñas *f* 110
nail scissors tijeras de uñas *f/pl* 110
name nombre *m* 23, 25, 79, 93
napkin servilleta *f* 36, 105
nappy pañal *m* 111
narrow estrecho(a) 116
nationality nacionalidad *f* 25
natural natural 83
natural history historia natural *f* 83
nausea náusea *f* 140
near cerca 14
near to cerca de 15
nearby cerca de aquí 77, 84
nearest más cercano(a) 78, 98
necessary necesario(a) 88
neck cuello *m* 30, 138
necklace collar *m* 121
need, to necesitar 29, 116
needle aguja *f* 27
negative negativo *m* 124
nephew sobrino *m* 94
nerve nervio *m* 138
nervous nervioso(a) 138
nervous system sistema nervioso *m* 138
Netherlands Países Bajos *m/pl* 146
never nunca 15
new nuevo(a) 14
newspaper periódico *m* 104, 105
newsstand quiosco de periódicos *m* 19, 67, 99, 104
New Year Año Nuevo *m* 152
New Zealand Nueva Zelandia *f* 146
next próximo(a) 14, 68, 73, 76, 149, 151
next to junto a 15, 77
niece sobrina *f* 94
night noche *f* 24, 26, 151
nightclub centro nocturno *m* 88
night cream crema de noche *f* 110
nightdress camisón *m* 117
nine nueve 147
nineteen diecinueve 147
ninety noventa 147
ninth noveno(a) 148
nipple *(feeding bottle)* tetina *f* 111
no no 9
noisy ruidoso(a) 25
nonalcoholic sin alcohol 60
none ninguno(a) 15
nonsmoker no fumadores *m/pl* 36, 69, 70
noon mediodía *m* 153
normal normal 30
north norte *m* 77
North America América del Norte *f* 146
nose nariz *f* 138
nosebleed hemorragia nasal *f* 141
not no 15, 163

note *(banknote)* billete *m* 130
notebook cuaderno *m* 105
note paper papel de cartas *m* 105
nothing nada 15, 17
notice *(sign)* indicación *f* 155
November noviembre *m* 150
now ahora 15
number número *m* 26, 65, 134, 136, 147
nurse enfermera *f* 144
nutmeg nuez moscada *f* 51

O

occupation ocupación *f* 94
occupied ocupado(a) 14, 70, 155
October octubre *m* 150
octopus pulpo *m* 46
office oficina *f* 19, 67, 99, 132, 156
oil aceite *m* 30, 37, 75, 111
oily graso(a) 30, 111
old viejo(a) 14
old town ciudad vieja *f* 81
olive aceituna *f* 41
olive oil aceite de oliva *m* 37
omelet tortilla *f* 44
on sobre, en 15
once una vez 148
one uno(a) 147
one-way *(ticket)* ida 65, 69
one-way street dirección única *f* 79
onion cebolla *f* 50
only sólo 80, 109
on request a petición 73
on time a la hora 68
onyx ónix *m* 122
open abierto(a) 14, 82, 155
open, to abrir 11, 17, 82, 108, 129, 131, 132, 142
open-air al aire libre 91
opera ópera *f* 87
opera house teatro de la ópera *m* 87
operation operación *f* 144
operator telefonista *m/f* 134
operetta opereta *f* 87
opposite enfrente 77
optician óptico *m* 99, 123
or o 15
orange naranja 113
orange naranja *f* 53, 64
orange juice jugo de naranja *m* 38, 60; zumo de naranja *m* 42
orangeade naranjada *f* 60
orchestra orquesta *f* 88; *(seats)* platea *f* 87
order, to *(meal)* pedir 36, 61; *(goods)* encargar 102, 103
oregano orégano *m* 51
ornithology ornitología *f* 83
our nuestro(a) 160
out of order estropeado(a) 78; averiado(a) 155
out of stock agotado(a) 103
outlet *(electric)* enchufe *m* 26
outside fuera 15, 36
overdone demasiado hecho(a) 61
overheat, to *(engine)* calentar demasiado 78
overtake, to adelantar 79
owe, to deber 144
oxtail rabo de buey *m* 47
oyster ostra *f* 42, 46

P

pacifier chupete *m* 111
packet paquete *m* 120; *(cigarettes)* cajetilla *f* 126
page *(hotel)* botones *m* 26
pail cubo *m* 128
pain dolor *m* 140, 141, 144
painkiller analgésico *m* 140, 144
paint pintura *f* 155
paint, to pintar 83
paintbox caja de pinturas *f* 105
painter pintor *m* 83
painting pintura *f* 83
pair par *m* 116
pajamas pijama *m* 118
palace palacio *m* 81
palpitation palpitación *f* 141
panties bragas *f/pl* 117
pants *(trousers)* pantalón *m* 117
panty girdle faja braga *f* 117
panty hose leotardos *m/pl* 117
paper papel *m* 104, 105
paperback rústica *f* 105
paper napkin servillete de papel *f* 105
paraffin *(fuel)* petróleo *m* 106
parcel paquete *m* 132
pardon perdone 10
parents padres *m/pl* 94
park parque *m* 81
park, to aparcar 26, 77
parking aparcamiento *m* 77; estacionamiento *m* 79
parking disc disco de aparcamiento *m* 77
parking meter parquímetro *m* 77

parliament cortes *f/pl* 81
parsley perejil *m* 51
parsnip chirivía *f* 50
part parte *f* 138; *(hair)* raya *f* 30
parting raya *f* 30
partridge perdiz *f* 48, 49
pass *(rail, bus)* pase *m* 72
pass, to *(car)* adelantar 79
passport pasaporte *m* 16, 17, 25, 156
passport photo foto para pasaporte *f* 124
pass through, to estar de paso 16
pasta pastas *f/pl* 40
paste *(glue)* engrudo *m* 105
pastry pastel *m* 64
pastry shop pastelería *f* 33, 99
path sendero *m* 155
patient paciente *m/f* 144
pay, to pagar 17, 62, 100, 102
payment pago *m* 131
pea guisante *m* 50
peach melocotón *m* 53, 54
peanut cacahuete *m* 53
pear pera *f* 53
pearl perla *f* 122
people gente *f* 79
pedestrian peatón *m* 79
peg *(tent)* estaca *f* 107
pen pluma *f* 105
pencil lápiz *m* 105
pencil sharpener sacapuntas *m* 105
pendant medallón *m* 121
penicilline penicilina *f* 143
penknife cortaplumas *m* 106
pensioner jubilado(a) *m/f* 82
pepper pimienta *f* 37, 38, 51, 64
peppers pimientos *m/pl* 42, 48, 50
per cent por ciento 148
perch perca *f* 46
per day por día 20, 32, 91
performance *(session)* función *f* 86
perfume perfume *m* 110
perfume shop perfumería *f* 108
perhaps quizá, tal vez 15
per hour por hora 77, 91
period *(monthly)* reglas *f/pl* 141
period pains dolores menstruales *m/pl* 141
permanent wave permanente *f* 30
permit permiso *m* 91
per night por noche 24
per person por persona 32
person persona *f* 32
personal personal 17
personal call llamada personal *f* 135
personal cheque cheque personal *m* 130
person-to-person call llamada personal *f* 135
per week por semana 20, 24
peseta peseta *f* 129
petrol gasolina *f* 75, 78
pewter peltre *m* 122
pheasant faisán *m* 48
phone teléfono *m* 28, 134
phone, to telefonear 134
phone booth cabina de teléfono *f* 134
phone call llamada 135, 136
phone number número de teléfono *m* 96
photo foto(grafía) *f* 82, 124, 125
photocopy fotocopia *f* 104
photograph, to fotografiar, tomar fotografías 82
photographer fotógrafo *m* 99
photography fotografía *f* 124
phrase expresión *f* 11
pickles pepinillos *m/pl* 50, 64
pick up, to recoger 80
picnic merienda *f* 63
picnic basket bolsa para merienda *f* 106
picture cuadro *m* 83; *(photo)* fotografía *f* 82
piece *(slice)* trozo *m* 52, 120
pigeon pichón *m* 49
pill píldora *f* 141, 143
pillow almohada *f* 27
pin alfiler *m* 121
pineapple piña *f* 53
pineapple juice zumo de piña *m* 42
pink rosa 113
pipe pipa *f* 126
pipe cleaner limpiapipas *m* 126
pipe tobacco tabaco para pipa *m* 126
pipe tool utensilios para pipa *m/pl* 126
pitcher botijo *m* 127
place lugar *m* 25
place of birth lugar de nacimiento *m* 25
plane avión *m* 65
plaster yeso *m* 140
plastic plástico *m* 107
plastic bag bolsa de plástico *f* 107
plate plato *m* 36, 61, 107
platform *(station)* andén *m* 67, 68, 69, 70

platinum platino *m* 122
play *(theatre)* pieza *f* 86
play, to jugar 90; *(music)* tocar 88
playground campo de juego *m* 32
playing card naipe *f* 105
please por favor 9
plimsolls zapatos de lona *m/pl* 116
plug *(electric)* clavija de enchufe *f* 29, 119
plum ciruela *f* 53
p.m. de la tarde 133
pneumonia neumonía *f* 142
poached hervido(a) 46
pocket bolsillo *m* 118
pocket watch reloj de bolsillo *m* 121
point punto *m* 80
point, to *(show)* señalar 11
poison veneno *m* 109
poisoning intoxicación *f* 142
police policía *f* 78, 156
police station comisaría de policía *f* 99, 156
pomegranate granada *f* 53
poplin popelín *m* 114
popular popular 80
pork cerdo *m* 47
port puerto *m* 74; *(wine)* oporto *m* 60
portable portátil 119
porter mozo *m* 18, 26, 71
portion porción *f* 61; ración *f* 54
Portugal Portugal *m* 146
possible posible 137
post *(letters)* correo *m* 133
post, to mandar por correo 28
postage franqueo *m* 132
postage stamp sello *m* 28, 126, 132
postcard tarjeta postal *f* 105, 126, 132
poste restante lista de correos *f* 133
post office oficina de correos *f* 99, 132
potato patata *f* 50, 64
pottery alfarería *f* 83
poultry aves *f/pl* 48
pound *(money)* libra *f* 18, 102, 130; *(weight)* libra *f* 120
powder polvo *m* 110
powder compact polvera *f* 121
prawn gamba *f* 41, 43; quisquilla *f* 42, 46; langostino *m* 42, 46
preference preferencia *f* 101
pregnant embarazada 141
premium *(gasoline)* super 75
prescribe, to recetar 143
prescription receta *f* 108, 143
present *(gift)* regalo *m* 120
press, to *(iron)* planchar 29
press stud broche de presión *m* 118
pressure presión *f* 75
price precio *m* 24
priest sacerdote *m* 84
print *(photo)* copia *f* 125
print, to imprimir 124
private privado(a) 155; particular 80, 92, 155
private toilet water particular *m* 23
processing *(photo)* revelado *m* 124
profession profesión *f* 25
profit ganancia *f* 131
programme programa *m* 87, 88
prohibit, to prohibir 32, 79, 92, 155
pronunciation pronunciación *f* 6, 11
propelling pencil lapicero *m* 121
Protestant protestante 84
provide, to conseguir 131
prune ciruela pasa *f* 53
public holiday día festivo *m* 152
pull, to tirar 155
pullover pullover *m* 117
puncture pinchazo *m* 75
purchase compra *f* 131
pure puro(a) 113
purple purpúreo(a) 113
push, to empujar 155
pyjamas pijama *m* 118

Q

quail codorniz *f* 48
quality calidad *f* 103, 114
quantity cantidad *f* 14, 103
quarter cuarto *m* 148; *(part of town)* barrio *m* 81
quarter of an hour cuarto de hora *m* 153
quartz cuarzo *m* 122
question pregunta *f* 10, 76
quick rápido(a) 14, 156
quickly rápidamente 137
quiet tranquilo(a) 23, 25

R

rabbi rabino *m* 84
rabbit conejo *m* 48, 49
race course/track pista de carreras *f* 91
racket *(sport)* raqueta *f* 91
radiator radiador *m* 78

radio *(set)* radio *f* 23, 28, 119
radish rábano *m* 42, 50
railroad crossing paso a nivel *m* 79
railway ferrocarril *m* 154
railway station estación (de ferrocarril) *f* 19, 21, 67, 70
rain, to llover 94
rain boot bota par la lluvia *f* 116
raincoat impermeable *m* 118
raisin pasa *f* 53
rangefinder telémetro *m* 125
rare *(meat)* poco hecho(a) 48
rash sarpullido *m* 139
raspberry frambuesa *f* 53
rate tarifa *f* 20; tasa *f* 131
razor máquina (navaja) de afeitar *f* 111
razor blade hoja de afeitar *f* 111
reading-lamp lámpara para leer *f* 27
ready listo(a) 29, 116, 123, 125
real auténtico(a) 121
rear trasero(a) 75
receipt recibo *m* 103, 144
recent reciente 149
reception recepción *f* 23
receptionist recepcionista *m/f* 26
recommend, to recomendar 35, 80, 86, 88, 137, 145; aconsejar 36, 41, 43, 50, 54
record *(disc)* disco *m* 127, 128
record player tocadiscos *m* 119
rectangular rectangular 101
red rojo(a) 113; *(wine)* tinto 58
redcurrant grosella roja *f* 53
red mullet salmonete *m* 46
reduction descuento *m* 24, 82
refill recambio *m* 105
refund, to devolver 103
regards recuerdos *m/pl* 152
register, to facturar 71
registered mail registrado(a) 133
registration inscripción *f* 25
registration form ficha *f* 25
regular *(petrol)* normal 75
religion religión *f* 83
religious service servicio religioso *m* 84
rent, to alquilar 20, 91, 92, 119, 155
rental alquiler *m* 20
repair reparación *f* 125
repair, to arreglar 29, 119, 121, 123, 145; reparar 116, 125
repeat, to repetir 11
report, to denunciar 156
reservation reserva *f* 19, 23, 65, 69
reservation office oficina de reservas *f* m 19, 67
reserve, to reservar 19, 23, 35, 86
restaurant restaurante *m* 19, 32, 34, 35, 67
return *(ticket)* ida y vuelta 65, 69
return, to *(give back)* devolver 103
reversed charge call llamada a cobro revertido *f* 135
rheumatism reumatismo *m* 141
rhubarb ruibarbo *m* 53
rib costilla *f* 138
ribbon cinta *f* 105
rice arroz *m* 45, 50, 54
ride, to *(horse)* montar a caballo 74
right derecho(a) 21, 63, 69, 77; *(correct)* correcto(a) 14
ring *(on finger)* sortija *f* 121
ring, to tocar el timbre 155; telefonear 134
river río 85, 91
road carretera *f* 76, 77, 79, 85
road map mapa de carreteras *m* 105
road sign señal de circulación *f* 79
roast asado(a) 48, 49
roll *(bread)* panecillo *m* 37, 64
roller skate patín de ruedas *m* 128
roll film carrete *m*, rollo *m* 124
roll-neck cuello vuelto *m* 117
room habitación *f* 19, 23, 24, 25, 27; *(space)* sitio *m* 32
room number número de la habitación *m* 26
room service servicio de habitación *m* 23
rope cuerda *f* 107
rosary rosario *m* 122, 127
rosé rosé 58
rosemary romero *m* 51
rouge colorete *m* 111
round redondo(a) 101
round *(golf)* juego *m* 91
round-neck cuello redondo *m* 117
roundtrip *(ticket)* ida y vuelta 65, 69
rowing-boat barca *f* 92
royal palace palacio real *m* 82
rubber *(eraser)* goma de borrar *f* 105
ruby rubí *m* 122
rucksack mochila *f* 107
ruin ruina *f* 82
ruler regla *f* 105
rum ron *m* 44, 60
running water agua corriente *f* 23

S

safe *(not dangerous)* sin peligro 92
safe caja fuerte *f* 27
safety pin imperdible *m* 111
saffron azafrán *m* 51
sage salvia *f* 51
sailing-boat velero *m* 92
salad ensalada *f* 43, 64
salami salchichón *m* 42, 64
sale venta *f* 131; *(bargains)* rebajas *f/pl* 101
sales tax impuesto *m* 102
salmon salmón *m* 42, 46
salt sal *f* 37, 38, 51, 64
salty salado(a) 61
sand arena *f* 91
sandal sandalia *f* 116
sandwich bocadillo *m* 64
sanitary towel/napkin paño higiénico *m* 109
sapphire zafiro *m* 122
sardine sardina *f* 42, 46
satin raso *m* 114
Saturday sábado *m* 151
sauce salsa *f* 49
saucepan cazo *m* 107
saucer platillo *m* 107
sausage salchicha *f* 47, 64
sautéed salteado(a) 46, 48
scallop venera *f* 46
scarf bufanda *f* 118
scarlet escarlata 113
school escuela *f* 79
scissors tijeras *f/pl* 107, 110
scooter escúter *m* 74
Scotch whisky escocés *m* 60
Scotland Escocia *f* 146
scrambled egg huevo revuelto *m* 38, 44
screwdriver destornillador *m* 107
sculptor escultor *m* 83
sculpture escultura *f* 83
sea mar *m* 23, 85
sea bream besugo *m* 45
seafood mariscos *m/pl* 45
season estación *f* 149
seasoning condimento *m* 37
seat asiento *m* 69, 70, 87; *(theatre, etc.)* localidad *f*, entrada *f* 86, 87, 89
seat belt cinturón de seguridad *m* 75
second segundo(a) 148
second segundo *m* 153
second class segunda clase *f* 66, 69
second hand segundero manecilla *m* 122
second-hand de segunda mano 104
secretary secretario(a) *m/f* 27, 131
see, to ver 12, 163
sell, to vender 100
send, to mandar 31, 78, 102, 132, 133; enviar 103
send up, to subir 26
sentence frase *f* 11
separately separadamente 62
September septiembre *m* 150
serge estameña *f* 114
serious serio(a) 139
service servicio *m* 24, 62, 98, 100; *(religion)* servicio *m* 84
serviette servilleta *f* 36
set *(hair)* marcado *m* 30
set menu plato combinado *m* 36, 39
setting lotion fijador *m* 30, 111
seven siete 147
seventeen diecisiete 147
seventh septimo(a) 148
seventy setenta 147
sew, to coser 29
shade sombra *f* 89; *(colour)* tono *m* 112
shampoo lavado *m* 30; champú *m* 30, 111
shape forma *f* 103
sharp *(pain)* agudo(a) 140
shave, to afeitar 30
shaver máquina de afeitar (eléctrica) *f* 26, 119
shaving cream crema de afeitar *f* 111
she ella 161
shelf estante *m* 120
sherry jerez *m* 43, 48, 55, 60
ship embarcación *f* 74
shirt camisa *f* 118
shirt-maker's camisería *f* 99
shiver escalofrío *m* 140
shoe zapato *m* 116
shoelace cordón (para zapato) *m* 116
shoemaker's zapatero *m* 99
shoe polish crema para zapatos *f* 116
shoe shop zapatería *f* 99
shop tienda *f*, comercio *m* 98, 99; *(big)* almacén *m* 98
shopping compras *f/pl* 97
shopping area zona de tiendas *f* 82, 100

shopping centre centro comercial *m* 99
short corto(a) 30, 116, 117
shorts pantalón corto *m* 118
short-sighted miope 123
shoulder espalda *f* 138
shovel pala *f* 128
show *(theatre)* función *f* 86; *(night-club)* atracciones *f/pl* 88
show, to enseñar 12, 13, 76, 100, 124; mostrar 119
shower ducha *f* 23, 32
shrimp quisquilla *f* 42, 46; gamba *f* 41, 43; langostino *m* 42, 46
shrink, to encoger 113
shut cerrado(a) 14
shutter *(window)* postigo *m* 29; *(camera)* obturador *m* 125
sick *(ill)* enfermo 140, 156
sickness *(illness)* enfermedad *f* 140
side lado *m* 30
sideboards/burns patillas *f/pl* 31
sightseeing tour recorrido turístico *m* 80
sign *(notice)* letrero *m* 155; *(road)* señal *f* 79
sign, to firmar 25
signature firma *f* 25
signet ring sortija de sello *f* 121
silk seda *f* 114
silver plateado(a) 113
silver plata *f* 121, 122
silver plate plata chapada *f* 122
silverware objetos de plata *m/pl* 122
simple sencillo(a) 124
since desde 15, 150
sing, to cantar 88
single soltero(a) 94; *(ticket)* ida 65, 69
single room habitación sencilla *f* 19, 23
sister hermana *f* 94
sit down, to sentarse 96
six seis 147
sixteen dieciséis 147
sixth sexto(a) 148
sixty sesenta 147
size tamaño *m* 124; *(clothes, shoes)* talla *f* 114, 115, 116
sketching block bloc de dibujo *m* 105
ski, to esquiar 91
skiing esquí *m* 90
ski lift telesquí *m* 91
skin piel *f* 138
skin-diving natación submarina *m* 92
skirt falda *f* 118
sleep, to dormir 71, 144
sleeping bag saco de dormir *m* 107
sleeping-car coche cama *m* 66, 68, 71
sleeping pill somnífero *m* 109, 143, 144
sleeve manga *f* 117
slice rebanada *f* 120
slide *(photo)* diapositiva *f* 124
slip combinación *f* 118
slipper zapatilla *f* 116
slow lento(a) 14; *(slowly)* despacio 11, 21, 79, 135
small pequeño(a) 14, 25, 54, 61, 101, 116
smoke, to fumar 155
smoked ahumado(a) 41, 42, 46
smoker fumadores *m/pl* 69, 70
snack tentempié *m* 63
snail caracol *m* 41
snap fastener broche de presión *m* 118
sneakers zapatos de lona *m/pl* 116
snorkel espantasuegras *m/pl* 128
snow, to nevar 94
snuff rapé *m* 126
soap jabón *m* 27, 111
soccer fútbol *m* 90
sock calcetín *m* 118
socket *(outlet)* enchufe *m* 26
soda water soda *f* 60
soft blando(a) 52; suave 123
soft-boiled *(egg)* pasado por agua 38
sold out *(theatre)* agotado(a) 87
sole suela *f* 116; *(fish)* lenguado *m* 46
solution solución *f* 123
some unos(as) 14
someone alguien 96
something algo 36, 54, 108, 112, 114, 125, 139
son hijo *m* 94
soon pronto 15
sore throat angina *f* 141
sorry *(I'm)* lo siento 10, 16, 87
sort clase *f* 52, 120
soup sopa *f* 43
south sur *m* 77
South Africa Africa del Sur *f* 146
South America América del Sur *f* 146
souvenir recuerdo *m* 127
souvenir shop tienda de objetos de regalo *f* 99

Soviet Union Unión Soviética *f* 146
spade pala *f* 128
spaghetti espaguetis *m/pl* 64
Spain España *f* 146
Spanish español(a) 11, 114, 104
spare tyre rueda de repuesto *f* 75
sparking plug bujía *f* 75
sparkling *(wine)* espumoso(a) 58
spark plug bujía *f* 75
speak, to hablar 11, 135, 162
speaker *(loudspeaker)* altavoz *m* 119
special especial 20, 37
special delivery urgente 133
specialist especialista *m/f* 142
speciality especialidad *f* 40, 43, 59
specimen *(medical)* muestra *f* 142
spectacle case estuche para gafas *m* 123
spend, to gastar 101
spice especia *f* 51
spinach espinaca *f* 50
spine espina dorsal *f* 138
spiny lobster langosta *f* 46
sponge esponja *f* 111
spoon cuchara *f* 36, 107
sport deporte *m* 90
sporting goods shop tienda de artículos de deporte *f* 99
sprain, to torcer 140
spring *(season)* primavera *f* 149
square cuadrado(a) 101
squid calamar *m* 41, 46
stadium estadio *m* 82
staff personal *m* 26
stain mancha *f* 29
stainless steel acero inoxidable *m* 107, 122
stalls *(theatre)* platea *f* 87
stamp *(postage)* sello *m* 28, 126, 132
staple grapa *f* 105
start, to empezar 80, 86, 88; *(car)* arrancar 78
starter entremés *m* 41; tapa *f* 63
station *(railway)* estación (de ferrocarril) *f* 21, 67, 70; *(underground, subway)* estación de metro *f* 73
stationer's papelería *f* 99, 104
statue estatua *f* 82
stay estancia *f* 31, 93
stay, to quedarse 16, 24, 25; hospedarse 93
steak filete *m* 47
steal, to robar 156
steamed cocido(a) al vapor 46
stewed estofado(a) 48
stew pot cacerola *f* 107
stiff neck tortícolis *f* 141
sting picadura *f* 139
sting, to picar 139
stock exchange bolsa *f* 82
stocking media *f* 118
stomach estómago *m* 138
stomach ache dolor de estómago *m* 141
stools heces *f/pl* 142
stop *(bus)* parada *f* 72, 73
stop! alto 79; deténgase 156
stop, to parar 21, 68, 70; detenerse 74
stop thief! al ladrón 156
store tienda *f* 98, 99; *(big)* almacén *m* 98
straight ahead (todo) derecho 21, 77
strange extraño(a) 84
strawberry fresa *f* 53, 54
street calle *f* 25, 76
street map mapa de la ciudad *m* 105
string cuerda *f* 105
strong fuerte 52, 143
student estudiante *m/f* 82, 94
stuffed relleno(a) 41
subway metro *m* 73
suede ante *m* 114, 116
sufficient suficiente 68
sugar azúcar *m* 37, 64
suit *(man)* traje *m* 118; *(woman)* vestido *m* 118
suitcase maleta *f* 18
summer verano *m* 149
sun sol *m* 89, 94
sunburn quemadura de sol *f* 108
Sunday domingo *m* 151
sunglasses gafas de sol *f/pl* 123
sunny soleado(a) 94
sunshade *(beach)* sombrilla *f* 92
sunstroke insolación *f* 141
sun-tan cream crema solar *f* 111
super *(petrol)* super 75
superb soberbio(a) 84
supermarket supermercado *m* 99
suppository supositorio *m* 109
surcharge suplemento *m* 69
sure *(fact)* cierto(a) 160
surfboard plancha de deslizamiento *f* 92
surgery *(consulting room)* consulta *f* 137

surgical dressing hilas *f/pl* 109
suspenders *(Am.)* tirantes *m/pl* 118
sweater suéter *m* 118
sweatshirt suéter de tela de punto *m* 118
sweet dulce 58, 61
sweet caramelo *m* 64, 126
sweet corn maíz *m* 50
sweetener edulcorante *m* 37, 64
sweet shop bombonería *f* 99
swell, to hinchar 139
swelling hinchazón *f* 139
swim, to nadar 91, 92; bañarse 92
swimming natación *f* 90
swimming pool piscina *f* 32, 91
swimming trunks bañador *m* 118
swimsuit traje de baño *m* 118
switch interruptor *m* 29
switchboard operator telefonista *m/f* 26
switch on, to *(light)* encender 79
swollen hinchado(a) 139
swordfish pez espáda *m* 46
synagogue sinagoga *f* 84
synthetic sintético(a) 114
system sistema *m* 138

T

table mesa *f* 35, 36, 107
tablet tableta *f* 109
taffeta tafetán *m* 114
tailor's sastre *m* 99
take, to llevar 18, 21, 67, 102; tomar 25, 72
take away, to *(carry)* llevar 63, 103
take off, to *(plane)* despegar 65
talcum powder polvo de talco *m* 111
tambourine pandereta *f* 127
tampon tampon higiénico *m* 109
tangerine mandarina *f* 53
tap *(water)* grifo *m* 28
tape recorder magnetófono *m* 119
tarragon estragón *m* 51
tart tarta *f* 54; tartaleta *f* 42
tax impuesto *m* 24, 102
taxi taxi *m* 19, 21, 31, 67
tea té *m* 38, 60, 64
tear, to desgarrar 140
tearoom salón de té *m* 34
teaspoon cucharilla *f* 107, 143
teat *(feeding bottle)* tetina *f* 111
telegram telegrama *m* 133
telephone teléfono *m* 28, 134
telephone, to telefonear 134
telephone booth cabina de teléfonos *f* 134
telephone call llamada *f* 135, 136
telephone directory guía de teléfonos *f* 134
telephone number número de teléfono *m* 96, 134, 136
telephoto lens lente de acercamiento *f* 125
television televisión *f* 23; *(set)* televisor *m* 28
telex télex *m* 133
telex, to mandar un télex 130
tell, to decir 12, 73, 76, 135, 136, 153
temperature temperatura *f* 92, 140, 142
temporary temporal 145
ten diez 147
tendon tendón *m* 138
tennis tenis *m* 91
tennis court pista de tenis *f* 91
tennis racket raqueta de tenis *f* 91
tent tienda (de campaña) *f* 32, 107
tent peg estaca *f* 107
tent pole mástil *m* 107
tenth décimo(a) 148
term *(word)* expresión *f* 131
terminus terminal *f* 72
terrible terrible 84
terrycloth tela de toalla *f* 114
tetanus tétanos *m* 140
than que 14
thank you gracias 10
that ése(a), aquél(la) 161
the el, la 159
theatre teatro *m* 86
theft robo *m* 156
their su 160
then entonces 15
there allí 14
thermometer termómetro *m* 109, 144
these éstos(as) 161
they ellos(as) 161
thief ladrón *m* 156
thigh muslo *m* 138
thin tenue 114
think, to *(believe)* creer 62, 95
third tercero(a) 148
third tercio *m* 148
thirsty, to be tener sed 13, 35
thirteen trece 147

thirty treinta 147
this éste(a) 161
those ésos(as), aquéllos(as) 161
thousand mil 148
thread hilo *m* 27
three tres 147
throat garganta *f* 138
throat lozenge pastilla para la garganta *f* 109
through train tren directo *m* 68, 69
thumb pulgar *m* 138
thumbtack chincheta *f* 105
Thursday jueves *m* 151
thyme tomillo *m* 51
ticket billete *m* 65, 69, 72, 156; *(theatre, etc.)* localidad *f*, entrada *f* 86, 87, 90
ticket office taquilla *f* 67
tide marea *f* 92
tie corbata *f* 118
tie clip sujetador de corbata *m* 122
tight ajustado(a) 116
tights leotardos *m/pl* 118
time tiempo *m* 80; *(clock)* hora *f* 137, 153; *(occasion)* vez *f* 143
timetable *(railway guide)* guía de ferrocarriles *f* 68
tin *(can)* lata *f* 120
tinfoil papel de estaño *m* 107
tin opener abrelatas *m* 107
tint tinte *m* 111
tinted ahumado(a) 123
tire neumático *m* 75
tired cansado(a) 13
tissue *(handkerchief)* pañuelo de papel *m* 111
tissue paper papel de seda *m* 105
to a, para 15
toast tostada *f* 38, 64
tobacco tabaco *m* 126
tobacconist's tabacos *m/pl* 99, 126; estanco *m* 99
today hoy 29, 151
toe dedo del pie *m* 138
toilet paper papel higiénico *m* 111
toiletry artículos de tocador *m/pl* 110
toilets servicios *m/pl* 27, 28, 32, 67
toll peaje *m* 79
tomato tomate *m* 50, 64
tomato juice zumo de tomate *m* 42; jugo de tomate *m* 60
tomb tumba *f* 82
tomorrow mañana 29, 151
tongue lengua *f* 138
tonic water tónica *f* 60
tonight esta noche 29, 86, 87, 96
tonsil amígdala *f* 138
too demasiado 14; *(also)* también 15
tool kit caja de herramientos *f* 107
tooth diente *m* 145
toothache dolor de muelas *m* 145
toothbrush cepillo de dientes *m* 111, 119
toothpaste pasta de dientes *f* 111
topaz topacio *m* 122
torch *(flashlight)* linterna *f* 107
torn desgarrado(a) 140
touch, to tocar 155
tough duro(a) 61
tourist information información turistica *f* 67
tourist office oficina de turismo *f* 80
towel toalla *f* 27
tower torre *f* 82
town ciudad *f* 21, 76, 105
town hall ayuntamiento *m* 82
tow truck grúa *f* 78
toy juguete *m* 120
toy shop juguetería *f* 99
tracing paper papel transparente *m* 105
tracksuit chandal de entrenamiento *m* 118
traffic *(car)* tráfico *m* 76
traffic light semáforo *m* 77
trailer caravana *f* 32
train tren *m* 66, 68, 69, 70, 73
tranquillizer sedante *m* 109
transfer *(bank)* transferencia *f* 131
transformer transformador *m* 119
translate, to traducir 11
transport transporte *m* 74
travel agency agencia de viajes *f* 99
traveller's cheque cheque de viajero *m* 18, 62, 102, 129, 130
travel sickness mareo *m* 108
treatment tratamiento *m* 143
tree árbol *m* 85
tremendous tremendo 84
trim, to *(beard)* recortar 31
trip viaje *m* 73, 94, 152
tripe callos *m/pl* 41, 47
trolley carrito *m* 18, 71
trousers pantalón *m* 118
trout trucha *f* 46
truffle trufa *f* 50
try, to probar 115; intentar 135
T-shirt camiseta *f* 118

tube tubo *m* 120
Tuesday martes *m* 151
tulle tul *m* 114
tuna atún *m* 41, 45
Tunisia Túnez *m* 146
tunny atún *m* 41, 45
turbot rodaballo *m* 46
turkey pavo *m* 48
turn, to *(change direction)* doblar 21, 77
turquoise turquesa 113
turquoise turquesa *f* 122
turtleneck cuello vuelto *m* 117
tuxedo smoking *m* 117
tweezers pinzas *f/pl* 111
twelve doce 147
twenty veinte 147
twice dos veces 148
twin bed dos camas *f/pl* 23
two dos 147
type *(kind)* clase *f* 140
typewriter máquina de escribir *f* 27
typewriter ribbon cinta para máquina *f* 105
typical típico(a) 35
typing paper papel de máquina *m* 105
tyre neumático *m* 75

U

ugly feo(a) 14, 84
umbrella paraguas *m* 118; *(beach)* sombrilla *f* 92
uncle tío *m* 94
unconscious inconsciente 139
under debajo 15
underdone *(meat)* poco hecho(a) 48, 61
underground *(railway)* metro *m* 73
underpants calzoncillos *m/pl* 118
undershirt camiseta *f* 118
understand, to comprender 12, 16; entender 12
undress, to desvestir 142
United States Estados Unidos *m/pl* 146
university universidad *f* 82
unleaded sin plomo 75
until hasta 150
up arriba 15
upper superior 70
upset stomach molestias de estómago *f/pl* 108
upstairs arriba 15, 69
urgent urgente 13, 145
urine orina *f* 142
use uso *m* 17, 109
use, to usar 134
useful útil 15

V

vacancy habitación libre *f* 23
vacant libre 14, 155
vacation vacaciones *f/pl* 151
vaccinate, to vacunar 140
vacuum flask termo *m* 107
vaginal vaginal 141
valley valle *m* 85
value valor *m* 131
vanilla vainilla *f* 51, 54
veal ternera *f* 47
vegetable verdura *f*, legumbre *f* 50
vegetable store verdulería *f* 99
vegetarian vegetariano(a) 37
vein vena *f* 138
velvet terciopelo *m* 114
venereal disease enfermedad venérea *f* 142
venison venado *m* 49
vermouth vermut *m* 55, 60
very muy 15
vest camiseta *f* 118; *(Am.)* chaleco *m* 118
veterinarian veterinario *m* 99
video cassette video-cassette *f* 119, 127
video-recorder video-grabadora *f* 119
video tape cinta video *f* 124
view vista *f* 23, 25
village pueblo *m* 76, 85
vinegar vinagre *m* 37
vineyard viñedo *m* 85
visit visita *f* 144
visit, to visitar 84
visiting hours horas de visita *f/pl* 144
V-neck cuello en forma de V *m* 117
volleyball balonvolea *m* 90
voltage voltaje *m* 119
vomit, to vomitar 140

W

waistcoat chaleco *m* 118
wait, to esperar 21, 96, 108
waiter camarero *m* 26, 36
waiting-room sala de espera *f* 67
waitress camarera *f* 26, 36
wake, to despertar 27; llamar 71
Wales País de Gales *m* 146

walk, to caminar 74; ir a pie 85
wall muro *m* 85
wallet cartera *f* 156
walnut nuez *f* 53
want, to *(wish)* desear, querer 12
wash, to lavar 29
washable lavable 113
wash-basin lavabo *m* 28
washing powder jabón en polvo *m* 107
watch reloj *m* 121, 122
watchmaker's relojería *f* 99, 121
watchstrap correa de reloj *f* 122
water agua *f* 23, 28, 32, 38, 75, 92
waterfall cascada *f* 85
water flask cantimplora *f* 107
watermelon sandía *f* 53
water-ski esquí acuático *m* 92
wave ola *f* 92
way camino *m* 76
we nosotros(as) 161
weather tiempo *m* 94
wedding ring anillo de boda *m* 121
Wednesday miércoles *m* 151
week semana *f* 16, 20, 24, 151
weekday día de la semana *m* 151
weekend fin de semana *m* 151
well *(healthy)* bien 10, 140
well-done *(meat)* muy hecho(a) 48
west oeste *m* 77
western *(film)* película del Oeste *f* 86
what qué 10; cómo 11; cuál 20
wheel rueda *f* 78
when cuándo 10
where dónde 10
which cuál 10
whisky whisky *m* 17, 60
white blanco(a) 58, 113
whitebait boquerón *m* 45
whiting pescadilla *f* 46
who quién 10
why por qué 10
wick mecha *f* 126
wide ancho(a) 116
wide-angle lens gran angular *m* 125
wife mujer *f* 94
wild boar jabalí *m* 49
wind viento *m* 95
windmill molino de viento *m* 85
window ventana *f* 28, 36, 69; *(shop)* escaparate *m* 100, 112
windscreen/shield parabrisas *m* 76
wine vino *m* 17, 56, 58, 61
wine list carta de vinos *f* 58
wine merchant's tienda de vinos *f*, bodega *f* 99
wine skin bota *f* 127
winter invierno *m* 149
wiper limpiaparabrisas *m* 75
wish deseo *m* 152
with con 15
withdraw, to *(bank)* retirar 131
without sin 15
woman señora *f* 115; mujer *f* 141, 156
wood alcohol alcohol de quemar *m* 107
woodcarving talla en madera *f* 127
woodcock becada *f* 48
wool lana *f* 114
word palabra *f* 11, 15, 133
work, to *(function)* funcionar 28, 119
working day día laborable *m* 151
worse peor 14
wound herida *f* 139
wrap, to envolver 102
wrapping paper papel de envolver *m* 105
wristwatch reloj de pulsera *m* 122
write, to escribir 11, 101
writing pad bloc de papel *m* 105
writing-paper papel de escribir *m* 27
wrong incorrecto(a) 14; equivocado(a) 77, 136

X

X-ray *(photo)* radiografía *f* 140

Y

year año *m* 149
yellow amarillo(a) 113
yes sí 9
yesterday ayer 151
yet todavía 15
yield, to *(traffic)* ceder el paso 79
yoghurt yogur *m* 64
you tú, usted 161
young joven 14
your tu, su, vuestro(a) 160
youth hostel albergue de juventud *m* 22

Z

zero cero *m* 147
zip(per) cremallera *f* 118
zoo zoo(lógico) *m* 82
zoology zoología *f* 83
zucchini calabacín *m* 50

Índice en español

FRANCE
Andorra
La Coruña
Gijón
Oviedo
Santander
Bilbao
San Sebastián
Vitoria
Pamplona
Vigo
León
Burgos
Ebro
Valladolid
Duero
Zaragoza
Barcelona
Tarragona
Salamanca
PORTUGAL
Avila
MADRID
Tajo
Toledo
Valencia
Menorca
Mahón
Mallorca
Palma
Ibiza
Ibiza
Lisbon
Guadiana
Albacete
Alicante
Elche
Murcia
Cartagena
Córdoba
Guadalquivir
MEDITERRANEAN SEA
Huelva
Sevilla
Granada
Málaga
Almería
Jerez de la Frontera
Cádiz
Gibraltar
ATLANTIC OCEAN
Tangier
Algiers
ALGERIA
Oran